Davis / Pinches

Canadian Financial Management

STUDY GUIDE

Third Edition

Alfred H.R. Davis

Queen's University

Francis Boabang

Saint Mary's University

Addison-Wesley Publishers Limited

Don Mills, Ontario • Reading, Massachusetts

Menlo Park, California • New York • Harlow, England

Sydney • Mexico City • Madrid • Amsterdam

Senior Editor: Brian Henderson
Managing Editor: Linda Scott
Editors: Gail Copeland, Madhu Ranadive, Suzanne Schaan
Desktopping: New Concept
Production Coordinator: Wendy Moran
Manufacturing Coordinator: Sharon Latta Paterson
Cover Design: Anthony Leung

Canadian Cataloguing in Publication Data

Davis, Alfred H.R., 1946–
    Study guide to accompany Davis/Pinches Canadian financial management, third edition

ISBN 0-673-99333-7

1. Finance – Canada.   2. Corporations – Canada – Finance.   3. Small business – Canada – Finance.   4.
International business enterprises – Finance.   I. Boabang, Francis.   II. Davis, Alfred H.R., 1946– . Canadian
financial management.   III. Title.

HG4090.D38 1997 Suppl.   658.15'0971   C97-931306-6

ISBN 0-673-99333-7

Printed and bound in Canada.

A B C D E -MP- 01 00 99 98 97

Contents

To the Student

The study of financial management is challenging and interesting; however, it can also be the source of difficulty, anxiety, and frustration. The purpose of this Study Guide is to promote your effective mastery of the material presented in *Canadian Financial Management* by Alfred Davis and George Pinches. It does this by presenting concisely, and in a different format, the key ideas covered in *Canadian Financial Management*. By applying yourself and using the Study Guide in addition to the text, you will gain a solid grasp of the financial concepts, terms, and applications that are so much a part of our daily lives.

The Study Guide is designed to assist in this process. It does this by presenting the following material for each chapter in which it is needed:

1. How This Chapter Relates to the Rest of the Text
2. Topical Outline
3. Formulas
4. What to Look For
5. Completion Questions
6. Problems
7. Answers to Completion Questions
8. Solutions to Problems

Before turning to this Study Guide, it is beneficial to read first the appropriate chapter in *Canadian Financial Management*. (Often it is useful to begin by skimming the chapter; once you have observed its key features, you can then read it in depth.) The first four elements of this Study Guide can be reviewed in order to expand upon the material in the chapter. The completion questions in this Study Guide are designed to reinforce key concepts by covering the main points in each chapter. Finally, the problems in this Study Guide are designed to supplement those in the book. By working through these additional problems, you will improve your mastery of the relevant concepts and gain understanding and confidence so you can master the problems in the book. The Study Guide also lets you verify immediately whether your answer is correct and see a step-by-step solution to the problem.

Acknowledgements

We would like to recognize the work that was done on the previous two editions of this Study Guide by David Ketcham. His conscientious work laid a solid foundation for us to build on. We would also like to express our thanks to the staff of Addison-Wesley, especially Brian Henderson and Suzanne Schaan, for their cooperation, understanding, and guidance. We of course are responsible for any errors and inconsistencies.

Finally, we acknowledge the continued love and support of our families. Without their understanding and patience, this project could not have been completed.

We would appreciate hearing comments from both students and instructors concerning the clarity of this Study Guide, any problems you might have or errors you may have discovered, and any suggestions for improvement you may wish to make. Good luck; we hope you find the study of financial management as interesting and as informative as we do.

Alfred H. R. Davis
Queen's University
Kingston, Ontario K7L 3N6
(613) 545-2353

Francis Boabang
Saint Mary's University
Halifax, Nova Scotia B3H 3C3

Chapter 1
Why Financial Management Matters

How This Chapter Relates to the Rest of the Text

Chapter 1 provides a definition of financial management and articulates the goal of the firm. Financial management is the acquisition, management, and financing of resources for firms by means of money. The chapter presents seven key ideas that form the foundation of the theory and practice of financial management. These are as follows: (1) The goal of the firm is to maximize its market value. (2) Financial markets are efficient. (3) Individuals act in their own self-interest. (4) Firms focus on cash flows and incremental effects. (5) A dollar today is worth more than a dollar tomorrow. (6) Risk and return go hand-in-hand. (7) Options are valuable.

Good financial management results in achieving the goal of the firm: maximization of its value. Since the firm can be thought of as a collection of assets, decisions affecting asset value will affect firm value. Value is a function of the size of cash flows, their timing, and riskiness. To achieve this goal, firms should operate in an ethical manner and recognize the impact that the internationalization of business has on financial management.

Topical Outline

I.   What is financial management?
   A.   The acquisition, management, and financing of resources for corporations.
   B.   Firms keep track of resources in terms of dollars.
   C.   The primary concern of financial management is the firm and its operations.
   D.   Financial markets make the final assessment about a firm's performance.
   E.   Although we concentrate on corporations, the tools of financial management are applicable to all forms of businesses.
   F.   Forms of business organization.
      1.   A proprietorship is an unincorporated business owned completely by one individual.
      2.   A partnership is similar to a proprietorship, except it involves more than one individual.
      3.   A corporation is an artificial person, created by law, with rights to contract and to own property.
         a.   A major benefit of the corporate form of business is limited liability, which limits the loss that owners can sustain to their investment in the corporation, if bankruptcy occurs.
         b.   Ownership of a corporation is evidenced by shares of common stock.
         c.   Firms can also raise funds by issuing bonds.
II.   Seven key ideas.
   A.   The goal of the firm is to maximize its market value.
      1.   The ingredients making up the firm include acquisition, financing, and management of resources.
      2.   The value of the firm is not determined solely by managers, but rather by what someone else is willing to pay for a claim on them.
      3.   The value of the firm is a function of the claims of both shareholders and bondholders: $V = S + B$. The values of S and B are determined in the financial markets.
      4.   For simplicity, we sometimes assume that firm value can be maximized by maximizing the value of S, shareholders' wealth.
      5.   Although the goal of maximizing the value of the firm should underlie all financial decisions, management does not always adhere to the goal, and sometimes the goal puts shareholders into conflict with bondholders, creditors, and others who are interested in the firm.
   B.   Financial markets are efficient.
      1.   An efficient market is one in which market prices adjust rapidly and accurately to the announcement of new information.
      2.   Characteristics that lead to efficient markets:

        a.   Many profit-maximizing individuals who analyze and value securities and who act independently.

        b.   New information arriving randomly.

        c.   Investors reacting quickly to new information, causing prices to change to reflect that new information.

    3.   Key lessons we learn from knowing that markets are efficient:

        a.   Trust market prices.

        b.   Start from the market price, and then look for factors that, if changed, could make the asset worth more or less.

C.   Individuals act in their own self-interest.

    1.   This results in agency problems or agency relationships.

    2.   An agency relationship is a contract under which principals (shareholders) engage an agent (manager) to act on the principals' behalf.

    3.   In a small business where the owner manages the firm, no agency problems occur.

    4.   In a corporation, an agency problem, or conflict of interest between agents and principals, may affect the firm's operations.

    5.   Conflicts between shareholders and managers.

        a.   Managers may increase perquisite consumption since they do not bear the total costs.

        b.   Managers may be satisfiers rather than maximizers.

        c.   Managers may prefer safe projects to a risky, but more profitable, one.

    6.   Agency relationships result in agency costs.

        a.   Financial contraction costs: the cost of structuring formal or informal contracts.

        b.   Cost of monitoring the performance of the agent.

        c.   Loss of wealth when agents pursue their own interest.

    7.   Agency costs are borne by the principals.

    8.   Conflicts between shareholders and bondholders.

        a.   Shareholders can increase the risk of bankruptcy, lowering the value of existing debt, by issuing new debt. This increases stock value at the expense of the bondholder.

        b.   Shareholders have an incentive to accept riskier projects than bondholders would like.

        c.   Constraints are often written into debt instruments to protect against expropriation.

        d.   In the absence of constraints, bondholders will demand higher rates of return, resulting in an agency cost.

    9.   Conflicts can also exist between bondholders and shareholders, managers, and stakeholders, such as customers, suppliers, the community, and government.

D.   Firms focus on cash flows and incremental effects.

    1.   The value of the firm or an asset is a function of the magnitude, timing, and riskiness of the future cash flows.

        a.   Cash flows are the actual cash receipts or payments.

        b.   We focus on incremental cash flows, new minus existing cash flows.

    2.   Cash flow is theoretically correct, unambiguous, and essential to the well-being of the firm.

    3.   Value is based on cash flow, not net income.

    4.   Because of different generally accepted accounting principles, net income can differ among identical firms.

    5.   Cash flow reflects the firm's ability to pay. Firms with higher net income can have difficulty paying bills if cash flow is low.

E.   A dollar today is worth more than a dollar tomorrow.

    1.   You are always better off taking a given cash flow (say $50) sooner than later.

    2.   We use present value and future value techniques to evaluate cash flows that occur at different points in time.

    3.   A standard procedure used to determine whether or not the future cash inflows associated with an investment are worthwhile is to calculate the investment's net present value, NPV.

> > a. NPV equals the present value of future cash flows, discounted at a rate based on foregone opportunities, minus the initial investment.
>
> F. Risk and return go hand-in-hand.
>
> > 1. Risk is the possibility of an undesirable outcome. Rational investors demand higher returns for exposing themselves to higher risks.
> > 2. The only way we can obtain a higher rate of return is to increase our exposure to risk.
>
> G. Options are valuable.
>
> > 1. An option exists any time an investor (whether it is an individual or a firm) has the opportunity, but not the obligation, to undertake some financial opportunity.
> > 2. Because an option can either be exercised or not, it has value.
> > 3. Options are embedded in many financial decisions.

III. Financial management and the firm.

> A. Financial management deals with the efficient use of a firm's resources.
> B. Only those management actions that positively affect the magnitude, timing, and riskiness of the future cash flows, while considering the self-interest of all shareholders, are desirable.
> C. Maximizing the value of the firm.
>
> > 1. This practice is theoretically correct and provides the proper basis for decision making.
> > 2. Firms can only maximize value subject to constraints.
> > 3. This provides a standard of comparison to evaluate managers' decisions.

IV. The finance function.

> A. There are many financial managers in a firm, including the financial vice-president and anyone else who makes or influences financial decisions.
> B. Financial management involves the acquisition, financing, and management of resources.

V. Finance, business, and ethics.

> A. Ethical behaviour in all forms of business activities now receives significant attention and rewards.
> B. Two types of ethical concerns.
>
> > 1. Taking actions to prevent illegal activities.
> > 2. Actions that deal with all stakeholders and societal considerations.

VI. The internationalization of business and financial management.

> A. Various trade agreements around the world have increased cross-border trade.
> B. There has been a move towards stateless firms that make decisions with little regard for national boundaries.
> C. International trade is a major aspect of the Canadian economy.
> D. Canada's major trading partner is the United States, which accounts for about 75 percent of both imports and exports.
> E. Exchange rates affect not only imports and exports but pricing and operating policies of Canadian firms.
> F. Canadian firms must compete for capital in the international markets.

What to Look For

Each year, hundreds of thousands of new businesses are incorporated and thousands fail. Effective financial management might have saved some of these firms.

Financial Management: Acquisition, Financing, and Management of Resources
Financial management is the acquisition, financing, and management of resources for firms by means of money. The goal of financial management is to maximize firm value.

Corporate resources can be classified as short-term assets, such as inventories and accounts receivable, or long-term assets, such as plant and equipment. Corporations acquire both types of assets in the course of doing business. While you might think that financial management will be difficult because of the variety of assets available, it is relatively straightforward. The value of any asset, and hence its desirability as an acquisition, is based on the asset's after-tax cash flow, its timing, and its riskiness.

With this in mind, the book first discusses the Canadian financial system, interest rates, and foreign exchange rates (Chapter 2). A detailed discussion of the fundamental concepts of financial management follows in the next four chapters. Chapter 3 examines timing and its effects on the value of money received or paid, and Chapter 4 discusses how to use cash flows, timing, and risk to value stocks and bonds. Chapter 5 discusses risk—what it is and how to measure it, while Chapter 6 shows how to determine a firm's opportunity cost of capital. This is the minimum rate of return the firm needs to earn in order to satisfy stockholders. Resources must produce more than this return for their investment to be worthwhile.

Chapters 7–9 show how the concepts of cash flow, valuation, and risk are combined to evaluate the feasibility of capital projects. Acquisitions require that a firm either generate funds internally or go to the capital market. Again, financial decisions are based on value. We will discuss how firms raise money by using common tock (Chapter 10) and long-term debt (Chapter 11). The mix of debt and equity, the firm's capital structure, and its effects on firm value are examined in Chapters 12 and 13, while the internal generation of funds and dividend policy is the subject matter of Chapter 14.

Leasing, an alternative means of financing capital projects, is discussed in Chapter 15. Another type of capital (long-term) investment occurs when one firm buys another. Consequently, we will apply the capital budgeting techniques developed in Chapters 7–9 to evaluate mergers and corporate restructuring in Chapter 16. In today's environment, internationalization of business activities is a way of life, not only for multinational corporations but also for domestic firms that import and export raw materials or finished goods. Chapter 17 shows how to adjust the capital budgeting process to accommodate investments in other countries and how import and export firms can hedge against foreign exchange rate fluctuations.

In recent years, derivative securities have become an important element of financial management. Chapter 18 introduces a popular form of derivative security, options, and shows how to value them. Chapter 19 applies the knowledge learned in Chapter 18 to value the many options that are embedded in securities and various corporate decisions. Chapter 20 values convertible bonds and warrants in an option pricing framework.

Like long-term assets, short-term assets, if carefully managed, will produce increased cash flows for the firm and a return to its shareholders. Consequently, the same basic procedures used to evaluate capital (long-term) projects are used in Chapters 21–23 to manage short-term assets. Chapter 24 discusses the cost of financing with short-term assets.

No matter how firms acquire assets, to be successful they must consistently manage their finances well. Chapter 25 provides us with a means of assessing the financial well-being of a firm based on an analysis of accounting statements, while Chapter 26 discusses financial planning and forecasting and points out some serious consequences of poor financial management. Chapter 27 relates what we have discussed about financial management to the operation of small businesses.

Seven Key Ideas

Seven key ideas help us understand the theory and practice of financial management. The recognition of these ideas in the decision-making process results in all corporate assets being used in the most efficient manner. Consequently, the following seven key ideas provide a framework for our discussion throughout the text.

1. The goal of the firm is to maximize its market value.
The objective of the firm is to acquire, finance, and manage resources in such a way as to maximize the value of both its shareholders and bondholders. The final judgement about how successful a firm's management is at achieving this goal is made by the financial markets. It is in the financial markets that it is determined how much someone else is willing to pay for claims on the firm, that is, for its stocks and bonds.

2. Financial markets are efficient.
An efficient market is one in which prices rapidly and correctly adjust to reflect new information. In order for a market to be efficient, there must be large numbers of value-maximizing participants, random arrival of new information, and investors who react quickly to new information. There is significant evidence that financial markets in developed countries, like Canada, are efficient. An efficient financial market means, among other things, that

market prices reflect the true value of the firm, and management should consider the impact of decisions on security prices.

The financial market's goal is the efficient transfer of money form borrowers to lenders. In the market, interest rates help allocate the scarce loanable funds. Chapter 2 discusses this mechanism. Managers must understand the workings of financial markets in order to plan the future financing needs or surpluses. The timing of these needs or surpluses can be critical, since the cost of funds can change drastically over the course of a year or two.

3. Individuals act in their own self-interest.

You will find that the goals of many individuals ultimately determine the kinds of decisions managers make. The shareholder wants to maximize his or her wealth. In a corporate setting, managers are hired to act as agents for the shareholders (principals). In theory, then, managers should act in the best interests of the shareholders and maximize the value of the firm. In practice, however, problems arise. Managers have their own interests, such as increasing salary or retaining their jobs, which can conflict with the goal of value maximization.

For example, managers may choose to consume excess perquisites (benefits such as company cars, luxurious office furnishings, etc.) rather than invest the money to the benefit of the shareholders. Managers may be satisfiers; that is, they may do just well enough to "get by" rather than maximize firm value. Finally, in an attempt to ensure further employment, managers may forego risky (but value-adding) projects in favour of those that are less risky. Shareholders can try to eliminate some of these agency problems through mandatory reporting requirements, outside audits, incentive plans, and bonuses.

Conflicts can also arise between shareholders and bondholders. Bondholders prefer the firm to have as little bankruptcy risk as possible. Shareholders might increase the risk of bankruptcy by issuing more debt or undertaking more risky projects. As risk increases, bond prices will fall and shareholders will be able to expropriate wealth from bondholders. Bonds often contain restrictions (called covenants) to prevent such activities. In the absence of covenants, bondholders require a higher required return, which is costly to the firm and its shareholders.

4. Firms focus on cash flows and incremental effects.

The timing, magnitude, and riskiness of a firm's future after-tax cash flows are critical. A shortage of cash can require a firm to seek additional and increasingly costly debt or equity, or can push the firm towards bankruptcy. Net income, as presented in GAAP financial statements, does not give a clear picture of the firm's cash position. For decision-making purposes, we focus on incremental cash flows, new minus existing cash flows. In addition, the financial markets determine the firm's value according to its expected future cash flow. Therefore, we will use cash flows rather than net income when evaluating the firm's financial management. Chapter 26 discusses cash flow.

5. A dollar today is worth more than a dollar tomorrow.

The cost of financing is the opportunity cost of money or interest. This opportunity cost is used to find the present value of future cash flows generated by an investment. For a firm to invest money in a project, the project's net present value must be positive. Chapter 3, on time value of money, helps us learn to calculate both the future and the present values of investments. We will use time values throughout the text.

6. Risk and return go hand-in-hand.

As the riskiness of a firm's future cash flow increases, so must its return. The return must compensate investors for bearing this additional risk. Bondholders' coupon payments come from pre-tax cash flows, while preferred and common shareholders' cash dividends come from after-tax cash flows. If investors fear for this coupon or dividend payment stream, they will demand a higher required rate of return. In Chapters 4 and 5, we work through these dynamics.

7. Options are valuable.

An option provides the firm with the right, but not the obligation, to undertake various financial opportunities. Options are also embedded in various securities and in many corporate decisions. Because an option allows the firm to walk away and not invest in the opportunity, if it chooses, the option has value.

Finance, Business, and Ethics

Ethical business practices enhance a firm's ability to maximize its long-run value. It may sometimes appear as if ethical business behaviour impedes value maximization by imposing additional costs on the firm. However, on closer scrutiny, we would recognize that this is a short-run situation. In the long run, a management team that acknowledges the interests of all of its stakeholders (shareholders, customers, suppliers, employees, and society in general) when making business decisions will prosper and, consequently, will maximize total firm value.

International Finance

While the emphasis of this book is on the financial management of Canadian firms, it should be remembered that businesses operate in an international marketplace. International trade is a major component of the Canadian economy, and Canada's major trading partner, the United States, accounts for 75 percent of imports and exports. Exchange rates affect not only imports and exports but also the pricing and operating policies of corporations, and Canadian firms, whether independent or multinational, must compete for funds in the international markets.

Completion Questions

1.1   _____ involves the _____, financing, and management of resources for corporations by means of money, but with due regard for the prices in external economic markets.

1.2   The financial manager's interest is in maximizing the _____ in the financial marketplace, not its book value.

1.3   Ownership in a corporation is evidenced by shares of _____.

1.4   Benefits of the corporate form include continual existence and _____ liability.

1.5   The investor determines the value of the firm by estimating the magnitude, timing, and riskiness of the firm's _____, rather than by looking at the firm's _____.

1.6   When we consider the timing of cash flows, we consider when the cash is _____.

1.7   The _____ of a firm is deeply involved in financial policy making, as well as in corporate or strategic planning.

1.8   Current assets include _____, _____, and _____, while current liabilities include all the payable accounts. The management of current assets and liabilities is called working capital management.

1.9   An _____ arises because there may be a conflict of interest between owners and managers.

1.10   If a manager's goal is to obtain an acceptable level of performance rather than firm value maximization, the manager is said to be a _____.

1.11   A conflict between bondholders and shareholders can arise if shareholders attempt to expropriate wealth through the issuance of new _____.

1.12   Many bonds contain _____ in an attempt to mitigate the agency problems associated with debt.

1.13   To ensure that management acts in their interest, shareholders use various incentives and monitoring devices; one such incentive that is tied in with the value of the firm is a _____ plan.

1.14   An investor is always better off taking a given cash flow _____ than _____.

1.15   _____ is a procedure to determine if a prospective investment is worthwhile or not.

1.16   Investors demand _____ to take on more risk.

1.17   Many business decisions have _____ embedded in them.

1.18   Ethical behaviour enhances a firm's ability to _____.

Answers to Completion Questions

1.1   Financial management; acquisition
1.2   value of the firm
1.3   common stock
1.4   limited
1.5   cash flows; earnings (or net income)
1.6   actually received or disbursed
1.7   financial vice-president (or chief financial officer)
1.8   cash; accounts receivable; inventory
1.9   agency problem
1.10   satisfier
1.11   debt
1.12   covenants
1.13   stock option
1.14   sooner; later
1.15   Net present value
1.16   higher returns
1.17   options
1.18   maximize its long-run value

Chapter 2
The Financial System, Interest Rates,
and Foreign Exchange

How This Chapter Relates to the Rest of the Text

Financial managers do not make decisions in a vacuum. The decisions they make and the results of these decisions are dependent upon the structure and operation of the financial marketplace in which firms operate. The Canadian financial system provides for the orderly transfer of funds from suppliers to demanders. The financial system consists of institutions such as chartered banks and markets such as the Toronto Stock Exchange.

Value (Chapter 4) is determined in the financial markets. An important component of value is the interest rate, which is a function of the supply and of the demand for loanable funds, expected inflation, and risk. While the later chapters, most notably Chapter 4, examine the relationship between value and rates of return, this chapter discusses the various components of interest rates.

Foreign exchange rates, or the conversion rates between currencies, are also determined in financial markets. Today many firms, both large and small, purchase from or sell to foreign firms. Therefore, foreign exchange rates are another important consideration for financial managers. Exchange rates are introduced in this chapter and then discusssed in detail in Chapters 17 and 19.

Topical Outline

I. The Canadian financial system.
    A. Goal of the financial system is to transform savings into investments.
        1. Savings come from individuals, business, and government.
        2. Financial institutions help channel the funds from suppliers to demanders of funds.
        3. Demanders of funds—individuals, business, and government—invest the funds in productive resources or services.
        4. Financial markets—the money market and the capital market—facilitate the issuance of financial assets.
    B. The transfer of funds creates financial assets for suppliers of funds and financial liabilities for demanders of funds.
        1. Money is a medium of exchange used to acquire goods and services or to pay debt.
        2. Debt is a promise to pay back a certain amount on a specified future date.
        3. Stock is an ownership in a business.
            a. Common stock has a residual claim on a business's assets.
            b. Preferred stock has a prior but limited claim on the assets and cash flows of the firm.
    C. Financial institutions.
        1. Bring suppliers and demanders of funds together in order to
            a. Provide liquidity and flexibility.
            b. Provide convenience.
            c. Provide expertise.
            d. Spread risks.
        2. Types of financial institutions.
            a. Chartered banks are the traditional financial "department store."
            b. Insurance companies and pension funds are also important.
            c. Investment companies include mutual funds, which allow individual investors to pool their funds. These funds are invested in stocks, bonds, and, more recently, money market instruments.
            d. Financial cooperatives include *caisses populaires* and credit unions, which accept deposits and make loans and investments.
            e. Other types of financial institutions include finance companies, mortgage loan

companies, trust companies, leasing companies, and venture capital firms, which are specialized loan sources.

    3.   Financial institutions are currently undergoing restructuring.

    4.   Investment dealers assist in the placement of new issues of bonds or stock.

    5.   Institutions help demanders indirectly meet suppliers in the financial markets.

  D.   Financial markets.

    1.   Money market securities mature in less than one year and include

        a.   Treasury bills issued by the federal and some provincial governments.

        b.   Day loans.

        c.   Certificates of deposit.

        d.   Commercial paper.

        e.   Bankers' acceptances.

        f.   Purchase and sale agreements.

    2.   Capital market securities mature in more than one year and include

        a.   Long-term government bonds.

        b.   Debt issued by firms.

        c.   Common and preferred stock.

    3.   Primary market: market for selling newly issued securities. This market is operated through investment dealers who provide assistance and advice to firms raising funds.

    4.   Secondary market: market for buying and selling seasoned securities.

        a.   Provides a ready market to ensure liquidity.

        b.   Provides a market in which issues trade when they have become seasoned.

        c.   Transactions occur on the organized exchanges (Alberta, Montreal, Toronto, Vancouver, and Winnipeg) or in the over-the-counter (OTC) market.

II.   The government's role.

  A.   The federal government has exclusive jurisdiction over banking operations, while the provinces regulate the securities markets. Insurance, trust and mortgage companies, financial cooperatives, and other financial institutions are regulated by both.

  B.   The Office of the Superintendent of Financial Institutions, the Canadian Co-operative Credit Society, Canadian Deposit Insurance Corporation, and other Crown corporations provide regulation and support.

  C.   The Bank of Canada system: tools to influence the operation of commercial banks.

    1.   Changing the reserve requirement can only be done through revision of the Bank Act.

    2.   Changing the bank rate affects interest rates.

    3.   Open market operations: If the Bank of Canada sells (buys) government securities, the money supply will contract (expand) and interest rates will increase (decrease).

  D.   Fiscal policy: government policies that influence business incentives, including taxation, investment tax credits, capital gains taxes, and any other policy positively or adversely affecting the business climate.

    1.   Increased deficits increase the demand for money and push up interest rates.

III.   Why is the financial system important?

  A.   The financial system provides an efficient means of bringing together suppliers and demanders of funds.

  B.   The financial system, through the secondary markets, provides liquidity to investors and enhances the capital-raising ability of firms.

  C.   The evolution of the financial system affords new opportunities to raise capital to astute firms.

  D.   Value is determined in the financial marketplace.

  E.   The financial system facilitates rapid reaction to new information about the firm's future prospects.

IV.   Interest rates and the required rate of return.

  A.   What are interest rates?

    1.   Interest rates are the prices paid when an individual, firm, or governmental unit borrows

money.

2.   Interest rates are costs or benefits, depending on whether you are a borrower or lender.

3.   Interest rates are almost always stated on an annual basis.

B.   The real rate of interest.

1.   In a world with no expected inflation or risk, the real rate of interest would be the cost of funds.

2.   The real rate is determined solely by the supply of and the demand for loanable funds and fluctuates over time.

C.   Inflation and its impact.

1.   As the purchasing power of the dollar is eroded by inflation, investors must be compensated by a higher rate of return to preserve their purchasing power.

2.   Fisher effect: The real rate of interest (between 2 and 3 percent) plus the expected rate of inflation equals the observed risk-free rate of interest.

a.   Those who borrowed at fixed rates when interest rates were low benefited at the expense of lenders when rates rose with unexpected inflation.

b.   Inflation has pushed lenders into variable interest rate financing strategies.

c.   Rapid inflation affects the validity of planning and pricing strategies, since not all cost increases can necessarily be passed on to customers.

d.   Accounting problems result during periods of high inflation, distorting reported profits, asset values, and liabilities.

e.   Higher inflation causes an increase in the cost of all funds obtained by firms.

f.   The yield on treasury securities with the same coupon and maturity is used as a proxy for the risk-free rate. This is done because treasury securities are

i.   default free

ii.   highly liquid, and

iii.   the most actively traded securities in the money and capital markets.

As such the yields on treasury securities are used to price other securities and to set yields on different sectors of the money and bonds markets.

D.   Maturity premium.

1.   The maturity premium is an additional return required by investors because long-term bonds are more sensitive to interest rate changes and thus are more risky.

2.   Graphs of the yield to maturity and term to maturity of securities of the same level of default risk are called yield curves and show the "term structure of interest rates."

V.   The term structure of interest rates.

A.   A yield curve shows the relationship between yield to maturity and term to maturity for securities with the same level of default risk.

1.   Yield curves shift up and down, depending on the general supply and demand for funds.

2.   The shape of the yield curve changes as investors' expectations of future rates of inflation change.

3.   Yield curves for firms will be above that for governments due to higher risk.

B.   Theories of the term structure of interest rates.

1.   The expectations theory asserts that the term structure can be explained solely on the basis of investors' expectations of future interest rates.

a.   Long-term rates are geometric averages of current and expected short-term rates.

b.   Forward rates (expected short-term rates) can be estimated using current returns on long-term bonds.

2.   The liquidity (maturity) preference theory suggests that investors find short-term securities preferable to long-term securities; thus, long-term securities must offer higher returns.

a.   Long-term securities have more risk.

b.   Firms must offer investors a premium on long-term securities to compensate for the additional risk.

3. The market segmentation hypothesis asserts that the short-, medium-, and long-term markets are independent of each other.
   a. Rates of return are determined by supply and demand conditions in each segment.
4. Although each of the three theories has been partially supported by empirical evidence, there is no consensus as to which theory is descriptive of reality.

C. The "risk premium."
   The risk premium of a firm is composed of a maturity premium, a default premium, a liquidity premium, and an issue-specific premium.
   1. A maturity premium is the premium required on long-term securities to compensate for the additional risk.
   2. A default premium is the additional return required to compensate for the risk that the firm will not be able to honour its promises (interest and principal payments) to bondholders.
   3. A liquidity premium arises if the market for the security is not active.
   4. An issue-specific premium arises from the type of security and its provisions.

D. The expected required return on an asset equals the nominal risk-free rate plus the risk premium. The higher the risk, the higher the risk premium and the higher the required return.

E. Foreign exchange.
   1. Exchange rates represent the conversion rates of currencies between countries.
   2. Exchange rates depend upon the relative supply and demand of the two currencies, the inflation expected in the two countries, and other factors.

F. Spot and forward rates.
   1. Spot rate: The price paid for the delivery of the currency today.
   2. Forward rate: The rate agreed upon today by the purchaser (seller) to take delivery of (to deliver) a foreign currency at a specified future date. Forward rates are computed from spot rates.

Formulas

Fisher Effect

$$\text{Nominal risk-free interest rate} = \text{real rate of interest} + \text{expected rate of inflation}$$

Long-Term Spot Rate

$$k_n = \left[(1 + k_1)(1 + f_2)(1 + f_3) \dots (1 + f_n) \right]^{1/n} - 1$$

Forward Rates

$$f_n = \frac{(1 + k_n)^n}{(1 + k_{n-1})^{n-1}} - 1$$

Expectation Theory of Foreign Exchange

$$\frac{F_{2/1}}{S_{2/1}} = \frac{E(S_{2/1})}{S_{2/1}}$$

Purchasing Power Parity

$$\frac{E\,(S_{2/1})}{S_{2/1}} = \frac{E\,(1 + i_2)}{E\,(1 + i_1)}$$

International Fisher Effect

$$\frac{E\,(1 + i_2)}{E\,(1 + i_1)} = \frac{1 + k_{RF2}}{1 + k_{RF1}}$$

Interest Rate Parity

$$\frac{1 + k_{RF2}}{1 + k_{RF1}} = \frac{F_{2/1}}{S_{2/1}}$$

Forward Rate of Exchange

$$F_{2/1} = \frac{S_{2/1}\,(1 + k_{RF2})}{1 + k_{RF1}}$$

What to Look For

Central to financial management are the financial markets. Chapter 2 introduces us to the financial markets and to their participants. Today's effective managers have learned their lessons about the financial markets and sometimes attempt to time their participation accordingly.

Briefly, financial markets bring borrowers of funds together with lenders of funds. Depending on the supply and demand of loanable funds, money can be relatively cheap or relatively expensive. That is, the real interest rates rise and fall according to the supply and demand for loanable funds. Also, inflation expectations will cause nominal rates to fluctuate. Managers who want to minimize their costs will attempt to time their financing accordingly. In the following section, we will review the financial markets, the securities traded in them, the participants, and the cost of borrowing.

Financial Markets and Their Respective Securities
The financial markets can be split into short-term and long-term markets.

The money market: short term
In the short-term or money market, such instruments as commercial paper, Canadian Treasury bills, certificates of deposit, bankers' acceptances, and day loans are traded. A firm might invest in commercial paper, Treasury bills, or certificates of deposit if it has excess cash over a short period. If a firm has an adequate credit rating, it may issue commercial paper for its own short-term credit needs. Import or export firms employ bankers' acceptances, which are another type of money market security.

The capital market: long term
Long-term financing for a firm is undertaken in the capital market. This financing can be in the form of debt or equity. Debt issues can be unsecured (debentures), or they can be secured with land, equipment, or some other collateral.

Firms can also issue debt with warrants or debt that is convertible into common stock. Warrants and the conversion feature sweeten the bond issue and induce investors to buy debt yielding a relatively low rate of interest.

Warrants and convertibles allow investors to exchange the firm's fixed-income security for its common stock, at a specific exchange rate over a specified period of time. Thus, the conversion feature and warrants are, as discussed in Chapter 20, "options" that give investors a chance to share in potential capital gains as the firm prospers.

Rather than issuing more debt, managers may decide to issue stock. Two types of stock exist—preferred and common stock. Preferred stockholders have a prior but limited claim to the income and the assets of the firm. Common stockholders, however, share in both the losses and the gains of the firm.

The primary market: issuing financial securities

In order to issue financial securities, firms must use the primary market, since the secondary markets are reserved for securities that have been previously traded. This issuance can take two forms.

To place a debt issue privately, a firm or its investment dealer might ask several insurance companies to buy the entire issue. Insurance companies would probably hold the issue until maturity. In recent years, roughly one-fourth of all debt issues are privately placed. (Common stock is seldom sold this way.)

New securities not privately placed will generally be sold through an investment dealer. The managing investment dealer and the other investment dealers underwriting the issue will plan the sale and distribution of the new issue. Depending upon the size and attractiveness of the issue, the underwriting syndicate will agree to sell the entire issue itself or to bring investment dealers into the selling syndicate. In many financial publications, you can observe public announcements of new security issues. These announcements list the investment dealers who are in the selling syndicate, and from whom you might get information about the new issue.

The secondary market: trading seasoned securities

The secondary markets are designed for trading in outstanding securities. These markets include the organized exchanges and the over-the-counter market. The organized exchanges include those in Alberta, Montreal, Toronto, Vancouver, and Winnipeg. Companies who meet the guidelines can list their stock for trading on one or more of these exchanges. Unlisted stocks trade in the over-the-counter market, an informal network of security brokers who buy and sell stock. Bonds trade primarily in the over-the-counter market. The secondary markets provide liquidity to the holders of securities and as well facilitate primary markets.

Financial Intermediaries

Financial institutions play the important role of bringing borrowers and lenders together. They gather lenders' deposits of varying maturities in order to match the borrowers' desired loan maturity. In addition, they combine many small deposits in order to make larger loans.

Each financial institution tends to specialize in specific types of lending. Mortgage loan companies provide real estate mortgage loans. Chartered banks primarily make commercial loans. Insurance companies, as we noted before, buy large blocks of new corporate debt, and, through various types of business insurance, bear some risk for corporations. Credit unions make consumer loans. As the text notes, financial institutions are going through rapid changes that are making them financial supermarkets. There is substantial overlap among the various financial institutions and the services they provide.

Interest Rates and Forces That Determine Their Level

Interest rates are the prices paid by individuals, corporations, and the government to borrow funds. The required rate of interest on an investment depends upon several factors.

Time and interest rates

Money has a time value, as Chapter 3 will show. Seldom can you borrow money without paying the lender some rate of return. If conditions in the economy are stable and your credit is flawless, the rate of interest on the loan should be a riskless or risk-free rate—the rate paid on Canadian Treasury securities. The treasury bill rate is the proxy for the riskless rate, since the repayment of these bills is virtually certain.

The economy is not stable, however. The riskless rate rises and falls as a result of supply and demand conditions. Facing a deficit, the Canadian government may decide to issue new government debt. This fiscal action will increase the demand for funds and will push interest rates upward. The Bank of Canada, in its role of stabilizing the economy, may decide to counteract inflationary forces by selling government securities in the open market. The resulting contraction of the money supply makes money more costly, pushing interest rates upward. On the other hand, if the Bank of Canada buys government securities, interest rates will fall in the short run, but the inflation that follows from money supply expansion often pushes interest rates up in the long run, as discussed below. The Bank of Canada can also raise interest rates by increasing the bank rate, the rate at which it lends funds. As you can see, interest rates are a complex subject.

The real rate of interest

Interest rates are the prices paid when an individual, firm, or governmental unit borrows money. These rates are usually stated as an annual percentage of the amount borrowed. In a world without risk or expected inflation, investors would expect to pay the real rate of interest, which is determined by the supply of and the demand for loanable funds.

Inflation and interest rates

Over time, the price level in the economy changes. We call an upward change in the price level inflation. If inflation exists, investors demand compensation for this upward change in the price level, since they want to achieve a desired rate of return, net of inflation. A useful way of looking at this net rate of return is with the Fisher effect. The Fisher effect shows the relationship between the expected rate of inflation and the observed or nominal rate of interest. The real rate of interest for a riskless investment (net of inflation) is about 3 or 4 percent. The equation for the observed rate of interest is below:

$$\begin{array}{ccc} \text{Nominal risk-free} \\ \text{interest rate} \end{array} = \begin{array}{c} \text{Real rate of} \\ \text{interest} \end{array} + \begin{array}{c} \text{Expected rate} \\ \text{of inflation} \end{array}$$

Generally, the Treasury bill rate is the measure of the observed or nominal rate of interest and is the base for the term structure of interest rates.

For longer-term government bonds, investors demand a maturity premium, an additional return that compensates investors because long-term bonds are more sensitive to changes in interest rates than short-term bonds. A useful tool in analyzing maturity premiums and interest rates is the yield curve, which shows the term structure of interest rates.

A yield curve shows the relationship between yield to maturity and term to maturity for bonds of equivalent default risk. The term structure of interest rates shown in the yield curve are changes over time due to supply and demand conditions and changes in inflationary expectations. At times, the term structure is upward sloping, at times flat, at times downward sloping, and on occasion, the term structure is humped. Three theories of term structure of interest rates have arisen.

Under the expectations theory, long-term rates are geometric averages of today's short-term rate and expected future short-term rates (or forward rates). For example, suppose you desired to invest $10,000 for two years. You see that one-year government bonds are paying 7 percent while two-year government bonds are paying 8 percent per year. Which of the two bonds you invest in will depend upon what you expect next year's interest rate to be.

If you invest in the two-year bond, your investment will be worth $10,000(1.08)^2 = $11,664 in two years. If you invest in a one-year bond, your investment will be worth $10,000(1.07) = $10,700 in one year. Now suppose that you expect that next year, one-year bonds will pay 10 percent. If you reinvest $10,700 at 10 percent, you'll have $10,700(1.10) = $11,770 after the end of the second year. Thus, you would be better off buying two one-year bonds, one today and one next year. If all investors thought that next year's one-year bond rate would be 10 percent, the prices of two-year bonds would fall (and one-year bonds would rise) until investors were indifferent between one- and two-year bonds.

Thus, if we observe one-year bonds paying 7 percent and two-year bonds paying 8 percent, we know that investors must expect that next year's one-year bond rate (or forward rate) will be

$$f_2 = \frac{(1.08)^2}{(1.07)} - 1 = .090093 \text{ or } 9.0093\%$$

under the expectations hypothesis. This theory assumes that short- and long-term bonds are perfect substitutes, which may not be true.

The liquidity (maturity) preference theory holds that investors prefer short-term to long-term bonds because short-term bonds are less sensitive to fluctuations in interest rates. In order to compensate investors for risk, longer-term bonds must offer higher returns than short-term bonds. A problem with this theory is that it implies that the term structure should always be upward sloping, which is not the case.

The market segmentation hypothesis asserts that the markets for short- and long-term bonds are separate. One class of investors—for example, money market funds—are interested only in short-term bonds. Another group—for example, life insurance companies—may be interested in long-term bonds. Under this theory, the term structure simply reflects supply and demand conditions in each market segment.

None of the three theories, by itself, explains the term structure to the satisfaction of researchers. Each, however, provides some insight into the determination of interest rates.

Risk and interest rates

The interest rates on most bonds have components other than the real rate of interest and an inflation premium. These components are called risk premiums and are designed to compensate investors for specific forms of risk associated with bonds.

Corporate bonds will also contain a default premium, which compensates investors for the risk that the issuer will be unable to pay interest or principal on the bonds. Corporate bonds are rated from AAA (very safe) to C and below. The higher the rating, the lower the default risk premium.

Other premiums include a liquidity premium, which arises if the market for the security is not very active, and an issue-specific premium, which compensates investors for risks associated with specific attributes of the security.

The required or expected return on an asset is the sum of two components. The first is the nominal (observed) risk-free rate of interest, which, according to the Fisher effect, is equal to the real rate of interest plus expected inflation. The second is the risk premium, which is the sum of maturity, default, liquidity, and issue-specific premiums. There is a positive relationship between risk and return; the higher the risk, the higher the required return. Understanding interest rates and their effects on asset values is an important tool in financial management.

Spot Rates and Forward Rates

A foreign exchange rate is the rate of conversion between currencies. Spot rates, or today's exchange rates, are quoted in either dollars needed to buy one unit of currency, or in units of currency needed to buy one dollar. For instance, you might be able to buy 349.65 Venezuelan bolivars with one dollar, or 0.00286 dollars with one bolivar. Using exchange rates found in the *Globe and Mail*, you can calculate exchange rates between any two currencies. For instance, if the spot rate for Chile's pesos were 311.92 per dollar, the exchange rate between bolivars and new pesos should be 311.92/349.65 = 0.89 pesos per bolivar.

If you wish to take delivery of a currency at some point in time in the future you can buy a forward contract. A forward rate is an exchange rate agreed upon today for delivery of foreign currency at some time in the future. Forward rates are also listed daily in the *Globe and Mail*. For example, a quote such as the following may appear:

Rate	Dollars required to buy one German mark
Spot	0.8763
30-day forward	0.8766
90-day forward	0.8770
180-day forward	0.8773

The purchaser of a 90-day forward contract agrees to take delivery of marks at an exchange rate of $0.8770 per mark ninety days from now. Note that the forward rates are all above the spot rate. The primary reason for this is the difference in the expected rate of inflation between the two countries. If the Canadian inflation rate is expected to be higher than that of Germany, the spot rate will be at a discount and the forward rates will increase.

Completion Questions

2.1   The price paid for delivery of a foreign currency today is its _____ rate. If an international businessperson does not want to risk the possibility that current exchange rates will change unfavourably, he or she might agree on a rate of exchange today—the _____ rate—for taking delivery of the foreign currency sometime in the future.

2.2   During periods of inflation, interest rates _____ in order to compensate lenders for the loss in _____ they experience by being paid back with dollars of lower value.

2.3   The Fisher effect states that the observed rate of interest is the sum of a real rate of interest plus _____. The real rate of interest is about _____.

2.4   Items that can be quickly and cheaply converted into money are called _____.

2.5   _____ refers to a promise to repay a certain amount on a certain date, often with a stated rate of interest.

2.6   _____ often come between suppliers and demanders of funds to accept deposits and make loans or investments.

2.7   _____ is the process of directly selling a new stock or bond issue to a financial institution rather than having the investment banking syndicate sell the issue.

2.8   A well-developed _____ allows investors to easily add or to liquidate their security holdings.

2.9   Any security that is not listed with an exchange will trade in the _____.

2.10   When the Bank of Canada conducts open-market operations to purchase government securities, the money supply _____; in response, interest rates will _____.

2.11   When budget deficits are funded with additional government borrowing, interest rates _____.

2.12   Under the _____ theory, long-term bond rates are geometric to short-term spot rates and _____ rates.

2.13   Under the market segmentation theory of the term structure of interest rates, the short-term and long-term markets are _____ of each other.

2.14   Under the _____ theory, long-term bonds have higher yields since they are more risky than short-term bonds.

2.15   The _____ rate is the rate of exchange between currencies today.

2.16   The _____ rate is the rate of exchange between currencies agreed upon today, for delivery in the future.

Problems

2.1   Recently, an economist forecast the following rates of inflation:

Year	Expected Inflation
1996	6.2%
1997	6.8
1998	5.4
1999	4.0

What should be the nominal risk-free rate of interest in each of the above years assuming a real rate of interest of 3 percent?

2.2   Suppose the real rate of interest is 2 percent and inflation is expected to be 6 percent per year over the next 15 years. All bonds have a maturity premium of 0.3 percent per year (that is, 0.3 percent for a 1-year bond, 0.6 percent on a 2-year bond, etc.). Corporate AAA bonds have a default premium of 2.5 percent, a liquidity premium of 0.8 percent, and an issue-specific premium of 2 percent. Calculate the interest rates for 1-, 5-, 10-, and 15-year government bonds and AAA corporate bonds.

2.3   Kandel Manufacturing, Ltd. and Durrough Industries, Ltd. are two firms with common stock trading on a major exchange. Premiums associated with each stock are as follow:

	Kandel	Durrough
Maturity premium	none	none
Default premium	4.0%	3.5%
Liquidity premium	3.1%	5.2%
Issue-specific premium	2.0%	2.5%

Which of the two securities has the highest level of risk?

2.4   The following spot rates were recently reported for government bonds.

Years to Maturity	Spot Rate
1	7.94%
2	8.10%
3	8.30%
4	8.47%
5	8.59%

a.   What factors account for the shape of the yield curve?
b.   What are the forward rates of interest implied by the yield curve?
c.   Suppose the expectations hypothesis holds.
    i.   What are the expected rates of inflation in each of the next 5 years, assuming that the real rate of interest is 3.5 percent?
    ii.   Determine the price of a 4-year 10 percent coupon bond that pays interest annually. (Assume this bond has no default risk, maturity risk, or issue-specific risk.)

2.5   Suppose you observe the following in the market:
    i.   6-month T-bill priced at 961.5384 per $1000 face value
    ii.   12-month T-bill priced at 933.511 per $1000 face value
    iii.   1 1/2-year treasury bond coupon rate 6.5 percent selling at par and paying semiannual interest
    iv.   2-year treasury bond coupon rate 5.75 percent selling at par and paying semiannual interest
a.   What are the six-month spot rates of interest?
b.   What are the six-month forward rates of interest implied by the yield curve?
c.   Given that the real rate of interest is 1.2 percent per 6-month period, what are the 6-month expected rates of inflation over the 2-year period?
d.   How would you price a 2-year, 8.75 percent coupon corporate bond that has no default risk, maturity risk, or issue-specific risk, and pays semiannual interest? What assumptions are invoked?

Answers to Completion Questions

2.1   spot; forward
2.2   rise; purchasing power
2.3   the expected rate of inflation; 2 to 3 percent
2.4   near money
2.5   Debt
2.6   Financial institutions (or intermediaries)
2.7   Private placement
2.8   secondary market
2.9   over-the-counter market
2.10   increases; fall
2.11   rise
2.12   expectations; forward
2.13   independent
2.14   liquidity (or maturity preference)
2.15   spot
2.16   forward

Solutions to Problems

2.1   According to the Fisher effect:

$$\text{Nominal rate of interest} = \text{Real rate of interest} + \text{Expected rate of inflation}$$

Year	Real Rate of Interest	+	Expected Rate of Inflation	=	Nominal Rate of Interest
1996	3.0%		6.2%		9.2%
1997	3.0		6.8		9.8
1998	3.0		5.4		8.4
1999	3.0		4.0		7.0

2.2   Step 1. Government bonds

	Year 1	Year 5	Year 10	Year 15
Real Rate of Interest +	2.0%	2.0%	2.0%	2.0%
Inflation Premium +	6.0	6.0	6.0	6.0
Maturity Premium	0.3% × 1 = 0.3	0.3% × 5 = 1.5	0.3% × 10 = 3.0	0.3% × 15 = 4.5
Interest Rate	8.3%	9.5%	11.0%	12.5%

Step 2. AAA corporate bonds

	Year			
	1	5	10	15
Real Rate of Interest	2.0%	2.0%	2.0%	2.0%
+ Expected Rate	6.0	6.0	6.0	6.0
+ Maturity Premium	0.3	1.5	3.0	4.5
+ Default Premium	2.5	2.5	2.5	2.5
+ Liquidity Premium	0.8	0.8	0.8	0.8
+ Issue-Specific Premium	2.0	2.0	2.0	2.0
Interest Rate	13.6%	14.8%	16.3%	17.8%

2.3 $\text{Risk premium} = \dfrac{\text{Maturity}}{\text{premium}} + \dfrac{\text{Default}}{\text{premium}} + \dfrac{\text{Liquidity}}{\text{premium}} + \dfrac{\text{Issue-specific}}{\text{premium}}$

Since Durrough Industries, Ltd., has a higher risk premium than Kandel Manufacturing, Ltd., it is more risky.

2.4   a.   This is an upward sloping yield curve. The shape can be explained in terms of the following:
      i.   Expectations theory: Expect rate of inflation to rise.
      ii.   Liquidity preference theory: In addition to expectation theory, an additional premium is required on longer-term bonds.
      iii. Market segmentation theory: Could arise from surplus of short-term investors and shortage of medium-term investors.
  b.   Forward rates implied by the yield curve.

$$f_2 = \frac{(1 + k_2)^2}{(1 + k_1)} - 1 = \frac{(1.0810)^2}{(1.0794)} - 1 = .0826 \text{ or } 8.26\%$$

$$f_3 = \frac{(1 + k_3)^3}{(1 + k_2)^2} - 1 = \frac{(1.0830)^3}{(1.0810)^2} - 1 = .0870 \text{ or } 8.70\%$$

$$f_4 = \frac{(1 + k_4)^4}{(1 + k_3)^3} - 1 = \frac{(1.0847)^4}{(1.0830)^3} - 1 = .0898 \text{ or } 8.98\%$$

$$f_5 = \frac{(1 + k_5)^5}{(1 + k_4)^4} - 1 = \frac{(1.0859)^5}{(1.0847)^4} - 1 = .0907 \text{ or } 9.07\%$$

c.   i.   From the Fisher effect,

$$\text{Nominal short-term interest rate} = \frac{\text{Real rate of}}{\text{interest}} + \frac{\text{Expected}}{\text{inflation}}$$

so, $\text{Expected inflation} = \frac{\text{Nominal short-term}}{\text{interest rate}} - \frac{\text{Real rate of}}{\text{interest}}$

Year	Expected Nominal Short-Term Rate of Interest	−	Real Rate of Interest	=	Expected Inflation
1	7.94%		3.50%		4.44%
2	8.26		3.50		4.76
3	8.70		3.50		5.20
4	8.98		3.50		5.48
5	9.07		3.50		5.57

ii.   Price $= 100/1.0794 + 100/(1.0810)^2 + 100/(1.083)^3 + 1100/(1.0847)^4$
       $= 1051.55$

OR Price $= 100/1.0794 + 100/(1.0794)(1.0826) + 100/(1.0794)(1.0826)(1.0870) +$
       $1100/(1.0794)(1.0826)(1.0870)(1.0898)$
       $= 1051.56$

2.5   a.   6-month spot rates of interest
       i.   6-month T-bill (selling at a discount)
             $961.5384 = 1000/(1 + k_1)$
                 $k_1 = 4\%$
       ii.   1-year T-bill (selling at a discount)
             1 year may be viewed as two periods of six months each.
             $933.511 = 1000/(1 + k_2)^2$
                 $k_2 = 3.5\%$
       iii. 1 1/2-year treasury bond selling at par
             1 1/2 years may be viewed as 3 periods of 6 months each.
             Coupon interest $= \$32.50$ per period.
             $1000 = 32.50/(1 + k_1) + 32.50/(1 + k_2)^2 + 1032.50/(1 + k_3)^3$
             $1000 = 32.50/1.04 + 32.50/(1.035)^2 + 1032.50/(1 + k_3)^3$
             $1000 = 31.25 + 30.34 + 1032.50/(1 + k_3)^3$
                 $k_3 = 3.24\%$
       iv.   2-year treasury bond selling at par
             $1000 = 28.75/1.04 + 28.75/(1.035)^2 + 28.75/(1.0324)^3$
                     $+ 1028.75/(1 + k_4)^4$
             $1000 = 27.64 + 26.84 + 26.13 + 1028.75/(1+k_4)^4$
                 $k_4 = 2.85\%$
       b.   6-month forward rates of interest
       i.

$$f_2 = \frac{(1 + k_2)^2}{(1 + k_1)} - 1 = \frac{(1.035)^2}{(1.04)} - 1 = 3\%$$

       ii.

$$f_3 = \frac{(1 + k_3)^3}{(1 + k_2)^2} - 1 = \frac{(1.0324)^3}{(1.035)^2} - 1 = 2.72\%$$

iii.

$$f_4 = \frac{(1 + k_4)^4}{(1 + k_3)^3} - 1 = \frac{(1.0285)^4}{(1.0324)^3} - 1 = 1.69\%$$

c.

Period	Expected 6-Month Spot Rates	Real Rate of Interest	Expected Rate of Inflation
1	4%	1.2%	2.8%
2	3%	1.2%	1.8%
3	2.72%	1.2%	1.52%
4	1.69%	1.2%	0.49%

d. Coupon interest = $43.75 per period of 6 months

Price = $43.75/1.04 + 43.75/(1.035)^2 + 43.75/(1.0324)^3 + 1043.75/(1.0285)^4$

= $1055.45

Assume expectations theory holds; that is, liquidity (maturity) premium is zero.

Chapter 3
Time Value of Money

How This Chapter Relates to the Rest of the Text

The time value of money is the first fundamental concept of finance discussed in this book. All valuation techniques such as bond and stock pricing (Chapter 4) and capital budgeting (Chapters 7–9) rely on present value. Time value concepts enable us to determine implied interest rates such as yield to maturity (Chapter 4) and the internal rate of return (Chapter 7). Other uses include leasing (Chapter 15) and working capital management (Chapter 23).

Topical Outline

I.   Basic concepts.
    A.   Present value or discounting.
        1.   Involves taking a future amount and figuring out what it is worth today when it is discounted at k percent each year or compounding period.
        2.   Useful for financial or investment planning and answering such questions as: How much would I have to put away at k percent today in order to have $X in 5 years to pay for a college education?
        3.   Equation: $PV_0 = FV_n/(1 + k)^n$ or $PV_0 = FV_n(PV_{k,n})$
        4.   Appendix Table B.1 at the end of the text has present value interest factors (PVs) for your use.
    B.   Future value or compounding.
        1.   Involves taking today's dollar amount and figuring what it will be worth sometime in the future if it earns a return of k percent each year or compounding period.
        2.   Use the formula: $FV_n = PV_0(1 + k)^n$ or $FV_n = PV_0(FV_{k,n})$
        3.   Appendix Table B.3 at the end of the text presents future value interest factors (FVs) for your use.
    C.   Comparing future value and present value.
        1.   Mathematically and theoretically, present value and future value are the inverse of each other.
           a.   Present value takes a future amount in period n and values it today, given a specific discount rate over time from period n to today.
           b.   Future value takes a present amount today and values it at time period n, given a specific compounding rate over the time from today to period n.
        2.   FV factors are the reciprocals of PV factors.
II.   Multiple cash flows: perpetuities, annuities, and uneven payments.
    A.   Perpetuities.
        1.   Fixed annuities into infinity, like preferred stock or a perpetual bond.
        2.   Formula:

$$PV_0 = \frac{\text{annual receipt}}{\text{discount rate}} = \frac{PMT}{k}$$

        3.   The present value of a perpetuity that grows at a constant rate of g percent per year (k is greater than g) is

$$PV_0 = \frac{PMT}{k - g}$$

    B.   Present value of an ordinary annuity.
        1.   Present value of a series of n annual payments of PMT dollars invested at k percent, the first receipt to be received in exactly one year.

2. Formula:

$$PV_0 = PMT \left[\frac{1 - [1/(1+k)^n]}{k} \right]$$

$$= PMT \, (PVA_{k,n})$$

3. Appendix Table B.2 at the end of the textbook has PVAs for you to use: $PV_0 = PMT(PVA_{k,n})$.

C. Present value of an annuity due assumes the first payment is made at the beginning rather than the end of the period.

$$PV_0 \text{ (annuity due)} = PMT \left[\frac{1 - [1/(1+k)]^n}{k} \right] (1 + k)$$

$$= PMT(PVA_{k,n})(1 + k)$$

D. Future value of an ordinary annuity.
1. An annuity is a series of fixed dollar payments for each of a number of periods.
2. Future value of an investment of a fixed dollar amount per period for n periods at k percent; the first payment at the end of the first period.
   a. Payments begin one year from now.
   b.

$$FV_n = PMT \left[\frac{(1 + k)^n - 1}{k} \right]$$

$$= PMT(FVA_{k,n})$$

3. Appendix Table B.4 at the end of the text has future value interest factors for annuities $(FVA_{k,n})$ for you to use: $FV_n = PMT(FVA_{k,n})$.
4. The FVAs are actually the sum of the FVs for the $n - 1$ number of periods plus 1.000.
5. An annuity due assumes the first payment is made at the beginning rather than the end of a period.

$$FV_n \text{ (annuity due)} = PMT \left[\frac{(1+k)^n - 1}{k} \right] (1 + k)$$

$$= PMT \, (FVA_{k,n}) \, (1 + k)$$

E. Present value of an uneven series.
1. Since the payments or receipts are uneven, PVs must be used instead of PVAs.
2. Each receipt must be discounted separately, unless some can be treated as an annuity.
   a. Use PVs on cash flows that are unlike the other cash flows in the series.
   b. If an even series of cash flows exists within the total series of cash flows, use a PVA (for the number of years it is received or paid) to discount these flows back to the period when these even flows begin; then discount this amount back to the present with a PV.

III. Determining interest rates.
A. Single cash flow.
1. If you borrowed $1,000 today and paid interest and principal in a $2,012.07 lump sum in five years, what would be the implied rate?
   a. Equation: $PV_0 = FV_n(PV_{k,n})$
   b. $PV_{k,n} = PV_0/FV_n = \dfrac{\$1,000.00}{\$2,012.07} = 0.497$
   c. When you have solved for PV, look in Appendix Table B.1 across the appropriate year row; in this case, the implied interest rate is 15 percent.
B. Annuities: Do as for a single cash flow, except $PVA_{k,n} = PV_0/PMT$.
C. Uneven series.
1. Trial-and-error approach. Choose an interest rate and use present value interest factors to attempt to exactly equal your present value; see Table 3.5 for an example.

IV.   Applications in financial management.
   A.   Investment decision making.
      1.   To evaluate the acceptablility of an investment project we can calculate either the project's net present value (NPV) or its internal rate of return (IRR).
         a.   NPV = (present value of future cash inflows) − (initial investment)

         $$NPV = \sum_{t=1}^{n} \frac{CF_t}{(1+k)^t} - PV_0$$

         b.   The project's IRR is obtained by solving for the unknown IRR in

         $$\sum_{t=1}^{n} \frac{CF_t}{(1+IRR)^t} = PV_0$$

         c.   Accept the project if its NPV is positive or if its IRR is greater than the discount rate.
      2.   There is a direct relation between the risk level of a project and its discount rate or required rate of return. In general riskier projects have a higher discount rate.
      3.   The discount rate or required rate of return is also referred to as the opportunity cost of capital or hurdle rate.
         a.   It is an opportunity cost of capital because it is the return foregone by investing in a specific asset rather than investing in some other equally risky investment.
         b.   It is a hurdle rate when it is used as the standard against which the IRR is compared.
   B.   Growth rates.
      1.   Determine the number of time periods involved—one less than the number of years (or periods) with which you are dealing.
      2.   Use the following formula:

         $$\text{Implied growth factor} = \text{rate associated with } PV_{k,n} = \frac{\text{beginning value}}{\text{ending value}}$$

      3.   Look in Appendix Table B.1 at the number of periods for the PV factor to find the implied growth rate.
   C.   Future sums.
      1.   You can determine annual funds necessary to accumulate a certain sum in the future.
      2. $$PMT = \frac{FV_n}{FVA_{k,n}}$$

   D.   Effective rate of interest.
      1.   Semiannual and other compounding and discounting periods.
         a.   For discounting, use

         $$PV_0 = \frac{FV_n}{[(1+k/m)]^{nm}}$$

         b.   m = number of periods per year; n = number of years.
         c.   For compounding, use the equation
         $$FV_n = PV_0[1+(k/m)]^{nm}$$

      2. $$k_{\text{effective annual}} = \left[1 + \frac{k_{nominal}}{m}\right]^m - 1$$

      3.   Mortgage payment calculations.
         a.   Canadian law requires interest on fixed rate mortgages to be compounded semiannually even if payments are made weekly, biweekly, or monthly.
         b.   The effective monthly rate is

         $$k_{EM} = \left(1 + \frac{k_{nominal}}{2}\right)^{1/6} - 1$$

c.   Calculate payments using

$$PV_0 = PMT\left[\frac{1 - \left[1/(1 + k_{EM})^{12n}\right]}{k_{EM}}\right]$$

V.   Continuous compounding.
   A.   Continuous compounding assumes that the compounding interval is infinitely small.
   B.   Present values of lump sums: $PV_0 = FV_n e^{-kn}$.
   C.   Future values of lump sums: $FV_n = PV_0 e^{kn}$, where $e = 2.71828$.
   D.   Present value of annuities:

$$PV_0 = PMT\left[\frac{1 - e^{-kn}}{k}\right]$$

   E.   Future value of annuities:

$$FV_n = PMT\left[\frac{e^{kn} - 1}{k}\right]$$

   F.   Effective interest rates: $k_{effective\ annual} = e^{k_{nominal}} - 1$

Formulas

Notation

PV_0 = present (or discounted) value of future amount that will be invested
k   = compounding or discount rate
Fvn   = future (or compounded) value of the present amount you will invest
n   = number of discounting or compounding periods or number of annuity periods
Σ = sigma, or take the sum of
PMT = annuity that starts in time period 1 and extends to time period n
m   = number of times per year the interest is compounded
t   = number of periods you invest the money
g   = constant growth rate per year
NPV = net present value
IRR = internal rate of return

Present Value

$$PV_0 = \frac{FV_n}{(1 + k)^n} = FV_n(PV_{k,n})\qquad\text{(Use Appendix Table B.1)}$$

Future Value

$$FV_n = PV_0(1 + k)^n\qquad\text{(Use Appendix Table B.3)}$$

$$= PV_0(FV_{k,n})$$

Present Value Versus Future Value

$$PV_{k,n} = \frac{1}{FV_{k,n}}$$

<u>Annuities or Perpetuities</u>
Present value:

$$PV_0 = PMT\left[\frac{1 - [1/(1 + k)^n]}{k}\right]$$

$$= PMT(PVA_{k,n}) \quad \text{(Use Appendix Table B.2)}$$

Future value:

$$FV_n = PMT\left[\frac{(1 + k)^n - 1}{k}\right]$$

$$= PMT(FVA_{k,n}) \quad \text{(Use Appendix Table B.4)}$$

Perpetuity:

$$PV_0 = \frac{PMT}{k}$$

Growing perpetuity:

$$PV_0 = \frac{PMT}{k - g}$$

Present value of an annuity due:

$$PV_0 = PMT\left[\frac{1 - [1/(1 + k)^n]}{k}\right](1 + k)$$

$$= PMT(PVA_{k,n})(1 + k)$$

Future value of an annuity due:

$$FV_n = PMT\left[\frac{(1 + k)^n - 1}{k}\right](1 + k)$$

$$= PMT(FVA_{k,n})(1 + k)$$

<u>Determining Interest Rates</u>
Rearrange the above equations as below:

$$PV_{k,n} = PV_0/FV_n$$

$$PVA_{k,n} = PVA_0/PMT$$

<u>Semiannual and Other Compounding and Discounting Periods</u>
Discounting:

$$PV_0 = \frac{FV_n}{[1 + (k/m)]^{m \times n}}$$

Compounding:

$$FV_n = PV_0[1 + (k/m)]^{m \times n}$$

Effective rate of interest:

$$k_{\text{effective annual}} = \left[1 + \frac{k_{\text{nominal}}}{m}\right]^m - 1$$

Net Present Value and Internal Rate of Return

$$NPV = \sum_{t=1}^{n} \frac{CF_t}{(1 + k)^t} - PV_0$$

$$\sum_{t=1}^{n} \frac{CF_t}{(1 + IRR)^t} = PV_0$$

Calculating Mortgage Payments

$$k_{EM} = \left(1 + \frac{k_{nominal}}{2}\right)^{1/6} - 1$$

$$PVA_0 = PMT\left[\frac{\left[1 - 1/(1 + k_{EM})^{12n}\right]}{k_{EM}}\right]$$

Continuous Compounding

Present value: $PV_0 = FV_n e^{-kn}$

Future value: $FV_n = PV_0 e^{kn}$

Present value of an annuity: $PV_0 = PMT\left[\frac{1 - e^{-kn}}{k}\right]$

Future value of an annuity: $FV_n = PMT\left[\frac{e^{kn} - 1}{k}\right]$

Effective interest rate: $k_{effective\ annual} = e^{k}_{nom} - 1$

What to Look For

Chapter 3 is the first of three critical chapters in this text; here we look at the time value of money. Up to now, we have made only general comments about interest or discount rates. In Chapter 3, we begin using interest rates. If your accounting class has covered the time value of money, you will find these concepts familiar. If you have never studied the time value of money, you will find it is a simple, common-sense approach for dealing with cash flows that occur at different points in time.

Terminology and Examples of Time Value

The study of time value will be easier if we understand a few terms.

Time value of money

Since money can be invested productively to earn a positive rate of return, a dollar received today is worth more than a dollar to be received sometime in the future. The difference in value depends upon the expected rate of return on that dollar received today.

Present value (PV$_0$)

A dollar to be received in 10 years is worth much less than if received today. This is the case because if we had the dollar today we could invest it and earn a rate of return. Therefore, its present value would be the future value, $1, discounted at the foregone rate of return—$1/(1 + k)^n—where k = the (foregone) rate of return and n = the number of discounting periods. Suppose that in delaying this $1 receipt by 10 years, we are foregoing a 15 percent annual rate of return on it. To find that future dollar's present value, we must discount it back to the present at the 15 percent discount rate:

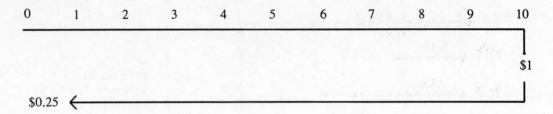

$$PV_0 = FV_n/(1 + k)^n = \$1\left[1/(1 + k)^n\right] = \$1(1/4.0455578)$$
$$= \$1(0.2471847) = \$0.2471847$$

So, a dollar to be received in 10 years is worth 25 cents today. This computation could be even simpler if you use the PVs from Appendix Table B.1 and the following equation:

$$PV_0 = FV_n(PV_{k,n}) = \$1(PV_{15\%,10yr}) = \$1(0.247) = \$0.247$$

Future value (FV)
Since the dollar received today can be invested, we can calculate the present dollar's future value by reversing the process we used for present value. In this case, its future value would be its present value, $1, compounded at the expected rate of return—$1(1 + k)n—where k = the rate of return and n = the number of compounding periods. If, as before, k = 15 percent and n = 10, what is the future value of the $1 received today earning 15 percent annually for 10 years?

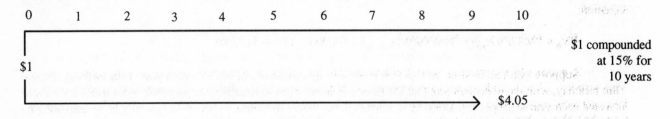

$$FV_{10} = PV_0(1 + k)^n = \$1(1 + 0.15)^{10} = \$1(4.0455578) = \$4.0455578$$

If you use the FVs in Appendix Table B.3 and the following equation, the computation is even simpler:

$$FV_n = PV_0(FV_{k,n}) = PV_0(FV_{15\%,10yr}) = \$1(4.046) = \$4.046$$

Annuity (PMT)
People who pay car or mortgage payments are often involved in paying an annuity. An annuity is a series of equal payments for a specified number of periods, typically years or months, with each payment occurring at the end of the period.

Suppose you are guaranteed that a university education (tuition) will cost $4,000 each year for four years and you will enter university on your 18th birthday. You would like to know how much of a nest egg you must have on your 18th birthday to make this series of tuition annuities. Let's remember that the money that you do not pay out in the first year's tuition stays invested until it is used sometime during the annuity series. What is the present value of this annuity of $4,000 for four years?

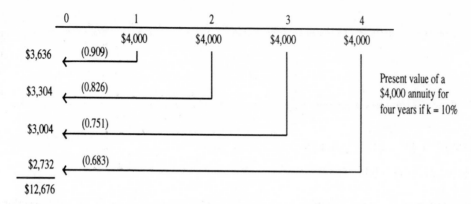

Present value of a $4,000 annuity for four years if k = 10%

or we can calculate the present value of this annuity as follows:

$$PV = PMT\left[\frac{1 - [1/(1 + k)^n]}{k}\right] = \$4,000\left[\frac{[1 - (1 + 0.10)^4]}{0.10}\right]$$

$$= \$4,000\left[\frac{1 - (1/1.4641)}{0.10}\right] = \$4,000\left[\frac{1 - 0.68301346}{0.10}\right]$$

$$= \$4,000(3.1698654) = \$12,679.462$$

By the time you reach 18, you would need a nest egg of $12,679.462 in order to pay your tuition. An even simpler method of calculating the present value of an annuity is to use the PVAs in Appendix Table B.2 and the following equation:

$$PV_0 = PMT(PVA_{k,n}) = \$4,000(PVA_{10\%, 4yr}) = \$4,000(3.170) = \$12,680$$

Suppose you received an annual gift from your grandparents of $1,500 from your 13th birthday to your 18th birthday, with the understanding that the money is to be saved to finance your university education. It would be invested each year at 10 percent annually in a bank. What would the future value of that annuity be by the time you were 18? This will be your university tuition nest egg. Will this nest egg be large enough to make your annual tuition payments? Let's calculate n first: end of 13th year (13th birthday) to the end of the 18th year (18th birthday) = 6 = n. We can calculate the future value of this annuity as follows:

Age	13	14	15	16	17	18	
	$1,500	$1,500	$1,500	$1,500	$1,500	$1,500	
					(1.100)	$1,650.00	$1,500 each year
					(1.210)	$1,815.00	for six years,
					(1.331)	$1,916.50	compounded at 10%
					(1.464)	$2,196.00	
					(1.611)	$2,416.50	
						$11,574.00	

or, using the equation 3.11, we can solve this as follows:

$$FV_n = PMT\left[\frac{(1+k)^n - 1}{k}\right] = \$1,500\left[\frac{[1+0.10)^6 - 1]}{0.10}\right]$$

$$= \$1,500\left[(1.771561 - 1)/0.10\right] = \$11,573.415$$

Again, the simpler method of calculating the future value of this annuity is to use the FVAs from Appendix Table B.4 and the following equation:

$$FVA_n = PMT(FVA_{k,n}) = \$1,500(FVA_{10\%,6yr}) = \$1,500(7.716) = \$11,574$$

You will need $12,679 to pay for your university education but will have a nest egg of only $11,574. Therefore, you must add $1,105 to your grandparents' contribution.

We can easily find the present value of an uneven series of payments or receipts. We should first look at the payments on a time line to get a better idea of how to solve for the present value. Look at the two time lines below; each represents an uneven series.

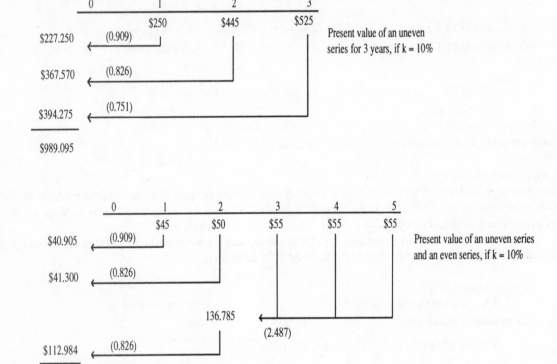

Using this approach and drawing time lines makes the calculation of the present value of any uneven time series easy.

Determining interest rates

Just as in any problem using time values, practice is necessary to feel comfortable with determining interest rates. This chapter discusses how to determine interest rates for single cash flows, annuities, uneven series, and growth rates. The key here is to try to solve for the interest factor and then match it to the implied rate. Examples in the text should help you in practising this type of problem.

Investment Decision Making

Net present value (NPV) and internal rate of return (IRR) are two methods that firms may use to evaluate the acceptability of investment projects. Both methods apply the concepts of time value of money. For NPV we must calculate the present value of the cash inflows generated by the project over its life and subtract from this the cost or initial investment required to undertake the project. On the other hand, for IRR we must determine the interest rate, or internal rate of return, that equates the present value of the cash inflows generated by a project over its life to the intital investment in the project. Consequently, the IRR of a project is that discount rate that makes NPV = 0. Examples in the text show how these procedures are carried out.

Changing the compounding period

To this point, we've assumed that interest is paid on an annual basis. That is, however, not always the case. For example, banks generally require monthly payments on loans. Suppose, for instance, that we spend $15,000 to purchase a car. A bank lends us the funds at 12 percent per year for five years but requires monthly payments. How much are those payments? (Assume monthly compounding of interest.)

First, we need to recognize that this is an annuity problem; our series of car payments is simply a stream of equal payments. Next, we need to calculate the number of payments (5 years $\times$ 12 months/year = 60 months) and the monthly interest rate (12%/year $\div$ 12 months/year = 1%/month). The problem can be solved as follows.

$$PV_0 = PMT(PVA_{k\%,n})$$

$$\$15,000 = PMT(PVA_{1\%,60months})$$

$$PMT = \frac{15,000}{44.955}$$

$$= \$333.67$$

The bank would require payments of $333.67 per month for 60 months.

Continuous compounding

Continuous compounding is a special case of changing the compounding period. In this approach, the compounding interval is infinitely small. Special computational formulas are used in continuous compounding; in all of the formulas presented earlier, the expression $(1 + k)^n$ is replaced with e^{kn} where e is 2.71828...

To show how continuous compounding affects value, suppose we deposited $1,000 in an account paying 6 percent and left it for 10 years. The value in the account after 10 years is

annual compounding:
$$FV_{10} = \$1,000(1.06)^{10} = \$1,790.85$$
semiannual compounding:
$$FV_{10} = \$1,000(1 + \frac{.06}{2})^{10(2)} = \$1,000(1.03)^{20}$$

$$= \$1,806.11$$
monthly compounding:
$$FV_{10} = \$1,000(1 + \frac{.06}{12})^{10(12)} = \$1,000(1.0005)^{120}$$

$$= \$1,819.40$$
continuous compounding:
$$FV_{10} = \$1,000e^{.06(10)} = \$1,000e^{0.6} = \$1,822.12$$

Changing the compounding period increases the speed at which we receive (or pay) interest and hence affects present and future value. Appropriate consideration of the compounding period is essential for good financial management.

Completion Questions

3.1   If you compare a dollar received today to a dollar received in one year, the dollar to be received _____ is more valuable, because money has _____.

3.2   You want to find out how much money you will have in 10 years if you leave $1,000 in a savings account earning 10 percent. To solve this problem, you must calculate the _____ of the $1,000.

3.3   You want to know how much money you will need when you are 21 in order to pay graduate school tuition of $5,000 for each of four years, given that the unused balance stays invested at 10 percent. For the solution to this problem, you need to find the _____ of the annuity.

3.4   The present value interest factors are actually the inverse of the _____ factors.

3.5   The _____ is the rate we use in calculating present value. It represents the required rate of return.

3.6   A _____ is an annuity that continues at a constant amount into infinity, like cash dividends on preferred stock.

3.7   If we want to know the cumulative savings after saving $15 per month at 12 percent for 3 years, we find the _____ of the annuity.

3.8   The value of a perpetuity is found by dividing the annuity by the _____.

3.9   Suppose you know the price and the expected uneven cash inflow series for an investment. You do not know the rate of return. You use the trial-and-error method to find the discount rate that makes the discounted present value of the cash inflows exactly equal to the investment's _____.

3.10   A project should be undertaken if its _____ is _____ or, alternatively, if its _____ is greater than _____.

3.11   By law, interest on fixed rate Canadian mortgages is compounded _____ even though payments are usually made _____.

Problems

3.1   Suppose you deposited $3,500 a year for 10 years in a savings account paying 12 percent interest, compounded annually. The first deposit will be made exactly one year from now. How much could you withdraw per year from years 11 through 20 if you wanted to have a balance of $1,000 one year after the last withdrawal (i.e., in year 21)?

3.2   Suppose your parents had decided to plan for your university education at a private university in the U.S. Their intent was to make equal deposits on each of your first 17 birthdays and give you $20,000 a year for 4 years starting on your 18th birthday. If the savings account paid 6 percent interest compounded annually, how much should the yearly deposits have been?

3.3   Mr. Michael Andrews will purchase one of two bonds. Bond A is a zero-coupon bond (that is, it is issued at a discount and pays no cash interest over its life, but it matures at a value greater than the issuance price). It will be issued for $295 and will pay a lump sum of $1,000 10 years from now. Bond B promises coupon payments of $100 per year for 10 years as well as the $1,000 principal repayment in the 10th year. What price would Andrews be willing to pay for bond B if he thought both bonds should offer the same compound rate of return?

3.4   Using an interest rate of 15 percent, calculate the present value of the following stream of cash inflows.

Year	Cash Inflows
1	$100
2	300
3	500
4	600
5	300
6	200

If this stream can be purchased for $900, what is its NPV? Finally, calculate the future value of this stream of payments in year 6. Use a time line to illustrate your calculations.

3.5   Suppose you deposited $2,000 in a savings account 15 years ago. For the first 5 years, the account paid 5 percent interest compounded annually. For the second 5 years, it paid 6 percent compounded semiannually. For the last 5 years, it paid 8 percent compounded quarterly.

a.   What is the balance in the account today?
b.   What is the average annual compound rate over the entire life of the deposit?

3.6   Many credit cards charge an interest rate of 1.5 percent per month, or a nominal rate of 18 percent per year. What is the effective annual interest rate on such credit cards?

3.7   Marion Willoughby recently purchased a new automobile for $12,500. She made a $1,000 down payment and financed the balance over 24 months using a loan with a 12 percent annual nominal rate of interest compounded monthly. What are her monthly payments?

3.8   Russell Gula recently obtained a $150,000 mortgage from Eastern Canada Bank with a nominal interest rate of 10 percent per year. If the mortgage requires 20 years of monthly payments, how much will Mr. Gula pay per month?

3.9   Many provinces in Canada now offer lotteries as a method of raising funds. Some lotteries offer prizes as either a lump sum or an annuity. Suppose you are offered your choice between a $50,000 lifetime annuity with the first payment a year from today or a prize of $1,000,000 today. If you expect to live 50 more years, at what interest rate would you be better off with the annuity? (Ignore any tax effects.)

3.10   Your rich friend has promised you an annuity of $360 every 3 months (quarterly) for the next 36 months. If payments are made at the end of each quarter, you expect to realize $4,828.35 at the end of the 36th month (assuming quarterly compounding of interest).

a.   What is the quarterly interest on your deposit?
b.   What is the effective annual interest on your deposit? Effective monthly rate on your deposit?
c.   What would be the balance in your account at the end of the 36th month if payments are made at the beginning of each quarter?
d.   Suppose you are also given the option to take a lump sum of $3,785.25 today or take the quarterly annuity of $360. Which option would you choose and why?

3.11   Suppose you have been promised an annuity of $200 per month for 2 years. Interest rate is 9 percent per year.

a.   Assuming the interest rate is compounded quarterly:
   i.   What is the balance in your account at the end of year 2 if payments are made at the end of each month?
   ii.   What is the balance in your account at the end of year 2 if payments are made at the beginning of each month?

b.   Redo part (a) assuming interest is compounded monthly.

c.   What accounts for the difference in your answers in parts (a) and (b)?

3.12   Suppose you wish to buy a house whose current market value is $150,000. You therefore approach a loan officer at the Bank of Nova Scotia (BNS) who offers 75 percent 25-year mortgage financing at a rate of 9.75 percent. Payments are to be made on a monthly basis even though the bank is required by law to compound interest semiannually.

a.   What are the *effective* annual and monthly rates of interest on the loan?

b.   Assuming that loan payments are due at the end of each month:

i.   Determine the size of the monthly loan payments.

ii.   Determine the amortization schedule for the first 3 months.

iii.   Determine the principal outstanding at the end of the 5th year.

c.   Redo part (b) sections (i) and (ii), assuming the loan payments are due at the beginning of each month.

3.13   Suppose you have $2,800 to invest today for the next 4 years. You expect interest rates to be 12 percent for the coming year, 14 percent for years 2 and 3, and 10 percent thereafter.

a.   What will the balance in your account be at the end of year 4, assuming annual interest compounding?

b.   What will the balance in your account be at the end of year 4, assuming interest is compounded monthly?

c.   What will the balance in your account be at the end of year 4 assuming continuous compounding of interest rate?

d.   For each of parts (a), (b), and (c), compute the annual yield or internal rate of return (IRR) on your investment over the 4-year period.

3.14   A Saint Mary's University professor is due to retire in 6 years. He expects to live for another 15 years after his retirement. During his retirement, he wants to draw $12,000 at the beginning of each year to finance his annual trip to the Caribbean. He currently has $8,500 in his savings account. Interest rates are expected to be 12 percent per year over the next 6 years. Thereafter the rates are expected to drop to 10 percent per year forever. Assume interest is compounded semiannually.

a.   How much will this professor have to accumulate in his savings account at the end of year 6 to meet the stated objective?

b.   How much will this professor have to deposit in his account at the end of each month for the next 6 years to accumulate this amount?

c.   What lump sum would he need to deposit in his account today to achieve the stated objective?

3.15   Maritime Investments is offering two investments, both maturing in 10 years. The first promises a 12.7 percent return, annual compounding. The second promises 12.0 percent, continuously compounded. Which investment will result in the highest value 10 years from now?

3.16   Recently, Ms. Barbara Wick inherited $1,000,000 from her aunt. Her desire is to put the money in a savings account paying 6.5 percent per year compounded continuously and draw funds out in equal installments 1 year apart over the next 30 years, starting 1 year from today. How much can she withdraw per year?

Answers to Completion Questions

3.1   today; time value

3.2   future value

3.3   present value

3.4   future value interest
3.5   discount rate
3.6   perpetuity
3.7   future value
3.8   discount rate (or rate of return)
3.9   present value (or price)
3.10   net present value (NPV); positive; internal rate of return (IRR); the discount rate
3.11   semiannually; monthly

Solutions to Problems

3.1   Step 1.   Find the balance in year 10.

$$FV_{10} = \$3,500(FVA_{12\%,10yr}) = \$3,500(17.549) = \$61,421.50$$

   Step 2.   Set this balance equal to the 10-year annuity plus the \$1,000 balance desired at the end of year 21, and solve for the annuity PMT.

$$FV_{10} = PMT(PVA_{12\%,10yr}) + \$1,000(PV_{12\%,11yr})$$

$$\$61,421.50 = PMT(5.650) + \$1,000(0.287)$$

$$PMT = \frac{\$61,421.50 - \$287.00}{5.650} = \$10,820.27$$

3.2   Step 1.   Find out how much money would have to be on deposit in year 17 to allow the withdrawal of \$20,000 a year for 4 years if the interest rate is 6 percent.

$$PV_{17} = \$20,000(PVA_{6\%,4yr}) = \$20,000(3.465) = \$69,300$$

   Step 2.   Now find the annuity that will give you a value of \$69,300 after 17 deposits.

$$FV_{17} = PMT(FVA_{6\%,17yr})$$

$$PMT = \frac{FV_{17}}{FVA_{6\%,17yr}} = \frac{\$69,300}{28.213} = \$2,456.31$$

3.3   Step 1.   Calculate the rate of return (or discount rate) on bond A, the zero-coupon bond.

$$PV_A = FV_n(PV_{k\%,10yr}), \text{ so } \$295 = \$1,000(PV_{k\%,10yr})$$

$$PV_{k\%,10yr} = \$295/\$1,000 = 0.295$$

   From Table B.1, k = 13%

   Step 2.   Bond B is a 10-year annuity of \$100 per year plus a lump sum of \$1,000 in year 10. At a discount rate of 13 percent:

$$PV_B = \$100(PV_{13\%,10yr}) + \$1,000(PV_{13\%,10yr})$$
$$= \$100(5.426) + \$1,000(0.295) = \$837.60$$

   Andrews would pay \$837.60.

3.4   Step 1.

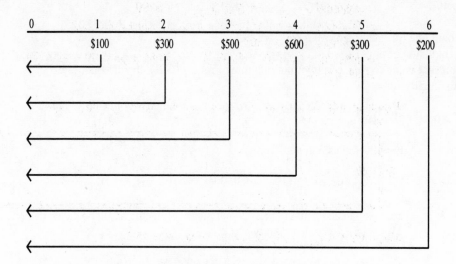

$$PV_0 = \$100(PV_{15\%,1yr}) + \$300(PV_{15\%,2yr}) + 500(PV_{15\%,3yr})$$
$$+ \$600(PV_{15\%,4yr}) + \$300(PV_{15\%,5yr}) + \$200(PV_{15\%,6yr})$$
$$= \$100(0.870) + \$300(0.756) + \$500(0.658) + \$600(0.572)$$
$$+ \$300(0.497) + \$200(0.432)$$
$$= \$87.00 + \$226.80 + \$329.00 + \$343.20 + \$149.10 + 86.40$$
$$= \$1,221.50$$

Step 2.   NPV = present value of future cash inflows − initial investment
= $1,221.50 − $900.00 = $321.50

Step 3.

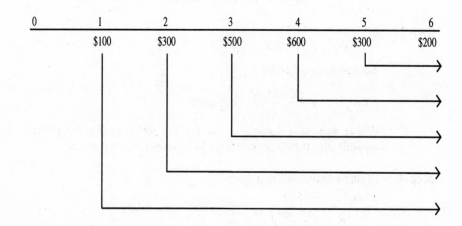

$$FV_6 = \$100(FV_{15\%,5yr}) + \$300(FV_{15\%,4yr}) + 500(FV_{15\%,3yr})$$
$$+ \$600(FV_{15\%,2yr}) + \$300(FV_{15\%,1yr}) + \$200$$
$$= \$100(2.011) + \$300(1.749) + \$500(1.521) + \$600(1.323)$$
$$+ \$300(1.150) + \$200$$
$$= \$201.10 + \$524.70 + \$760.50 + \$793.80 + \$345.00 + \$200.00$$
$$= \$2,825.10$$

However, a far easier way is to start from the answer to step 1. Thus,

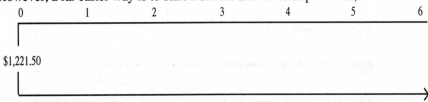

$$FV_6 = PV_0(FV_{15\%,6yr}) = \$1,221.50(2.313) = \$2,825.33$$

3.5   a.   Step 1.

Years (n)	Annual Rate (k)	Periodic Rate (k/m)	Number of Periods (m − n)
1–5	5%	5%	5
6–10	6%	6%/2 = 3%	2 × 5 = 10
11–15	8%	8%/4 = 2%	4 × 5 = 20

Step 2. $FV_{15} = \$2,000(FV_{5\%,5\ periods})(FV_{3\%,10\ periods})(FV_{2\%,20\ periods})$
$= \$2,000(1.276)(1.344)(1.486) = \$5,096.81$

or $FV_{15} = \$2,000(1.05)^5 \left(1 + \dfrac{0.06}{2}\right)^{2 \times 5} \left(1 + \dfrac{0.08}{4}\right)^{4 \times 5}$

$= \$2,000(1.05)^5(1.03)^{10}(1.02)^{20} = \$5,097.44$

b.   Step 3.

$$FV_{15} = PV_0(FV_{k\%,15yr})$$

$$\$5,096.81 = \$2,000(FV_{k\%,15yr})$$

$$FV_{k\%,15yr} = \frac{\$5,096.81}{\$2,000} = 2.5484$$

Using Appendix Table B.3, the factor is between 6 and 7 percent. By inspection, it is slightly closer to 6 percent than to 7 percent, say 6.4 percent.

Step 4.   Using a financial calculator:
$(1+k)^{15} = 2.5484$

$$k = [2.5484]^{1/15} - 1$$
$$k = [1.06435] - 1 = 6.435\%$$

3.6 $k_{effective\ annual} = \left(1 + \dfrac{k_{nominal}}{m}\right)^m - 1$

$= \left(1 + \dfrac{0.18}{12}\right)^{12} - 1$

$= (1.015)^{12} - 1 = 0.1956$ or 19.56%

3.7   Step 1. $PV_0 = \$12,500 - \$1,000 = \$11,500$

$k = \dfrac{12\%}{12mo} = 1\%/\,month$

Step 2. $PMT = \dfrac{PV_0}{PVA_{k,n}} - \dfrac{\$11,500}{PVA_{1\%,24}} = \dfrac{\$11,500}{21.243} = \$541.35/\,month$

3.8   Step 1. $k_{EM} = \left(1 + \dfrac{k_{nominal}}{2}\right)^{1/6} - 1$

$= \left(1 + \dfrac{.10}{2}\right)^{1/6} - 1$

$= (1.05)^{1/6} - 1$

$= 1.0081648 - 1$

$= .0081648$

Step 2. $PVA_0 = PMT\left[\dfrac{1 - \left[1/(1 + k_{EM})^{12n}\right]}{k_{EM}}\right]$

$150,000 = PMT\left[\dfrac{1 - \left[1/1.0081648^{240}\right]}{.0081648}\right]$

$= PMT\left[\dfrac{1 - 1/7.0399115}{.0081648}\right]$

$= PMT\left[\dfrac{1 - 0.1420472}{.0081648}\right]$

$= PMT\left[\dfrac{0.85795276}{.0081648}\right]$

$= PMT[105.0795]$

$PMT = \dfrac{150,000}{105.0795}$

$= \$1,427.49$

3.9   Step 1.   If the present value of the annuity equals $1,000,000, you should be indifferent between the two payment plans. Find the rate where

$\$1,000,000 = \$50,000(PVA_{k\%,50yr})$

$PVA_{k\%,50yr} = \dfrac{\$1,000,000}{\$50,000} = 20.000$

Step 2.   From the PVA table, 20.000 lies between the factors for 4 percent and 5 percent.
Via financial calculator, the rate is 4.427%.
If you could reinvest at a rate greater than 4.427 percent, you would be better off with the $1,000,000. For rates greater than 4.427 percent, the present value of the annuity is less than $1,000,000.

3.10   a.   Let k denote the quarterly rate of interest. Then we equate the future value of an annuity of $360 for 12 quarters (36/3) to $4,828.35:

$360[((1 + k)^{12} − 1)/k] = \$4,828.35$
or
$360FVA_{k\%,12 \text{ periods}} = \$4,828.35$
$FVA_{k\%,12 \text{ periods}} = 13.4121$
From Table B.4, k = 2%
Hence, the quarterly rate is 2 percent.

b.   i. $k_{\text{effective annual}} = (1.02)^4 − 1 = 8.24\%$
ii. $k_{\text{effective monthly}} = (1.02)^{1/3} − 1 = 0.662\%$

c.   If payments are made at the begining of each quarter, then
$FV = \$4,828.35(1.02)^4$
$= \$4,828.35(1.0824) = \$5226.21$

d.   If the lump sum of $3,785.25 is invested for 3 years at 8.24 percent per year, then
$FV = \$3,785.25(1.0824)^3$
$= \$4800.12$
Take the quarterly annuity since its future value is greater.

3.11   a.   If interest is compounded quarterly, then the effective rate per quarter = 0.09/4 = 0.0225.
Therefore, the effective monthly rate, $k_{EM} = (1.0225)^{1/3} − 1 = 0.00744$
Recognizing that there are 24 months in two years,
i. $FV_{24} = \$200[((1.00744)^{24} − 1)/0.00744]$
$= \$5,234.58$
ii.   If payments are made at the beginning of each month, then
$FV_{24} = \$5,234.58(1.00744)$
$= \$5,273.53$

b.   If interest is compounded monthly,
$k_{EM} = 0.09/12 = 0.0075$
i.   If payments are made at the end of each month, then
$FV_{24} = \$200[((1.0075)^{24} − 1)/0.0075]$
$= \$5,237.69$
ii.   If payments are made at the beginning of each month, then
$FV_{24} = \$5,237.69(1.0075) = \$5276.98$

c.   The differences in the results of parts (a) and (b) are due to the compounding effect of interest rates. The higher the frequency of compounding of interest rates, the greater the terminal value of the annuity. Thus, monthly compounding of interest should yield a higher future value than quarterly compounding of interest.

3.12   Since BNS is required by law to compound interest semiannually, the effective rate for 6-month period is 4.875 percent (9.75/2).

a. $k_{\text{effective annual}} = (1.04875)^2 - 1 = 0.09988$
$k_{EM} = (1.09988)1/12 - 1$
$= 0.007965$
or $k_{EM} = (1.04875)^{1/6} - 1$
$= 0.007965$

b.   i.   Total number of monthly payments = 25 ¥ 12 = 300
$k_{EM} = 0.007965$
Amount of loan = 0.75($150,000) = $112,500
Let PMT = size of loan payment

$$\$112,500 = PMT\left[\frac{1 - [1/(1.007965)^{300}]}{0.007965}\right]$$

$112,500 = PMT(113.9300)$

PMT = $987.45

Monthly payments amount to $987.45.

ii.   Loan amortization schedule

Month	Beginning Balance	Monthly Payment	Interest	Principal Repayment	Remaining Balance
1	$112,500	$987.45	$896.06	$91.39	$112,408.61
2	112,408.61	987.45	895.33	92.12	112,316.49
3	112,316.49	987.45	894.60	92.85	112,223.64

iii.   At the end of year 5, you have made 60 monthly payments, leaving 240 payments to go.

$$\text{Remaining principal} = \$987.45\left[\frac{1 - [1/(1.007965)^{240}]}{0.007965}\right]$$

$= \$987.45(106.85)$

$= \$105,505.59$

c.   i.   If loan payments are due at the beginning of each month, then monthly payment
= $987.45(1.007965) = $995.32.

ii.   Loan amortization schedule when loan payments are made at the beginning of each month

Month	Beginning Balance	Monthly Payment	Interest	Principal Repayment	Remaining Balance
1	$112,500	$995.32		$995.32	$111,504.65
2	111,504.68	995.32	$888.13	107.19	111,397.49
3	111,397.49	995.32	887.28	108.04	111,289.45

3.13   a.   If we assume annual compounding of interest, then
$FV_4 = \$2,800(1.12)(1.14)^2(1.1)$
$= \$4,483.10$

b.   If interest is compounded monthly, then
the effective annual rate for year 1 = $(1 + 0.12/12)^{12} - 1 = (1.01)^{12} - 1 = 0.126825$,
the effective annual rates for year 2 and 3 = $(1 + 0.14/12)^{12} - 1 = (1.01167)^{12} - 1 = 0.14934$, and
the effective annual rate for year 4 = $(1 + 0.10/12)^{12} - 1 = (1.00833)^{12} - 1 = 0.1047$.
$FV_4 = \$2,800(1.126825)(1.14934)^2(1.1047)$
$= \$4,604.27$

c. If interest is compounded continuously, then
the effective rate for year $1 = e^{0.12} - 1 = 0.1275$,
the effective rates for year 2 and $3 = e^{0.14} - 1 = 0.1503$, and
the effective rate for year $4 = e^{0.1} - 1 = 0.1052$.
$FV_4 = \$2,800(1.1275)(1.1503)^2(1.1052)$
$= \$4,616.64$

d. i.   Annual compounding of interest
$\$2,800 = \$4,483.10/(1 + IRR)^4$

$$IRR = \left(\frac{\$4,483.10}{\$2,800}\right)^{1/4} - 1$$

$IRR = 0.1249\ (12.49\%)$

ii. Monthly compounding of interest
$\$2,800 = \$4,604.27/(1 + IRR)^4$

$$IRR = \left(\frac{\$4,604.27}{\$2,800}\right)^{1/4} - 1$$

$IRR = 0.1324\ (13.24\%)$

iii. Continuous compounding of interest
$\$2,800 = \$4,616.64/(1 + IRR)^4$

$$IRR = \left(\frac{\$4,616.64}{\$2,800}\right)^{1/4} - 1$$

$IRR = 0.1332\ (13.32\%)$

3.14 Note that as soon as the professor retires at the end of year 6, he will need \$12,000 immediately to finance his first trip to the Caribbean.

a. Effective annual rate for year 7 and beyond is 10.25 percent.

$$PV_0\ (\text{annuity due}) = \$12,000\left[\frac{1 - [1/(1.1025)^{15}]}{0.1025}\right](1.1025)$$

$$= \$99,208.55$$

b. Since interest for the next 6 years is expected to be 12 percent compounded semiannually, the effective rate for 6 months is 6 percent.

Effective monthly rate $= (1.06)^{1/6} - 1$

$= 0.009759$

$$PMT\left[\frac{(1.009759)^{72} - 1}{0.009759}\right] = 99,208.55$$

$$PMT(103.7223) = \$99,208.55$$

$$PMT = \$956.48$$

The professor needs to deposit \$956.48 each month for the next 6 years.

c. $PV_0 = \$99,208.55/(1.06)^{12}$
$PV_0 = \$49,303.61$
or $PV_0 = \$99,208.55(PV_{6\%, 12\text{ periods}})$
$= \$99,208.55(0.497) = \$49,306.65$
A lump sum of \$49,303.61 deposited today will achieve the same result in 6 years as a monthly deposit of \$956.48.

3.15   Step 1.   For the first investment,

$FV_{10} = \$10,000(1.127)^{10}$

$= \$10,000(3.305515)$

$= 33,055.15$

Step 2.   For the second investment,

$FV_{10} = \$10,000e^{0.12(10)}$

$= \$10,000e^{1.2}$

$= \$10,000(3.320117)$

$= \$33,201.17$

The continuously compounded investment offers the highest future value.

3.16 $\$1,000,000 = PMT\left[\dfrac{1 - e^{-kn}}{k}\right]$

$\$1,000,000 = PMT\left[\dfrac{1 - e^{-.06(30)}}{.06}\right]$

$= PMT\left[\dfrac{1 - e^{-1.8}}{.06}\right]$

$= PMT\left[13.911685\right]$

$PMT = \dfrac{\$1,000,000}{13.911685}$

$= \$71,882.02$ per year

Chapter 4
Valuation of Bonds and Stocks

How This Chapter Relates to the Rest of the Text

Common stocks and bonds are the two main sources of external capital for a firm (Chapters 10–11). The value of these assets is a function of their cash flows, timing (Chapter 3), and riskiness (Chapter 5). The firm's opportunity cost of capital or required return (Chapter 6) is a function of the returns on stocks and bonds. Many managerial decisions such as capital budgeting (Chapters 7–9) and capital structure (Chapters 12 and 13) have an impact on the value of the firm's securities.

Topical Outline

I.   Financial assets.
   A.   Financial assets are created when demanders of funds, such as firms or governments, raise funds in financial markets.
   B.   The major forms of financial assets are bonds and stocks.
II.   Determining bond values and yields.
   A.   Bond characteristics.
      1.   Promissory notes are issued by a firm or government.
      2.   Issued for the short term (less than one year), intermediate term (1 to 10 years), or long term (10 to 30 years).
      3.   Par value or stated face value of a bond is generally $1,000; this is the maturity value of the bond.
      4.   The coupon interest rate is the stated interest rate that will be paid annually (with the exception of securities, like treasury bills, or zero-coupon bonds, which are sold at a discount originally and pay no periodic interest).
      5.   Maturity is the length of time in years until repayment of the bond is legally due.
      6.   New issues are bonds that have not been in the market before and are sold in the primary market to generate funds for the issuer.
      7.   Outstanding issues are bonds traded in the secondary market, providing no new money to the issuer.
      8.   The market price of coupon bonds will typically be at or close to par when newly issued; an outstanding bond's market price may be far from par value.
   B.   The bond valuation model.
      1.   The value of a bond is the present value of its expected cash flows in terms of interest and maturity repayment.
      2. $B_0 = I(PVA_{k_b,n}) + M(PV_{k_b,n})$
      3.   Some bonds sell at a premium (discount) because the current market interest rate for bonds of that risk level is less (greater) than the bond's coupon interest rate. Prices of shorter maturity bonds fluctuate less than those of longer maturity bonds as market interest rates change.
   C.   Interest rates and bond prices.
      1.   Bond prices move inversely with interest rates. As interest rates increase, bond prices decrease.
      2.   The required rate of return on bonds will change if the expected inflation and maturity, default, liquidity, or issue-specific premiums change.
   D.   Yield to maturity. This is the discount rate that equates the present value of the bond's future cash flows to its current price. To estimate this discount rate, do the following:
      1.   Use the bond valuation formula above.
         a.   Set up a relationship among missing present value interest factors, cash flows, and the market price.
         b.   Use the tables to find the correct discount rate to balance the equation.
      2.   In searching for the correct discount rate, remember that as the discount rate increases, the

present value decreases.

- E. Bonds with semiannual interest.
    1. Most bonds pay interest semiannually.
    2. For semiannual interest payments:

$$B_0 = \sum_{t=1}^{2n} \frac{I}{2} \left[\frac{1}{1 + (k_b/2)} \right]^t + M \left[\frac{1}{1 + (k_b/2)} \right]^{2n}$$

$$= \frac{I}{2} (PVA_{k_b/2, \, 2n}) + M(PV_{k_b/2, \, 2n})$$

- F. Bond valuation and financial management.
    1. Bonds are one of the main sources of capital for firms; understanding the valuation process is important for financial managers.
    2. Determining the firm's opportunity cost of capital (Chapter 6), and capital structure (Chapters 12 and 13) requires knowledge of bond pricing.
    3. Managers must understand bond valuation in order to determine the appropriate form of financing for the firm.
- G. Consol bonds and preferred stock.
    1. A consol bond is a perpetual coupon rate bond.
    2. For consols,

$$B_0 = \frac{I}{k_b}$$

    3. Preferred stock is similarly valued with dividends replacing the coupon rate

III. Determining common stock values.
- A. The value of common stock is the present value of their expected cash flows; it is adjusted for expected growth in the stock price and cash dividends.
- B. The dividend valuation model
    1. Value of common stock is equal to the present value of the expected cash dividends and future market price.
    2. Value $= P_0 = \sum_{t=1}^{n} \frac{D_t}{\alpha(1 + k_s)^t} + \frac{P_n}{(1 + k_s)^n}$

        a. Each year's cash dividend is discounted separately with its own PV factor.
        b. When you assume infinite dividends, the future market price component, P_n, drops out.

$$P_0 = \sum_{t=1}^{\infty} \frac{D_t}{(1 + k_s)^t}$$

- C. No growth in cash dividends.
    1. An unrealistic, but useful simplification for calculating common stock value is to suppose no growth in cash dividends.
    2. Value $= P_0 = D/k_s$
- D. Constant growth in cash dividends.
    1. Dividends are assumed to grow at a constant rate for a given period. This makes sense for the following reasons:
        a. Inflation tends to erode the purchasing power of future dividends. To reduce the effect, dividends are allowed to grow.
        b. Internally generated cash retained by the firm rather than paying them as dividends should be reflected in future dividends.
    2. $P_0 = \dfrac{D_1}{k_s - g} = \dfrac{D_0 (1 + g)}{k_s - g}$
    3. Use cash dividends for next year and not current cash dividends.

E.   Nonconstant growth in cash dividends.
1.   The example in the text shows a situation where dividends grow at 10 percent for three years followed by a constant dividend growth of 3 percent.
2.   Calculate each dividend until the assumption of constant growth is valid. Calculate the stock price one period before the first constant growth dividend is received, and discount this price and all earlier dividends back to t = 0.
3.   The text gives step-by-step directions to calculate the present value of these dividends; Figure 4.4 may be helpful.

F.   To invest or not to invest.
1.   The common stock valuation procedures can help us determine if we should invest in (buy) a stock or not.
2.   Net present value (NPV) approach.
   a.   Based on equation 4.5, P_0 represents the present value of all future dividends (or cash inflows).
   b.   The current market price of the common stock represents the initial investment.
   c.   NPV = P_0 – market price
   d.   If: NPV > 0, buy the stock.
        NPV < 0, do not buy or sell the stock if owned.
3.   Internal rate of return (IRR) approach.
   a.   The rate of return that we expect to earn by owning a common stock is the IRR that will be earned by investing in the stock.
   b.   Using the constant growth model, the expected rate of return is

$$k_x = \frac{D_1}{P_0} + g$$

   c.   If: k_x > the required rate of return, buy.
        k_x < the required rate of return, do not buy or sell if owned.

G.   Nondividend paying stocks.
1.   Estimate when dividends will be paid, their size and growth and proceed as before.
2.   Estimate a future market price and discount.
3.   Use an earnings multiple approach.

IV.   The present value of growth opportunities.
A.   Expected growth is valuable. The larger the expected growth of a firm, the higher the market price of its stock.
B.   Price/earning (P/E) ratios.
1.   P/E ratio is the market price of common stock divided by earnings per share (EPS).
2.   Dividend payout ratio is cash dividends per share of common stock divided by EPS.
3. $D_1 = EPS_1$ (dividend payout ratio). Therefore, using the constant growth equation,

$$\frac{P_0}{EPS_1} = \frac{\text{dividend payout ratio}}{k_s - g}$$

4.   P/E ratio is a function of the firm's dividend payout ratio, investors' required rate of return, k_s, and the firm's expected future growth, g.
5.   A high P/E ratio may indicate the expectation of high future growth or it may be due to very low earnings.
C.   Growth opportunities and value creation.
1.   Positive net present value projects and value creation are synonymous.
   a.   To increase the value of the firm, it must accept positive NPV projects.
   b.   Accepting projects with NPV = 0 does not create value.
   c.   Accepting projects with NPV < 0 destroys value; i.e., the firm suffers a loss in value.
   d. $P_0 = \begin{array}{c}\text{present value of}\\\text{assets in place}\end{array} + \begin{array}{c}\text{present value of}\\\text{growth opportunities}\end{array}$

V.   Returns and financial management.

       A.   While *ex ante* returns are always positive, *ex post* or realized returns may be negative. Managers may be able to take actions that increase the chance that the firm is a winner rather than a loser.

       B.   Value has three components: the magnitude, timing, and riskiness of cash flows. Most managerial actions have an impact on at least one of these components and hence, stock values.

Formulas

Notation

B_0	=	current market price of the bond
I	=	dollar amount of interest expected to be received each year (or par value $\times$ coupon interest rate)
n	=	number of years to maturity of the bond
k_b	=	required rate of return for the bond
M	=	par or maturity value of the bond (typically $1,000)
D_t	=	annual amount of cash dividends expected to be received on common stock in the tth year
D_0	=	cash dividend just paid on the common stock
D_1	=	cash dividend on common stock expected in one year
k_s	=	required rate of return on a common stock, based on the risk-free rate and a risk premium appropriate to the particular stock
P_t	=	market price of the stock at time t
P_0	=	market price of common stock today (t = 0) right after receipt of the cash dividend D_0
P_1	=	market price of common stock one year from now after receiving the cash dividend D_1
g	=	expected (compound) growth rate for a common stock's cash dividend
k_x	=	expected rate of return on a common stock
EPS	=	earnings per share
PVGO	=	present value of growth opportunities

Bond Valuation Model

$$\text{Value} = B_0 = \sum_{t=1}^{n} \frac{I}{(1 + k_b)^t} + \frac{M}{(1 + k_b)^n}$$

$$= I\,(PVA_{k_b,n}) + M(PV_{k_b,n})$$

Yield to Maturity

Use formula above. In trial-and-error form, use PVAs and PVs for year n, one interest rate at a time. *Hint:* If B_0 is below par, the yield is below the coupon rate. When you achieve B_0, you have found the yield to maturity. Interpolate if necessary.

Common Stock Valuation

Dividend valuation model for valuing common stock:

$$P_0 = \sum_{t=1}^{n} \frac{D_t}{(1 + k)^t} + \frac{P_n}{(1 + k_s)^n}$$

Fundamental common stock valuation model if we assume that cash dividends go on forever:

$$P_0 = \sum_{t=1}^{\infty} \frac{D_t}{(1 + k_s)^t}$$

No-growth dividend valuation model:

$$P_0 = \frac{D_1}{k_s}$$

Constant growth dividend valuation model:

$$P_0 = \frac{D_1}{k_s - g} = \frac{D_0(1 + g)}{k_s - g}$$

Nonconstant growth in cash dividends: See four-step procedure in the text.

Expected rate of return:

$$k_x = \frac{D_1}{P_0} + g$$

Present Value of Growth Opportunites

Price/Earning ratio:

$$P_0 = \frac{EPS_1 \text{ (dividend payout ratio)}}{k_s - g}$$

$$\frac{P_0}{EPS_1} = \frac{\text{dividend payout ratio}}{k_s - g}$$

Growth opportunities:

$$P_0 = \frac{EPS_1}{k_s} + PVGO$$

Returns

$$k = \frac{D_1 + P_1 - P_0}{P_0}$$

What to Look For

Valuation: How We Use It

The value of any investment results from the present value of its expected cash flows. You first measure the cash flows, measure their riskiness (Chapter 5), determine the appropriate rate of return given the risk (Chapter 6), and use the appropriate rate to discount these expected cash flows back to the present (Chapter 3). We will use this procedure for many types of valuation problems in this course.

Bond Valuation

Bond value is merely the present value of the expected cash flows from a bond. Bond cash flows come from two sources, coupon interest and repayment of the principal. Since bond cash flows occur through time, present value factors help us discount these cash flows back to the present. The time line below illustrates a 10 percent coupon bond's cash flows. The bond has five years until maturity, and the going market rate of interest is 10 percent. The interest for this year has just been paid.

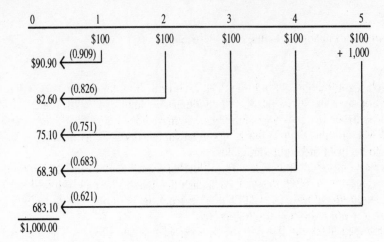

A simpler method of calculating the bond value is to use the following equation:

$$B_0 = I(PVA_{k_b,n}) + M(PV_{k_b,n})$$

$$= \$100(PVA_{10\%,5\ yr}) + \$1,000(PVA_{10\%,5\ yr})$$

$$= \$100(3.791) + \$1,000(0.621) = \$379.10 + \$621 = \$1,000.10 \cong \$1,000$$

The present value of this particular bond is its par value, since the coupon interest rate equals the current market-determined required rate of return (or yield to maturity). Once a bond is issued, its stated coupon rate does not change, although the market-determined required rate of return may rise or fall. If the required rate of return rises above the coupon rate, investors buying the bond on the secondary market can achieve their required rate of return only if they pay less than par for the bond. So, as the required rate rises above the coupon rate, the bond's market value falls below par. The required rate on a bond, k_b, will rise as the term structure of interest rates rises or as the risk of the bond itself increases. This process works in reverse as the required rate of return falls below the coupon rate. The two examples below, where k_b = 15 percent and where k_b = 8 percent, illustrate this process for a five-year 10 percent coupon bond:

$$15\%: \ B = \$100(PVA_{15\%,5\ yr}) + \$1,000(PV_{15\%,5\ yr})$$

$$= \$100(3.352) + \$1,000(0.497) = \$335.20 + \$497 = \$832.20$$

$$8\%: \ B = \$100(PVA_{8\%,5\ yr}) + \$1,000(PV_{8\%,5\ yr})$$

$$= \$100(3.993) + \$1,000(0.681) = \$399.30 + \$681 = \$1080.30$$

It is possible to know a bond's value or current market price and not its yield to maturity, k_b. However, by trial and error, you can plug PVAs and PVs into the equation above until you come close to the bond's price. Remember, if your price is below par, the yield to maturity is above the coupon rate and vice versa. Suppose you have a four-year 6 percent coupon bond selling for $830. What is the yield to maturity? It must be above 6 percent, but how much? We will use trial and error.

$$\text{Try } 12\%: \quad B = \$60(PVA_{12\%,\ 4\ yr}) + 1,000(PV_{12\%,\ 4\ yr})$$

$$= \$60(3.037) + \$1,000(0.636) = \$182.22 + \$636.00 = \$818.22$$

$$\text{Try } 11\%: \quad B = \$60(PVA_{11\%,\ 4\ yr}) + 1,000(PV_{11\%,\ 4\ yr})$$

$$= \$60(3.102) + \$1,000(0.659) = \$186.12 + \$659.00 = \$845.12$$

The yield is between 11 and 12 percent. By financial calculator, 11.54 percent.

Common Stock Valuation Techniques

In common stock valuation, you again are looking at cash flows. The cash flow on common stock is in the form of cash dividends and the ending market price. The dividends may be nonexistent, stable, growing evenly, or growing unevenly. The valuation technique used depends upon the assumptions you make concerning the dividend cash flows. Let's review the basic common stock valuation techniques, based upon the various dividend assumptions above. Here we will assume that cash dividends do occur for all common stocks.

Suppose we want to use a basic equation that will work no matter what the dividend assumptions. If we follow the same format as for bond valuation, we will discount each cash dividend to be received until the year we expect to sell the stock, and then discount the stock's expected market price. This is Equation 4.4; we must use this formula if cash dividends are uneven or if some selling price is expected.

Suppose, however, that we expect cash dividends to be $2 next year and to grow at 5 percent each year thereafter. It would be a waste of your time to discount each year's dividends separately. Instead, we can use the constant growth formula, Equation 4.7. Assume $k_s = 13$ percent.

$$P_0 = D_1/(k_s - g) = \$2.00/(0.13 - 0.05) = \$25$$

Sometimes dividends do not actually grow at a constant rate, but the assumption of constant growth makes the valuation calculations simple.

If we assume that a firm's dividend will continue at the same amount forever—i.e., $g = 0$, we can price the stock as a perpetuity. Here, we divide the cash dividends by the required rate of return: $P_0 = D_1/k_s$. This same formula is also useful for valuing preferred stock and consol bonds.

Finally, if we expect a firm's cash dividends to grow unevenly, we must discount all dividends separately. If we have a series of equal dollar dividends, these can be discounted as an annuity. Suppose you are valuing the shares of Vic Chemical Limited, and you have the following expectations for cash dividends:

Year 1 = $2.00   The constant
Year 2 = $2.15   dividend growth of
Year 3 = $2.15 (1 + 0.08) = $2.322   8 percent, then,
Year 4 = $2.15 (1 + 0.08)^2 = $2.50776 = $2.508   begins in Year 3.
Year n = $2.15 (1 + 0.08)$^{n-2}$

How would we value this dividend cash flow if our required return on Vic Chemical were 16 percent? First, we discount back to time zero the cash dividends for Years 1 and 2 separately, since they are uneven. Then, we discount the constant growth dividend series back to Year 2 (the year before the constant growth series begins) using the constant growth model. Once we have a value for the constant growth dividend series, we discount that value back two years to time zero. The value of Vic Chemical is then the sum of the first two present values, plus the series' present value: $1.724 + $1.597 + $21.566. The calculations and the timeline below will clarify the process:

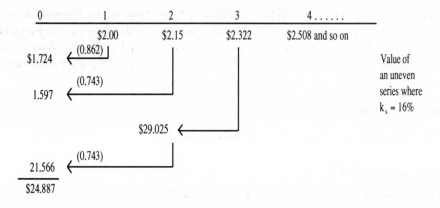

The calculation for Years 3 through infinity is

$$P_2 = \frac{D_3}{k_s - g} = \frac{\$2.322}{0.16 - 0.08} = \$29.025$$

Changes That Affect Required Return and Valuation

Uncertainty is a fact of life, and it will affect an investment's required return and valuation. Most people are risk averse, that is, people generally require more return for bearing more risk. Therefore, the required rate of return on risky securities includes a premium above the riskless rate. The size of this premium depends upon the riskiness of the individual security. For example, a stock with high return variability would likely have a higher required return than a stock with very low return variability.

The risk premium depends upon investors' current attitudes toward bearing risk. For example, during a recession, investors become more reluctant to bear risk, since their uncertainty about the economy and their own livelihood has increased. As a result, they raise their risk premiums. The risk premium of relatively more risky investments may rise more than that of relatively less risky investments, while the riskless rate may be unaffected.

As the required rate of return on a security increases, the value or market price of the security decreases. To see this, compare the constant growth valuation based on a k_s of 12 percent to one based on a k_s of 14 percent. Assume that D_1 is \$2.50 and g is 6 percent:

$$P_0 = D_1/(k_s - g) = \$2.50/(0.12 - 0.06) = \$42.67$$

versus $P_0 = \$2.50/(0.14 - 0.06) = \$31.25$

You can see that the dividend growth assumptions and the required rate of return can have a marked effect upon the stock's market price. Since the managers' objective is to maximize firm value, they must pay attention to how their decisions affect the magnitude, timing, and riskiness of their firm's expected cash flows.

Completion Questions

4.1   As the risk of a financial asset increases, its required rate of return _____. So, the financial asset's market value must _____.

4.2   In bond valuation, the coupon payment can be thought of as an _____, while the par value can be thought of as a _____ payment.

4.3   Coupon interest is the stated amount of interest. To calculate the amount of the annuity in dollars, multiply the stated coupon rate times the _____.

4.4   If a 10 percent coupon bond is currently selling at par, its yield to maturity must be _____.

4.5   If an 8 percent coupon rate bond is yielding 12 percent, its current market price must be _____ its par value.

4.6   In comparing the price variability of bonds of various maturities, market prices of bonds with longer maturities vary _____ than prices of bonds with shorter maturities in response to general market interest rate changes.

4.7   The yield to maturity is that discount rate which makes the present value of the bond's expected cash flows equal to _____.

4.8   A _____ is a bond that pays a periodic interest payment but never matures.

4.9   When the rate of expected inflation increases, the risk-free rate _____, and all other required rates of return _____.

4.10   Suppose a firm has been expecting constant growth in its cash dividends. The marketing department announces that a newly tested product should increase net income substantially for the next five years and that cash dividends too will increase substantially. Experts believe this prediction. The market price for this firm will _____ in response to this news.

4.11   In the dividend valuation model, the present market value of a share of common stock is equal to the present value of _____.

4.12   When we value a share of common stock which is expected to provide constant growth in its cash dividends, we divide the expected cash dividend for the _____ year by the difference between the required rate of return and the _____.

4.13   When looking at the relationship between the growth rate in expected cash dividends and the current market value of the stock, we expect the value of a no-dividend-growth stock to be _____ than that of a growing dividend stock, all other things being equal.

4.14   If   the   _____ of a common stock is less than your _____, you should not buy the common stock.

4.15   A _____ does not necessarily imply the prospect of high growth.

4.16   The stock price of a firm may be thought of as the sum of _____ and _____.

4.17   For a company to grow, it must invest in _____.

Problems

4.1   Vancouver Mining Limited has outstanding a bond with 17 years to maturity. The coupon rate on the bond is 11 percent, the face value is $1,000, and the current market price is $809.03. What is its yield to maturity?

4.2   The bonds of Scott Chemical Limited promise annual interest payments of $120, have a $1,000 face value, mature in 15 years, and are priced to yield 8 percent. If interest payments are made semiannually, what is the price of the bond?

4.3   Ketch-Me Productions is expected to pay a cash dividend of $2.31 per share next year. The company is quite risky; its required return is 22 percent and $P_0 = \$19.25$. What is this year's (at $t = 0$) cash dividend, assuming a constant growth rate in cash dividends until infinity?

4.4   Solar Energy Research Limited is a new enterprise and is not expected to pay any cash dividends for the next five years. Its first dividend (D_6) is expected to be $2, and dividends are expected to grow for the next four years (through $t = 10$) at 25 percent. After that, dividends are expected to grow at a more normal 5 percent. If $k_s = 18$ percent over the entire time period, what is P_0?

4.5   Processed Food Limited is a well-established firm that pays a cash dividend of $5 per share and has experienced no growth for several years. Its current required rate of return (without the new investment described below) is 14 percent. The firm has asked shareholders to forgo the cash dividend payment for the next five years to free funds for investment in a new process that will ultimately allow the firm to increase the $5 dividend by 10 percent per year. If the firm intends to resume the dividend in year 6 (at $5.50, or 5.00×1.10) and the new $k_s = 18$ percent, will the present shareholders be better or worse off?

4.6   Exactly two years ago, you purchased at par, a 10-year 10 percent coupon bond, face value $1,000, that pays annual interest. Today the market rate of interest is 6 percent and you are considering selling the bond.
   a.   What was the market rate of interest at the time you purchased the bond?
   b.   Suppose you wish to sell the bond today
      i.   How much should you sell the bond for?
      ii.   What is the current yield on the bond?
      iii.   What will be your holding period return (yield) on the bond?
   c.   Suppose your friend offers you a price of $1,125 for the bond. Would you be willing to sell the bond to him/her? Explain your answer.

      d.   Given that this bond is freely callable at 12 percent premium. With the market rate of interest currently at 6 percent, does the price computed in part (b) seem reasonable? Explain?

4.7   B-Line Ltd. has just paid a dividend of $2. These dividends are expected to grow at 4 percent a year indefinitely. If the firm has a current market price of $25 and you require a rate of return of 11 percent, is B-Line a good investment?

Answers to Completion Questions

4.1   increases; decrease
4.2   annuity; lump sum
4.3   par (or face) value
4.4   10 percent
4.5   below
4.6   more widely
4.7   current market price
4.8   consol
4.9   increases; increase also
4.10   increase immediately
4.11   all future cash dividends
4.12   next; compound growth rate
4.13   less
4.14   expected rate of return; required rate of return
4.15   high P/E ratio
4.16   present value of assets in place; present value of growth opportunities
4.17   positive NPV projects

Solutions to Problems

4.1   Step 1.   Since the bond is selling at a discount, the yield to maturity must be greater than the coupon rate.

           Step 2.   at 12%: $B_0 = \$110(PVA_{12\%, 17\,yr}) + \$1,000(PV_{12\%, 17\,yr})$

                             $= \$110(7.120) + \$1,000(0.146) = \$929.20$, which is too high

                   at 13%: $B_0 = \$110(PVA_{13\%, 17\,yr}) + \$1,000(PV_{13\%, 17\,yr})$

                             $= \$110(6.729) + \$1,000(0.125) = \$865.19$, which is still too high

                   at 14%: $B_0 = \$110(PVA_{14\%, 17\,yr}) + \$1,000(PV_{14\%, 17\,yr})$

                             $= \$110(6.373) + \$1,000(0.108) = \$809.03$

           The yield to maturity is 14 percent.

4.2   For semiannual interest payments:

$$B_0 = \frac{I}{2}(PVA_{k/2,\ 2n}) + M(PV_{k/2,\ 2n})$$

$$= \frac{\$120}{2}(PVA_{8\%/2,\ 2 \times 15}) + \$1,000(PV_{8\%/2,\ 2 \times 15})$$

$$= \$60(PVA_{4\%,\ 30}) + \$1,000(PV_{4\%,\ 30})$$

$$= \$60(17.292) + \$1,000(0.308)$$

$$= \$1,037.52 + \$308.00 = \$1,345.52$$

4.3   Step 1.   Assuming constant growth:

$$P_0 = \frac{D_1}{k_s - g}$$

$$\$19.25 = \frac{\$2.31}{0.22 - g}$$

$$0.22 - g = \frac{\$2.31}{\$19.25}$$

$$g = 0.22 - \frac{\$2.31}{\$19.25} = 0.22 - 0.12 - 0.10$$

Step 2.   Since
$$D_1 = D_0(1 + g)$$

$$D_0 = \frac{D_1}{(1 + g)} = \frac{\$2.31}{\$1.10} = \$2.10$$

4.4   Step 1. $D_6 = \$2.00$

$D_7 = \$2.00 (1.25) = \$2.50$

$D_8 = \$2.50 (1.25) = \$3.125$

$D_9 = \$3.125 (1.25) = \$3.906$

$D_{10} = \$3.906 (1.25) = \$4.883$

$D_{11} = \$4.883 (1.05) = \$5.127$

Step 2. $$P_{10} = \frac{D_{11}}{k_s - g} = \frac{\$5.127}{0.18 - 0.05} = \$39.438$$

Step 3. $P_0 = \$2.00(PV_{18\%,6\ yr}) + \$2.50(PV_{18\%,7\ yr})$

$+ \$3.125(PV_{18\%,8\ yr}) + \$3.906(PV_{18\%,9\ yr})$

$+ \$4.883(PV_{18\%,10\ yr}) + \$39.438(PV_{18\%,10\ yr})$

$= \$2.00(0.370) + \$2.50(0.314) + \$3.125(0.266) + \$3.906(0.225)$

$+ \$4.883(0.191) + \$39.438(0.191)$

$= \$0.7400 + \$0.7850 + \$0.8312 + \$0.8788 + \$0.9327 + \$7.5327$

$= \$11.70$

4.5   Step 1.   With no investment:

$$P_0 = \frac{D_1}{k_s} = \frac{\$5.00}{0.14} = \$35.71$$

Step 2.   With the investment:

$$P_5 = \frac{D_6}{k_s - g} = \frac{\$5.50}{0.18 - 0.10} = \$68.75$$

Step 3. $P_0 = (P_5)(PV_{18\%, 5 \text{ yr}}) = \$68.75(0.437) = \$30.04$

The current shareholders will be worse off. The shareholders will lose \$5.67 (\$35.71 − \$30.04) per share.

4.6   Note that the bond was purchased 2 years ago for \$1,000 (at par).

   a.   Since the bond was orginally purchased at par, the coupon rate at that time was the same as the market rate of interest.

   Market rate of interest = 10%

   b.   i.   Since the bond was purchased 2 years ago, it has 8 years remaining to maturity.

   $B_0 = \$100(PVA_{6\%, 8 \text{ yr}}) + \$1,000/(PV_{6\%, 8 \text{ yr}})$

   $= \$100(6.210) + \$1,000(0.627)$

   $= \$1,248$

   Given the market rate of 6%, the bond should sell for \$1,248.

   ii.   Current yield = annual coupon rate/current market price

   $= \$100/\$1,248 = 8.01\%$

   iii.   If you sell the bond today for \$1,248, then your holding period return k_b is given as:

   $\$1,000 = \$100/(1 + k_b) + (\$100 + \$1,248)/(1 + k_b)^2$

   By financial calculator, $k_b = 21.21\%$.

   c.   No, since the current price is \$1,248, which represents the minimum price you should accept.

   d.   No. The call price is \$1,120. This means that for a freely callable bond, the maximum price investors are willing to pay for the bond is \$1,120. Thus the bond will trade in the market for price range equal to or less than \$1,120.

4.7 $D_0 = \$2.00$

$D_1 = D_0(1 + g) = \$2.00(1.04) = \$2.08$

The maximum you would be willing to pay for B-Line is

$$P_0 = \frac{D_1}{k_s - g} = \frac{\$2.08}{0.11 - 0.4} = \$29.71$$

NPV = P_0 − market value = \$29.71 − \$25 = \$4.71

Since NPV is positive, the stock is a good buy.

The same conclusion can be reached by using the current market price of \$25 to calculate your expected rate of return, k_x, as follows:

$$k_x = \frac{D_1}{P_0} + g = \frac{\$2.08}{\$25} + 0.04 = 12.32\%$$

Since your expected return, k_x, is greater than your required return of 11 percent, B-Line is a good buy.

Chapter 5
Risk and Return

How This Chapter Relates to the Rest of the Text

The relationship between risk and expected return is another fundamental concept of finance. Risk and return influence the value of financial assets (Chapter 4) and the opportunity cost of capital (Chapter 6) and are an important consideration in capital budgeting (Chapters 7–9). The capital asset pricing model, which shows the relationship between risk and return, enables a financial manager to identify profitable (or undervalued) investments. In fact, this tradeoff between risk and expected return underlies all financial decisions—both corporate and personal.

Topical Outline

I.   Measuring risk.
    A.   Risk arises whenever the outcomes of an event are unknown or at least not known with certainty.
    B.   Probability distributions show the chances of various outcomes occurring.
    C.   Expected value or mean is the probability weighted average of possible outcomes.
    D.   Standard deviation measures dispersion around the mean; this total risk measure contains both diversifiable and nondiversifiable risk.
    E.   When considering risk of a security in a diversified portfolio, other measures of risk should be used.
II.   Portfolio risk and diversification.
    A.   A portfolio's return is the average return of the securities in the portfolio weighted by the proportion of the portfolio invested in each security.
    B.   Portfolio risk.
        1.   When you combine securities in a portfolio, the total riskiness is generally less than the average risk of the individual risks.
        2.   The risk of a portfolio is a function of the risk of individual securities and the correlations between returns of securities in the portfolio. Correlation measures the degree with which two variables, such as the return on two securities, move together.
    C.   Two-security portfolios.
        1.   Perfect positive correlation: no risk reduction; portfolio standard deviation is a weighted average of the individual standard deviations.
        2.   Perfect negative correlation: maximum risk reduction; risk can be completely eliminated.
        3.   Negative correlation or positive correlation that is less than perfect: some benefits from diversification in terms of risk reduction.
        4.   The returns on most assets are positively correlated, since they tend to move with the general movements of the economy.
    D.   The efficient frontier.
        1.   The efficient frontier is the set of portfolios that offer the highest expected return at a given level of risk or the lowest risk at a given level of return.
        2.   Since portfolios on the efficient frontier dominate all others, they should be preferred by investors.
    E.   Diversifiable and nondiversifiable risk.
        1.   Portfolio risk declines to a minimum level as more randomly selected securities (up to 20 or 25) are added.
        2.   Risk can be divided into two parts.
            a.   Diversifiable risk relates to events specific to companies or industries, such as strikes, product developments, or new patents.
            b.   Nondiversifiable risk relates to general economic conditions, the impact of monetary and fiscal policy, and inflation.
III. Riskless borrowing and lending.
    A.   Inclusion of the riskless asset alters the shape of the efficient frontier.
        1.   Investors can form portfolios consisting of the risk-free security and a risky but efficient

portfolio.

2. Investors are made best off by holding portfolios consisting of the risk-free security and portfolio M (the tangent portfolio).

    a. M is called the market portfolio and is a value-weighted portfolio of all risky assets.

    b. Investors obtain lending portfolios by buying both the market portfolio and the risk-free security.

    c. Investors obtain borrowing portfolios by borrowing at k_{RF} and using the proceeds to buy the market portfolio.

3. The capital market line (CML) shows the relationship between risk and expected return for efficient portfolios only.

    a. $$\overline{K}_p = k_{RF} + \left[\frac{\overline{k}_M - k_{RF}}{\sigma_M} \right] \sigma_p$$

    b. The slope of the CML is the market price of risk.

    c. The return to the TSE 300 is often used to measure $\overline{k}_M$.

B. Beta is the measure of how security returns move with the returns on the market.

1. Beta measures the nondiversifiable risk remaining for the individual stock after a portion of its total risk has been diversified away by forming a portfolio of securities.

2. Since individuals are basically risk-averse, they require a higher expected return to invest in higher beta stocks.

    a. The treasury bill rate is considered the risk-free rate.

    b. The risk premium is the return required over and above the risk-free rate to compensate the investor for additional risk.

    c. We measure this additional risk with beta—a comparison of the variability in returns on the security with the variability in returns for the market portfolio as a whole.

C. Beta as the measure of diversifiable risk.

1. Beta is the measure of the stock's price volatility relative to the volatility of the market as a whole as measured by some market index, such as the TSE 300.

2. Beta is the measure of nondiversifiable risk for stocks in a diversified portfolio.

3. The market has a beta of 1.0; it is our frame of reference.

4. Less risky firms with stable cash flows have betas of less than 1.0, since their market prices fluctuate less than the market as a whole.

5. More risky firms, whose cash flows are more volatile, have more volatile market prices than the market index; thus, they have betas greater than 1.0.

D. The capital asset pricing model (CAPM).

1. Assumptions.

    a. All investors are expected wealth maximizers who evaluate portfolios on the basis of means and standard deviations.

    b. All investors can lend or borrow at k_{RF}.

    c. Homogeneous expectations.

    d. The markets are frictionless and there are no taxes.

    e. The markets are perfectly competitive.

2. The required return on any security is given by the security market line (SML):

$$\overline{k}_j = k_{RF} + \beta_j(k_M - k_{RF}) = \begin{array}{l} \text{required return for} \\ \text{riskless investment} \end{array} + \begin{array}{l} \text{risk premium} \\ \text{appropriate to} \\ \text{the investment} \end{array}$$

E. Using the capital asset pricing model (CAPM).

1. Components: risk-free rate (k_{RF}), expected return on the market (k_M), and the stock's beta (β_j). The value of each component changes as conditions change.

    a. Risk-free rate depends upon expected inflation, economic conditions, and monetary policy.

    b. Expected return on the market can be estimated based on expected inflation, expected real growth in the economy, and the risk premium commanded for owning common stocks rather than bonds.

    c. Betas for stocks change over time but can be found in some published sources, reports from stockbrokers, or by using the techniques outlined in the book.

  2. Beta measures nondiversifiable (market or systematic) risk.

  F. Calculating beta.

    1. Use linear regression to fit a least-squares regression line in the form $Y = \alpha + \beta X$.

      a. The "α" is the return on the stock when the market risk premium is zero—the Y-intercept.

      b. The "β" is the sensitivity of the returns of the security relative to the returns of the market index (beta).

      c. The "Y" is the required return on stock; "X" is the expected return on the market.

    2. Beta equals the covariance between the stock's return and the market's returns divided by the variance of the market's returns.

      a. Covariance of the returns of the security and the market is equal to the standard deviation of the security times the standard deviation of the market times the correlation between the security and the market: $Cov_{jM} = \sigma_j\ \sigma_M\ Corr_{jM}$.

      b. Use the standard deviation of the stock's return, the standard deviation of the market's returns, and the correlation between the two returns: $\beta_j = (\sigma_j\ Corr_{jM})\ \sigma_M$.

  G. A portfolio's beta is the weighted average of the betas of the securities within that portfolio.

IV. More on the capital asset pricing model.

  A. Changes in risk and price.

    1. The CAPM helps us to see the impact of a change in risk on investors' required rate of return and, in turn, on a firm's stock price.

    2. Other things being equal, an increase in risk increases investors' required rate of return, resulting in a decrease in stock price, and a decrease in risk increases stock price.

  B. The equilibrium nature of the CAPM.

    1. In equilibrium, the expected rate of return equals the required rate of return.

    2. In disequilibrium, the stock is either overpriced or underpriced, providing an actual rate of return less or greater than the return required.

      a. In an efficient market, investors will see the possibilities of excess return from an underpriced stock and will bid up the price, driving down the expected return.

      b. Investors will do just the opposite to overpriced stocks.

  C. Words of caution when using the CAPM.

    1. The CAPM is an *ex ante* model (variables in the market are unobservable); using historical data without adjustment for future expectations invites trouble.

    2. Both the SML and beta can shift over time.

    3. Persistent evidence on the risk–return tradeoffs for small-capitalization stocks and low P/E stocks, as well as seasonal effects, casts some doubt as to the efficiency of the markets and the validity of the CAPM.

V. The efficient market hypothesis.

  A. The efficient market hypothesis states that prices react accurately and quickly to new information.

  B. Three streams of research.

    1. Tests for return predictability: Future returns are to some extent, predictable from past returns, dividend yields, and various term structure variables.

    2. Tests for return movement: With respect to firm-specific events, stock prices react quickly to all publicly available information.

    3. Tests for private information: After considering transaction costs and the cost of generating unique information, the informal investor does not earn returns greater than expected based on the amount of risk taken.

    C.   Implications of the efficient market hypothesis for managers.
        1.   The best estimate of the value of a firm is the market value of its stocks and bonds.
        2.   When estimating value, start with market value, if it exists, and then consider the impact of subsequent corporate actions on the value.
        3.   The only way to increase firm value is to find investments that provide a rate of return greater than the required return.
        4.   In an efficient market you should expect to pay an equilibrium rate for the financing obtained.

VI.   Arbitrage pricing theory (APT).
    A.   The arbitrage pricing theory is based on fewer assumptions than the CAPM.
    B.   In the APT, stock returns are assumed to be a linear function of a number of factors common to all securities.
        1.   Equation:

$$k_j = k_{RF} + \sum_{n=1}^{N} b_{jn}(k_n - k_{RF})$$

        2. k_n is the required return on the nth factor.
    C.   A problem with APT is that the factors are unknown *ex ante*.
    D.   The CAPM is a single factor APT.

VII.   Appendix 5A: Calculating covariances and correlations.
    A.   Covariance measures the degree of linear relationship between any two random variables.
        1.   Formula for calculating covariance from expected returns:

$$Cov_{AB} = \sum_{i=1}^{n} (k_{Ai} - \overline{k}_A)(k_{Bi} - \overline{k}_B)P_i$$

        2.   Formula for calculating covariance from historical returns:

$$Cov_{FG} = \frac{\sum_{t=1}^{n} (k_{Ft} - \overline{k}_F)(k_{Gt} - \overline{k}_G)}{n - 1}$$

    B.   The correlation coefficient ranges from −1 to +1 and measures the degree of linearity between two random variables.

$$Corr_{AB} = \frac{Cov_{AB}}{\sigma_A \sigma_B}$$

Formulas

Notation

k	= return
P_0	= price at $t = 0$
D_1	= dividend at $t = 1$
$\overline{k}$	= the expected value or expected return
k_i	= rate of return or outcome associated with the ith possible state
n	= number of possible states of the economy
p_i	= probability of the ith state or outcome occurring
σ	= standard deviation—how tightly the probability distribution is centred around the expected return or expected value. Also, the square root of the variance
σ^2	= variance, the square of the standard deviation
W_i	= proportion of portfolio invested in stock i
β_j	= beta coefficient for asset j
k_M	= expected return on the market in general
k_{RF}	= risk-free rate of return, generally measured by the return on Canadian treasury bills

$(k_M - k_{RF})$ = market risk premium required to encourage investment in the market rather than in riskless securities

$\beta_j(k_M - k_{RF})$ = risk premium required for the security in question

$Corr_{AB}$ = correlation between the returns on securities A and B

α = Y-intercept of the characteristic line, the return on the stock when risk or beta is zero

$Cov_{j\,M}$ = covariance between returns on security j and returns on the market

$b_{j,n}$ = the sensitivity of security j to factor n

Holding Period Return on Stock

$$k = \frac{D_1 + P_1 - P_0}{P_0}$$

Expected Value or Mean Rate of Return

$$\text{Expected Value} = \overline{k} = \sum_{i-1}^{n} k_i P_i$$

Standard Deviation

$$\sigma = \left[\sum_{i-1}^{n} (k_i - \overline{k})^2 P_i \right]^{0.5}$$

Portfolio Return

$$\overline{k}_p = W_A \overline{k}_A + W_B \overline{k}_B + \dots + W_Z \overline{k}_Z$$

Standard Deviation of a Two-Security Portfolio

$$\sigma_p = \left[W_A^2 \sigma_A^2 + W_B^2 \sigma_B^2 + 2W_A W_B \sigma_A \sigma_B Corr_{AB} \right]^{0.5}$$

Capital Market Line

$$\overline{K}_p = k_{RF} + \left[\frac{\overline{k}_M - k_{RF}}{\sigma_M} \right] \sigma_P$$

Security Market Line:

$$\overline{k}_j = k_{RF} + \beta_j \left[\overline{k}_M - k_{RF} \right]$$

Fitted Regression or Characteristic Line for Estimating Beta

$$k_j = \alpha + \beta k_M$$

Calculation of Beta

$$\beta_j = \frac{Cov_{jM}}{\sigma_M^2} = \frac{\sigma_j \sigma_M Corr_{jM}}{\sigma_M^2} = \frac{\sigma_j Corr_{jM}}{\sigma_M}$$

Calculation of Covariance

$$Cov_{jM} = \sigma_j \sigma_M Corr_{jM}$$

Portfolio Beta

$$\beta_p = \sum_{j-1}^{n} W_j \beta_j$$

Arbitrage Pricing Model

$$k_j = k_{RF} + \sum_{n=1}^{N} b_{jn} \left[k_n - k_{RF} \right]$$

What to Look For

We will discuss risk, economic forces resulting in risk, measures of risk, and required rates of return in order to develop the concepts of risk and return. Although we want to understand risk from a business standpoint, we begin by seeing it from an investor's viewpoint. The investor's viewpoint is essential for the manager; the firm's required return is determined by the perceived riskiness of the firm's cash flows.

Risk

As you will note, risk is a multifaceted term. Let's begin by splitting risk into two major categories—diversifiable risk and nondiversifiable risk. Diversifiable risk is risk particular to an individual firm, security, or industry. For example, you can diversify away the financial risk of a debt-heavy firm by buying stock of firms that are not debt heavy. By buying a diversified portfolio of up to 20 or 25 stocks, an investor can eliminate virtually all diversifiable risk.

Nondiversifiable risk is risk that every firm faces and that cannot be avoided in any investment. Nondiversifiable risk results from participation in the marketplace, where certain economic forces are at work. The main risk resulting from these forces is the possibility that the cash flows and hence the rate of return on investments may change.

Economic forces that affect risk levels

As noted in Chapter 2, monetary policy set by the Bank of Canada controls the money supply, helps stabilize the economy, and affects interest rates. For example, when the Bank of Canada wants to cool down a hot economy, it conducts open market operations to sell government securities to banks. The money supply shrinks. Money becomes more expensive, and interest rates rise. Since the cost of borrowing has risen, managers postpone capital spending projects, and the economy cools. The risk comes from not being able to predict Bank of Canada policy and its full effect on the economy. In some cases, the market may believe that a Bank of Canada decision will have serious effects on business, so investors push up their required returns.

Monetary policy may be reinforced or counteracted by a second force, fiscal policy. Fiscal policy may mean raising taxes or borrowing money to fund the budget. Sometimes the goals of fiscal and monetary policy conflict, so the decisions counteract one another. Again, the risk results from not knowing what the effect of the actions may be.

Inflation is a third force active in the market environment. Inflation results from too many dollars chasing too few goods in the marketplace. As you can probably guess, inflation can result in a heated economy in which the money supply has increased too fast. Inflation expectations increase investors' required rate of return, since they want to achieve a certain rate of return, net of inflation.

Measurement of risk: a practical example

Risk measurement is difficult to describe in the abstract. We know we expect higher risk, but how do we measure this risk? In Chapter 5, we use standard deviation or variance to measure the variability of a firm's return. We associate a probability with each of a spectrum of states of the economy. For example, the probability of an expansion might be 40 percent. With each of these states of nature, we associate a potential rate of return for each stock. Below, for example, we predict that in an expansion, Molson will return 20 percent, while BC Tel will return 14 percent. Remember, these are just predictions, not actual returns. Given this probability distribution and these return estimates, we can find the probability-weighted expected return for these two stocks and discover the predicted variability around these expected returns.

Let's measure the variability of two stocks' returns to see how risk is measured and how it affects the expected rate of return. Suppose you had access to information through an investment advisory service. Suppose those experts made some informed guesses about next year's economy and the probable return on the common stock of Molson and BC Tel.

Step 1: Calculate expected return.

State of the Economy	Associated Probability P_i	Associated Molson Total Return k_i	Molson Expected Return $\overline{k}$
Recession	0.20	8.0%	1.6%
Normal	0.40	14.0%	5.6%
Expansion	0.40	20.0%	8.0%

Molson's mean or expected return = $\overline{k}$ = 15.2%

State of the Economy	Associated Probability P_i	Associated BC Tel Total Return k_i	BC Tel Expected Return $\overline{k}$
Recession	0.20	8.0%	1.6%
Normal	0.40	11.0%	4.4%
Expansion	0.40	14.0%	5.6%

BC Tel's mean or expected return = $\overline{k}$ = 11.6%

Now you have calculated the expected return on these two stocks. You know that in the next period you might expect, on average, a 15.2 percent return on Molson and an 11.6 percent return on BC Tel. Take time to note a few things about the return distributions of these two firms. Over the course of the business cycle, the returns on BC Tel are expected to range less widely (6 percent) than those of Molson (12 percent).

Step 2: Calculate variance and standard deviation.
The wider return variability of the Molson stock is a sign of the greater total risk in holding such stock as one's sole investment. We can measure this variability with the use of the variance or standard deviation. We will use the return values from the previous table.

Molson:

Outcome – Expected Value (deviation from mean $(k_i - \overline{k})$	Deviation Squared $(k_i - \overline{k})^2$	$\times$	Probability of ith Outcome P_i	$=$	$P_i(k_i - \overline{k})^2$
8.0 – 15.2 = – 7.2	51.84		0.20		10.368
14.0 – 15.2 = – 1.2	1.44		0.40		0.576
20.0 – 15.2 = 4.8	23.04		0.40		9.216

Molson variance = σ^2 = 20.160

Molson standard deviation = $\sigma = (\sigma^2)^{0.5}$ = 4.490

BC Tel:

Outcome − Expected Value (deviation from mean $(k_i - \bar{k})$	Deviation Squared $(k_i - \bar{k})^2$	×	Probability of ith Outcome P_i	=	$P_i(k_i - \bar{k})^2$
$8.0 - 11.6 = -3.6$	12.96		0.20		2.596
$14.0 - 11.6 = -3.6$	0.36		0.40		0.144
$20.0 - 11.6 = 2.4$	5.76		0.40		2.304

BC Tel variance $= \sigma^2 = 5.040$

BC Tel standard deviation $= \sigma = (\sigma^2)^{0.5} = 2.245$

As you can see, the standard deviation of Molson is twice that of BC Tel. Over the course of the business cycle, BC Tel's return seems to be the less variable or risky. Logically, Molson requires a higher return—15.2 percent versus 11.6 percent.

Risk and diversification

Most individuals hold portfolios of securities rather than just one individual stock. While the return to a portfolio is simply the weighted average of the returns of the stocks in the portfolio, a portfolio's risk is not. A portfolio's risk is a function of the risk of the stocks and of their correlations. If stocks are less than perfectly positively correlated, the portfolio's risk will be less than the weighted average of the stocks' risk. For example, suppose you own some Chrysler Canada stock. You estimate that if gasoline prices rise, car sales (and hence Chrysler's profitability) will fall. Holding Chrysler stock alone exposes you to risk.

Now, suppose that you sell half of your Chrysler Canada stock and purchase shares of Petro Canada with the proceeds. If gasoline prices rise, Chrysler Canada profitability falls, but Petro Canada's profits should rise. By diversifying your holdings, you have eliminated some of the risk to which you were exposed.

The key to diversification is the correlation between the returns to the securities in your portfolio. In the above example, suppose:

	Chrysler	Petro Canada
Expected return	15%	21%
σ	20%	40%

and that $\text{Corr}_{C,P} = -0.50$. What is the expected return and risk of a portfolio of 50 percent Chrysler stock and 50 percent Petro Canada stock?

$$\bar{k}_P = W_C k_C + W_P k_P = 0.50(15\%) + 0.50(21\%) = 18\%$$

$$\sigma_P = \left[W_C^2 \sigma_C^2 + W_P^2 \sigma_P^2 + 2W_C W_P \sigma_C \sigma_P \text{Corr}_{C,P} \right]^{0.5}$$

$$= \left[(0.5)^2(20)^2 + (0.5)^2(40)^2 + 2(0.5)(0.5)(20)(40)(-0.5) \right]^{0.5}$$

$$= \left[100 + 400 - 200 \right]^{0.5} = (300)^{0.5} = 17.32\%$$

Note that because the correlation is negative, the risk of the portfolio is less than the risk of either stock.

Investors are faced with choices concerning literally thousands of risky investments, which can be formed into an infinite number of portfolios. Rational, risk-averse investors attempt to hold efficient portfolios of these securities, that is, those portfolios offering the highest return for a given level of risk (or the lowest risk for a given level of return). By holding these portfolios, investors have diversified away as much risk as possible.

Risk reduction through diversification is an important concept. Portfolio risk declines on average to a minimum level as more and more randomly selected stocks (up to 25) are added. Since investors can eliminate part of the portfolio's risk through diversification, they do not expect to be compensated for it. Only nondiversifiable risk, associated with general economic conditions, is priced in the market.

The Capital Asset Pricing Model

Individuals have the ability to invest in both the risk-free security and efficient but risky portfolios. The text shows that the optimal portfolio of risky assets to hold is portfolio M, which is on a line drawn from k_{RF} and tangent to the efficient frontier. Portfolio M is the market portfolio that is a value-weighted portfolio of all risky assets. Investors can hold lending portfolios by buying both M and the risk-free security. Or, they can purchase borrowing portfolios by borrowing at k_{RF} and investing the proceeds in M.

The Capital Market Line

Because investors are better off holding portfolios that are linear combinations of the risk-free security and the market portfolio, we can write an expression for the relationship between return and risk for efficient portfolios. This relationship is the capital market line (CML), and is

$$\overline{K}_p = k_{RF} + \left[\frac{\overline{k}_M - k_{RF}}{\sigma_M} \right] \sigma_p$$

The slope of the CML is the market price of risk.

To see how the CML is used, suppose we hold a portfolio with $\sigma_p = 18\%$. If $\sigma_M = 15$, $\overline{k}_M = 19\%$ and $k_{RF} = 8\%$, our portfolio should earn

$$\overline{K}_p = 8\% + \left[\frac{19\% - 8\%}{15} \right] \times 18 = 21.2\%$$

The Security Market Line

Assuming investors hold efficient portfolios, we can price the risk of individual assets in the market portfolio. This pricing relationship is called the security market line (SML), or

$$k_j = k_{RF} + \beta_j \left[k_M - k_{RF} \right]$$

where beta (β_j) is the measure of the security's undiversifiable risk.

The stock market is the reference point for beta calculation. Let's assume k_M equals 13 percent. If a firm has a beta above (below) 1.0, its required return is above (below) k_M. Let us suppose that we have calculated the betas for Molson and BC Tel. Since Molson's 15.2 percent expected return is above k_M, we would expect its beta to exceed 1.0. Likewise, since BC Tel's 11.6 percent expected return is below k_M, we would expect its beta to be below 1.0. Let's assume the calculated betas would be 1.55 for Molson and 0.65 for BC Tel.

Security Market Line and the Capital Asset Pricing Model

We can take these betas and plug them into the security market line equation. If the risk-free rate, k_{RF}, equals 9.0 percent, these are the required returns for both stocks:

Security market line = $k_j = k_{RF} + \beta_j (k_M - k_{RF})$
For Molson: k = 9.0% + 1.55(13.0% − 9.0%) = 15.2%
For BC Tel: k = 9.0% + 0.65(13.0% − 9.0%) = 11.6%

We can graph the security market line below, using the directions in Chapter 5:

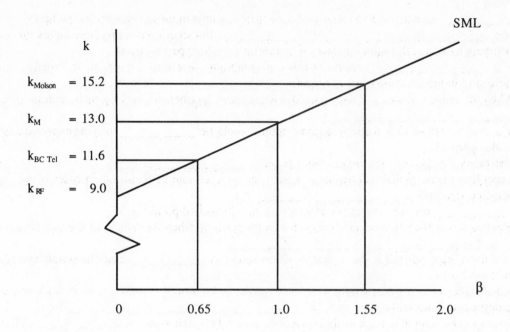

The capital asset pricing model states that in a competitive market the expected risk premium varies proportionately with beta, as we see above. The model goes on to suggest that everyone could buy the same portfolio of assets, the market portfolio, and they could vary the risk of the portfolio by borrowing or lending at the risk-free rate. If the market is not at equilibrium—that is, if some asset is returning more than is required, investors will bid up the price of that asset and push its return down to the required level.

The Efficient Market Hypothesis
You have no doubt heard someone say "you get what you pay for" or "there's no such thing as a free lunch." While most individuals are willing to accept both statements, most have problems with the notion of an efficient market.

In an efficient market, security prices rapidly and accurately reflect all relevant information about that security. Research into the efficient market hypothesis has followed three streams:
1.   Tests for return predictability: This research is based on all historical information concerning a security. Evidence suggests that future returns are, to some extent, predictable from past returns, dividend yields, and various term structure variables.
2.   Tests for return movement: In this research, all publicly available information such as earnings and dividend announcements form the information base. If the results indicate that trading on company-specific information, such as that announced in the *Globe and Mail*, is not profitable, the market is efficient.
3.   Tests for private information: This research focuses on private information, such as insider trading, or unique security analysis, to see if trading on this information is profitable or not. The findings suggest that, after considering transaction costs, trading on private information is not profitable.

The results of this research should mean two things to financial managers. The first is "you get what you pay for." That is, the price of an asset is an unbiased estimate of its actual worth. Thus, the prices of a firm's stocks and bonds (and changes in those prices upon the announcement of new information) accurately reflect what investors think a firm is worth; maximizing these values is the appropriate goal for financial managers.

Second, "there is no such thing as a free lunch." In an efficient market, the only way to earn increased returns is to bear additional risk. For both investors and managers this is extremely important and should be considered in making an informed investment decision.

Completion Questions

5.1   _____ measures the sensitivity of a security's returns to movements in the market.

5.2   The _____ of a security measures how tightly the probability distribution of possible return outcomes is centred around the expected return.

5.3   _____ is the process of combining assets in a portfolio in order to reduce the variability in the total investment's return.

5.4   When the returns of stock A and stock B tend to move together, we can say their returns are positively _____.

5.5   If a stock's beta is 0.95, then its required return would be _____ than the expected return on the market portfolio.

5.6   The proxy for the risk-free rate is the rate on _____.

5.7   According to the capital asset pricing model, the required rate of return on an asset is the sum of the risk-free rate and a _____.

5.8   _____ measures nondiversifiable risk in a diversified portfolio.

5.9   Maximum risk reduction occurs in a two-security portfolio when the returns of the two securities move _____.

5.10   In a diversified portfolio, the riskiness of the stocks is _____ than the simple average of their individual risks.

5.11   If a stock is providing expected returns over its required return, it is underpriced. A stock cannot remain underpriced, since investors will _____.

5.12   If two stocks' returns move exactly opposite to each other, their correlation is _____. The returns on most assets, however, are _____.

5.13   The _____ shows the relationship between risk and return for efficient portfolios; the _____ shows the relationship between risk and return for all assets.

5.14   The market portfolio is a _____ portfolio of all assets.

5.15   After _____, trading on _____ is not profitable.

Problems

5.1   The following is a probability distribution of possible security returns for Dixon Medical Supply:

State	Probability	Return
Boom	0.15	16.0%
High growth	0.20	14.0
Normal growth	0.30	9.0
Recession	0.25	7.0
Deep recession	0.10	3.5

What is the expected security return and standard deviation?

5.2   Vidmar Industries and Mansfield Manufacturing have the following distributions of rates of return:

		Distribution of Security Returns	
State	Probability	Vidmar Industries	Mansfield Manufacturing
1	0.10	40%	−10%
2	0.20	20	−5
3	0.30	16	6
4	0.25	9	18
5	0.15	3	30

a.   Calculate the expected return and standard deviation for both companies.
b.   What is the covariance between the two companies?
c.   Construct a portfolio composed of 60 percent Vidmar Industries and 40 percent Mansfield. What is the expected return and standard deviation of the portfolio?

5.3   Bachman, Ltd., a manufacturer of home building products, is currently in an equilibrium situation with an expected return of 18 percent. The expected market return is 16 percent and the risk-free rate is 8 percent.
a.   What is the stock's beta?
b.   If a situation now arises such that the firm is no longer in equilibrium, and the firm now has a beta of 0.8 and an expected return of 13.6 percent, what can you say about the firm's stock?

5.4   First Investment Trust is a mutual fund investing in the common stock of six firms. The firms, market value of shares held, and beta of each stock are as follows:

	Market Value of Shares Held	
Firm	(in millions)	Beta
Anderson Industries	$ 90	0.6
Evans International	110	1.2
Yukon Power, Ltd.	60	0.7
Omicron, Ltd.	130	1.8
P.E.I. Trucking, Ltd.	70	0.9
Space Satellite, Ltd.	40	2.5
	$500	

a.   Calculate the beta of the mutual fund.
b.   Suppose $k_M = 16\%$ and $k_{RF} = 6\%$; what is the expected portfolio return?
c.   Using the individual security betas, calculate the expected return for each security. Show that the weighted average of the individual security returns equals the expected return of the portfolio calculated above.

5.5   Walter Abercrombie has invested $10,000 in the stock of Montreal Brewing Company and $15,000 in the stock of Amalgamated Aluminum. The expected return on Montreal Brewing is 18.6 percent and its standard deviation is 19 percent. The expected return on Amalgamated is 25.8 percent and its standard deviation is 31 percent. If the correlation between the two securities' returns is 0.45, what is the expected return and standard deviation of his portfolio?

5.6   Consider the following information.

Stock	Expected Return	Standard Deviation	Corr$_{jM}$
Michaelson, Ltd.	16.80%	12.5%	0.88
Williams, Ltd.	13.00	17.5	0.40
Woods Computers	24.00	27.5	0.64
Miller Grain, Ltd.	19.52	20.0	0.72
Market portfolio	16.00	10.0	1.00

a.   Calculate the beta for each stock.
b.   Suppose $k_{RF} = 8\%$. Calculate the required security returns implied by the CAPM and compare these to the expected returns to determine if the securities are correctly priced.

5.7   Suppose an efficient portfolio has a return of 14 percent. If $k_M = 16\%$, $k_{RF} = 8\%$, and $\sigma_M = 10$, what is the risk (σ_p) of the portfolio?

5.8   The following data relates to three Canadian securities labelled A, B, and C.

Stock	Cov (k_i, K_M)	σ_i^2
A	0.40	0.64
B	0.60	0.49
C	0.70	0.36

Given the following: $Corr_{AB} = 0.25$, $Corr_{BC} = 0.8$, $Corr_{AC} = 0.30$, and $\sigma_m^2 = 0.50$

a.   Compute betas for securities A, B, and C.
b.   What are the values of the covariances between the pairs of securities A, B, and C?
c.   Given that the risk-free rate (k_{RF}) is 8 percent and the average return on the TSE 300 index is 12 percent, what are the beta, expected return, and standard deviation for an equally weighted portfolio of stocks A, B, and C?

5.9   MTT just paid dividends of $1.80 per share on its stock. Management expects this level of dividends to grow at 8 percent forever. Investors require 12 percent return on MTT stock. Given that the risk-free rate (k_{RF}) is 6 percent and that the expected return on the market portfolio (k_M) is 10 percent:
a.   How much are you willing to pay for MTT stock?
b.   How does the market assess the riskiness of MTT stock?
c.   Suppose you purchase MTT stock today, hold it for one year, and realize $53.46 from the sale of the stock
    i.   What is your (holding period) return on the stock?
    ii.   What does your realized return suggest about the riskiness of MTT stock compared with the market?
    iii. How much of your realized return comes from dividend yield? From capital gains yield?

5A.1   Consider the following probability distributions for Applegate Industries and the market portfolio.

State(i)	P$_i$	k$_{Applegate}$	k$_{market}$
Depression	0.1	−20%	−10%
Recession	0.3	50%	10%
Normal economy	0.4	30%	25%
Boom	0.2	10%	35%

     a.   Calculate the correlation between the returns on Applegate and the market.

     b.   What is the beta for Applegate?

     c.   Given that the risk-free rate is 8 percent, what is the required return on Applegate?

Answers to Completion Questions

5.1	Beta
5.2	standard deviation
5.3	Diversification
5.4	correlated
5.5	less
5.6	treasury bills
5.7	risk premium
5.8	Beta
5.9	exactly opposite one another
5.10	less
5.11	buy the stock and bid the price up
5.12	−1.0; positively correlated
5.13	capital market line; security market line
5.14	value-weighted
5.15	transaction costs; private information

Solutions to Problems

5.1   Step 1.   Expected return:

Probability	×	Security Return	=	Expected Return
0.15		16.0%		2.40%
0.20		14.0		2.80
0.30		9.0		2.70
0.25		7.0		1.75
0.10		3.5		0.35

$$\text{Expected return} = \overline{k} = 10.00\%$$

Step 2.   Standard deviation:

$(k_i - \overline{k})$	$(k_i - \overline{k})^2$	×	Probability	=	$(k_i - \overline{k})^2 P_i$
6.0%	36		0.15		5.400
4.0	16		0.20		3.200
−1.0	1		0.30		0.300
−3.0	9		0.25		2.250
−6.5	42.25		0.10		4.225

$$\text{Variance} = \sigma^2 = 15.375\%$$
$$\sigma = (15.375\%)^{0.5} = 3.920\%$$

5.2   a.   Step 1.   Vidmar Industries:

$$\overline{k} = 0.10(40\%) + 0.20(20\%) + 0.30(16\%) + 0.25(9\%) + 0.15(3\%)$$

$$= 4\% + 4\% + 4.8\% + 2.25\% + 0.45\% = 15.5\%$$

Step 2. $\sigma^2 = 0.10(40 - 15.5)^2 + 0.20(20 - 15.5)^2 + 0.30(16 - 15.5)^2$
$\qquad\qquad + 0.25(9 - 15.5)^2 + 0.15(3 - 15.5)^2$
$\qquad = 0.10(24.5)^2 + 0.20(4.5)^2 + 0.30(0.5)^2 + 0.25(-6.5)^2 + 0.15(-12.5)^2$
$\qquad = 60.025 + 4.05 + 0.075 + 10.5625 + 23.4375 = 98.15$
$\qquad \sigma = (98.15\%)^{0.5} = 9.91\%$

Step 3.   Mansfield Manufacturing:
$\qquad \overline{k} = 0.10(-10\%) + 0.20(-5\%) + 0.30(6\%) + 0.25(18\%) + 0.15(30\%)$
$\qquad\quad = -1\% - 1\% + 1.8\% + 4.5\% + 4.5\% = 8.8\%$

Step 4. $\sigma^2 = 0.10(-10 - 8.8)^2 + 0.20(-5 - 8.8)^2 + 0.30(6 - 8.8)^2$
$\qquad\qquad + 0.25(18 - 8.8)^2 + 0.15(30 - 8.8)^2$
$\qquad = 0.10(353.44) + 0.20(190.44) + 0.30(7.84) + 0.25(84.64)$
$\qquad\qquad + 0.15(449.44)$
$\qquad = 164.36\%$
$\qquad \sigma = (164.36\%)^{0.5} = 12.82\%$

b. $\mathrm{Cov}(k_{\mathrm{Vidmar}}, k_{\mathrm{Mansfield}}) = 0.1(40 - 15.5)(-10 - 8.8) + 0.2(20 - 15.5)(-5 - 8.8)$
$\qquad\qquad\qquad\qquad\quad + 0.3(16 - 15.5)(6 - 8.8) + 0.25(9 - 15.5)(18 - 8.8)$
$\qquad\qquad\qquad\qquad\quad + 0.15(3 - 15.5)(30 - 8.8)$
$\qquad\qquad\qquad\qquad\quad = -113.7\%$

c.   Step 1.   Calculate portfolio returns:

State	Vidmar Return	× Weight	+	Mansfield Return	× Weight	= Return
1	40%	0.6		-10%	0.4	20.0%
2	20	0.6		-5	0.4	10.0
3	16	0.6		6	0.4	12.0
4	9	0.6		18	0.4	12.6
5	3	0.6		30	0.4	13.8

Step 2.   Expected portfolio return:

State	Probability	×	Portfolio	=	Expected Return
1	0.10		20.0%		2.00%
2	0.20		10.0		2.00
3	0.30		12.0		3.60
4	0.25		12.6		3.15
5	0.15		13.8		2.07
			Expected return	=	12.82%

Step 3.   Standard deviation:

$$\sigma^2 = 0.10(-20 - 12.82)^2 + 0.20(10 - 12.82)^2 + 0.30(12 - 12.82)^2$$
$$+ 0.25(12.6 - 12.82)^2 + 0.15(13.8 - 12.82)^2$$
$$= 0.10(51.55) + 0.20(7.95) + 0.30(0.67) + 0.25(0.05) + 0.15(0.96)$$
$$= 7.10\%$$
$$\sigma = (7.10\%)^{0.5} = 2.67\%$$

Alternatively, expected return and standard deviation of the portfolio may be computed as follows:

Step 1.   Expected return:

$$K_{portfolio} = W_{Vidmar} \times k_{Vidmar} + W_{Mansfield} \times k_{Mansfield}$$
$$= 0.6(15.5\%) + 0.4(8.8\%) = 12.82\%$$

Step 2.   Standard deviation:

$$\sigma^2 = W^2_{Vidmar}\,\sigma^2_{Vidmar} + W^2_{Mansfield}\,\sigma^2_{Mansfield} + 2W_{Vidmar}W_{Mansfield}Cov(k_{Vidmar},k_{Mansfield})$$
$$= (0.6)^2(98.15\%) + (0.4)^2(164.36\%) + 2(0.6)(0.4)(-113.6\%)$$
$$= 7.1035\%$$
$$\sigma = (7.1035)^{0.5} = 2.665\%$$
Note: $Cov(k_{Vidmar},k_{Mansfield}) = \sigma_{Vidmar}\,\sigma_{Mansfield}Corr_{Vidmar,Mansfield}$

5.3   a.   Since $k_j = k_{RF} = \beta_j(k_M - k_{RF})$

$$k_j - k_{RF} = \beta_j(k_M - k_{RF})$$

$$\beta_j = \frac{k_j - k_{RF}}{k_M - k_{RF}} = \frac{18\% - 8\%}{16\% - 8\%} = \frac{10\%}{8\%} = 1.25$$

b.   With a stock beta of 0.8, the firm's required rate of return is

$$k_j = k_{RF} + \beta_j(k_M - k_{RF})$$

$$= 8\% + 0.8\%(16\% - 8\%) = 14.4\%$$

Since the stock has an expected return of 13.6 percent, it is overpriced (or overvalued) in the market.

5.4   a.   Step 1.   Calculate the beta of the mutual fund.

$$\beta_p = \frac{\$90}{\$500}(0.6) + \frac{\$110}{\$500}(1.2) + \frac{\$60}{\$500}(0.7) + \frac{\$130}{\$500}(1.8) + \frac{\$70}{\$500}(0.9)$$

$$+ \frac{\$40}{\$500}(2.5)$$

$$= 0.18(0.6) + 0.22(1.2) + 0.12(0.7) + 0.26(1.8) + 0.14(0.9) + 0.08(2.5)$$

$$= 0.108 + 0.264 + 0.084 + 0.468 + 0.126 + 0.200 = 1.25$$

b.   Step 2. $K_p = k_{RF} + \beta_p(k_M - k_{RF}) = 6\% + 1.25(16\% - 6\%) = 18.5\%$

c.   Step 3. $k_j = k_{RF} + \beta_j(k_M - k_{RF})$

Anderson Industries: $k_j = 6\% + 0.6(16\% - 6\%) = 12\%$

Evans International: $k_j = 6\% + 1.2(16\% - 6\%) = 18\%$

Yukon Power, Ltd.: $k_j = 6\% + 0.7(16\% - 6\%) = 13\%$

Omicron, Ltd.: $k_j = 6\% + 1.8(16\% - 6\%) = 24\%$

P.E.I. Trucking, Ltd.: $k_j = 6\% + 0.9(16\% - 6\%) = 15\%$

Space Satellite, Ltd.: $k_j = 6\% + 2.5(16\% - 6\%) = 31\%$

Step 4.

Firm	Expected Return to Security	×	Market Value Weight	=	Expected Portfolio Return
Anderson Industries	12%		$90/$500		2.16%
Evans International	18		$110/$500		3.96
Yukon Power, Ltd.	13		$60/$500		1.56
Omicron, Ltd.	24		$130/$500		6.24
P.E.I. Trucking, Ltd.	15		$70/$500		2.10
Space Satellite, Ltd.	31		$40/$500		2.48

Total portfolio return = 18.50%

5.5   Step 1.   Let Montreal Brewing = A and Amalgamated Aluminum = B
Total investment = $10,000 + $15,000 = $25,000

$$W_A = \frac{\text{Investment in A}}{\text{Total investment}} = \frac{\$10,000}{\$25,000} = 0.4$$

$$W_B = \frac{\text{Investment in B}}{\text{Total investment}} = \frac{\$15,000}{\$25,000} = 0.6$$

Step 2. $\overline{K}_p = W_A \overline{k}_A + W_B \overline{k}_B$

$= 0.4(18.6\%) + 0.6(25.8\%) = 7.44\% + 15.48\% = 22.92\%$

Step 3. $\sigma_p = \left[W_A^2 \sigma_A^2 + W_B^2 \sigma_B^2 + 2W_A W_B \sigma_A \sigma_B \text{Corr}_{AB} \right]^{0.5}$

$= \left[(0.4)^2(19)^2 + (0.6)^2(31)^2 + 2(0.4)(0.6)(19)(31)(0.45) \right]^{0.5}$

$= \left[(0.16)(361) + (0.36)(961) + 127.224 \right]^{0.5}$

$= \left[57.76 + 345.96 + 127.224 \right]^{0.5}$

$= (530.944)^{0.5} = 23.04\%$

5.6   a.   Step 1.   Calculate the betas for each stock.
From Equation 5.15:

$$\beta_j = \frac{\sigma_j \, \text{Corr}_{jM}}{\sigma_M}$$

Michaelson, Ltd.:
$$\beta_j = \frac{12.5\%(0.88)}{10\%} = 1.1$$

Williams, Ltd.:

$$\beta_j = \frac{17.5\%(0.40)}{10\%} = 0.7$$

Woods Computers:

$$\beta_j = \frac{27.5\%(0.64)}{10\%} = 1.76$$

Miller Grain, Ltd.:

$$\beta_j = \frac{20\%(0.72)}{10\%} = 1.44$$

b.   Step   2.   Michaelson, Ltd.: $k_j = 8\% + 1.1(16\% - 8\%) = 16.8\%$. The security is correctly priced, since the required rate of return is equal to the expected return.

Williams, Ltd.: $k_j = 8\% + 0.7(16\% - 8\%) = 13.6\%$. The security is overpriced; the expected return of 13.0 percent is below the required return of 13.6 percent.

Woods Computers: $k_j = 8\% + 1.76(16\% - 8\%) = 22.08\%$. The security is underpriced; its expected return of 24 percent is higher than the required return of 22.08 percent.

Miller Grain, Ltd.: $k_j = 8\% + 1.44(16\% - 8\%) = 19.52\%$. The security is correctly priced, since its expected and required rates of return are equal.

5.7   Step 1.   From the CML,

$$\overline{K}_p = k_{RF} + \left[\frac{\overline{k}_M - k_{RF}}{\sigma_M} \right] \sigma_p$$

$$14\% = 8\% + \left[\frac{16\% - 8\%}{10} \right] \sigma_p$$

$$6\% = [0.8]\, \sigma_p$$

$$\sigma_p = \frac{6}{0.8} = 7.5$$

5.8   a. $\beta_A = \text{Cov}(k_A, k_M)/\sigma^2_M = 0.4/0.5 = 0.8$
      $\beta_B = \text{Cov}(k_B, k_M)/\sigma^2_M = 0.6/0.5 = 1.2$
      $\beta_C = \text{Cov}(k_C, k_M)/\sigma^2_M = 0.7/0.5 = 1.4$

b.   Noting that $\text{Corr}_{AB} = \text{Cov}(k_A, k_M)/\sigma_A \sigma_B$

$\text{Cov}(k_A, k_B) = \sigma_A \sigma_B\, \text{Corr}_{AB}$
$\qquad\qquad = (0.8)(0.7)(0.25)$
$\qquad\qquad = 0.14$
$\text{Cov}(k_A, k_C) = (0.8)(0.6)(0.30) = 0.144$
$\text{Cov}(k_B, k_C) = (0.7)(0.6)(0.8) = 0.336$

c.   Given $W_A = 1/3$, $W_B = 1/3$, and $W_C = 1/3$
      Portfolio beta

$$\beta_p = 1/3(0.8) + 1/3(1.2) + 1/3(1.4) = 1.133$$

Expected return

$$K_p = k_{RF} + \beta_p(k_M - k_{RF})$$
$$= 8\% + (12\% - 8\%)(1.13) = 12.53\%$$

Standard deviation

$$\sigma_p^2 = W_A^2\sigma_A^2 + W_B^2\sigma_B^2 + W_C^2\sigma_C^2 + 2W_AW_BCov_{k_Ak_B} + 2W_AW_CCov_{k_Ak_C}$$

$$+ 2W_BW_CCov_{BC}$$

$$= 1/9(0.64) + 1/9(0.49) + 1/9(0.36) + 2(1/9)(0.14) + 2(1/9)(0.144)$$

$$+ 2(1/9)(0.336) = 0.3033$$

$$\sigma_p = (0.3033)^{0.5}0.5508$$

5.9   a.   Note that $D_1 = \$1.80(1.08) = \$1.944$

$P_0 = D_1/(k_s - g) = 1.944/(0.12 - 0.08) = \$48.60$

b. $k_{MTT} = k_{RF} + (k_M - k_{RF})\beta_{MTT}$

$12\% = 6\% + (10\% - 6\%)\beta_{MTT}$

$\beta_{MTT} = 6\%/4\% = 1.5\%$

MTT stock is more risky than the market.

c.   i.   If you purchase MTT stock today for $48.60, at the end of the year you realize dividends $D_1 = 1.944$ along with proceeds of $53.46 from the sale of the stock. Using Equation 4.11:

$$k_s = \frac{D_1 + (P_1 - P_0)}{P_0} = \frac{\$1.944 + (\$53.46 - \$48.60)}{\$48.60}$$

$$= 14\%$$

Holding period return is 14 percent.

ii. $k_s = k_{RF} + \beta_{MTT}(k_M - k_{RF})$

$14\% = 6\% + \beta_{MTT}(10\% - 6\%)$

$\beta_{MTT} = 8\%/4\% = 2.0$

MTT stock is now twice as risky as the market.

iii.   Realized return = 14%

Dividend yield $D_1/P_0 = 1.944/\$48.60 = 4\%$

Capital gains $(P_1 - P_0)/P_0 = (\$53.46 - \$48.60)/\$48.60 = 10\%$

5A.1.   a.   Step 1.   Calculate expected returns:

$$\overline{k} = \sum_{i=1}^{n} k_i P_i$$

$$\overline{k}_{Applegate(A)} = 0.1(-20\%) + 0.3(50\%) + 0.4(30\%) + 0.2(10\%)$$

$$= 27\%$$

$$\overline{k}_{market(M)} = 0.1(-10\%) + 0.3(10\%) + 0.4(25\%) + 0.2(35\%)$$

$$= 19\%$$

Step 2.   Calculate standard deviations:

$$\sigma_{Applegate(A)} = [0.1(-20 - 27)^2 + 0.3(50 - 27)^2 + 0.4(30 - 27)^2 + 0.2(10-27)^2]^{0.5}$$

$$= (220.9 + 158.7 + 3.6 + 57.8)^{0.5} = (441)^{0.5} = 21$$

$$\sigma_{market(M)} = [0.1(-10 - 19)^2 + 0.3(10 - 19)^2 + 0.4(25 - 19)^2 + 0.2(35-19)^2]^{0.5}$$

$$= (84.1 + 24.3 + 14.4 + 51.2)^{0.5} = (174)^{0.5} = 13.19$$

Step 3.   Calculate the covariance:

$$Cov_{A,M} = (k_{A,i} - \overline{k}_A)(k_{M,i} - \overline{k}_M)P_I$$

State	P_i ×	$(k_{A,i} - \overline{k}_A)$ ×	$(k_{M,i} - \overline{k}_M)$	$= (k_{A,i} - \overline{k}_A)(k_{M,i} - \overline{k}_M) P_i$
Depression	0.1	(− 20 − 27)	(− 10 − 19)	136.3
Recession	0.3	(50 − 27)	(10 − 19)	−62.1
Normal	0.4	(30 − 27)	(25 − 19)	7.2
Boom	0.2	(10 − 27)	(35 − 19)	−54.4
				$Cov_{A,M} = 27.0$

Step 4.   Calculate the correlation:

$$Corr_{A,M} = \frac{Cov_{A,M}}{\sigma_A \sigma_M}$$

$$Corr_{A,M} = \frac{27}{(21)(13.19)} = \frac{27}{276.99} = 0.0975$$

b. $\beta_{Applegate} = \dfrac{Cov_{A,M}}{\sigma_M^2} = \dfrac{27}{174} = 0.16$

c. $K_{Applegate} = 8 + (19 - 8)(0.16) = 9.76\%$

Chapter 6
The Opportunity Cost of Capital

How This Chapter Relates to the Rest of the Text

A major component of a project's NPV (Chapters 7–9) is the firm's opportunity cost of capital. Calculation of the opportunity cost of capital requires knowledge of common stocks (Chapter 10), bonds and preferred stock (Chapter 11), and the valuation process (Chapter 4). A firm's opportunity cost of capital is dependent on its capital structure (Chapters 12 and 13). It is also useful in lease evaluation (Chapter 15) and accounts receivable and inventory decisions (Chapter 23).

Topical Outline

I. The concept of opportunity cost of capital.
   A. Financial decision making requires an understanding of capital budgeting. An important component of NPV is the opportunity cost of capital to be used as the discount rate for the project.
   B. If project risk is the same as risk to the firm as a whole, the proper rate of return can be viewed in two fashions.
      1. The opportunity cost of capital is the rate of return that the firm, or its investors, could earn if it invested its funds in alternative uses.
      2. The weighted average cost of capital is the average after-tax cost of funds to the firm.
   C. Definitions and calculations of the opportunity cost of capital.
      1. Opportunity cost of capital = $k_i W_{debt} + k_{ps} W_{preferred\ stock} + k_s W_{common\ equity}$
      2. The Ws are the proportions of funding to be raised by debt, preferred stock, and common equity.
      3. k_i is the after-tax cost of issuing new debt: $k_i = k_b (1 - T)$.
      4. k_{ps} is the after-tax cost of issuing new preferred stock.
      5. k_s is the after-tax cost of internally generated equity capital.
   D. Basic assumptions in order to use the opportunity cost of capital for decision making.
      1. The project's risk must be typical of the firm's risk.
      2. The firm will not materially change its financing policies to undertake the investments.
II. Calculating specific costs and financing proportions.
   A. Cost of debt.
      1. Interest is a tax-deductible expense, so the cost of debt is reduced by that tax deduction (assuming the firm is profitable).
         a. $k_i = k_b (1 - T)$
         b. $B_{np} = I(PVA_{k_b, n}) + M(PV_{k_b, n})$
      2. Debt is the least costly of the three sources, since bondholders have a fixed legal claim, and since interest is tax deductible for profitable firms.
   B. Cost of preferred stock.
      1. Cash dividends paid on preferred stock are not a tax-deductible expense.
      2. $k_{ps} = D_{ps}/P_{np}$
   C. Cost of common equity.
      1. The cost of internally generated funds.
         a. Actually, this is an opportunity cost, because shareholders forgo cash dividends in lieu of the retention of cash flows.
            i.   Management can distribute the cash flows or reinvest them in the firm.
            ii.   Shareholders could have invested the dividend payments for some rate of return if the cash flows had been paid out as cash dividends rather than retained.
            iii. If a firm cannot earn a return of at least k_s on reinvested internally generated funds, it should distribute the funds to investors so they can invest them in other assets of

similar risk to provide a return equal to k_s.

iv. Estimating the cost of equity capital requires both judgment and an understanding of what the firm's shareholders expect of the firm.

  b. Three approaches to calculating k_s.

    i. Dividend valuation approach:
$$k_s = (D_1/P_0) + g$$

    ii. CAPM approach:
$$k_s = k_{RF} + \beta_j (k_M - k_{RF})$$

    iii. Bond yield plus risk premium approach:
$$k_s = \text{bond yield} + \text{risk premium}$$

      a. Useful for firm that does not pay cash dividends.

      b. Useful when stock is not traded.

2. Cost of new common stock, k_e (external common equity).

  a. The cost of newly issued common stock is the same as the cost of internally generated equity, except for the adjustment for flotation costs and the underpricing that occurs when new common stock is sold.

  b. $k_e = (D_1/P_{np}) + g$

D. The financing proportions.

1. The weights should be determined by the current proportions of the market values of the firm's outstanding securities.

2. We assume that in investing in assets, the firm will not significantly change its financing mix.

III. The opportunity cost of capital in practice.

  A. Steps in calculating the weighted average cost of capital.

    1. Calculate the cost of long-term debt, preferred stock, and internally generated funds using the formulas above.

      a. The before-tax cost of debt is what the firm would have to pay to raise additional debt.

      b. In calculating the opportunity cost of capital, the manager is interested in the after-tax cost of debt.

      c. In estimating the cost of internally generated common equity via the dividend valuation approach, the manager should begin by estimating the expected growth in cash dividends.

    2. Calculate the market value proportions of financing to be employed.

      a. Multiply the market price per bond by the number of bonds outstanding; if no current market price is available, use the term structure of interest rates to estimate the required yield and price.

      b. Multiply the common stock market price by the number of shares outstanding.

      c. Multiply the preferred stock market price by the number of shares outstanding.

      d. Add all these market values, and divide each by this base to get the proportions of each.

    3. Use the formula, given before, to calculate the opportunity cost of capital.

    4. The opportunity cost of capital can be used to discount cash flows of projects that are as risky as the firm; projects with a positive NPV are candidates for selection.

    5. The opportunity cost of capital can be used as a hurdle rate for IRR calculations on projects as risky as the firm.

    6. Accepting projects with less return than the opportunity cost of capital is not consistent with the goal of value maximization.

  B. How often should the opportunity cost of capital be calculated?

    1. When the financing proportions have changed or are expected to change.

    2. When economic conditions have changed.

IV.   Divisional and project-specific opportunity cost.

A.   Reasons for calculating divisional costs of capital.

1.   Riskiness varies among divisional cash flows.

2.   If a firm uses a firm-wide opportunity cost of capital, it may be too low for high-risk projects and too high for low-risk projects.

3.   A firm-wide opportunity cost of capital will under-allocate funds to low-risk divisions and over-allocate funds to high-risk divisions.

B.   Steps in calculating divisional opportunity costs of capital.

1.   Determine the firm's cost of debt, k_i, and use as the cost of debt for the division.

2.   Identify one or more publicly traded firms that are similar in terms of product line and capital structure. (If the capital structure differs, an adjustment to the beta used will be necessary.)

$$\beta_{asset} = \frac{\beta_{levered\ firm}}{1 + (1 - T)B/S}$$

3.   Calculate the division's cost of equity capital, using the beta of the publicly traded firm.

4.   Estimate the division's target or appropriate capital structure as if it were a free-standing firm.

5.   Calculate the division's opportunity cost of capital as though you were calculating the firm-wide opportunity cost of capital.

C.   Divisional costs in practice.

1.   Estimating each division's opportunity cost of capital requires a thorough understanding of the firm's divisions and appropriate publicly traded firms similar to the divisions.

2.   Since some bonds might not be publicly traded, you might estimate the rating and yield to maturity of newly issued bonds for the firm.

D.   Project-specific opportunity cost of capital can be calculated using the same basic steps used in calculating divisional opportunity cost of capital.

Formulas

Notation

k_b = before-tax cost of new debt issued by the firm

k_e = after-tax cost of newly issued common stock

k_i = after-tax cost of new debt issued by the firm, $k_b(1 - T)$

k_{ps} = after-tax cost of new preferred stock issued by the firm

k_s = after-tax cost of internally generated funds (equity capital)

W_i = weights indicate the future financing proportions to be employed by the firm for debt, preferred stock, and common equity

I = annual dollar interest on a bond

M = maturity value (typically $1,000) of a bond

B_{np} = net proceeds from the sale of a bond after considering any premium or discount in price and the flotation costs involved

n = number of years to bond's maturity

D_{ps} = cash dividend expected on the preferred stock

k_{RF} = risk-free rate; often use Canadian treasury bill rate as proxy

k_M = expected return on the market portfolio

β_j = market risk measure for security j (beta)

g = expected compound percentage growth in cash dividends

D_1 = expected cash dividend for next year

P_0 = current value or price

Opportunity Cost of Capital

Opportunity cost of capital $= k_i W_{debt} + k_{ps} W_{ps} + k_s W_s$

Before-Tax Cost of Debt, k_b

$$B_{np} = I\ (PVA_{k_b,n}) + M\ (PV_{k_b,n})$$

After-Tax Cost of Debt, k_i

$$k_i = k_b\ (1 - T)$$

Cost of Preferred Stock, k_{ps}

$$k_{ps} = (D_{ps}/P_{np})$$

Cost of Internally Generated Funds, k_s (Opportunity Cost)

Dividend valuation approach:
$$k_s = (D_1/P_0) + g$$
CAPM approach:
$$k_s = k_{RF} + \beta_j (k_M - k_{RF})$$
Bond yield plus risk premium approach:
$$k_s = \text{bond yield} + \text{risk premium}$$

Cost of Externally Generated Funds

$$k_e = (D_1/P_{np}) + g$$

Divisional Cost of Capital

$$\text{Divisional cost of equity} = k_{RF} + \beta_{similar\ firm} (k_M - k_{RF})$$

Unlevered Beta

$$\beta_{asset} = \frac{\beta_{levered\ firm}}{1 + (1 - T)\,B/S}$$

What to Look For

Any craftsman will tell you that you must have the right tool for the job at hand in order to complete the task well. Financial management is an art and a science. Managers use techniques such as the time value of money (Chapter 3) and cash flow to make valuation estimates for short-term and long-term asset investments. The discount rate they use in these calculations is determined by a combination of theory and guess work. If the discount rate is wrong, the valuation results will be wrong, no matter how accurate the cash flow estimates. Chapter 6 addresses the craft of estimating the discount rate. While we want to be as precise as possible, errors of 1 to 2 percent in a firm's discount rate rarely make any important difference in practice.

We know the discount rate by several names—the opportunity cost of capital, the required rate of return, the weighted average cost of capital, and the hurdle rate. We use these terms interchangeably in this chapter.

The Theory Underlying Opportunity Cost of Capital

During the life of a firm, managers invest the firm's borrowed and equity funds in short- and long-term assets. If every opportunity presented is accepted, the firm will not remain a going concern. Managers must decide among investment alternatives, as we will see in Chapters 7–9. The key criterion for selecting investments is that the investment should increase or maximize the value of the firm.

Net present value (NPV) and internal rate of return (IRR) are two discounting procedures managers can use to value investment alternatives (Chapter 7). If the proposed project's NPV is negative, or if the IRR does not exceed the opportunity cost of capital for that project, acceptance of the project will reduce the value of the firm.

What is this opportunity cost of capital, however? In Chapter 6, we calculate the financing costs of generating new capital. This opportunity cost of capital (weighted average cost of capital) is the cost of the last dollar of additional funds and is used as a hurdle rate or as the discount rate for making investment decisions for projects with risk similar to the firm.

As you know, investors require a higher return from common stock than from preferred stock or debt, since there is no stated cash dividend rate, and they share in both the good and bad times of the firm. So, in calculating the component costs of financing, the cost of equity will be higher than that of preferred stock or debt. Changes in economic risk, inflation risk, firm- and issue-specific risk, and international risk will also increase the firm's cost of some or all of the capital components and thus increase the opportunity cost of capital.

The Art of Estimating the Opportunity Cost of Capital

Many of the values used in calculating the component costs of capital are rough estimates. The more skillful the manager, the closer the estimates will be to the actual values. In calculating any of the component costs, the proceeds, net of flotation costs and any discount (or underpricing), must be estimated. Discounts and flotation costs increase the effective cost of new capital. In addition, the manager must estimate the expected interest, I, or cash dividend, D_{ps} or D_1, on the new debt or stock, and the expected compound growth in common stock cash dividends, g. If the economy and the financial markets are especially unstable, this estimate may need frequent revision to reflect changes in the supply of and demand for money and possible internally generated cash flows available for distribution as common stock cash dividends.

Managers must also estimate the future required return on the stock market, k_M, the future risk-free rate, k_{RF}, and the firm's future beta, β_j. Chapter 6 discusses how to approximate k_M; we will go through the process in the next section. A careful study of the term structure of interest rates can help in approximating k_{RF}. Some financial services can give a reasonable estimate of the firm's beta, but remember that betas for individual firms are not stable and may change over time.

Calculating the Opportunity Cost of Capital

Now, let's run through an opportunity cost of capital calculation for a hypothetical company, Webb Bicycle Limited. The firm's bonds are rated AA, as is its preferred stock. Its beta is 1.2. Suppose we look at the financial section of the *Globe and Mail* and find that AA industrial bonds are yielding 12 percent, while AA preferred stock is yielding 13.25 percent. We look at the trends in the Canadian treasury bill rate and deduce that the risk-free rate is 9 percent. Finally, we project the expected rate of inflation (8 percent) and the real rate of return in the economy (2 percent). Then, we add the historical risk premium of stocks over bonds (about 4 percent) and we get an expected k_M of 14 percent. The firm currently has outstanding

    1)   5,000 bonds with a $1,000 par value, 8.5 percent coupon rate, and 9 years to maturity.

    2)   10,000 shares of $200 par value preferred stock with an 18.75 percent dividend..

    3)   1,000,000 no par value common stock that were originally sold for $10.

In selling new bonds, we estimate that the proceeds, B_{np}, will be $980. We predict that the proceeds from each new $100 par preferred share, P_{np}, will be $96. Finally, the current market price, P_0, of Webb Bicycle common stock is $30 per share. First, calculate the bond price:

$$B_{np} = I(PVA_{k_b, n}) + M(PV_{k_b, n})$$

$$= \$85(PVA_{12\%, 9yr}) + \$1,000(PV_{12\%, 9yr})$$

$$= \$85(5.328) + \$1,000(0.361) = \$452.88 + \$361.00 = \$813.88$$

Now, calculate the price of preferred stock:

$$D_{ps} = \$200(0.1875) = \$37.50$$

$$P_{np} = D_{ps}/k_{ps} = \$37.50/0.1325 = \$283.02$$

Following is the capital structure of Webb Bicycle Limited and the calculation of its market value weights:

Liabilities and Stockholders' Equity for Webb Bicycle Limited

	Book Value	Market Price	×	Number Outstanding	=	Market Value
Debt:						
8.5 percent coupon rate due in 9 years, $1,000 par, 5,000 bonds	$5,000,000	$813.88		5,000		$ 4,069,400
Preferred stock:						
18.75 percent dividend, 10,000 shares, $200 par	1,000,000	283.02		10,000		2,830,200
Stockholders' equity:						
Common stock, no par, 1,000,000 shares outstanding	10,000,000	30.00		1,000,000		30,000,000
Total						$36,899,600

The market value weights are: Debt = $4,069,400/$36,899,600 = 11.03%; preferred stock = $2,830,200/$36,899,600 = 7.67%; and common stock = $30,000,000/$36,899,600 = 81.30%.

We can calculate the opportunity cost of capital on Webb Bicycle by using the equations in Chapter 6. Let's list again the estimates we made above: M = $1,000; B_{np} = $980; P_0 = $96; k_{RF} = 9%; k_M = 14%; β_j = 1.2; and let's suppose D_1 = $1.50 and g = 10.5%. We will assume that the new bonds are 15-year bonds and the firm's marginal corporate tax rate is 25 percent. Finally, the firm can finance its common equity needs with internally generated funds.

Now, let's calculate the component costs of capital:

Cost of debt: 12 percent coupon, 15 years to maturity
$$B_{np} = I(PVA_{k_b, 15yr}) + M(P_{k_b, 15yr})$$

at k_b = 12%
$$B_{np} = \$120(6.811) + \$1,000(0.183) = \$1,000.32$$

at k_b = 13%
$$B_{np} = \$120(6.462) + \$1,000(0.160) = \$775.44 + \$160.00 = \$935.44$$

Via financial calculator, k_b = 12.30%.
$$k_i = k_b(1 - T) = 12.30\%(1 - 0.25) = 9.23\%$$
Cost of preferred stock: 13.25 percent dividend rate
$$k_{ps} = D_{ps}/P_{np} = \$13.25/\$96 = 13.80\%$$

Cost of internally generated funds:
CAPM approach:
$$k_s = k_{RF} + \beta_j (k_M - k_{RF}) = 9\% + 1.2(14\% - 9\%) = 15\%$$

Dividend valuation approach:
$$k_s = D_1/P_0 + g = (\$1.50/\$30) + 10.5\%$$
$$= 15.5\%$$
Bond yield plus risk premium approach:
$$k_s = \text{bond yield} + \text{risk premium}$$
$$= 12.28\% + 4\% = 16.28\%$$

We will use the average of the three approaches (15.59 percent). Now, using the market value weights, we can weight these costs to find the opportunity cost of capital.

$$\text{Opportunity cost of capital} = k_i W_{debt} + k_{ps} W_{preferred\ stock} + k_s W_{common\ equity}$$
$$= 0.1103\ (9.23\%) + 0.0767\ (13.80\%) + 0.8130\ (15.59\%) = 14.75\%$$

Webb Bicycle Limited can use 14.75 percent as the discount rate for NPV or hurdle rate for IRR calculations if the projects have the same level of risk as the firm.

Divisional Costs of Capital

It is possible to calculate opportunity costs of capital or hurdle rates for divisions. If, for example, Webb Bicycle had three divisions of varying risk, the most risky division would have more opportunity to invest in risky projects than the least risky division. If the firm used an overall opportunity cost of capital, the most risky division would get more capital budgeting money than the moderately risky and the least risky divisions, simply because of this risk–return difference. To estimate divisional opportunity costs of capital, the firm could find other companies that produce the same product line as the most risky division, some that produce the same product as the moderately risky division, and so on. Using the capital structure and beta of the comparable firms, the original firm could calculate divisional costs of equity and then divisional opportunity costs of capital for use in capital budgeting, just as we did above. Each division would have an appropriate discount rate to use when evaluating possible capital investment projects. Managers should take care when using this method, however, since one or more firms similar to the firm's divisions must be found.

Completion Questions

6.1 The _____ is the minimum acceptable rate of return on new investments of average risk.

6.2 The opportunity cost of capital is the weighted average of the firm's _____ _____.

6.3 In making investment decisions, projects should be chosen that _____ _____. Any projects whose return is _____ the opportunity cost of capital should be rejected, since they will impair the firm's value.

6.4 As inflation and other sources of risk increase, the firm's opportunity cost of capital will _____. In response, the market value of the firm's debt and equity outstanding will _____.

6.5 During the calculation of opportunity cost of capital, the relevant cost of debt is the _____ _____, since it is the cost to the firm.

6.6 In order to calculate the cost of _____, the returns demanded by existing equity investors must be estimated. This cost is an _____, since the cash flows are reinvested in the firm's projects at some rate of return rather than paid out as cash dividends.

6.7   _____ increase the cost of new common equity, making it a more costly source of financing than internally generated funds.

6.8   The cost of common equity is _____ the cost of preferred stock or the cost of debt. From the investor's standpoint, there is _____ risk, since the common shareholders participate in both the good and bad times of the firm.

6.9   The weights used in calculating the opportunity cost of capital are based on the current proportions of the _____ of the firm's outstanding securities.

6.10   The firm's opportunity cost of capital should be recalculated at least _____ or _____.

6.11   Since the riskiness of divisions may vary, the firm might calculate _____ _____ to evaluate possible capital projects. This procedure can help prevent more risky divisions from receiving _____ than their share of capital investment funding.

6.12   When the internal rate of return method is used for screening capital projects, the _____ or some appropriate _____ is the hurdle rate that must be met.

6.13   In calculating the firm's cost of equity with CAPM, the future return on the market can be approximated by adding the _____, _____ _____ and _____. The rate on _____ _____ is used as a proxy for the risk-free rate.

Problems

6.1   Winchester Limited has outstanding only one bond issue, which will mature in 10 years. The bond is presently selling for $764.23 even though its face value is $1,000. Winchester has estimated its after-tax cost of debt for a new debt issue at 7.7 percent. What are the yearly interest payments on the outstanding bonds if the tax rate is 30 percent?

6.2   Washington Petroleum Ltd. is planning to issue new preferred stock. The present preferred is selling for $58.50 and pays dividends of $7 per year. The new preferred will carry the same dividend, but the net proceeds of the sale are expected to be $3.50 lower than the current market price. What is the percentage cost of new preferred stock?

6.3   Howard Software Limited's common stock is currently selling for $45 a share. In 1997, the cash dividend on common stock is expected to be $5.85 per share, an increase over the 1996 dividend of $5.09 per share. What is the cost of internally generated funds using the dividend valuation approach? (Round to the nearest whole percent.)

6.4   Hanson Piano Limited wishes to estimate its opportunity cost of capital. The following financial data have been provided.

Balance Sheet for 1996 (in thousands)

Total assets	$3,710	Accounts payable	$ 200
		Notes payable	300
		Bonds ($1,000 par)	800
		Preferred stock (10,000 shares)	100
		Common stock (1 million shares)	1,000
		Retained earnings	1,310
			$3,710

Common stock
    1989 cash dividend = $0.20
    1996 cash dividend = $0.30
    Current price = $2.375
    Beta = 1.05

Debt
    Term to maturity = 8 years
    Yearly interest rate = 10%
    Market price = $900 ($1,000 par)

Preferred stock
    Dividend = $2.00
    Current price = $14.00

Market data
    k_{RF} = 8%
    k_M = 19%

Because of Hanson's good credit rating, both the accounts payable and notes payable have costs (before tax) of approximately 2 percent over the risk-free rate. The tax rate is 30 percent.

a.   Determine the after-tax cost of long-term debt.
b.   Determine the cost of preferred stock.
c.   Determine the after-tax cost of short-term debt.
d.   Assuming the firm can finance its common equity needs from internally generated funds, use both the dividend valuation approach and the CAPM approach to estimate the cost of common equity. Take as your estimate the average of the two approaches.
e.   Assuming that short-term debt is valued at its face value, what are the market-value proportions of each component of Hanson's capital structure?
f.   Determine the opportunity cost of capital.

6.5   A firm wishes to raise $6 million in new capital in the following component portions: 30 percent debt, 20 percent preferred shares, and 50 percent from common equity. This firm is currently faced with the following market conditions. New 10-year bonds may be issued at par, with issuing and underwriting expenses of 5 percent of par value. The bonds would have a 14 percent coupon rate paying semiannual coupons.

    New preferred shares par value $100 may be sold at a 3 percent discount from par value, and issuing and underwriting expenses amount to 1.5 percent of par value. The expected dividend rate will be 15 percent.

    New common shares can be issued at a 2 percent discount from the current market price of $20 a share. Issuing and underwriting expenses will amount to 3 percent of market price. The company has just paid a year-end dividend of $2 per share and anticipates sustaining a long-term average growth rate in dividends of 8 percent. Assume the firm's tax rate is 40 percent and that all flotation costs are tax-deductible in the issuance year.

a.   Determine the company's after-tax cost (in percent) of each source of new financing.
b.   What is the firm's opportunity cost of capital if it raises all of the common equity portion of new financing from internally generated funds?
c.   What is the firm's opportunity cost of capital if it raises all of the common equity portion of new financing by issuing new common shares?

Answers to Completion Questions

6.1   opportunity cost of capital
6.2   after-tax cost of new financing
6.3   maximize the value of the firm; below
6.4   increase; decrease
6.5   after-tax cost
6.6   internally generated funds; opportunity cost
6.7   Flotation costs and underpricing
6.8   more than; more

6.9   market value

6.10   every two years; when economic conditions change

6.11   divisional costs of capital; more

6.12   opportunity cost of capital; required rate of return

6.13   expected real growth in the economy; next year's expected inflation; a risk premium for riskiness of common stock over bonds; Canadian treasury bills

Solutions to Problems

6.1   Step 1.   From Equation 6.2,

$$k_i = k_b(1 - T) \quad \text{or} \quad k_b = \frac{k_i}{(1 - T)} = \frac{7.7\%}{1 - 0.30} = 11.0\%$$

Step 2.

$$B_{np} = I(PVA_{11\%,\ 10yr}) + \$1,000(PV_{11\%,\ 10yr})$$

$$\$764.23 = I(5.889) + \$1,000(0.352)$$

$$I(5.889) = \$764.23 - \$352.00$$

$$I = \$412.23/5.889 = \$70.00$$

6.2   Step 1.   The proceeds from the sale will be $58.50 - $3.50 = $55.00 = P_{np}

Step 2. $k_{ps} = D_{ps}/P_{np} = \$7.00/\$55.00 = 12.73\%$

6.3   Step 1.   To estimate g, recall that $D_1 = D_0(1 + g)$ or $1 + g = (D_1/D_0)$

Step 2.

$$B_{np} = I(PVA_{11\%,\ 10yr}) = \$1,000(PV_{11\%,\ 10yr})$$

$$\$764.23 = I(5.889) + \$1,000(0.352)$$

$$I(5.889) = \$764.23 - \$352.00$$

$$I = \$412.23/5.889 = \$70.00$$

Step 2. $k_s = (D_1/P_0) + g = (\$5.85/\$45.00) + 14.93\% = 13\% + 14.93\% = 27.93\%$

6.4   a.   Step 1.   To estimate k_b,

$$\$900 = \$100(PVA_{k_b\%,\ 8yr}) + \$1,000(PV_{k_b\%,\ 8yr})$$

at 12%,

$$B_{np} = \$100(PVA_{12\%,\ 8yr}) + \$1,000(PV_{12\%,\ 8yr})$$

$$= \$100(4.968) + \$1,000(0.404) = \$900.80$$

at 13%,

$$B_{np} = \$100(PVA_{13\%,\ 8yr}) + \$1,000(PV_{13\%,\ 8yr})$$

$$= \$100(4.799) + \$1,000(0.376) = \$855.90$$

By financial calculator, $k_b = 12.01\%$.

Step 2. $k_i = k_b(1 - T) = 12.01\%(1 - 0.30) = 8.41\%$

b.   Step 3. $k_{ps} = D_{ps}/P_0 = \$2/\$14 = 14.29\%$

c.   Step 4.   The after-tax cost of short-term debt from the last paragraph of the problem is equal to 8% + 2% = 10% before tax or 10(1 - 0.3) = 7.0% after tax.

d.   Step 5.   Dividend valuation approach:
                Estimate g:

$$D_{1996} = (PV_{?\%, \, 7yr}) = D_{1989}$$

$$PV_{?\%, \, 7yr} = \frac{D_{1989}}{D_{1996}} = \frac{\$0.20}{\$0.30} = 0.667$$

From the PV tables, g is approximately 6%.

Or alternatively,

$$g = \left(\frac{D_{1996}}{D_{1989}}\right)^{1/7} - 1$$

$$= \left(\frac{\$0.30}{\$0.20}\right)^{1/7} - 1$$

$$= 0.0596 \approx 6\%$$

Step 6. $D_1 = D_0 (1 + g) = \$0.30(1.06) = \$0.318$

Step 7. $k_s = (D_1/P_0) + g = (\$0.318/\$2.375) + 6\% = 19.39\%$

Step 8.   From the CAPM,
           $k_j = k_{RF} + \beta(k_M - k_{RF}) = 8\% + 1.05(19\% - 8\%) = 19.55\%$

The estimate of $k_s = (19.39\% + 19.55\%)/2 = 19.47\%$

Step 9.   (In thousands)
           Market value of short-term debt:
               Accounts payable + notes payable = \$200 + \$300 = $ \$ \ 500
           Market value of long-term debt:
               (Number of bonds)(B_0) = (800)(\$900)   =   720
           Market value of preferred:
               (Number of shares)(P_0) = (10)(\$14)   =   140
           Market value of common:
               (Number of shares)(P_0) = (1,000)(\$2.375)   =   2,375
                                          Total market value = \$3,735

Step 10.

Component	Market Value of Component	÷	Total Market Value	=	Market Value Proportions
Short-term debt	$ 500		$3,735		0.1339
Long-term debt	720		3,735		0.1928
Preferred stock	140		3,735		0.0375
Common stock	2,375		3,735		0.6358

f.   Step 11.   The opportunity cost is just the after-tax cost of each component weighted by the market-value proportions.

Opportunity cost of capital = 0.1339(7.0%) + 0.1928(8.41%) + 0.0375(14.29%)
+ 0.6358(19.47%)
= 0.9373% + 1.6214% + 0.5359% + 12.3790% = 15.47%

6.5   a.   After-tax component costs:

New debt issue:

Issuing and underwriting (flotation) cost per bond = 0.05($1,000) = $50
After-tax flotation cost = $50(0.6) = $30
Net proceeds per bond = $1,000 – $30 = $970

The next step is to compute the before-tax cost of new bond issue from the following relationship:

$$\$970 = \$70(PVA_{k_{b/2},20}) + \$1,000(PV_{k_{b/2},20})$$

By financial calculator, $k_{b/2}$ = 7.29%.
Hence k_b = 14.58%
After-tax cost of new debt = 14.58(0.6) = 8.75%

New preferred stock issue:

Discount = 0.03($100) = $3.00
Issuing and underwriting expenses = 0.015($100) = $1.50
Flotation costs per share = $4.50
After-tax flotation costs per share = $4.50(0.6) = $2.70
Net proceeds = $100 – $2.70 = $97.30
k_{ps} = $15/$97.30 = 15.42%

New common stock:

Flotation costs per share = 0.02($20) + 0.03($20) = $1.00
After-tax flotation costs per share = $0.60
Net proceeds = $20 – $0.6 = $19.40

For internal equity financing:

$k_s = [D_0(1 + g)/P_0] + g = [\$2(1.08)/\$20] + 0.08 = 18.8\%$

For external equity financing:

$k_e = [D_0(1 + g)/P_{np}] + g = [\$2(1.08)/\$19.4] + 0.08 = 19.13\%$

b.   Since the firm finances equity internally, k_s = 18.8%, and

Opportunity cost of capital = 0.3(8.75%) + 0.2(15.42%) + 0.5(18.80%)
= 2.625% + 3.084% + 9.4% = 15.109%

c.   Since the firm finances equity externally, k_e = 19.13%, and

Opportunity cost of capital = 0.3(8.75%) + 0.2(15.42%) + 0.5(19.13%)
= 15.274%

Chapter 7
Capital Budgeting Techniques

How This Chapter Relates to the Rest of the Text

Capital budgeting techniques are used to evaluate proposed investment in long-term assets and build on the concepts of cash flow, timing (Chapter 3), and risk (Chapter 5). As we saw in Chapters 1 and 3 the net present value (NPV) of an asset is simply the discounted present value of its future cash inflows less its initial investment or cost. It is through accepting only positive NPV projects that a manager increases the firm's stock price (Chapter 4). Another decision criterion also introduced in Chapter 3, the IRR, is mathematically the same as the project's implied rate of return, or the yield to maturity on a bond (Chapter 4). Managers should accept projects with IRRs greater than the firm's opportunity cost of capital (Chapter 6) or the project's risk-adjusted discount rate (Chapter 9). Chapters 8 and 9 further examine the process of capital budgeting.

Topical Outline

I.   Introduction.
   A.   Capital budgeting techniques are used to evaluate proposed investment in long-term assets, those whose return is expected to extend beyond one year.
   B.   Annually, firms should complete an economic forecast, a sales budget, and a production budget in order to estimate internal cash flows and determine external financing needs.
II.   Capital budgeting and the value of the firm.
   A.   Project classifications.
      1.   One method is to classify projects as expansion, replacement, or regulatory.
      2.   Another method is to classify projects as mutually exclusive, interrelated, or independent.
         a.   Mutually exclusive projects cannot be undertaken simultaneously and must be considered as a group of alternative projects whose individual paybacks, internal rates of return, or net present values can be compared.
         b.   Independent projects are evaluated in isolation.
         c.   The cash flow of interdependent projects may interact negatively or positively.
   B.   Value maximization.
      1.   There are similarities between the valuation process discussed in Chapter 4 and capital budgeting.
      2.   A project's net present value is the present value of the cash inflows, discounted at the opportunity cost of capital, less the project's cost.
      3.   Only by accepting positive NPV projects can a firm increase its long-run market value.
III.   Overview of the capital budgeting process.
   A.   Search and identify growth opportunities from all areas of the firm.
   B.   Develop forecasts of costs, benefits, and risks of each project.
      1.   In this chapter, we will assume all projects have identical risk; in Chapter 9, we will adjust the discount rate for the riskiness of the cash flows.
   C.   Select from among proposed projects using net present value or internal rate of return.
   D.   A post-completion audit compares the projections with the project's actual cash flows, suggesting changes in the capital budgeting process.
   E.   When working through steps B and C above, given equal risk, all projects use the same hurdle or discount rate.
      1.   The discount rate, k, is the required rate of return on the project.
      2.   The minimum required rate of return is the firm's opportunity cost of capital (Chapter 6).
IV.   Selecting capital budgeting projects.
   A.   Payback period.
      1.   Payback period is the number of years it takes for the firm to recover its initial investment.

2. Payback period is the time (τ) such that

$$\sum_{t=1}^{\tau} CF_t = CF_0$$

3. When the cash inflows are unequal, interpolation is necessary. Example: $500 project with cash inflows of $80, $100, and $400.
    a. Determine the number of whole years of payback: $500 – $80 – $100 = $320, so the payback is 2 years plus some fraction.
    b. Determine the fraction of the last year before full recovery: $320/$400 = 0.80 years.
    c. Payback is 2.80 years.

4. The firm establishes a stated or benchmark payback period; projects whose payback exceeds this benchmark are not accepted.

5. Advantages of payback include its simplicity and its rough indication of the riskiness of the project; projects with faster payback may have more certainty.

6. Disadvantages of payback are that it does not consider the timing of the cash flows (time value of money) nor cash flows that occur after the payback period.

B. Net present value is the discounted cash inflows less the initial investment.

1. The equation for net present value is

$$NPV = \sum_{t=1}^{n} \frac{CF_t}{(1 + k)^t} - CF_0$$

2. Projects with positive NPV are candidates for selection; the mutually exclusive project with the higher NPV is preferred. If projects are independent, select all that have positive NPVs.

3. Net present value will lead to a correct capital budgeting decision; payback can lead to erroneous decisions.

4. A present value profile, based upon varying discount rates, can show how sensitive the net present value is to increases or decreases in the discount rate.

5. Projects with the same cash flows can have different net present values if their discount rates differ; the more risky the cash flows, the higher the discount rate.

C. Internal rate of return (IRR).

1. The IRR is the discount rate that equates the present value of the project's cash inflows to its initial investment.

2. The formula is

$$\sum_{t=1}^{n} \frac{CF_t}{(1 + IRR)^t} = CF_0, \quad \text{or} \quad \sum_{t=1}^{n} \frac{CF_t}{(1 + IRR)^t} - CF_0 = 0$$

3. If the IRR exceeds the firm's opportunity cost of capital or hurdle rate, the project is a candidate for acceptance.

4. Review the steps for determining interest rates (Chapter 3).

5. For the present value profile in Figure 7.2, the internal rate of return occurs where the profile passes through the x (or horizontal) axis, and the net present value equals zero.

D. Why NPV is preferred.

1. The IRR calculations can produce multiple internal rates of return when the cash flow series involves more than one change in sign.

2. When ranking mutually exclusive projects, IRR and NPV sometimes do not provide consistent rankings; the firm wants to choose the project that will maximize its value.
    a. The initial outlays for mutually exclusive projects may differ significantly, causing the ranking problems.
    b. The timing of the mutually exclusive projects' cash inflows may differ significantly, causing ranking problems.
    c. The cause of the NPV–IRR conflict is the implied assumption about the rate at which cash flows are reinvested.

i. IRR assumes that all intermediate cash flows can be reinvested at the same rate of return as the IRR on the project; this assumption can be faulty, especially for longer-term projects.

ii. NPV assumes that the intermediate cash flows are reinvested at the firm's opportunity cost of capital; this assumption leads toward value maximization.

3. The modified internal rate of return (MIRR) calculates the future value of cash flows at a specified reinvestment rate, then finds the MIRR that sets the present value of the reinvested cash flows equal to the project's costs.

a.

$$\text{MIRR} = \left(\frac{FV_n}{CF_0} \right)^{1/n} - 1$$

b. The MIRR approach does not overcome ranking problems associated with size disparities.

4. To reconcile the NPV–IRR conflict, use the five-step incremental approach described in the text.

V. What leads to positive NPVs?

 A. Positive NPVs for capital budgeting projects must come from bad data or unique attributes of the firm or project.

  1. Some studies suggest that managers are over-optimistic in formulating cash flow and risk estimates. Incorrect specification of these items leads to incorrect NPVs—"garbage in, garbage out."

  2. Unique attributes arise because labour and product markets are less than perfectly competitive and hence inefficient. An effective capital budgeting process includes analysis of these imperfections.

VI. Interrelated projects—the acceptance of one project can partially affect (either positively or negatively) the cash flows of other possible projects.

 A. Joint cash flows for two or more interrelated projects must be analyzed together.

 B. Identify all possible combinations of interrelated projects.

 C. Determine the initial investment and after-tax cash flow stream for each combination, in addition to the total NPV for each project.

 D. Choose the combination with the greatest NPV.

VII. Mutually exclusive projects with unequal lives.

 A. In order to make a valid comparison, the lives of mutually exclusive projects must be equalized.

 B. Two approaches to the unequal life problem:

  1. Replacement chain approach: Assume that you can reinvest in each project to the point that the lifetimes are equal. For example, if you are comparing a four-year project and an eight-year project, assume that you reinvest in the shorter project in year four. The chain then has a life of eight years.

   a. Calculate the NPV of each replacement chain and choose the one with the highest NPV.

   b. If the replacement chains are long, use the equivalent annual NPV approach.

  2. Equivalent annual NPV method.

   a. Converts the net present value to a yearly annuity.

   b. Formula:

$$\text{Equivalent annual NPV} = \frac{NPV_n}{PVA_{k,n}}$$

   c. Choose the project with the highest equivalent annual annuity.

 C. Remember, unequal lives are a problem only in deciding among mutually exclusive alternatives.

 D. When only cash outflows exist.

  1. The objective is to minimize the discounted cash outflows.

  2. You must calculate the equivalent annual cost.

  3. Select the project with the minimum equivalent annual cost.

VIII.   Capital rationing occurs when the firm sets a dollar limit to the capital budget, generally due to a limit on the amount of external funds a firm can raise.

A.   The goal in capital rationing is to maximize the net present value of the projects accepted.

B.   For small numbers of projects, one can list all feasible combinations of projects within the budget constraint and choose the combination with the largest NPV.

C.   For large numbers of projects, linear programming can produce an optimal combination of projects.

Formulas

Payback Period

$$\text{Payback, such that } \sum_{t=1}^{\tau} CF_t = CF_0$$

Net Present Value (NPV)

$$NPV = \sum_{t=1}^{n} \frac{CF_t}{(1+k)^t} - CF_0$$

Internal Rate of Return (IRR)

$$\text{Rate so that } \sum_{t=1}^{n} \frac{CF_t}{(1+IRR)^t} - CF_0 = 0$$

Modified Internal Rate of Return (MIRR)

$$MIRR = \left(\frac{FV_n}{CF_0}\right)^{1/n} - 1$$

Equivalent Annual NPV

$$\text{Equivalent annual NPV} = \frac{NPV_n}{PVA_{k,n}}$$

What to Look For

In this chapter, we begin to look at investment in capital assets, assets whose life is expected to extend beyond one year. Capital budgeting decisions are important, since they shape the future of the firm for years to come. In addition, they may represent a relatively large commitment of the firm's resources.

In Chapter 7, we discuss the basics of capital budgeting and assume that all capital budgeting projects have equally risky cash flow streams. In Chapter 8, we consider techniques for evaluating the various types of capital budgeting projects. In Chapter 9, we relax that assumption and consider variations in risk. In capital budgeting, as in all financial management, the firm's goal is to maximize the value of the firm.

The Capital Budgeting Process

The capital budgeting processs can be looked at as four distinct steps:

1.   Search for and identification of growth opportunities
2.   Estimation of the magnitude, timing, and riskiness of cash flows
3.   Selection or rejection
4.   Control and postcompletion audit

While steps 1 and 4 are important stages of the process, measuring the magnitude, timing, and risk of the cash flows associated with a capital project is often the most difficult stage of the capital budgeting process. The measuring of cash flows is left until Chapter 8. Here we focus on the various selection criteria available to assess the acceptability of a project.

Selection Techniques

Two selection techniques that consider the timing as well as the magnitude and riskiness of the cash flows are net present value (NPV) and the internal rate of return (IRR). The payback period does not consider the timing or riskiness of the cash flows, but it implies that a shorter payback makes a project less risky.

The net present value calculation allows the manager to discount the proposed project's expected cash flows using the firm's market-determined opportunity cost of capital. (Chapter 6 discusses how to calculate the firm's opportunity cost of capital.) In calculating net present value, the manager is not only considering the riskiness of the project, but also assuming that its cash flows are reinvested at the firm's opportunity cost of capital.

When choosing among independent projects, the manager chooses all projects with a positive net present value. If two projects are mutually exclusive, the manager chooses the project that will increase the value of the firm more—the project with the higher net present value. By doing so, the manager maximizes the value of the firm.

The internal rate of return (IRR) is the rate of return the project's inflows must earn in order to exactly offset the initial investment. The project is accepted if the IRR exceeds the hurdle rate or opportunity cost of capital. The IRR method assumes that the intermediate cash flows are reinvested at the IRR of that specific project. This assumption can be unrealistic if the IRR is relatively high and if the project's life is long.

In ranking mutually exclusive capital projects, NPV and IRR do not always give consistent results. NPV, however, always gives a value-maximizing decision. We'll demonstrate both the calculation of NPV and IRR and their ranking differences. Breckenridge Manufacturing is considering two capital projects, project A and project B. Both were due to the marketing department's suggestions to expand production.

Project A is a completely automated bottling system, while project B uses the company's current technology. The two projects are mutually exclusive and have five-year lives.

Project A

The initial investment is $185,000, and the after-tax cash flows generated by the project in years 1 through 5 are $43,900, $48,220, $46,276, $44,721, and $114,832, respectively. The firm's opportunity cost of capital, k, is 12 percent.

With these data, we can calculate the NPV and IRR of project A. Since k = 12%:

Time	Cash Flow	$PV_{12\%,n}$	Present Value of Cash Flows
1	$43,900	0.893	$ 39,202.70
2	48,220	0.797	38,431.34
3	46,276	0.712	32,948.51
4	44,721	0.636	28,442.56
5	114,832	0.567	65,109.74

Present value of cash flows = $204,134.85

Net present value = $204,134.83 – $185,000 = $ 19,134.85

Using a financial calculator, the IRR = 15.5368%

Project B:

Project B calls for an initial investment of $105,000 and is expected to generate after-tax cash flows of $26,100, $28,500, $27,420, $26,556, and $67,729 in years 1 through 5, respectively.

With these data, we can calculate the NPV and IRR of project B. Since k = 12%:

Time	Cash Flow	$PV_{12\%,n}$	Present Value of Cash Flows
1	$26,100	0.893	$ 23,307.30
2	28,500	0.797	22,714.50
3	27,420	0.712	19,523.04
4	26,556	0.636	16,889.62
5	67,729	0.567	38,402.34

Present value of cash flows = $120,836.80

Net present value = $120,836.80 – $105,000 = $ 15,836.80

Using a financial calculator, the IRR =   17.1118%

Net present value ranks project A above project B, but IRR ranks project B above project A. However, IRR has not been used properly. To reconcile this conflict, the IRR must be used on an incremental basis. Since project B costs significantly less, it is set up as the "defender," and project A is the "challenger." Calculating the annual incremental cash flows of the challenger over the defender shows us that, in order to invest in project A, the firm would need to invest an additional $185,000 – $105,000 = $80,000. For this additional investment, the firm gets larger cash flows.

The incremental cash flows for years 1 through 5 are shown below.

Time	CF_A	–	CF_B	=	ΔCF
1	$43,900		$26,100		$17,800
2	48,220		28,500		19,720
3	46,276		27,420		18,856
4	44,721		26,556		18,165
5	114,832		67,729		47,103

Thus, the incremental project (A – B) can be represented as

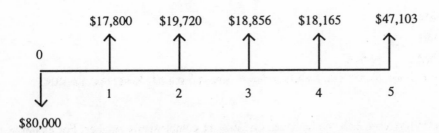

If the IRR for this incremental project (A – B) is greater than the firm's opportunity cost of capital, then the firm should select project A, the challenger. If not, B should be chosen. Using a financial calculator, the IRR of the incremental investment equals 13.428 percent. Since this is greater than the firm's opportunity cost of capital (12 percent), the firm is better off if it invests in project A. This is the same decision as we would have reached using NPV.

Both the NPV approach and the IRR approach make implicit assumptions about reinvestment of the cash flows. The NPV approach assumes that the firm invests cash flows at the firm's required return while the IRR approach assumes that the cash flows are invested at the IRR. For example, suppose that a firm faces a five-year project costing $2,745 and promising after-tax cash flows of $1,000 per year. If the firm's opportunity cost of capital is 15 percent, the project's NPV is

$$
\begin{aligned}
\text{NPV} &= \$1,000 \ (\text{PVA}_{15\%,5\text{yr}}) - \$2,745 \\
&= \$1,000 \ (3.352) - \$2,745 \\
&= \$607.00
\end{aligned}
$$

The IRR can be found by solving:

$$
0 = \$1,000(\text{PVA}_{\text{IRR},5\text{yr}}) - \$2,745
$$

$$
\text{PVA}_{\text{IRR}} = \frac{2,745}{1,000} = 2.745
$$

Using Table B.2, IRR = 24%.

The project will add $607 to the firm value if the firm can invest the $1,000 cash flows at 15 percent, but the project will only earn 24 percent if the firm can invest those cash flows at 24 percent. The former assumption about reinvestment is more realistic.

We can modify the IRR to allow for different assumptions about reinvestment. Suppose in the above example, the firm can only reinvest cash flows at 15 percent. The future value of the cash flows at the end of five years is

$$
\begin{aligned}
\text{V}_5 &= \$1,000 \ (\text{FVA}_{15\%,5\text{yr}}) \\
\text{F} &= \$1,000 \ (6.742) \\
&= \$6,742
\end{aligned}
$$

The modified IRR (MIRR) is the rate that equates the future value of the cash flows to the project's cost. That is,

$$
\text{MIRR} = \left(\frac{\text{FV}_5}{\text{CF}_0}\right)^{1/5} - 1
$$

$$
\begin{aligned}
\text{MIRR} &= \left[\frac{\$6,742}{\$2,745}\right]^{1/5} - 1 \\
&= [2.45624]^{1/5} - 1 \\
&= 1.1969 - 1 \\
&= 0.1969 \quad \text{or} \quad 19.69\%
\end{aligned}
$$

The MIRR is lower because we assume that cash flows are reinvested at a rate lower than the IRR.

Interrelated Projects

Many projects cannot be analyzed independently as one project complements another. For example, suppose a developer owns a large tract of land and is considering three projects: a restaurant, a shopping centre, and an apartment building. Unless the developer intends to accept only one project, he must consider the interrelationship between projects in order to decide how the land should be developed. The restaurant will do more business if the apartment building or the shopping centre is nearby. Likewise, the proximity to shopping may be an important consideration for those moving into the apartment building, and so on. The developer would need to evaluate the joint cash flows from seven possible combinations of projects in order to reach the optimal decision. These combinations are

1. Restaurant alone.
2. Shopping centre alone.
3. Apartment building alone.
4. Restaurant and shopping centre.
5. Restaurant and apartment building.

6.   Shopping centre and apartment building.
7.   Shopping centre, apartment building, and restaurant.

After identifying all the possible combinations, the developer must determine the initial investment and cash flow stream for each combination and calculate the NPV. The appropriate decision is to choose the combination with the highest NPV.

Mutually Exclusive Projects with Unequal Lives

Firms must often make decisions between mutually exclusive projects with unequal lives. Simply choosing the project with the highest NPV can be suboptimal; longer-lived projects have more time to build up positive NPVs. In order to make a valid comparison, it is necessary to equalize the lives of the projects.

The first method is called the replacement chain approach. In this approach, we assume that we reinvest in the projects at the end of their lives until the lifetimes of the replacement chains are equal. For instance, assume a three-year project has an NPV of $1,500 and a four-year project has an NPV of $1,650. If we assume that we invest in the first project in years 0, 3, 6, and 9 and the second in years 0, 4, and 8, both alternatives have equal lives. Assuming a required return of 14 percent, we can now calculate the NPV of the replacement chain for each alternative. For the first alternative:

$$
\begin{aligned}
\text{NPV} &= \$1,500 + \$1,500\ (\text{PV}_{14\%,3yr}) + \$1,5000\ (\text{PV}_{14\%,6yr}) \\
&\quad + \$1,5000\ (\text{PV}_{14\%,9yr}) \\
&= \$1,5000 + \$1,5000\ (0.675) + \$1,5000\ (0.456) + \$1,5000\ (0.308) \\
&= \$1,500 + \$1,012.50 + \$684.00 + \$462.00 = \$3,658.50
\end{aligned}
$$

For the second alternative:

$$
\begin{aligned}
\text{NPV} &= \$1,650 + \$1,650\ (\text{PV}_{14\%,4yr}) + \$1,650\ (\text{PV}_{14\%,8yr}) \\
&= \$1,650 + \$1,650\ (0.592) + \$1,650\ (0.351) \\
&= \$1,650 + \$976.80 + \$579.15 = \$3,205.95
\end{aligned}
$$

Since the three-year project has a higher NPV with the replacement chain, it should be taken over the four-year project.

The replacement chain approach will be difficult if the chains are long. In that case, it is easier to use the equivalent NPV approach. This method converts the original NPVs to yearly net present value figures. The equivalent annual NPV is

$$
\text{Equivalent annual NPV} = \frac{\text{NPV}_n}{\text{PVA}_{k,n}}
$$

For the three-year project:

$$
\text{Equivalent annual NPV} = \frac{\$1,500}{\text{PVA}_{14\%,3yr}} = \frac{\$1,500}{2.322} = \$643.22
$$

For the four-year project:

$$
\text{Equivalent annual NPV} = \frac{\$1,650}{\text{PVA}_{14\%,4yr}} = \frac{\$1,650}{2.914} = \$566.23
$$

You should choose the three-year project since it provides the highest equivalent annual NPV.

Remember that only in the case of mutually exclusive projects do we worry about unequal lives. For independent projects, you should choose the ones with positive NPVs.

Capital Rationing

Capital rationing occurs when the firm places a limit on the money available for investment in long-term projects. In this case, not all positive NPV projects can be accepted. If this happens, you should choose the set of projects that fits the capital budget and has the highest total NPV. If the number of projects is small, this can be done by listing all possible combinations and calculating the NPV of each combination. If there is a large number of projects, linear programming should be used.

When using single-value estimates of initial investment, inflows, outflows, ending values, project life, and so forth, managers should consider how sensitive the project rankings are to variations from these expected values. In Chapter 9, we will adjust NPV calculations for this variability, and look at other methods of analyzing project risk.

Completion Questions

7.1   Long-term investments have a major impact on the magnitude, timing, and riskiness of the firm's _____.

7.2   In searching for and identifying capital project ideas, managers must be certain that the projects are in line with the firm's _____.

7.3   The _____ contains estimates of the cash flows for long-term projects.

7.4   _____ projects are those designed to improve the firm's ability to produce and market its products. _____ projects are those designed to take the place of existing assets that have become obsolete.

7.5   When two capital projects are _____, the acceptance of one precludes the acceptance of the other. The firm would choose that project whose NPV was _____.

7.6   The _____ is a nondiscounted cash-flow technique measuring the number of years it takes for the firm to recover its initial investment. It does not, however, consider the cash flows that _____.

7.7   The net present value is determined by discounting the _____ back to the present and then _____.

7.8   Among the three selection techniques, the _____ technique provides the correct ranking decisions.

7.9   On the present value profile, the internal rate of return is where the net present value would be _____.

7.10   If one of several _____ projects is undertaken, the cash flows to all related projects also increase.

7.11   The joint cash flows for two or more interrelated projects must be _____.

7.12   In deciding among _____ projects, you must ensure that the lifetimes are equal.

7.13   Two methods for equalizing lifetimes are _____ and _____.

7.14   When the firm sets a limit on the size of the capital budget, it is faced with _____. In order to select from among the alternative projects, the firm will consider all possible combinations of positive net present value projects within the budget limit. The set of projects with the _____ will be selected.

7.15   The NPV approach assumes cash flows are reinvested at the firm's _____ _____, while the IRR approach assumes cash flows are reinvested at the _____.

Problems

7.1   Kiser Kitchenware is considering the construction of a new assembly line requiring an initial investment of $1,500,000. The assembly line is expected to last for 10 years, and the firm expects constant yearly after-tax cash flows (CF) over the life of the project. The payback period on the assembly line is 4.92 years. Assuming an opportunity cost of capital of 12 percent, what is the project's NPV? What is its IRR?

7.2   Miles Office Supply is considering two mutually exclusive inventory management systems, each with five-year lives. Project A is an office computing system to facilitate record-keeping, costing $20,000 and yielding a CF of $6,540.22 per year. Project B is a fully automated system costing $100,000 with a CF of $29,832.94 per year.

    a.   Calculate the IRR of each project and select the preferred project.

    b.   Assuming that the opportunity cost of capital is 10 percent, which project is preferable?

    c.   At what discount rate would the firm be indifferent between the two projects?

7.3   Verdun Bridge Company is considering the purchase of a paint sprayer. The project costs $15,000 and has expected CF of $3,337.78 per year for the next 10 years. What is the project's NPV if Verdun's opportunity cost of capital is 12 percent? What is the IRR? What is the modified IRR if the firm can only reinvest the cash flows at 12 percent?

7.4   Suppose a firm has available to it the following projects:

Project	Initial Investment	After-Tax Cash Flow per Year	Life
A	$100,000	$ 50,000	3
B	250,000	75,000	8
C	350,000	100,000	5
D	60,000	10,000	10
E	85,000	30,000	4
F	150,000	60,000	5
G	500,000	150,000	6
H	275,000	65,000	8

    If the market-determined opportunity cost of capital is 18 percent, and the firm has available for investment only $600,000, which projects should be chosen?

7.5   Imported Auto Repair Centre has recently purchased a plot of land to allow for expansion. Three possible projects are under consideration: a parts store, a gas station, and an automobile dealership. Each project has an expected life of 15 years. The parts store will cost $2 million and is expected to produce after-tax cash flows of $375,000 per year. The gas station would cost $500,000 and will produce after-tax cash flows of $85,000 per year. The dealership would cost $4 million and produce after-tax cash flows of $718,000 per year. Because of certain scale economies, the parts store could be combined with the dealership for a total cost of $5 million and would produce after-tax cash flows of $900,000. The gas station could be combined with any of the projects, but it is not expected that such a combination will result in any investment savings or changes in the cash flows. If Imported's opportunity cost of capital is 16 percent, what should it do?

7.6   Milliken Manufacturing Company, a producer of airplane parts, is considering two different plans for moving raw materials into its work area. Plan A is to invest $6 million in a fully automated assembly line that will result in annual after-tax cash flows of $2.7 million per year. Plan B is for a system of conveyor belts to bring raw materials into the work area where they will be moved manually into the appropriate work station. The conveyor belts are less costly, requiring an investment of $3 million; however, because of the labour intensity, the annual after-tax cash flows will be only $1.02 million per year. If the fully automated assembly line has a useful lifetime of 3 years and the conveyors have a lifetime of 5 years, which plan should the firm undertake if its opportunity cost of capital is 12 percent? Use both the replacement chain approach and the equivalent annuity approach to show your answer is correct.

Answers to Completion Questions

7.1	cash flows
7.2	strategic goals and objectives
7.3	capital budget
7.4	Expansion; Replacement
7.5	mutually exclusive; greater (assuming both NPVs are positive)
7.6	payback period; occur after the payback period
7.7	expected cash inflows; subtracting the initial investment
7.8	net present value
7.9	zero
7.10	complementary
7.11	analyzed together
7.12	mutually exclusive
7.13	the replacement chain approach; the equivalent NPV approach
7.14	capital rationing; maximum total NPV
7.15	opportunity cost of capital; IRR

Solutions to Problems

7.1   Step 1.   When cash flows are constant,

$$\text{Payback period} = \frac{\text{Initial investment}}{CF_t}$$

so, $CF_t = \dfrac{\text{Initial investment}}{\text{Payback period}} = \dfrac{\$1,500,000}{4.92} = \$304,878.05 \text{ per year}$

Step 2. $NPV = \displaystyle\sum_{t=1}^{n} \frac{CF_t}{(1+k)^t} - \text{cost}$

$= \$304,878.05 \, (PVA_{12\%,10yr}) - \$1,500,000$

$= \$304,878.05 \, (5.650) - \$1,500,000$

$= \$1,722,560.99 - \$1,500,000$

$NPV = \$222,560.99$

Step 3.   IRR: At the IRR, $\displaystyle\sum_{t=1}^{n} \frac{CF_t}{(1+IRR)^t} - \text{initial investment} = 0$

so, $\$304,878.05 \, (PVA_{IRR,10yr}) - \$1,500,000 = 0$

$PVA_{IRR,10yr} = \dfrac{\$1,500,000}{\$304,878.05} = 4.920$

Step 4.   Using Table B.1, we can see that the $PVA_{IRR,10yr}$ lies between the factors for 15 percent and 16 percent. Visually it appears to be about 15.5%. By financial calculator it is 15.52%.

7.2   a.   Step 1.   Project A
$20,000   = \$6,540.33$ (PVA$_{?\%,5yr}$)
(PVA$_{?\%,5yr}$)$= (\$20,000 / \$6,540.22) = 3.058$

From Appendix Table B.2, this PVA is associated with 19 percent.
Thus, the IRR for project A is 19 percent.

Project B
(PVA$_{?\%,5yr}$) $= (\$100,000 / \$29,832.94) = 3.352$; from Table B.2 IRR = 15%
Select project A since it has the higher IRR.

   b.   Step 2.   Calculate the NPV for each project.

NPV$_A$ = \$6,540.22 (PVA$_{10\%,5yr}$) $- \$20,000$
   = \$6,540.22 (3.791) $- \$20,000$
   = \$24,793.97 $- \$20,000 = \$4,793.97$
NPV$_B$ = \$29,832.94 (3.791) $- \$100,000$
   = \$113,096.68 $- \$100,000 = \$13,096.68$

Since our goal is to maximize the value of the firm, select project B, which has the larger NPV.

   c.   Step 3.   Set the two projects equal to each other and solve for the discount rate.
$6,540.22 (PVA$_{?\%,5yr}$) $- \$20,000$ = \$29,832.94 (PVA$_{?\%,5yr}$) $- \$100,000$
   $23,292.72 (PVA$_{?\%,5yr}$) = \$80,000$
   PVA$_{?\%,5yr}$ = \$80,000 / \$23,292.72 = 3.435$
The rate associated with a PVA of 3.517 is 13 percent, while that associated with 3.433 is 14. By financial calculator the rate is 13.98%.

7.3   Step 1.   NPV = \$3,337.78 (PVA$_{12\%,10yr}$) $- \$15,000$
   = \$3,337.78 (5.650) $- \$15,000$
   = \$18,858.46 $- \$15,000$
   = \$3,858.46

   Step 2.   IRR can be found by solving
   $15,000   = \$3,337.78$ (PVA$_{IRR,10yr}$)

   $$PVA_{IRR,10yr} = \frac{\$15,000.00}{\$3,337.78}$$

   = 4.494

From Table B.2, IRR = 18%.

Step 3.   MIRR can be found by solving

$$\$15,000 = \frac{\displaystyle\sum_{t=1}^{n} \$3,337.78 \, (1.12)^{t-1}}{(1 + MIRR)^{10}}$$

$$\$15,000 = \frac{\$3,337.78 \, (FVA_{12\%,10yr})}{(1 + MIRR)^{10}}$$

$$\$15,000 = \frac{\$3,337.78 \, (17.549)}{(1 + MIRR)^{10}}$$

$$\$15,000 = \frac{\$58,573.82}{(1 + MIRR)^{10}}$$

$$MIRR = \left[\frac{\$58,573.82}{(\$15,000)}\right]^{1/10} - 1$$

$$= [3.90492]^{1/10}$$

$$= 1.1459 - 1$$

$$= .1459 \text{ or } 14.59\%$$

7.4   Step 1.   Calculate the NPV of each project.

NPV_A = $50,000 $(PVA_{18\%,3yr})$ − $100,000 = $50,000 (2.174) − $100,000
        = $8,700
NPV_B = $75,000 $(PVA_{18\%,8yr})$ − $250,000 = $75,000 (4.078) − $250,000
        = $55,850
NPV_C = $100,000 $(PVA_{18\%,5yr})$ − $350,000 = $100,000 (3.127) − $350,000
        = −$37,300
NPV_D = $10,000 $(PVA_{18\%,10yr})$ − $60,000 = $10,000 (4.494) − $60,000
        = −$15,060
NPV_E = $30,000 $(PVA_{18\%,4yr})$ − $85,000 = $30,000 (2.690) − $85,000
        = −$4,300
NPV_F = $60,000 $(PVA_{18\%,5yr})$ − $150,000 = $60,000 (3.127) − $150,000
        = $37,620
NPV_G = $150,000 $(PVA_{18\%,6yr})$ − $500,000 = $150,000 (3.498) − $500,000
        = $24,700
NPV_H = $65,000 $(PVA_{18\%,8yr})$ − $275,000 = $65,000 (4.078) − $275,000
        = −$9,930

Step 2.   Since projects C, D, E, and H have negative NPVs, the firm would never accept them. Consider only the remaining projects.

Project	Cost	NPV
A	$100,000	$ 8,700
B	250,000	55,850
F	150,000	37,620
G	500,000	24,700

Step 3.   The firm can invest in combination A, B, F or combination A and G and remain within the capital budget.

$$NPV_{ABF} = NPV_A + NPV_B + NPV_F$$
$$= \$8,700 + \$55,850 + \$37,620 = \$102,170$$
$$NPV_{AG} = NPV_A + NPV_G + = \$8,700 + \$24,700 = \$33,400$$

The appropriate combination is projects A, B, and F. Note that the firm does not exhaust its capital budget with this combination.

Alternatively the firm can use the profitability index to rank the projects.

$$PI = \frac{\sum \frac{CF_t}{(1 + k)^t}}{CF_0}$$

$$PI_A = \frac{\$108,700}{\$100,000} = 1.087$$

$$PI_B = \frac{\$305,850}{\$250,000} = 1.223$$

$$PI_F = \frac{\$187,620}{\$150,000} = 1.251$$

$$PI_G = \frac{\$524,700}{\$500,000} = 1.049$$

Ranking the projects in decending order of PI we have: B, F, A, and G. By undertaking projects B, F, and A we use only \$500,000 of our capital budget and achieve a total NPV of \$102,170. We do not have enough money to include project G, with its cost of \$500,000, and the combination of projects A and G (total cost \$600,000) yields a lower total NPV of \$33,400. Therefore the best combination is projects B, F, and A.

7.5   Step 1.   Calculate the NPVs of the following projects:
The parts store
The gas station
The automobile dealership
The dealership and the parts store
If the NPV of the parts store is positive, we can add it to the alternative with the highest NPV.

Step 2.   Parts store
$$NPV = \$375,000 \ (PVA_{16\%,15yr}) - \$2,000,000$$
$$= \$375,000 \ (5.575) - \$2,000,000 = \$90,625$$

Gas station
$$NPV = \$85,000 \ (PVA_{16\%,15yr}) - \$500,000$$
$$= \$85,000 \ (5.575) - \$500,000 = -\$26,125$$

Dealership
$$NPV = \$718,000 \, (PVA_{16\%,15yr}) - \$4,000,000$$
$$= \$718,000 \, (5.575) - \$4,000,000 = \$2,850$$

Dealership and parts store
$$NPV = \$900,000 \, (PVA_{16\%,15yr}) - \$5,000,000$$
$$= \$900,000 \, (5.575) - \$5,000,000 = \$17,500$$

Imported should build just the parts store. (Note: If the gas station had a positive NPV, the combinations to consider would increase since the gas station would have to be evaluated with each of the projects above.)

7.6   Step 1.   Project A (in units of $1,000):
$$CF_0 = \$6,000$$

Step 2. $$NPV = CF_{1-5} \times PVA_{12\%,3yr} - CF_0$$
$$= \$2,700 \, (2.402) - \$6,000$$
$$= \$6,485.40 - \$6,000$$
$$= \$485.40$$

Step 3.   The replacement chain is 15 years long, so
$$NPV = \$485.40 + \$485.40 \, (PV_{12\%,3yr}) + \$485.40 \, (PV_{12\%,6yr})$$
$$+ \$485.40 \, (PV_{12\%,9yr}) + \$485.40 \, (PV_{12\%,12yr})$$
$$= \$485.40 + \$485.40 \, (0.712) + \$485.40 \, (0.507) + \$485.40 \, (0.361)$$
$$+ \$485.40 \, (0.257)$$
$$= \$485.40 + \$345.60 + \$246.10 + \$175.23 + \$124.75$$
$$= \$1,377.08$$

Step 4.   Equivalent annual annuity:
$$\frac{NPV_n}{PVA_{12\%,3yr}} = \frac{\$485.40}{2.402} = \$202.08 \text{ or } \$202,080$$

Step 5.   Project B (in units of $1,000):
$$CF_0 = \$3,000$$

Step 6. $$NPV = CF_{1-5} \times PVA_{12\%,5yr} - CF_0$$
$$= \$1,020 \, (3.605) - \$3,000$$
$$= \$3,677.10 - \$3,000$$
$$= \$667.10$$

Step 7.   The replacement chain is 15 years long, so
$$NPV = \$677.10 + \$677.10 \, (PV_{12\%,5yr}) + \$677.10 \, (PV_{12\%,10yr})$$
$$= \$677.10 + \$677.10 \, (0.567) + \$677.10 \, (0.322)$$
$$= \$677.10 + \$383.92 + \$218.03$$
$$= \$1,279.05$$

Step 8.   Equivalent annual annuity:

$$\frac{NPV_n}{PVA_{12\%,5yr}} = \frac{\$677.10}{3.605} = \$187.82 \text{ or } \$187,820$$

Step 9.   Project A is preferable; although its NPV is less, both the NPV of the replacement chain and the equivalent annual annuity for project A are greater than those for project B.

Chapter 8
Application of Capital Budgeting Techniques

How This Chapter Relates to the Rest of the Text

Chapter 7 discussed the techniques of capital budgeting. The net present value of a project is a function of its cash flows, their timing (Chapter 3), and riskiness (Chapter 5). In this chapter, we examine the application of the tools of capital budgeting to the types of projects a firm might undertake, such as expansion projects, replacement projects, and the divestiture decision. We also introduce corporate taxation in this chapter. Although the Canadian tax system is complex, it is important to understand it. Taxes affect the firm's cash flows not only for capital budgeting, but also for cash budgets (Chapter 26). Taxes affect the opportunity cost of capital (Chapter 6), and the tax benefits of debt (Chapter 11) affect the firm's capital structure decision (Chapter 12). Taxes are also an important consideration in evaluating leases (Chapter 15) and corporate restructuring (Chapter 16). The final chapter in this section (Chapter 9) discusses risk and capital budgeting.

Topical Outline

I.   Corporate taxes.
    A.   The Capital Cost Allowance (CCA) specifies the amount of depreciation that can be deducted from revenue for tax purposes.
        1.   Depreciation for tax purposes (CCA) differs from GAAP depreciation.
        2.   Depreciable assets are grouped into one of 44 different asset classes.
        3.   Each class has a maximum CCA rate that is applied to the undepreciated capital cost (UCC) of the class.
        4.   One-half of the capital cost (purchase price + installation costs) is added to the UCC of the other assets in the same class in the year the asset is put in use; the remaining half is added in the following year.
        5.   If an asset is sold, the lesser of the net proceeds from the sale or the capital cost of the asset is deducted from the pool.
        6.   The 50% Rule states that if assets are bought and sold from the same class in the same year (i.e., assets are replaced), one-half of the net acquisition (capital cost of the new asset minus the lesser of the net proceeds from the sale or the capital cost of the old) is added to the pool.
        7.   When all the assets in the pool are sold, the pool is terminated and the firm subtracts the lesser of the net proceeds or the total capital cost from the UCC of that class.
            a.   If the balance is positive, the firm can deduct the terminal loss from income.
            b.   If the balance is negative, the firm must report the CCA recapture as income and possibly a capital gain if the asset is sold for more than its original cost.
        8.   While the CCA generally uses a declining balance method, some classes of assets can be completely written off in one to two years.
    B.   The disposal of an asset results in tax effects only if the asset pool is terminated.
    C.   If the asset pool survives, the firm receives CCA deductions (and thus cash flows) from the asset, even after it is disposed of.
    D.   Other important provisions.
        1.   Federal tax rates on corporate income vary from 12 percent to 28 percent.
            a.   Firms also pay a 4 percent surcharge to the federal government.
            b.   Provincial tax rates vary from 8.9 percent to 17 percent.
        2.   Dividend and interest income.
            a.   Interest income is taxed as ordinary income as is dividend income from non-Canadian corporations.
            b.   Dividend income earned from investments in Canadian corporations is not taxed.
        3.   Interest and dividends paid.
            a.   Interest paid on bonds and loans is an expense of doing business and is deductible for tax purposes.

        b.   Dividends paid on common and preferred stock and interest paid on income bonds must be paid out of net income and are not tax-deductible.

    4.   Capital gains occur when a firm sells a financial asset or depreciable asset for more than its purchase price; a capital loss occurs when a firm sells a financial asset for less than its cost.

        a.   3/4 of net capital gains will be taxed at the firm's marginal rate.

    5.   Tax loss carrybacks and carryforwards.

        a.   A firm incurs an operating loss if its allowable expenses exceed revenues.

        b.   Operating losses are carried back to reduce all types of income (including capital gains) for the three previous years.

        c.   If all the losses cannot be used, they are carried forward for seven years from the year of origin.

        d.   A net capital loss can be carried back three years to offset *only* capital gains.

        e.   If all the capital losses cannot be used, they can be carried forward indefinitely to offset capital gains.

II.   How to estimate cash flows.

    A.   The capital cost allowance (CCA) is an important component of cash flows since it is a noncash expense that reduces a firm's tax liability.

    B.   Express cash inflows and outflows on an after-tax basis.

    C.   Ignore all irrelevant costs and benefits, such as overhead.

    D.   Divide cash flows into three types:

        1.   Initial investment at time zero—the initial cash outflow.

        2.   Operating net cash flows for each year in the economic life of the investment—the periodic cash flows.

        3.   Ending cash flows occur when the project is terminated.

    E.   Opportunity costs are the cost associated with an alternative or forgone opportunity bypassed in choosing another alternative.

III.   Expansion projects.

    A.   Estimate initial investment.

        1.   Consider opportunity costs, increases (or decreases) in working capital, and other start-up costs as well as the cost of the asset.

    B.   Estimate operating cash flows (CF).

        1. $CF = CFBT (1 - T) + T \times CCA$.

    C.   Estimate the ending cash flows (ECF).

        1.   Consider tax effects if the asset pool is eliminated.

        2.   If working capital is released, ECF increases.

    D.   Calculate the project's net present value.

        1.   Formula:

$$NPV = \sum_{t=1}^{n} \frac{CFBT_t (1 - T)}{(1 + k)^t} + \left\{ \left[\frac{TdC_0}{k + d} \right] \left[\frac{1 + 0.5k}{1 + k} \right] - \left[\frac{1}{(1 + k)^n} \right] \left[\frac{TdRV}{k + d} \right] \right\}$$

$$+ \frac{ECF}{(1 + k)^n} - CF_0$$

IV.   Replacement decisions—focus on incremental cash flows; cash flows related to the new equipment less cash flows related to the old.

    A.   For initial flows, consider the increase in net working capital, the tax effects of the sale or disposal of the replaced asset, and the purchase price and installation costs.

    B.   For operating flows, consider the changes in cash inflows, cash outflows, and CCA.

        $\Delta CF_t = \Delta CFBT_t (1 - T) + \Delta CCA_t (T)$

    C.   In calculating the ending flows, consider the tax effects of the sale or disposal of the asset if the pool is eliminated and the release of net working capital.

D.   If the net present value of the incremental cash flows is positive, the existing asset should be replaced.

V.   More on cash flow estimation.

A.   Inflation.

1.   Inflation affects both cash flow and the opportunity cost of capital. Only in the case where both CFs and the opportunity cost of capital properly anticipate and adjust for the same percentage rate of inflation will the effects cancel each other out.

2.   If inflation is accounted for in the opportunity cost of capital, but not CF, NPVs will be downward biased.

3.   In adjusting for inflation, managers should remember the following:

a.   Be consistent; make sure inflation consequences are built into both CFs and the opportunity cost of capital.

b.   Even if gross inflows and outflows change in line with inflation, CF will not due to Canada's tax structure.

c.   Inflation is not constant across sectors of the economy.

d.   Differential price changes may occur due to supply and demand. These changes are due to factors other than inflation and should be considered.

B.   Financing costs should, under most cases, be excluded from the calculation of CFs. Capital budgeting and financing decisions are separate.

C.   Abandonment.

1.   In order to ensure that all alternatives have been examined, consider abandonment.

2.   The selling price of an asset is an opportunity cost that must be considered.

3.   An additional alternative is to consider modernization. The relevant set of cash flows for this decision is the combination of existing and new cash flows.

VI.   Appendix 8A: Adjusted present values.

A.   The adjusted present value method separates the effects of the investment (capital budgeting) decision from the effects of the financing decision.

1.   Calculate the base case net present value of the project's operating cash flows using the unlevered cost of equity capital.

2.   The adjusted present value equals the base case NPV plus the present value of financing benefits.

B.   Financing effects.

1.   Calculate the present value of interest tax shields using the unlevered cost of equity.

2.   Subtract any issuing costs.

3.   Subsidized debt yields two benefits; interest tax shields and lower loan payments.

C.   When APV comes in handy.

1.   The adjusted present value method comes in handy when the firm is in a temporary loss position; tax shields that can be taken can be built into the APV approach but not the NPV method.

2.   The APV approach should be used when specialized financing cannot be incorporated into the opportunity cost of capital.

3.   In general, it is easier to use NPVs.

D.   If the tax system is symmetrical, if market values of debt and equity are employed, and if the project's debt capacity is determined by the present value of the operating and financing cash flows, the NPV approach and the APV approach produce the same answers.

Formulas

Notation

UCC	=	undepreciated capital cost
CCA	=	capital cost allowance
T	=	the firm's marginal tax rate
d	=	the CCA rate
C, C_0	=	the capital cost of the new asset
k	=	the firm's market-based marginal cost of capital
RV	=	net resale value
n	=	the useful life of the project
$CFBT_t$	=	annual operating cash flows before tax
ECF	=	ending cash flows
CF_0	=	initial investment
CF_t	=	cash flow after tax in year t
β_S^U	=	unlevered beta
β_S^L	=	levered equity beta
k_S^U	=	unlevered cost of equity
S	=	market value of the firm's common stock
B	=	market value of the firm's bonds

Taxable Income

Taxable income = Revenue − Expense − Depreciation for tax purposes

Undepreciated Capital Cost at the Beginning of Year n

$$UCC_n = \begin{cases} 1/2\ C & \text{for } n = 1 \\ C\,(1 - d/2)(1 - d)^{n-2} & \text{for } n \geq 2 \end{cases}$$

Capital Cost Allowance in Year n

$$CCA_n = d \times UCC_n$$

Initial Investment

Initial investment = cost of equipment and land + costs related to purchase + additional net working capital required + opportunity costs (net of taxes).

Operating Cash Flows

$$CFBT_t = \text{cash inflows}_t - \text{cash outflows}_t$$
$$CF_t = CFBT_t(1 - T) + CCA_t(T)$$

Ending Cash Flows

Ending cash flows = funds realized from sale of asset plus a tax benefit if it is expected to be sold at a loss or, minus a tax liability if it is expected to be sold at a gain + release of net working capital − disposal costs (net of taxes).

Net Present Value

$$NPV = \sum_{t=1}^{n} \frac{CFBT_t(1-T)}{(1+k)^t} + \left\{ \left[\frac{TdC_0}{k+d}\right]\left[\frac{1+0.5k}{1+k}\right] - \left[\frac{1}{(1+k)^n}\right]\left[\frac{TdRV}{k+d}\right] \right\}$$

$$+ \frac{ECF}{(1+k)^n} - CF_0$$

Incremental Operating Cash Flows

$$\Delta CF_t = \Delta CFBT_t(1-T) + \Delta CCA_t(T)$$

NPV of the Replacement Decision

$$NPV = \sum_{t=1}^{n} \frac{\Delta CFBT_t(1-T)}{(1+k)^t} + \left\{ \left[\frac{Td(\Delta C_0)}{k+d}\right]\left[\frac{1+0.5k}{1+k}\right] - \left[\frac{1}{(1+k)^n}\right]\left[\frac{Td(\Delta RV}{k+d}\right] \right\}$$

$$+ \frac{\Delta ECF}{(1+k)^n} - \Delta CF_0$$

Appendix 8A

Unlevered Equity Beta

$$\beta_S^U = \beta_S^L \left[\frac{S}{B+S}\right]$$

Unlevered Cost of Equity Capital

$$k_S^U = k_{RF} + \beta_S^U(k_M - k_{RF})$$

Base Case NPV

$$NPV = \sum_{t=1}^{n} \frac{CF_t}{(1+k_S^U)^t} - CF_0$$

Adjusted Present Value

APV = Base case NPV + present value of financing benefits

Present Value of Interest Tax Shields

$$PV = \sum_{t=1}^{n} \frac{T(interest_t)}{(1+k_S^U)^t}$$

What to Look For

In Chapter 7, we examined basic capital budgeting techniques. Managers must be able to apply these techniques to a variety of different types of decisions such as expansion, replacement, or divestiture. However, before applying the techniques the manager must have knowledge of the Income Tax Act provisions that impact on the estimation of the relevant cash flows. In this chapter, we apply the net present value criterion to the cash flows of various types of projects. In all cases, our goal is to maximize the the value of the firm, which is accomplished by choosing positive NPV projects.

Capital Cost Allowance

An important component of cash flows is capital cost allowance (CCA). CCA is a noncash expense that is deductible for tax purposes and as such, affects the tax liability of the firm. Under the Income Tax Act, all depreciable assets are placed into one of forty-four classes and each class has its own Capital Cost Allowance (CCA) rate. This rate is applied to the undepreciated capital cost (UCC) to figure out the amount of CCA allowed. When an asset is purchased, one-half of the capital cost is added to the pool in the year the asset is put in use and one-half in the following year.

To see how this works, consider the case of Gowan Fisheries, Ltd. The firm wishes to build three new wooden wharves, one in 1997 costing $100,000, one in 1998 costing $110,000, and one in 1999 costing $125,000. Wooden wharves are in Class 6, which has a CCA rate of 10 percent. Let's assume that the pool has a UCC of $300,000 at the end of 1996 and calculate the CCA for the pool over the next few years.

	1997	1998	1999	2000	2001
Beginning UCC	$300,000	$315,000	$378,000	$445,950	$457,605
Add:					
1/2 capital cost of wharf 1	50,000	50,000	—	—	—
1/2 capital cost of wharf 2	—	55,000	55,000	—	—
1/2 capital cost of wharf 3	—	—	62,500	62,500	—
UCC end of year	350,000	420,000	495,500	508,450	457,605
CCA (0.10)(UCC end of year)	(35,000)	(42,000)	(49,550)	(50,845)	(45,760)
UCC beginning of next year	$315,000	$378,000	$445,950	$457,605	$411,845

This, of course, assumes that Gowan Fisheries does not dispose of any assets in the pool. If they had, the lesser of the capital cost or the proceeds from the sale of the asset would be deducted from the UCC. The Income Tax Act also specifies the tax proceedures for terminating a pool of assets. When this happens, the firm may incur a terminal loss, a capital gain, or a CCA recapture, each of which affects the company's taxes. Table 8.6 in your text shows several different cases of pool termination and the impact they have on taxable income.

Since taxes can have a big effect on the firm's cash flow, it is important for you understand how the tax system works. By understanding the impact of taxes, managers are better able to determine how decisions will affect the value of the firm and thus, they are better able to undertake projects that possibly affect share price.

Corporate Taxes

Since corporations pay taxes on income, it is important to understand the nuances of corporate taxes so that we can determine how projects will affect the value of the firm.

Corporate taxes vary across firm size, with small businesses being taxed at lower rates. Corporations face tax rates ranging from 12 percent to 28 percent at the federal level, and additional provincial rates from 8.9 percent to 17 percent. Small business tax rates apply to the first $200,000 of income for all corporations.

Corporations must make adjustments to income in order to calculate their tax liability. Interest paid by corporations is treated as a business expense and is deducted from taxable income, but interest earned is taxable. Dividends are paid out of after-tax earnings and are not deductible for tax purposes, while dividends received from other Canadian firms are not taxable. Corporations also earn capital gains and experience capital losses. Net capital gains are taxed at three-quarters of the firm's tax rate.

To see how this works, suppose that Gowan Fisheries, Ltd., is located in the Yukon. The company had $3 million in revenues and $1.8 million in expenses in 1997, as well as $300,000 in capital cost allowance (CCA). The firm paid $250,000 in interest expense and earned $15,000 in interest on government of Canada securities. The company also received $25,000 in dividends from U.S. corporations, $30,000 in dividends from Canadian corporations, and earned a net capital gain of $45,000 from the sale of a boat. The calculation of their tax liability (assuming that they are classified as a basic corporation, and that the territorial tax rate is 10 percent), is as follows:

Revenues		$3,000,000.00
Less: Expenses		1,800,000.00
Income from operations		1,200,000.00
Less: Capital cost allowance		300,000.00
Less: Interest paid		250,000.00
		650,000.00
Add: Interest income		15,000.00
Add: Dividends from U.S. corporations		25,000.00
Add: 3/4 capital gain		33,750.00
Taxable income		723,750.00
Taxes: Federal (12% of the first $200,000)	24,000.00	
Federal ($723,750 – $200,000)(0.28)	146,650.00	
Provincial ($723,500 × 0.10)	72,350.00	
Less: Total taxes		243,000.00
Add: Dividends from Canadian corporations		30,000.00
Net income		$510,750.00

Measuring the Relevant Cash Flows

In making capital budgeting choices, we take into account the timing, magnitude, and riskiness of each project's cash flows. It is easier to estimate a project's expected cash flows if we break the flows down into initial, operating, and ending. Initial flows are all those necessary to get the project off the ground. These might include (1) purchase of land, building, and equipment; (2) installation and freight; (3) special training for using new equipment; (4) increases in net working capital such as an increase in accounts receivable and inventory, less increases in accounts payable and accruals; and (5) tax effects of selling a replaced asset. For simplicity, we assume these flows all occur at time zero, so their net outflow is immediate. In order for a project to be acceptable, the present value of the operating flows plus ending flows must exceed the initial investment.

Intermediate cash flows are also on an after-tax basis, so we must adjust the operating cash flows (inflows – outflows) for taxes. Since CCA is a noncash expense that decreases taxable income, we must consider its effect on operating cash flows. The CCA of a project is an important component of CF and must be considered over the entire life of the project.

Ending flows are those flows that result at the end of the project. These include (1) funds realized from sale of an asset; (2) the tax benefit if the asset is sold at a loss; (3) the release of net working capital; (4) the tax liability if the asset is sold at a gain. Some of these are a concern only if the asset is the only one in the pool and the pool is terminated.

Cash Flow: A Comprehensive Example

The following example will demonstrate more fully CCA, taxes, and cash flow. We will look at the after-tax cash flows throughout the life of an investment, after calculating the component cash inflows and outflows.

Initial investment

Suppose your company purchases some IBM PCs for $13,500, and you expect to use them for three years. Installation expenses are $1,500 and the corporate tax rate is 34 percent. The initial investment will be $13,500 + $1,500 = $15,000.

Operating cash flows

Out-of-pocket costs each year are $1,500 in materials and maintenance, while out-of-pocket savings per year in time and personnel costs are $4,000. The machines will be the only equipment in CCA Class 10, which has a CCA rate of 30 percent. The yearly CCAs are as follows:

	Year 1	Year 2	Year 3
UCC beginning of year	$ 0.00	$5,250.00	$8,925.00
Add: 1/2 capital cost	7,500.00	7,500.00	—
UCC	7,500.00	12,750.00	$8,925.00
CCA = UCC × 0.30	(2,250.00)	(3,825.00)	(2,677.50)
UCC end of year	$5,250.00	$8,925.00	$6,247.50

Ending cash flow

Suppose that at the end of three years, you decide to sell all of the computers for $10,000. Since you are selling the machines for more than the UCC (but less than the computers' capital cost), the sale results in a CCA recapture of $10,000 – $6,247.50 = $3,752.50, which is taxed as ordinary income. The tax liability arising from this recapture is $3,752.50 × 0.34 = $1,275.85, so the ending cash flow (ECF) is $10,000 – $1,275.85 = $8,724.15.

Net cash flows

The chart and figure below will help us find the net after-tax cash flows for each period.

Time	Type	Cash Flow Calculations	Net Cash Flows
Year 0	Initial	–$13,500 – $1,500	–$15,000.00
Year 1	Operating	($4,000 – $1,500)(1 – 0.34) + ($2,250)(0.34)	2,415.00
Year 2	Operating	($4,000 – $1.500)(1 – 0.34) + ($3,825)(0.34)	2,950.50
Year 3	Operating	($4,000 – $1,500)(1 – 0.34) + ($2,677.50)(0.34)	2,560.35
Year 3	Ending	$10,000 – $1,275	$8,724.15

$2,560.35
+ 8,724.15

$2,415.00 $2,950.50 $11,284.50

```
         0
                1              2              3

   $15,000
```

Expansion Decisions

Firms grow through expanding production of existing product lines or expanding into new product lines. How do we use capital budgeting techniques to decide if such expansion is warranted?

    Consider New Brunswick Potato Packers (NBPP). The company presently has an unused warehouse that it rents to a storage company for $50,000 per year. New Brunswick wants to convert the warehouse into a facility to bag potatoes. The packing equipment will cost $900,000 and it will cost the company $30,000 to install the machinery. If NBPP installs the machinery, they will not, of course, be able to rent out the warehouse.

    The new equipment will enable NBPP to increase revenues by $700,000 per year, but will increase expenses by $200,000. The company will also be required to increase working capital by $100,000. The equipment has a useful life of 5 years and is expected to have a resale value of $100,000. If the firm's marginal tax rate is 45 percent, and their opportunity cost of capital is 15 percent, should they expand?

    To answer this question, we need to identify the various after-tax cash flows associated with the project. The initial investment, for instance, is

CF_0 = cost of equipment + costs related to purchase + additional net working capital

+ tax effects of gain or sale on replaced assets

= \$900,000 + \$30,000 + \$100,000 + \$0

= \$1,030,000

While this represents out-of-pocket cash, it is not the complete outlay. If NBPP installs the equipment, they cannot continue to rent the warehouse to the storage company. Thus, they suffer an additional opportunity loss equal to the foregone rent $\times$ (1 − tax rate) or \$50,000(1 − 0.45) = \$27,500. So, CF_0 = \$1,030,000 + \$27,500 = \$1,057,500. Likewise, the CFBT from operations is: Revenues − expenses − opportunity loss of rent = \$700,000 − \$200,000 − \$50,000 = \$450,000.

An important component of cash flows is the Capital Cost Allowance (CCA). The CCA is a noncash expense which shields revenues from taxes. Packing equipment falls in Class 8 which has a CCA rate of 20 percent. While we could calculate the CCA rate for each year, Chapter 8 tells us that assuming that the disposal of the equipment will not result in the termination of a pool, we can calculate the present value of the tax shields from the CCA as a perpetuity (Equation 8.8 in the text). To do so, we need only to know the CCA rate (d = 0.20), the capital cost (\$930,000 = cost + installation), and the resale value (\$100,000).

The last cash flow we need to calculate is the ending cash flow (ECF). This cash flow equals the proceeds from the sale of the asset plus any net working capital recovered, plus the tax effects of the gain or sale of the assets. In our case, ECF = \$100,000 + \$100,000 + \$0 = \$200,000. Now, let's calculate the NPV using Equation 8.9.

$$NPV = \sum_{t=1}^{n} \frac{CFBT_t(1-T)}{(1+k)^t} + \left\{ \left[\frac{TdC_0}{k+d} \right] \left[\frac{1+0.5k}{1+k} \right] - \left[\frac{1}{(1+k)^n} \right] \left[\frac{TdRV}{k+d} \right] \right\}$$

$$+ \frac{ECF}{(1+k)^n} - CF_0$$

$$= \sum_{t=1}^{5} \frac{\$450,000(1-0.45)}{(1.15)^t} + \left\{ \left[\frac{(0.45)(0.2)(\$930,000)}{0.15+0.2} \right] \left[\frac{1+0.5(0.15)}{1.15} \right] \right.$$

$$\left. - \left[\frac{1}{(1.15)^5} \right] \left[\frac{(0.45)(0.2)(\$100,000)}{0.15+0.2} \right] \right\} + \frac{\$200,000}{(1.15)^5} - \$1,057,500$$

$$= \$247,500(PVA_{15\%,5yr}) + \{\$223,546.58 - \$25,714.29(PV_{15\%,5yr})\}$$

$$+ \$200,000(PV_{15\%,5yr}) - \$1,057,500$$

$$= \$247,500(3.325) + \{\$223,546.58 - \$25,714.29(0.497)\}$$

$$+ \$200,000(0.497) - \$1,057,500$$

$$= \$829,620 + (\$223,546.58 - \$12,780.00) + \$99,400 - \$1,057,500$$

$$= \$82,286.58$$

The addition of the new packing equipment and the expansion has a positive net present value, so New Brunswick Potato Packers should expand.

Replacement Decisions

Firms are often faced with the alternative of keeping or replacing an existing asset due to normal wear or technological innovation. The replacement decision is especially complex because the manager must concentrate on incremental cash flows, that is, the cash flows related to the new equipment less those associated with the old.

In calculating incremental cash flows, a variety of factors need to be considered. The initial investment includes cost of equipment, all other costs related to the investment, additional working capital required, and any tax effects and opportunity costs. The change in operating CF contains the change in CFBT as well as the change in

CCA due to the new equipment. It is also important to consider any terminal cash flows associated with the new project such as recovery of working capital. If the NPV of the incremental cash flows is positive, replacement should take place.

For example, suppose that Northwest Lumber, Ltd. is considering the replacement of a plywood glue machine. Their present machine was purchased three years ago for $500,000. The machine could be sold today for $250,000, but for only $50,000 in five years. The new gluer costs $800,000, has a five year useful life, and an expected salvage value of $100,000. The new machine will require additional net working capital of $50,000, but will result in labour savings of $150,000 per year. Both machines have a CCA rate of 20 percent. If the opportunity cost of capital is 12 percent and the corporate tax rate is 35 percent, should Northwest buy the new equipment?

Replacement decisions are similar to expansion projects, except we need to concentrate on incremental cash flows. In fact, Equation 8.11 is identical to Equation 8.9 except it uses changes (Δ) in cash flows. Let's calculate the various cash flows we need to calculate the NPV of the replacement.

Step 1.	Cost of new asset		$800,000
	Less: Net proceeds from sale of old asset		250,000
	Incremental capital cost (ΔC_0)		550,000
	Add: Increase in net working capital		50,000
	Incremental initial investment (ΔCF_0)		600,000
Step 2.	Incremental before-tax savings (Δ CFBT)		$150,000
Step 3.	Net resale value, new asset		$100,000
	Less: Net resale value, old asset		50,000
	Incremental net resale value (Δ RV)		50,000
	Add: Release of net working capital		50,000
	Incremental ending cash flows (Δ ECF)		$100,000

Step 4. Calculating the net present value of the incremental cash flows, using Equation 8.11

$$NPV = \sum_{t=1}^{5} \frac{(\$150,000)(1 - 0.35)}{(1.12)^t} + \left\{ \left[\frac{(0.35)(0.2)(\$550,000)}{0.12 + 0.20} \right] \right.$$

$$\times \left[\frac{1 + 0.5(0.12)}{1 + 0.12} \right] - \left[\frac{1}{(1.12)^5} \right] \left[\frac{(0.35)(0.2)(\$50,000)}{0.12 + 0.20} \right] \right\}$$

$$+ \frac{\$100,000}{(1.12)^5} - \$600,000$$

$$= \quad \$97,500 \, (PVA_{12\%,5yr}) + [\$113,867.19 - \$10,937.50(PV_{12\%,5yr})]$$

$$+ \$100,000(PV_{12\%,5yr}) - \$600,000$$

$$= \quad \$97,500 \, (3.605) + [\$113,867.19 - \$10,937.50 \, (0.567)]$$

$$+ \$100,000 \, (0.567) - \$600,000$$

$$= \quad \$351,487.50 + [\$113,867.19 - \$6,201.56] + \$56,700 - \$600,000$$

$$= -\$84,146.87$$

The firm is better off with the old glue machine since the incremental cash flows from the new machine have a negative net present value.

More on Cash Flow Estimation

To this point, we've ignored some issues in cash flow estimation that are important. First, how do we adjust for inflation? If inflation affects both after-tax cash flows and the opportunity cost of capital proportionally, we can ignore the effects. In other cases, we must incorporate our estimates into both. It is not an easy task, but it must be done in order to reach appropriate decisions.

Another issue is financing costs. Since interest on debt is tax-deductible, you would think that we should account for its effect in calculating cash flows. This is generally not the case. For most projects, the capital budgeting decision is separate from the decision on how to finance the project.

Financial managers must make sure that they have examined all of the alternatives available to the firm. One alternative often ignored is the alternative to abandon an existing asset. If the firm can sell an asset for more than the present value of its CF, shareholders will be better off if the asset is sold. If modernization is an option, the relevant set of cash flows for decision making is the combination of existing cash flows and new cash flows due to modernization.

Completion Questions

8.1 Depreciation for _____ can differ substantially from _____ depreciation.

8.2 For a corporation, dividend income from _____ companies is taxable, while dividend income from _____ companies is tax exempt.

8.3 Firms incurring operating losses can carry the loss back _____ years or forward _____ years.

8.4 The _____ rate is the maximum rate of write-off applied to a specific asset class.

8.5 When a new asset is purchased, one-half the _____ of the asset is added to the _____ in the year the asset is put in use, and one-half in the following year.

8.6 The effective tax rate on net capital gains for corporations is three-quarters the firm's _____ _____.

8.7 If a pool is terminated, the lesser of the _____ or the proceeds from the sale of the asset is _____ from the UCC.

8.8 In a pool termination, the firm suffers a _____ if the proceeds from the sale are less than the capital cost and greater than the undepreciated capital cost.

8.9 With limited exceptions, only the _____ method of capital cost allowance is allowed.

8.10 So long as the firm never terminates an asset pool, the capital cost allowance for a new investment can be treated as a _____.

8.11 The tax benefits arising from the sale of replaced assets and costs related to purchases are all part of the _____.

8.12 The _____ is the cost of a forgone opportunity, such as the loss of rental income when a firm decides to use its own warehouse space.

8.13 The release of net working capital occurs in the _____.

8.14 If a firm recovers working capital at the end of a project, the _____ will be greater than the _____.

8.15 In replacement decisions, the appropriate cash flows to analyze are the _____ cash flows.

8.16 Incremental operating CF includes the after-tax change in CFBT and _____.

8.17 If both CFs and _____ are proportionally affected by inflation, inflation will not affect the capital budgeting decision.

8.18 The capital budgeting decision is separate from the _____ decision.

8.19 In cases in which inflation might be a factor, the project's _____ and _____ should be adjusted to reflect inflation.

8.20 A project should be abandoned if the present value of the cash flows is less than the project's _____.

8.21 An alternative to NPV is the _____ which includes the effects of project financing on value.

Problems

8.1   North Bay Iron, a basic corporation, expects to have revenues of $10 million and expenses of $6 million in 1998. The company expects to pay interest on debt of $1.5 million and earn interest on its marketable securities of $150,000. The company also owns 50,000 shares of U.S. Steel, which plans on paying a dividend of $5 per share. The company will incur a loss of $600,000 on the sale of securities, a capital gain of $900,000, and a CCA recapture of $200,000 on the termination of an asset pool. What is the firm's federal tax bill assuming it has CCA expenses of $1,450,000?

8.2   Green Thumb Nursery just purchased its only van for $14,000. What will be the undepreciated capital cost in 10 years? (Calculate the UCC as of the beginning of year 10.)

8.3   Yukon Air Carriers is a new company that plans on purchasing one airplane per year for the next four years for $800,000 per plane. Calculate the undepreciated capital cost and the capital cost allowance for each of the next six years.

8.4   Niagara Falls Rentals has received an offer of $10,000 for its 550 canoes and row boats. The sale of these assets would liquidate the asset pool. If the assets had a capital cost of $8,000, and an undepreciated cost of $3,860, what are the CCA recapture and the capital gain on the termination of the pool?

8.5   Manson Electronics is considering converting an existing warehouse into a production facility. For the new facility, Manson must buy manufacturing equipment for $1,500,000. The new facility will allow Manson to increase sales by $3,000,000 per year. The following should be considered in the analysis.
   1.   Expenses associated with the new facility are:
         Fixed cash flows = $100,000
         Variable cash flows = 60 percent of sales
   2.   The manufacturing equipment will be written off at a CCA rate of 30 percent.
   3.   Manson Electronics can lease the warehouse to a local moving company for $100,000 (before taxes) per year, starting from the beginning of year 2. The lease payments would be received in advance, i.e., at the end of the previous year.
   4.   The new facility will require a $500,000 increase in raw materials inventory. Manson expects to recover this at the end of the project's life.
   5.   The equipment can be sold at the end of five years for its undepreciated capital cost.
   6.   Manson's tax rate is 30 percent.
   What are the cash flows associated with the above project?

8.6   Baker Publishing, Ltd., is considering converting a warehouse to enable the firm to increase production. The renovation will require the purchase of $3,000,000 worth of printing and binding equipment that will have a CCA rate of 20 percent. The warehouse is currently being rented out for $75,000 per year.
       The new facility has an expected lifetime of 10 years and zero resale value. Because of the increased productive capability, Baker expects additional sales of $2,000,000 in year 1, and sales are expected to increase (primarily due to inflation) by 5 percent per year. The fixed costs associated with this facility are $100,000 per year, and variable costs are 60 percent of sales. If the corporate tax rate is 35 percent, and the discount rate is 16 percent, should the warehouse be renovated?

8.7   Hebert Manufacturing is considering the replacement of a lathe used to make table legs. The machine, which was purchased three years ago for $50,000 still has a useful life of five years. A more efficient lathe with a cost of $75,000 is being considered because the new machine will result in a reduction of expenses of $30,000 per year over its five-year life. Both machines are in CCA Class 43, CCA rate 30 percent. The old machine could be sold now for $25,000, but will be worthless at the end of five years. The new machine has an expected resale value of $10,000 and will require a $10,000 increase in working capital. If the opportunity cost of capital is 10 percent, should the machine be replaced? The corporate tax rate is 40 percent.

8.8   Winnipeg Caterers is considering the purchase of three more vans to enable it to expand its business. Each van costs $20,000 and will be written off at a CCA rate of 30 percent. The company expects to sell the vans in three years for $8,000 each. Assuming that the firm needs additional working capital of $6,000 (total) to utilize the vans, k = 18 percent, and the marginal tax rate is 46 percent, what is the minimum cash flow before-tax the vans need to generate over the next three years to be a profitable investment. (Assume that CFBT will be a constant for each of the next three years).

8.9   Jacobson Luggage Company is unhappy with the performance of its designer luggage division. Full capacity has been reached, which means that the firm can only expect CFs of $600,000 per year, with no growth prospects. A proposal to expand the plant has been put forth. The expansion will require investments of $2.5 million per year for the next two years, during which time the CFs will remain as above. After that (starting in year 3), CFs will be able to grow at a rate of 10 percent per year. The division presently has $2 million in debt, and no new debt will be added should the company expand. A competitor has offered to pay Jacobson $5 million (after-tax) for the division. If the discount rate is 15 percent, what should Jacobson do?

8.10   Ben and Bennie's Ice Cream is trying to decide if it should remain in operation. The forecasts of CFs are as follows: $CF_1 = \$4,000$, $CF_2 = \$4,500$, $CF_3 = \$6,000$, and growth beyond year 3 is expected to be 5 percent per year. The firm presently has $20,000 in debt, and the assets can be sold for $38,000 (after-tax). If the appropriate discount rate is 20 percent, should the store be abandoned?

8A.1   Kate's Pet Foods is considering the building of a new food processing plant for $5 million. The plant will last five years and the company expects that it will generate CFs of $1.5 million per year over its life. The new plant will have the same risk as the firm's other assets. Presently, Kate's has a debt to total value ratio of 0.20 and its stock has a beta of 1.75. The firm intends to partially finance the plant with $1 million of subsidized debt paying 6 percent interest annually and the principal paid at the end of five years. The flotation costs of the debt are $50,000 and the firm's tax rate is 45 percent. If k_{RF} = 9 percent, k_M = 14 percent, and the firm normally pays 10 percent (before-tax) on debt, what is the plants adjusted present value?

Answers to Completion Questions

8.1   tax purposes; GAAP
8.2   foreign-owned; Canadian
8.3   three; seven
8.4   capital cost allowance
8.5   capital cost; undepreciated capital costs of the pool
8.6   marginal tax rate
8.7   capital cost; subtracted
8.8   CCA recapture
8.9   declining balance
8.10   perpetuity
8.11   initial investment
8.12   opportunity cost
8.13   ending cash flow
8.14   ending cash flow; net resale value
8.15   incremental
8.16   the tax rate times the change in CCA rate

8.17   opportunity cost of capital
8.18   financing
8.19   cash flows; opportunity cost of capital
8.20   market value
8.21   adjusted present value

Solutions to Problems

8.1

Revenues		$10,000,000
Expenses		6,000,000
Income from operations		4,000,000
Less: CCA		1,450,000
		2,550,000
Less: Interest expense		1,500,000
		1,050,000
Add: Interest earned		150,000
		1,200,000
Add: Dividends earned (50,000 × $5)		250,000
		1,450,000
Add: CCA recapture		200,000
		1,650,000
Capital gains:		
3/4 capital gain (3/4 × $900,000)	675,000	
Less: 3/4 capital loss (3/4 × $600,000)	450,000	
Net capital gain	225,000	225,000
Taxable income		1,875,000
Federal tax ($200,000 × 0.12)	24,000	
Add: ($1,875,000 − $200,000)(0.28)	469,000	
Total taxes paid		$ 493,000

8.2   Using Equation 8.1,
$$UCC_n = C(1 - d / 2) (1 - d)^{n-2}$$
Since vans are in Class 10, the CCA rate (d) = 30 percent so,
$$UCC_n = \$14,000 (1 - 0.30 / 2) (1 - 0.70)^{10-2}$$
$$= \$14,000 (0.85) (0.0576)$$
$$= \$685.44$$

8.3   Airplanes are in Class 9, so the CCA rate = 25%.

	Year			
	1	2	3	4
UCC end of previous year	0	300,000	825,000	1,218,750
Add: 1/2 capital cost:				
Airplane 1	400,000	400,000	–	–
Airplane 2	–	400,000	400,000	
Airplane 3	–	–	400,000	400,000
Airplane 4	–	–	–	400,000
UCC current year	400,000	1,100,000	1,625,000	2,018,750
CCA: (UCC × 0.25)	(100,000)	275,000	406,250	504,687
UCC end of year	300,000	825,000	1,218,750	1,514,063

	Year	
	5	6
UCC end of previous year	1,515,063	1,435,547
Add: 1/2 capital cost:		
Airplane 1	–	–
Airplane 2	–	–
Airplane 3	–	–
Airplane 4	400,000	–
UCC current year	1,914,063	1,435,547
CCA: (UCC × 0.25)	478,516	358,887
UCC end of year	1,435,547	1,076,660

8.4   Capital gain   = net proceeds from sale − capital cost
$$= \$10,000 - \$8,000 = \$2,000$$
CCA recapture = capital cost − undepreciated capital cost
$$= \$8,000 - \$3,860 = \$4,140$$

8.5   Step 1.   (in thousands)

Initial investment

Manufacturing equipment	$1,500
Inventory	500
Net initial cash outflow	$2,000

Step 2.   For years 1–5:

CFBT = sales − variable cash flows − fixed cash flows
$$= [\$3,000 - (0.60)(\$3,000) - \$100] = \$1,100$$

Step 3.   Capital cost allowance

	Year 1	1/2 capital cost	$ 750.00
		$CCA_1 = (\$750 \times 0.3)$	(225.00)
		UCC at end of year 1	$ 525.00
	Year 2	Add 1/2 capital cost	750.00
		UCC beginning of year 2	1,275.00
		$CCA_2 = (\$1{,}275 \times 0.3)$	382.50
		UCC at end of year 2	$ 892.50
	Year 3	$CCA_3 = (\$892.50 \times 0.3)$	267.75
		UCC at end of year 3	$ 624.75
	Year 4	$CCA_4 = (\$624.75 \times 0.3)$	187.43
		UCC at end of year 4	$ 437.32
	Year 5	$CCA_5 = (\$437.32 \times 0.3)$	131.20
		UCC at end of year 5	$ 306.12

Step 4.

CFBT	$1,100.00	$1,100.00	$1,100.00	$1,100.00	$1,100.00
CFBT(1 – T)	770.00	770.00	770.00	770.00	770.00
CCA	525.00	382.50	267.75	187.43	131.20
T × CCA	157.50	114.75	80.33	56.23	39.36
CF = CFBT(1 – T) + T × CCA	927.50	884.75	850.33	826.23	809.36
Opportunity cost					
$100 (1 – 0.30) = $70	(70.00)	(70.00)	(70.00)	(70.00)	(70.00)
Recovery of inventory					500.00
Sale of equipment					552.96
CF	$ 857.50	$ 814.75	$ 780.33	$ 756.23	$1,545.48

Step 5.   The total cash flow stream is

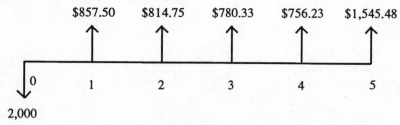

8.6   Step 1.   Cash Flows Year 0: Capital cost of equipment, C_0 = $3,000,000
Add: Opportunity cost of lost rent $75,000(1 – 0.35) =   48,750
Initial investment, CF_0 = $3,048,750

Step 2.   CFBT

Year	Sales	− Variable Cost	Opportunity Cost of − Fixed Cost	− Rent	= CFBT
1	$2,000,000	$1,200,000	$100,000	$75,000	$625,000
2	2,100,000	1,260,000	100,000	75,000	665,000
3	2,205,000	1,323,000	100,000	75,000	707,000
4	2,315,250	1,389,150	100,000	75,000	751,100
5	2,431,012	1,458,607	100,000	75,000	797,405
6	2,552,563	1,531,538	100,000	75,000	846,025
7	2,680,191	1,608,115	100,000	75,000	897,076
8	2,814,201	1,688,521	100,000	75,000	950,680
9	2,954,911	1,772,947	100,000	75,000	1,006,964
10	3,102,656	1,861,594	100,000	75,000	1,066,062

Step 3.   Operating Cash Flows

Year	CFBT	CFBT(1 − T)	× $PV_{16\%,nyrs}$	= PV of CFBT(1 − T)
1	$ 625,000	$406,250	0.862	$ 350,187.50
2	665,000	432,250	0.743	321,161.75
3	707,000	459,550	0.641	294,571.55
4	751,100	488,215	0.552	269,494.68
5	797,405	518,313	0.476	246,716.99
6	846,025	549,916	0.410	225,465.68
7	897,076	583,099	0.354	206,385.19
8	950,680	617,942	0.305	188,472.31
9	1,006,964	654,527	0.263	172,140.60
10	1,066,062	692,940	0.227	157,297.38
		Present value of CFBT(1 − T)	=	$2,431,893.51

Step 4.

$$ NPV = \sum_{t=1}^{n} \frac{CFBT_t\,(1-T)}{(1+k)^t} + \left\{ \left[\frac{TdC_0}{k+d} \right] \left[\frac{1+0.5k}{1+k} \right] - \left[\frac{1}{(1+k)^n} \right] \left[\frac{TdRV}{k+d} \right] \right\} $$

$$ + \frac{ECF}{(1+k)^n} - CF_0 $$

$$ = \$2,431,873.51 + \left\{ \left[\frac{(0.35)\,(0.2)\,(\$3,000,000)}{0.16 + 0.20} \right] \left[\frac{1 + 0.5\,(0.16)}{1.16} \right] \right. $$

$$ \left. - \left[\frac{1}{(1.16^{10})} \right] \left[\frac{(0.35)\,(0.20)\,(0)}{0.16 + 0.20} \right] \right\} + \frac{0}{(1.16)^{10}} - \$3,048,750 $$

$$ = \$2,431,873.51 + \left[\frac{\$210,000}{0.36} \right] \left[\frac{1.08}{1.16} \right] - \$3,048,750 $$

$$ = \$2,431,873.51 + \$543,103.43 - \$3,048,750 $$

$$ = -\$73,773.06 $$

Step 5.   Baker should not convert the warehouse since the net present value of the project is negative.

8.7   Step 1.

	Cost of new asset		$75,000
Less:	Net proceeds from sale of old asset		25,000
	Incremental capital cost (ΔC_0)		50,000
Add:	Increase in working capital		10,000
	Incremental initial investment (ΔCF_0)		$60,000

Step 2.   Incremental operating cash flows (Δ CFBT) $30,000

Step 3.

	Net resale value, new asset		$10,000
Less:	Net resale value, old asset		0
	Incremental resale value (Δ RV)		$10,000
Add:	Release of net working capital		10,000
	Incremental ending cash flows (Δ ECF)		$20,000

Step 4.

$$NPV = \sum_{t-1}^{n} \frac{\Delta\, CFBT\, (1 - T)}{(1 + k^t)} + \left\{ \left[\frac{Td(\Delta\, C_0)}{k + d} \right]\left[\frac{1 + 0.5k}{(1 + k)} \right] - \left[\frac{1}{(1 + k)^n} \right]\left[\frac{Td\, (\Delta\, SV)}{k + d} \right] \right\}$$

$$+ \frac{\Delta\, ECF}{(1 + k)^n} - CF_0$$

$$= \$30,000\, (1 - 0.40)\, PVA_{10\%,5yr} + \left\{ \left[\frac{(0.40)(0.30)(\$50,000)}{0.10 + 0.30} \right] \times \right.$$

$$\left. \left[\frac{1 + (0.5)\,(0.10)}{1.10} \right] - \left[\, PV_{10\%,5yr} \right]\left[\frac{(0.40)\,(0.30)\,(\$10,000)}{0.10 + 0.30} \right] \right\}$$

$$+ 20,000\, (PV_{10\%,5yr}) - \$60,000$$

$$= \$18,000\, (3.791) + \{(\$15,000)\, (0.955) - (\$3,000)\, (0.621)\}$$

$$+ \$20,000\, (0.621) - \$60,000$$

$$= \$68,238 + \{\$14,325 - \$1,863\} + \$12,420 - \$60,000$$

$$= \$33,120$$

Step 5.   Hebert should replace the lathe; the net present value of the incremental cash flows is positive.

8.8   Step 1.

	Initial capital cost (C_0) ($20,000 $\times$ 3)		$60,000
Add:	Increase in working capital		6,000
	Initial investment (CF_0)		$66,000

Step 2.

	Resale value (RV) ($8,000 $\times$ 3)		$24,000
Add:	Recovery of working capital		6,000
	Ending cash flow (ECF)		$30,000

Step 3.

$$NPV = \sum_{t-1}^{n} \frac{CFBT_t\, (1 - T)}{(1 + k)^t} + \left\{ \left[\frac{TdC_0}{k + d} \right]\left[\frac{1 + 0.5k}{1 + k} \right] - \left[\frac{1}{(1 + k)^n} \right]\left[\frac{TdRV}{k + d} \right] \right\}$$

$$+ \frac{ECF}{(1 + k)^n} - CF_0$$

Since the project is minimally acceptable when NPV = 0,

$$0 = \text{CFBT} (1 - 0.46)\, \text{PVA}_{18\%,3yr} + \left\{ \left[\frac{(0.46)\,(0.30)\,(\$60,000)}{0.18 + 0.30} \right] \times \right.$$

$$\left. \left[\frac{1 + (0.5)\,(0.18)}{1.18} \right] - \left[\text{PV}_{18\%,3yr} \right] \left[\frac{(0.46)\,(0.30)\,(\$24,000)}{0.18 + 0.30} \right] \right\}$$

$$\$30,000\,(\text{PV}_{18\%,3yr}) - \$66,000$$

$$= \text{CFBT}(0.54)(2.174) + \{(\$17,500)\,(0.924) - (\$6,900)\,(0.609)\}$$

$$+ \$30,000\,(0.609) - \$66,000$$

$$= (1.1740)\,\text{CFBT} + \$16,170 - \$4,202.10 + \$18,270 - \$66,000$$

$$0 = (1.1740)\,\text{CFBT} - \$35,762.10$$

$$\text{CFBT} = \frac{\$35,762.10}{1.1740} = \$30,461.75 \text{ per year}$$

8.9   Step 1.   No expansion:
NPV = \$600,000/0.15 − \$2,000,000 = \$2,000,000. The net proceeds from divesting would be \$5 million − \$2 million in debt = \$3 million. Without the possibility of expanding the division, the decision would be to divest it since the net divestiture proceeds of \$3 million exceed the net present value of continuing to operate of \$2 million.

   Step 2.   With expansion:

NPV = (\$600,000 − \$2,500,000)(PV$_{15\%,1yr}$) + (\$600,000 − \$2,500,000)(PV$_{15\%,2yr}$)
    + [\$600,000(1.10)/(0.15 − 0.10)](PV$_{15\%,2yr}$) − \$2,000,000
  = −\$1,900,000(0.870) − \$1,900,000(0.756) + \$13,2000,000(0.756) − \$2,000,000
  = \$4,889,800

Jacobson should proceed with the expansion since its value is greater than the net proceeds from selling. The shareholders would receive only \$3 million from divestment since the \$2 million in debt must be paid off.

8.10   Step 1.   NPV = \$4,000(PV$_{20\%,1yr}$) + \$4,500(PV$_{20\%,2yr}$) + \$6,000(PV$_{20\%,3yr}$)
    + [\$6,000(1.05)/(0.20 − 0.05)](PV$_{20\%,3yr}$) − \$20,000
  = \$4,000(0.833) − \$4,500(0.694) + \$6,000(0.579) + \$42,000(0.579) − \$20,000
  = \$14,247

   Step 2.   The net proceeds for the sale would be \$38,000 − debt or \$38,000 − \$20,000 = \$18,000. Since the NPV of continuing to operate is less than the net proceeds, the company should abandon the store.

8A.1   Step 1.   Calculate the unlevered beta.

$$\beta_s^U = \beta_s^L \left[\frac{S}{B + S} \right] \quad \text{Since } B/(S + B) = 0.2,\ S/(S + B) = 0.8$$

$$= \quad 1.75(0.8)$$

$$= \quad 1.40$$

Step 2.   Calculate the unlevered cost of equity.

$k_S^U = k_{RF} + (k_M - k_{RF})\beta_S^U$

$= 9\% + (14\% - 9\%)(1.40)$

$= 16\%$

Step 3.   Calculate the base case NPV.

$NPV = PMT \times PVA_{16\%,5yr} - CF_0$

$= \$1,500,000(3.274) - \$5,000,000$

$= \$4,911,000 - \$5,000,000$

$= -\$89,000$

Step 4.   Calculate the present value of the interest tax shields on the subsidized debt at the unlevered cost of equity.

Year	Principal	Interest (Principal Interest × 0.06)	Tax Shield Interest × 0.45	$PV_{16\%,nyrs}$	PV of Interest Tax Tax Shields
1	$1,000,000	$60,000	$27,000	0.862	$23,274
2	1,000,000	60,000	27,000	0.743	20,061
3	1,000,000	60,000	27,000	0.641	17,307
4	1,000,000	60,000	27,000	0.552	14,904
5	1,000,000	60,000	27,000	0.476	12,852
				Total	$88,398

Step 5.   Calculate the present value of the subsidized debt financing at the after-tax cost of the unsubsidized debt.

$k_i = k_b(1 - T)$

$= 10\%(1 - 0.45)$

$= 5.5\%$

Year	Principal Repayment	Interest	After-Tax Interest Outflow (interest × 1 − 0.45)	Principal + After-Tax Interest	Present Value at 5.5%
1		$60,000	$33,000	$ 33,000	$ 31,279.62
2		60,000	33,000	33,000	29,648.93
3		60,000	33,000	33,000	28,103.25
4		60,000	33,000	33,000	26,638.15
5	$1,000,000	60,000	33,000	1,033,000	790,383.79
				Total	$906,053.74

Savings from standardized loan = $1,000,000 − $906,053.74

= $93,946.26

Step 6.   Calculate the APV.

APV = Base case NPV + present value of financing decision

= −$89,000 − issue costs + present value of interest tax shields

+ savings from subsidized loan

= −$89,000 − $50,000 + $88,398 + $93,946.26

= $43,344.26

Chapter 9
Risk and Capital Budgeting

How This Chapter Relates to the Rest of the Text

As we have seen in Chapters 7 and 8, capital budgeting decisions are based on cash flows, their timing (Chapter 3), and the valuation process (Chapter 4). An important factor in determining value is the opportunity cost of capital, which is a function of risk (Chapter 6). This chapter discusses various methods of adjusting the required return to reflect the riskiness of the project. If the project is similar in risk to the firm, the firm's opportunity cost of capital (Chapter 6) can be employed. The riskiness of a project affects the business risk (Chapter 12) of the firm. Risk in international capital budgeting is discussed in Chapter 17.

Topical Outline

I.   Risk and strategic decisions.
      A.   Strategic decisions.
            1.   All sources of risk are important in the capital budgeting process.
            2.   Taking into account risk is one of the most difficult aspects in capital budgeting, but it cannot be ignored.
            3.   Risk may be beneficial; firms must expose themselves to risk in order to earn positive NPVs.
            4.   It is a mistake to think that discount rates must be increased in order to account for the greater riskiness of distant cash flows; the use of any rate above k_{RF} recognizes that more distant cash flows are proportionately more risky.
      B.   Factors to consider when estimating risk.
            1.   Fudge factors should not be used to adjust the firm's opportunity cost of capital to reflect risk.
            2.   Any cyclicality in a project's cash flows must be considered.
            3.   Operating leverage or the level of fixed operating costs used by the firm.
            4.   Financial leverage or the level of fixed financial costs used by the firm.
II.   Opportunity cost of capital for capital budgeting decisions.
      A.   Firm, divisional, and project-specific opportunity costs.
            1.   Some corporations use a single, firm-wide opportunity cost of capital, reflecting the cost of funds to the firm. That is, some firms use the opportunity cost of capital approach (Chapter 6).
            2.   The divisional cost of capital approach assigns different required returns to projects in different divisions, based on the perceived risk of that division.
            3.   Project-specific discount rates are based on the riskiness of the individual project.
                a.   One such approach is the CAPM.
                b.   The stand-alone principle states that a proposed project should be evaluated on its own merits; consider the opportunity costs of investing in another project of the same risk.
                c.   Project-specific required returns are hard to estimate; part science and part judgement.
      B.   What about portfolio effects?
            1.   Investors diversify their own portfolios, so diversification should not be the goal of the firm.
            2.   However, cash flow interactions among projects should be considered, since these interactions can affect the actual cash flows and their estimates.
      C.   When a single discount rate cannot be used; sequential analysis.
            1.   Probability distributions can produce the sequential outcomes of cash flows related to a capital budgeting project.
            2.   The sum of the joint probabilities times the respective NPVs result in the project's NPV.
III.   Information about project riskiness.
      A.   Sensitivity analysis determines how sensitive NPV is to changes in input variables (cash flows, costs, discount rates, etc.).
      B.   Break-even analysis: The break-even point occurs when the present value of inflows equals the present value of outflows.

1. Use present values of cash inflows and outflows.
2. Break-even points calculated using GAAP ignore the opportunity cost of the initial investment and provide biased estimates of the actual break-even point.

C. Simulation is a technique that allows for changing all of the relevant variables in an analysis.
    1. Specify the relevant variables and interdependencies.
    2. Specify a probability distribution of possible values for each relevant variable.
    3. Randomly select values for each relevant variable.
    4. Calculate NPVs using the values selected.
    5. Repeat the simulation, using new randomly selected variables, and graph NPVs.
    6. Problems with simulation.
        a. Simulations are costly, time-consuming, and usually require computers.
        b. It is difficult to correctly specify interdependencies.
        c. Results are often difficult to interpret.

Formulas

Required Return
Opportunity cost of capital = risk-free rate + risk premium based on project risk

Operating Leverage

$$\text{Operating leverage} = \frac{(\text{sales} - \text{variable costs})}{\text{EBIT}}$$

Capital Asset Pricing Model
$$\text{Risk-adjusted discount rate} = k_{project} = k_{RF} + \beta_{project}(k_M - k_{RF})$$

What to Look For

If we could predict the future accurately, we would not need to adjust our required returns for risk. We could have our fortunes made. Chapters 7 and 8 assumed that we could predict cash flows accurately. The discounting process we conducted merely adjusted the capital project cash flows for the time value of money and the firm's cost of funds, since we could invest in something else if we did not invest in the project.

In Chapter 9, we recognize that actual cash flows will probably vary from the expected cash flows. Managers must assign probabilities to the possible levels of cash flow and assign a discount rate appropriate to the cash flow riskiness. This discount rate increases as the cash flows' variability or risk increases. We will look at several methods of considering project risk, including firm-wide, divisional, and project-specific opportunity cost of capital, break-even analysis, sequential analysis, and sensitivity analysis.

Risk-Adjusted Discount Rates
Essentially, the opportunity cost of capital or required return should be the risk-free rate plus some risk premium appropriate to the project. We use this just as we used the opportunity cost of capital in Chapters 7 and 8 when we calculated net present value. The opportunity cost of capital approach implicitly compensates for risk by assuming it increases as a function of time. If you suspect that a project's risk will vary for other reasons, you might assign a different rate for each year's cash flows. Although it is difficult to decide how and when the risk of a project will change, this adjustment is necessary and appropriate. However, managers must avoid using fudge factors by focusing first on producing the best estimates of the project's cash flows as possible.

Measuring Project Risk
In Chapter 5, we considered risk as variability from the expected value. This variability is due to economic factors and the amount of fixed operating and financing costs used by the firm. These factors can significantly affect the

variability of the project's expected cash flows and the appropriate discount rate to be used. For example, a recession can reduce expected sales revenue, or a Bank of Canada tightening of money can push inflation down and increase the whole structure of interest rates.

Firms use a variety of approaches to analyze risk in capital budgeting. The technique used depends on your assumptions about risk. For instance, some approaches assume that risk is constant throughout the project's life. They are:

Firm-wide opportunity cost of capital
The firm-wide opportunity cost of capital approach suggests that the return from an acceptable project will exceed the firm's cost of the last dollar of new funds. This rate is appropriate for projects such as replacement projects that are similar to the firm.

Divisional opportunity cost of capital
The divisional opportunity cost of capital approach requires that the risk involved in each division's projects be evaluated. Each division is then assigned an appropriate required return, assuming risk is the same for all projects within the division. For example, consider Xerox Corporation. They have a division that produces office equipment, such as copiers, and a division that retails office products, such as paper. Each division has associated with it certain risk characteristics and it is likely that each should use its own discount rate.

Project-specific opportunity cost of capital
Each project is unique, and as such, has its own risk characteristics. Appropriate capital budgeting requires that this risk be reflected in discount rates. One method of doing so is to employ the CAPM using the project's beta. However, in practice, this procedure can be difficult to implement since project betas are hard to calculate.

Other Techniques for Analyzing Project Risk

Sequential analysis
Sequential analysis uses the probability distribution information to consider sequential cash flow outcomes and NPVs for a capital budgeting project. The sum of the joint probabilities times the net present values give the project's expected NPV. Use of sequential analysis is limited since it cannot easily consider all possible outcomes in many realistic situations.

Sensitivity analysis
Sensitivity analysis focuses on how sensitive the NPV or IRR is to change in any of the input variables, such as initial investment or the discount rate. Managers can ask "what if" questions and look at how much variability can occur in each variable before the project's NPV becomes negative. They can then focus on these critical variables. Recent advances in computer technology have made this kind of analysis much more available.

Break-even analysis
Break-even analysis enables you to determine the point at which the present value of the cash inflows equals the present values of the outflows; the point at which NPV equals zero. From this point, you can calculate the minimum level of sales needed to justify the project.

For example, Moonbeam Herbal Tea is considering the addition of a new tea bag packaging machine. The machine costs $10,000 and is expected to last ten years. It will be depreciated using straight-line CCA (ignore the half-year rule). Costs of goods sold amount to 80 percent of sales and fixed costs are $2,000. If the tax rate is 30 percent, and the opportunity cost of capital is 16 percent, what kind of sales are necessary?

To solve this problem, first calculate the annual cash flow level, CF_t, that will generate the zero NPV point:

Zero NPV = PV of inflows − PV of outflows = 0

$$CF_t(PVA_{16\%,10yr}) - \$10,000 = 0$$

$$CF_t = \frac{\$10,000}{4.833} = \$2,069.10$$

The machine needs to generate cash inflows of $2,069.10 per year to break even.

The volume of sales needed to generate these annual cash flows is determined as follows:

Sales − (variable + fixed costs) − taxes = CF_t

Variable costs = (0.80) (sales)

Taxes = [sales − (variable + fixed costs) − CCA](T)

$$= \left[\text{sales} - [(0.80)(\text{sales}) + \$2,000] - \frac{\$10,000}{10 \text{ yrs}} \right] (0.30)$$

= (0.06)(sales) − $900

Sales − [(0.80)(sales) + $2,000] − [(0.06)(sales) − $900] = $2,069.10

(0.14)(sales) − $1,100 = $2,069.10

Sales = $3,169.10/0.14 = $22,636.43

If the company can increase sales by more than $22,636.43 per year, the new machine will have a positive NPV.

Simulation

The advent of modern computers has allowed more firms to use simulation to evaluate capital budgeting projects. In a simulation, all relevant variables can be changed and a profile of possible values of NPVs can be generated. Although difficult, simulation is useful in determining the likelihood that a project will have a positive NPV. With this additional information, managers can make more informed decisions about project acceptability.

Completion Questions

9.1   Since the actual returns from a project are not known until after the firm invests in the project, _____ exists.

9.2   Firms unable to pass on the impact of inflation to their customers have _____ inflation risk than those which can readily increase their prices.

9.3   A project employing advanced state-of-the-art technology would have more _____ than a replacement project.

9.4   The CAPM is a _____ model which is not entirely appropriate for making long-term capital budgeting decisions.

9.5   The risk premium approach assumes that risk changes purely as _____. The opportunity cost of capital is equal to the risk-free rate and _____. To take into account risk changes that are not time related, _____ may be employed.

9.6   _____ is the risk apparent in the cash flows associated with a project resulting from sensitivity to the economy and other risk sources.

9.7   A project less risky than the firm as a whole would have a required return that is _____ the firm's opportunity cost of capital.

9.8   _____ uses probability distribution information to consider cash flow outcomes and NPVs for a capital budgeting project.

9.9   _____ does not formally quantify risk, but focuses on determining which factors have the greatest effect on net present value.

9.10   The _____ is the point where the present value of cash inflows equals the present value of the outflows and the NPV equals zero.

9.11   In an efficient market, firms should ignore _____ effects since investors can diversify themselves.

Problems

9.1   J. M. Richardson Company has under consideration a project with a cost of $50,000 and the following cash flows:

Year	CF
1	$10,000
2	14,000
3	18,000
4	15,000
5	14,000
6	21,849

If k_{RF} = 8 percent and k_M = 16 percent, what is the maximum beta the project could have and still be acceptable?

9.2   Snap-Tight Tool Limited is considering a project with a cost of $100,000 and CFs of $22,500 per year for the eight year life of the project.
  a.   If the k_{RF} is 10 percent and the risk premium is 3 percent, should the project be accepted?
  b.   Suppose the firm used a firm-wide opportunity cost of capital approach. If the opportunity cost of capital for Snap-Tight is 17 percent and the risk premium is the same, should the project be accepted?

9.3   Miller Snack Stand is considering the installation of ice cream making equipment with a cost of $150,000 and an expected life of nine years. The machine has expected CFs of $40,000 for each year of its life. Since Miller does not currently make ice cream, the manager regards this as a risky venture, at least initially. He has determined the appropriate discount rates are as follows:

Years	Required Return
1–3	20%
4–6	16
7–9	10

Calculate the NPV and determine if the equipment should be bought.

9.4   Morely Vacuum Cleaners is considering an expansion project that will enable them to make vacuum cleaner bags. The necessary equipment will require an initial cash outflow today of $100,000 and an increase in working capital of $20,000 *next* year. The equipment will be depreciated over five years using straight-line CCA (ignore the half-year rule) and the working capital investment will be recovered in year 5. Costs of goods sold amount to 60 percent of sales and fixed costs are $10,000 per year. If the required return on the investment is 14 percent, and the tax rate is 35 percent, what is the break-even level of sales?

9.5   CK Enterprises is considering a two-phase project to enable them to produce bottled soft drinks. Phase 1 requires a cash outflow of $1 million in year 0 and is expected to generate CFs in year 1 of $1.2 million with probability 0.6 or $0.5 million with probability 0.4. If, in fact, the year 1 cash flow is $1.2 million, the firm will invest (also in year 1) another $5 million in Phase 2, which is expected to yield CFs of $1.5 million per year for five years (in years 2–6). Since Phase 1 is more risky, its required return is 15 percent; Phase 2's required return is 10 percent. Using sequential analysis, determine if this project is acceptable.

Answers to Completion Questions

9.1   uncertainty (or risk)
9.2   more

Solutions to Problems

9.1   Step 1.   Find the IRR of the project using the technique presented in Chapter 8. To find the average cash flow:

$$\overline{CF} = \frac{\$10,000 + \$14,000 + \$18,000 + \$15,000 + \$14,000 + \$21,849}{6}$$

$$= \$15,474.83$$

The simulated annuity IRR is found where

$$\$15,474.83(PVA_{IRR,6yr}) - \$50,000 = 0$$

$$PVA_{IRR,6yr} = 50,000/\$15,474.83 = 3.231$$

The factor lies between 21 percent and 22 percent in the PVA tables. Thus, the simulated annuity based IRR is between 21 and 22 percent. This provides a starting point for determining the actual IRR on the project.

Step 2.   Starting at 21 percent:

$$NPV = \$10,000\ (PV_{21\%,1yr}) + \$14,000\ (PV_{21\%,2yr}) + \$18,000\ (PV_{21\%,3yr})$$

$$+ \$15,000\ (PV_{21\%,4yr}) + \$14,000\ (PV_{21\%,5yr}) + \$21,849\ (PV_{21\%,6yr})$$

$$- \$50,000$$

$$= \$10,000\ (0.826) + \$14,000\ (0.683) + \$18,000\ (0.564)$$

$$+ \$15,000\ (0.467) + \$14,000\ (0.386) + \$21,849\ (0.319) - \$50,000$$

$$= \$8,260 + \$9,562 + \$10,152 + \$7,005 + \$5,404 + \$6,970 - \$50,000$$

$$= -\$2,647$$

Since the NPV is negative, the IRR is lower than 21 percent.

Step 3.   Try 19 percent:

$$NPV = \$10,000\ (0.840) + \$14,000\ (0.706) + \$18,000\ (0.593)$$

$$+ \$15,000\ (0.499) + \$14,000\ (0.419) + \$21,849\ (0.352) - \$50,000$$

$$= \$8,400 + \$9,884 + \$10,674 + \$7,485 + \$5,866 + \$7,691 - \$50,000$$

$$= 0$$

The IRR is 19 percent. (By financial calculator IRR is also 19 percent.)

Step 4.   From the CAPM,

$$k_{project\ j} = k_{RF} + \beta_j\ (k_M - k_{RF})$$

$$19\% = 8\% + \beta_j\ (16\% - 8\%)$$

$$\beta_j = \frac{19\% - 8\%}{16\% - 8\%} = \frac{11\%}{8\%} = 1.375$$

If the project's beta is greater than 1.375, its opportunity cost of capital (or discount rate) will be greater than its IRR, and its NPV will be negative.

9.2   a.   Step 1. $k = k_{RF}$ + risk premium = 10% + 3% = 13%

Step 2.   NPV = CF_{1-8} ($PVA_{13\%,8yr}$) − CF_0 = $22,500 (4.799) − $100,000

= $7,977.50

Since the NPV is positive, the project is acceptable.

b.   Step 3.   NPV = CF_{1-8} ($PVA_{17\%,8yr}$) − CF_0 = $22,500 (4.207) − $100,000

= −$5,342.50

Since the NPV is negative, the project should not be accepted.

9.3   NPV = CF_{1-3} ($PVA_{20\%,3yr}$) + CF_{4-6}($PVA_{16\%,3yr}$)($PV_{20\%,3yr}$)

+ CF_{7-9} ($PVA_{10\%,3yr}$) ($PV_{16\%,3yr}$) ($PV_{20\%,3yr}$) − CF_0

= $40,000 (2.106) + $40,000 (2.246) (0.579) + $40,000 (2.487) (0.641)

(0.579) − $150,000

= $84,240 + $52,017.36 + $36,920.91 − $150,000 = $23,178.27

Since the NPV is positive, the project should be accepted.

9.4   Step 1.   Calculate the present value of the cash outflows less the present value of the inflow from the recovery of working capital. (This accounts for all cash flows that do not occur *each* year). The answer is the present value of the investment we need to recoup.

PV_0 = $100,000 + $20,000 ($PV_{14\%, 1yr}$) − $20,000 ($PV_{14\%, 5yr}$)

= $100,000 + $20,000 (0.877) − $20,000 (0.519)

= $100,000 + $17,540 − $10,380

= $107,160

Step 2.   Calculate the annual cash flows so NPV = 0.

PV of inflows − PV of outflows = 0

CF_t($PVA_{4\%, 5yr}$) = $107,160

CF_t = $107,160/3.433

= $31,214.68

Step 3.   Calculate CCA.

CCA_{1-5} = $100,000/5 = $20,000

Step 4.   To solve for the break-even sales, express CF_t in terms of sales.

$31,214.68   = sales − (variable + fixed costs) − taxes

= sales − [(0.60)(sales) + $10,000] − [sales − (0.60)(sales) − $10,000 − $20,000](0.35)

= (0.40)(sales) − $10,000 − [(0.14)(sales) − $10,500]

= (0.26)(sales) + $500

(0.26)(sales) = $31,214.68 − $500

Sales = $30,714.69/0.26 = $118,133.39

9.5   Step 1.   We can represent the cash flows in the following fashion (using units of $1,000):

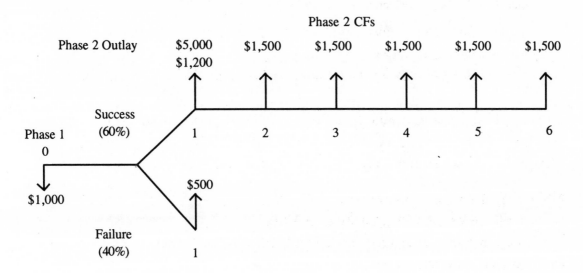

Step 2.   Phase 2 NPV (in year 1) = $1,500 (PVA$_{10\%,5yr}$) − $5,000

(if successful)   = $1,500 (3.791) − $5,000

= $5,686.50 − $5,000 = $686.50

Step 3.   Phase 2 Expected Present Value in year 1 = 0.6 (686.50) = $411.90

Step 4.   Phase 2 Expected NPV in year 0 = $411.90 (PV$_{15\%,1yr}$)

= $411.90 (0.870) = $358.35

Step 5.   Phase 1 Expected CF in year 1 = 0.6 ($1,200) + 0.4 ($500)

= $720 + $200 = $920

Step 6.   Phase 1 NPV in year 0 = $920 (PV$_{15\%,1yr}$) − $1,000

= $920 (0.870) − $1,000

= $800.40 − $1,000 = −$199.60

So NPV = $358.35 − $199.60 = $158.75 and the project is acceptable.

Chapter 10
Raising Long-Term Funds

How This Chapter Relates to the Rest of the Text

Chapters 7–9 provided us with the tools needed to evaluate long-term capital projects. In order to take advantage of positive NPV projects, firms often must raise funds in the capital markets. In Chapter 2, we saw how these markets operate; in this chapter, we see how they relate to long-term financing and common stock. Other long-term sources of funds—bonds and preferred stock—are covered in Chapter 11. Short-term sources of funds are discussed in Chapter 24. The opportunity cost of capital (Chapter 6), capital structure (Chapters 12 and 13), and dividend policy (Chapter 14) are closely related to the firm's ability and need to secure external financing.

Topical Outline

I. Raising long-term funds.
   - A. Internal funds are generated through retention of cash flows from continuing operations.
   - B. External funds are secured from creditors and investors.
   - C. Firms need more external financing during economic downturns.
II. Means of raising external funds.
   - A. Cash offerings.
     1. Offered for sale to the general public (cash offer) or through privileged subscription (rights offering).
     2. Typically uses an investment dealer.
   - B. Private placements provide funds from financial institutions such as insurance companies.
   - C. A bought deal is when an investment dealer lines up potential buyers and approaches the issuing firm.
   - D. When raising external capital, firms must plan in order to provide flexibility and to be able to minimize financing costs.
III. Cash offerings.
   - A. Role of investment dealers.
     1. Firm commitment offering.
        - a. An investment dealer purchases the issue from the firm at a fixed price and then resells it.
        - b. The risk of the issue not selling is borne by the investment dealer.
        - c. The firm is guaranteed a fixed dollar amount from the issue.
     2. Best efforts offering.
        - a. The investment dealer agrees to sell as much of the issue as he or she can for a fixed commission.
        - b. Large, well-known firms that feel the issue will sell easily may use a best efforts offering.
        - c. Very small firms use best efforts offerings when the risks and costs are too great for underwriting.
     3. Direct placement is generally through a rights offering to stockholders. It may or may not require an investment dealer.
   - B. Selection of an investment dealer.
     1. The negotiated underwriting process involves simply selecting or negotiating with one investment dealer.
     2. Competitive bidding involves announcing an intention to sell the securities, and inviting bids to select the investment dealer.
   - C. The underwriting process.
     1. At the pre-underwriting conferences, the issuing firm and the investment dealer discuss the general details of the issue.
        - a. They discuss the amount of capital needed, the type(s) of security to issue, and the terms of the agreement.

b. The investment dealer, a specialist in selling new securities, offers advice.

c. The investment dealer begins the underwriting investigation, which will be followed up by an auditor and lawyers.

d. The firm and the underwriter draw up an underwriting agreement after the investigation.

e. The underwriting agreement may also contain an out clause that causes the contract to be void if the security's market price falls below a predetermined level.

2. The prospectus filed with the provincial securities commission presents all the facts of the issue and the issuing firm.

a. The securities commission will judge the factual accuracy of the prospectus.

b. During the registration period, a preliminary prospectus (or red herring) must be distributed in Alberta, Saskatchewan, Manitoba, and Ontario. In other provinces, only a final prospectus is required.

c. During this period, the underwriters can make oral offers and discover the interest of potential buyers, but the price is decided after the registration period.

   i. When a new issue of existing stock is sold, the investment dealer might buy the security at a few points below the closing price of the security on the last day of its registration.

   ii. If the new stock issue is for a firm just going public, the investment dealer and the issuer must negotiate on a price.

   iii. For bonds and preferred stock, the ratings services rate the issue, and the issue is priced according to the current rate of return on that rating of security.

d. After the registration period, the underwriting firm will often run a tombstone advertisement in the financial newspapers, telling from whom the prospectus may be obtained.

3. An underwriting syndicate (wholesalers) and a selling group (retailers) are formed in order to spread the risk and ensure nationwide marketability.

IV. Costs of flotation to the issuing firm.

A. Costs include the underwriting fee and all other expenses related to the offering.

B. Total selling costs are the difference between what the securities are sold for and what the firm actually receives.

C. The cost of selling common stock is substantially greater than for selling preferred stock and debt.

1. Common stock is sold to a large number of investors, whereas preferred stock and debt are issued in large blocks and are sold to fewer investors.

2. The price of common stock is more erratic, and entails greater risk for the investment dealer.

V. Private placements.

A. Advantages of private placements.

1. The issuing firm saves the time, expense, and trouble of having to register the issue with any securities commission.

2. The firm can maintain a lower profile, since it need not go through the registration process.

3. The firm can discuss the financing problem directly with the lender and often make modifications in the offering.

B. Disadvantages of private issues.

1. The lender may monitor the firm's activities more closely, either directly or through loan provisions.

2. If common stock financing is used, the investor is likely to gain substantial influence on or even control of the firm.

3. The cost of privately placed debt is generally higher than on public issues.

4. It is more difficult to raise large amounts of capital through private placements.

C. A bought deal is where one underwriter or group of underwriters buys an issue from a firm and sells the securities to investors.

1. No syndicate is formed.

2.   The procedure is conducted without an out clause.

3.   The cost of issuing securities is less than underwriting.

D.   Provinces from Quebec westward allow qualified firms access to the capital markets without filing full prospectuses.

1.   Requirements vary across provinces; in Ontario, firms must have publicly traded equity with a market value of $75 million and have filed financial statements with the securities commission for 36 months.

2.   Firms file a simplified document called a short-form prospectus at the time of issue.

E.   Investment dealers are required to maintain high ethical standards.

1.   Their continued business and profitability are tied directly to their reputation.

2.   The costs to restore their business and reputation may be substantial.

VI.   Rights and privileges of common shareholders.

A.   Common shareholders have a residual right to the income of the firm.

1.   Creditors, lessors, the government, and preferred stockholders receive their claims before common shareholders receive cash dividends.

2.   Firms are not obligated to pay cash dividends.

3.   Since risk is greater for common stock, so is the expected return.

B.   In theory, shareholders control the firm through election of the board of directors, but this control is limited.

1.   Individual shareholders generally hold only a small fraction of the total shares.

2.   Management often nominates only enough directors to fill the board positions, requesting stockholders to vote for this slate.

3.   Outside or dissident groups may challenge management and propose a different slate of directors.

4.   The board is selected either by majority voting or cumulative voting.

a.   Majority voting requires that the shareholders place only one vote per share per director; the candidates with the most votes win.

b.   Cumulative voting allows investors to distribute their total votes among the candidates in any manner they wish, allowing minority groups to elect representatives on the board.

C.   Cumulative voting.

1.   Each share is entitled to one vote per director to be elected.

a.   Shareholders can distribute these per share votes in any manner they wish, allowing minority groups to amass enough votes to elect representatives on the board.

b.   The equations in the chapter help in calculating the number of votes required to elect a desired number of directors and the number of directors that can be elected with shares owned by the minority group.

2.   The firm can partially thwart the intent of cumulative voting by reducing the size of the board or electing only a portion of it each year.

D.   Shareholders have the right to obtain information from management about the firm's operations.

E.   Common shareholders can (in most circumstances) lose no more than their initial investment, since they have no liability for the debts incurred by the firm.

F.   Shareholders may have the preemptive right to buy new shares of common stock in the same percentage as their current ownership.

1.   Some corporate articles have eliminated this right in order to make mergers and acquisitions easier.

G.   Common shareholders may transfer ownership of shares to other investors in the secondary market.

VII.   Features of common stock.

A.   Authorized and outstanding shares.

1.   The firm's charter states the maximum number of shares the firm is authorized to issue without amending the charter.

      2.   Under the Canada Business Corporations Act (CBCA) and many provincial acts there is no limit to the number of shares that can be issued.

      3.   Outstanding shares are those held by the public.

  B.   Par value and book value.

      1.   Common stock used to be issued with or without par value.

          a.   The common shareholder was responsible to creditors for the difference between par value and the issuance price if that price is below par value, so par value was generally low.

          b.   If the firm did not state a par value, it used some stated value for accounting purposes.

          c.   The difference between the issuance price and the par (or stated) value was recorded on the firm's balance sheet as additional paid-in capital.

          d.   Under the CBCA and most new provincial acts, par value shares are not permitted; the full amount paid for new shares is reported in the common stock account.

      2.   The book value per share reflects the common shareholder's equity divided by the number of shares outstanding.

          a.   Due to the effects of inflation, this figure has little economic meaning.

          b.   Some analysts prefer to use net working capital to estimate the value of the firm in potential liquidation.

  C.   Forms of common stock.

      1.   Sometimes the firm issues a nonvoting class and reserves the voting class for the founders' group.

      2.   The founders' class of stock may have more votes per share than the class of stock for other shareholders, so that founders can maintain their voting power.

      3.   Voting and nonvoting stocks of a firm generally trade at similar price levels.

VIII.   Common stock financing.

  A.   Recent studies have indicated that issuing new common stock causes a stock price decline of approximately 3 percent. Debt issues leave stock prices unaffected.

      1.   The decline may be due to information asymmetries. Managers should be inclined to issue (sell) new shares if they feel that the firm's stock is overpriced. A new issue signals this belief to investors and stock prices fall.

      2.   Investors may interpret the issue as a signal about the firm's investment prospects. If the prospects are good, investors would prefer debt financing since the gains from the prospect would not have to be shared with new stockholders.

  B.   Initial public offerings (IPOs) are often underpriced by 15–20 percent due to difficulties in selling the issue or lack of information about the firm.

  C.   Pricing new issues.

      1.   For firms having outstanding shares, the new shares typically are priced a few dollars below the closing price on the day the stock clears registration.

      2.   For firms initially going public, no market exists for the stock, so the investment dealer must determine the issue price.

          a.   Estimate what the total market value of the firm would be after the issue.

             i.   Use a valuation approach appropriate to the firm, such as the constant dividend growth approach:

$$S_0 = D_1/(k_s - g).$$

             (a)   The D_1 estimate depends upon the firm's projected net income and dividend payout.

             (b)   The g estimate depends upon the firm's expectations for earnings and dividend growth.

             (c)   Estimating k_s is difficult; the investment dealer might use some approach such as adding a risk premium to the expected interest rate on long-term bonds.

          (d)   This approach is not very helpful, since both k_s and D_1 are difficult to determine for a new issue.

      ii.   Use the comparative P/E approach for valuation.

          (a)   Examine the P/E ratios for publicly traded firms in the same industry and of firms that have recently gone public.

          (b)   Compare other pertinent information.

              (i)   Financial condition, growth prospects, quality and stability of management, and size.

              (ii)   Some of these comparisons are qualitative rather than quantitative.

          (c)   Establish an appropriate P/E ratio, and determine the value of the firm:

$$S_0 = \text{(expected net income) (expected P/E per share)}.$$

    b.   Divide this total market value by the number of shares that will be outstanding, including privately held or founders' shares.

  D.   Recording a stock issue on the firm's balance sheet.

    1.   Increase the common stock account by the number of shares times the issue price per share.

    2.   Increase cash by the amount of the new capital raised.

IX.   Rights offering.

  A.   The rights offering is the issuance of new shares of common stock, with the firm's current stockholders having first option to buy the issue.

  B.   The importance of rights offerings has diminished.

    1.   Some firms have eliminated the preemptive right.

    2.   Investors have increased participation in dividend reinvestment plans.

    3.   Short-form prospectus procedures have been introduced.

  C.   The number of rights needed to purchase an additional share can be calculated using the formula presented in the chapter.

  D.   Value of stock and rights.

    1.   Rights-on is the period of time when the right is attached and purchasable with the share of common stock.

    2.   Ex rights day is the day the stock and the right begin trading separately; the price of the stock drops by the value of the right.

  E.   Effect on the position of the shareholders.

    1.   As long as shareholders take positive action, they do not suffer any loss from a rights offering.

    2.   If they let the rights expire, they incur a loss equal to the value of the rights.

  F.   Pricing the offering.

    1.   If the firm wants to lower its per share price substantially, it would set a low subscription price.

    2.   If the firm does not want to lower its price much, the subscription price will be set just low enough to ensure the market price remains above it during the rights offering.

X.   Listing the stock.

  A.   Small firms generally do not list their stock but trade on the over-the-counter market.

  B.   In order to apply for listing, a firm must meet certain conditions, file a listing application, pay a listing fee, and agree to meet the additional financial reporting requirements.

XI.   Regulation of public issues.

  A.   Primary market issues are regulated by the provincial securities acts.

Formulas

<u>Notation</u>

S   = value of an all-equity firm

D_1 = expected cash dividend to be paid to shareholders next year

k_s = common stock investors' required return

g   = the expected (compound) growth rate in cash dividends

P/E   = price/earnings ratio

EPS   = earnings per share

<u>Estimated Selling Price for Common Stock of a Firm Going Public</u>

Value of firm after the issue/number of shares of common stock

<u>Constant Growth Formula for Valuing the Firm</u>

$S = D_1 / (k_s - g)$

<u>Comparative P/E Approach to Valuing the Firm</u>

S = (expected net income) $\times$ (expected P/E of stock)

<u>Cumulative Voting</u>

Minimum number of shares required to elect a desired number of directors $= \dfrac{\left[\begin{array}{c}\text{total shares outstanding} \\ \text{and entitled to vote}\end{array}\right] \times \left[\begin{array}{c}\text{number of directors} \\ \text{desired}\end{array}\right]}{\text{total number of directors to be elected} + 1} + 1$

Number of directors that can be elected with shares owned $= \dfrac{\left[\begin{array}{c}\text{number of shares} \\ \text{owned} - 1\end{array}\right] \times \left[\begin{array}{c}\text{total number of directors} \\ \text{to be elected} + 1\end{array}\right]}{\text{total shares outstanding and entitled to vote}}$

<u>Rights Offerings</u>

Notation

v_r = value of one right

P_o = rights-on market price per share

P_s = subscription price

N = number of rights needed to purchase one additional share

P_x = ex rights stock price per share

Number of Rights Needed to Purchase an Additional Share

Number of additional shares, N = funds to be raised/subscription price, P_s

Number of rights to buy one additional share = existing shares/additional shares

Cost to shareholders for one additional share of stock = P_s + required rights per share

Value of stock and rights

Rights-on:

Value of one right $= \dfrac{\text{market value of stock, rights-on} - \text{subscription price}}{\text{number of rights needed to purchase one share} + 1}$

$v_r = (P_o - P_s)/(N + 1)$

Ex rights:

$$\text{Value of one right} = \frac{\text{market value of stock, ex rights} - \text{subscription price}}{\text{number of rights needed to purchase one share}}$$

$$v_r = (P_x - P_s)/(N)$$

Combining the two definitions given for the value of one right, we obtain the third definition for the value of one right:

$$v_r = P_o - P_x$$

What to Look For

We have spent the last three chapters preparing to make long-term financing decisions by evaluating the capital budget (Chapters 7–9). Now, we are ready to look for long-term funding sources. In this chapter, we see that firms can generate equity internally by retaining cash flows. In order to maintain their operation, however, firms may also need to find sources of external long-term financing. In Chapter 10, we focus on the process of obtaining these long-term external funds.

Obtaining External Long-Term Funds

Cash offerings

Firms that offer new securities publicly have several alternatives. They can place the issue directly with current shareholders through a rights offering. They can hire an investment dealer to underwrite the issue, shifting the risk of the sale to the investment dealer. Finally, they can hire an investment dealer to sell the issue on a best efforts basis. To select an investment dealer, the firm could simply negotiate with a single investment dealer or accept competitive bids.

In the underwriting process, the issuing firm and the investment dealer hold pre-underwriting conferences and discuss the type of security issue, how much capital to raise, and the terms of the agreement. In many provinces the firm, through its underwriter, files a preliminary prospectus or red herring. After an audit and legal examination, firms file a final prospectus stating the terms of the offering and the investment dealer forms a syndicate to spread risk and ensure nationwide marketability.

Private placements

Private placements occur when the firm issues securities directly to financial institutions, such as insurance companies, banks, or pension funds. Firms can privately place either debt or equity. Firms that place equity privately transfer a substantial amount of control to the investor, so firms are often reluctant to place equity privately. For small and medium-size firms, a potential buyer of privately placed equity is a venture capitalist (Chapter 27). Firms choosing to place equity privately with a venture capitalist should choose the investor carefully, looking for one that will not only provide the funds, but also nurture and wisely advise the firm.

The interest rate paid on privately placed debt is often 10 to 40 basis points (or 0.10 to 0.40 percent) higher than on a public offering. Some privately placed debt is in the form of term loans (Chapter 11). Lending institutions protect themselves by attaching restrictive covenants to privately placed debt.

It is also possible for firms to issue stocks through a bought deal. In a bought deal, one underwriter (or a small group of underwriters) purchases the securities and sells them to investors without forming a syndicate. Bought deals are generally less expensive to the issuing firm than a traditional public offering and do not contain an out clause.

Since 1982, the process of issuing securities in provinces from Quebec westward has been facilitated by the adoption of the Prompt Offering Prospectus System (or POP system). Qualifying firms can issue securities after filing a short-form prospectus that contains less information. This procedure is easier and has reduced the registration period from several weeks to five days.

Long-Term Funding and Managers

A broad array of decisions face managers in the process of obtaining long-term external funds. First, they must decide which type of funding they want to use: common stock, preferred stock, debt, warrants, or convertibles. They must then decide whether to place the issue privately or to offer it publicly.

If they choose a public offering, they must decide whether to use an investment dealer. If an investment dealer is used, managers must decide whether the issue should be underwritten (insured) or sold on a best efforts basis. They must also decide whether to choose an investment dealer or to have competitive bidding. In all these choices, the goal is to maximize the value of the firm, so managers should weigh the costs and benefits of each of these decisions.

Managers must have greater sophistication today than in the recent past when raising long-term capital. Inflation has risen and then fallen, as have interest rates. To protect themselves, lenders have shifted much of the interest rate risk to their customers through the use of variable-rate loans. In addition, larger firms are increasingly using short-form prospectus procedures to time the issuance of new securities. The use of the short-form prospectus may result in bypassing the investment dealer in the registration procedure.

Rights of Common Stockholders

Shareholders, in theory, control the firm through the election of the firm's board of directors. As the text notes, the control of the individual shareholder is limited. Two voting systems exist: majority voting and cumulative voting. In the majority voting system, shareholders may cast one vote per share for a candidate for each director's position. For example, if a shareholder held 200 shares of stock, and the firm was electing 8 directors, the shareholder could vote a total of 1,600 votes—with 200 per director candidate. In the cumulative voting system, the same shareholder could vote 1,600 votes any way desired; the shareholder could even cast all 1,600 votes for a single director candidate. Through this concentration of votes, the cumulative voting system allows minority groups to place representatives on the board of directors.

A minority group can discover how many votes it needs to vote in a representative. For example, suppose the firm was electing 8 directors, and the minority group wanted 3 representatives on the board. The group would need to amass a minimum number of voting shares from the total 180,000 voting shares outstanding:

$$\text{Minimum number of shares required to elect 3 directors} = \frac{(180{,}000 \text{ shares}) (3 \text{ directors})}{8 \text{ directors} + 1} + 1 = \frac{60{,}001}{\text{votes}}$$

If the group has 40,001 voting shares, how many directors can it elect?

$$\text{Number of directors minority group can elect with shares owned} = \frac{(40{,}001 \text{ shares} - 1) (8 \text{ directors} + 1)}{180{,}000 \text{ shares}} = 2 \text{ directors}$$

The firm can reduce the power of cumulative voting by reducing the number of directors on the board or by electing a smaller portion of the board each year.

Shareholders have the right to receive information about the operations of the firm. Management screens this information in order to protect the firm's competitive position in its industry.

All About Common Stock

What do the balance sheet figures mean?

The details in the shareholders' equity section of the balance sheet may be confusing. Authorized shares are shares the firm's charter allows the firm to issue. Outstanding shares are the shares held by the public. Par value of common stock is the value stated in the firm's charter. Under the Canada Business Corporations Act, firms can issue an unlimited number of shares that have no par value. In this case, any new funds raised by an issue are added to the common stock account. Finally, as you already know, the retained earnings account is equal to the sum of all income (over the years) from the firm's income statements less all cash dividends paid. Remember, there is no cash in the retained earnings account.

How does a firm price a new issue of common stock?

Firms with outstanding stock tend to price new issues a few dollars below its price on the day the stock cleared registration with the provincial securities commission. Firms going public with an initial stock offering, however, have more trouble pricing their issues. The firm should use several methods to value the firm. These methods are subjective, but if several are employed, they should produce a usable value.

The firm divides this calculated market value by the number of shares to be issued in order to obtain an issuance price. The setting of the issuance price is important. If the price is set too high, it will be difficult to sell the issue; a price that is too low will not bring in enough capital for the firm. Remember, the firm's capital proceeds from selling common stock are based on the issuance price, not the subsequent market price after the stock is outstanding.

When a firm with existing outstanding shares issues new stock, the holdings of current shareholders can be diluted. Some firms will issue new shares via a rights offering. A rights offering gives current shareholders the first option of buying new shares. These options can be traded, and so long as a shareholder takes some action (by selling the rights or buying new shares) he or she will be protected against the effects of the new issue.

Completion Questions

10.1   Firms have two primary sources of funds. They can generate funds internally from continuing operations or _____.

10.2   When firms publicly offer new issues of long-term capital, they frequently use the services of an _____ _____, who helps register the new issue and assist in its distribution and sale.

10.3   Investment dealers can be hired either to _____ the issue or to sell the issue on a _____ basis.

10.4   To select an investment dealer and the issue price, some firms (especially those in the public utility industry) use _____.

10.5   A _____ can be distributed prior to the issue's approval by the provincial securities commission.

10.6   When the issuing firm has outstanding stock, the investment dealer firm typically buys the new issue at _____.

10.7   _____ is a streamlined procedure that qualifying firms can use for issuing both debt and equity issues.

10.8   Among new issue securities, _____ involves higher flotation costs, since it involves more risk and is distributed to more investors.

10.9   Common shareholders play two roles. They both own the firm and provide _____ for the firm.

10.10   Common shareholders have a _____ to the income of the firm. This claim comes _____ the claims of creditors, lessors, the government, and preferred stockholders.

10.11   Under the majority voting system, each shareholder has _____ vote per director per share. Under _____ voting, the shareholder has the same number of votes as the majority voting system, but can distribute these votes to any director(s) as deemed appropriate.

10.12   The _____ is a provision granting shareholders the right to purchase new shares of common stock in the same proportion as their current ownership. When shareholders have this option, the stock issuance is called a _____ offering.

10.13   _____ shares are the shares a firm is allowed to issue without amending its charter. _____ shares are the shares currently issued.

10.14   If a firm is making an initial stock offering, the pricing of the issue is difficult since there is no _____ for the stock. In this case, the firm or investment dealer may use a _____ approach like those in Chapter 6 or the _____ approach.

Problems

10.1 Deighton Bank intends to issue 2 million shares of common stock. The bank's investment dealer has offered two alternatives:

Plan A: A best efforts offering at $16 per share subject to an underwriting commission of 2 percent of the expected gross proceeds plus $300,000. The investment dealer firm expects 93 percent of the issue will be sold.

Plan B: An underwritten offer at $15.50 per share plus an underwriting fee of 7 percent of the gross proceeds.

Which plan offers the highest net proceeds to Deighton Bank?

10.2 Gray Enterprises is considering the issuance of 1 million shares of common stock. The stock is expected to pay a $2.50 cash dividend next year and cash dividends and earnings are expected to grow at a rate of 8 percent per year. If k_s is 20 percent and the cost of issuing the stock is 7 percent of the gross proceeds from the sale, how much should Gray expect to receive if 100 percent of the issue is sold?

10.3 Stevenson Industries is planning its first issue of common stock. The company expects to pay a cash dividend of $2.28 per share next year—a dividend payout ratio of 60 percent. Firms in the same industry typically have a P/E ratio of 22 times and earnings growth of 6 percent.
a. What price should Stevenson expect per share of stock?
b. Assuming that the price in part (a) is correct, what is the required return (k_s) for Stevenson?

10.4 Lawrence Fisheries, Ltd. has 1,000,000 shares outstanding and will elect 7 directors at its next annual meeting. If you control 225,000 shares of Lawrence, how many directors can you elect under cumulative voting assuming all shares vote?

10.5 Converse Industries, in order to protect existing stockholders, has decided to attach a rights offering to its latest equity issue. The firm presently has 2 million shares of common stock and is attempting to raise $8.5 million by issuing an additional 400,000 shares. At present, the company's EPS is $2.50 per share and its P/E ratio is 10 times. Determine the value of the right and the ex rights price of the stock.

10.6 NSPC common stock is priced at $44 a share in the market. There are 100,000 shares of common stock outstanding. Notice is given that shareholders may purchase one new share of NSPC at a price of $32 for every 5 shares held.
a. What is the value of a right?
b. What is the ex rights price?
c. How many additional shares of NSPC were issued?

10.7 ABC Industries is planning a rights offering of 50,000 shares at $40 each. The following timetable is planned
February 10 - announcement date
March 15 - ex rights date
March 17 - record date
April 16 - rights expire
The market price on February 10 is $50 a share and 4 rights are required for each additional share to be purchased. Assume there are no changes in the market value except as a result of the rights offering.
a. What is the value of one right?
b. How many shares of common stock will ABC have outstanding after the rights offering?
c. Trace the market price per share from February 10 to April 16.

d.   Suppose you own 200 shares of ABC stock. On April 15, you decide to take the following actions:
   i.   Exercise the rights.
   ii.   Sell the rights.
   iii. Allow the rights to expire.
Discuss the effects of such actions on your current wealth.

10.8   In 1996 Beaver Inc. issued rights to buy one new share at $5 for every four shares held. Before the issue, there were 10 million shares outstanding and the share price was $6.
   a.   What is the total amount of new funds raised?
   b.   How many rights are needed to buy one new share?
   c.   What is the value of one right?
   d.   What is the prospective ex rights price?
   e.   How far could the total value of the company fall before shareholders would be unwilling to take up their rights?
   f.   Show that Beaver's shareholders are just as well off if it issues the new shares at $4 per share rather than $5 per share.

Answers to Completion Questions

10.1   secure them externally from creditors or investors
10.2   investment dealer
10.3   underwrite; best efforts
10.4   competitive bidding
10.5   preliminary prospectus
10.6   a few dollars below the securities' closing price on the last day of the registration period
10.7   Short-form prospectus
10.8   common stock
10.9   long-term capital
10.10   residual right; after
10.11   one; cumulative
10.12   preemptive right; rights
10.13   Authorized; Outstanding
10.14   existing market; valuation; comparative P/E

Solutions to Problems

10.1   Step 1.   Plan A: Expected gross proceeds = (2,000,000) ($16) (0.93) = $29,760,000
                              Commissions:
                                    Underwriting = ($29,760,000) (0.02) = $595,200
                                    Fee   300,000
                                    Total commissions $895,200
                              Net proceeds = $29,760,000 - $895,200 = $28,864,800
        Step 2.   Plan B: Expected gross proceeds = (2,000,000)($15.50) = $31,000,000
                              Underwriting = ($31,000,000)(0.07) = $2,170,000
                              Net proceeds = $31,000,000 − $2,170,000 = $28,830,000
                              The net proceeds from Plan A are greater by $34,800.

10.2 Step 1. Total dividends paid next year = (1,000,000 shares) ($2.50 per share)

$$= \$2,500,000$$

Step 2. $S = D_1/(k_s - g)$

$$= \frac{\$2,500,000}{0.20 - 0.08} = \frac{\$2,500,000}{0.12} = \$20,833,333$$

The net proceeds = $\$20,833,333(1 - 0.07) = \$19,375,000$

10.3 a. Step 1. Dividends per share = (earnings per share) × (dividend payout)
So EPS = DPS/dividend payout = $2.28/0.60 = $3.80 per share

Step 2. $P_0 = (EPS) \times (P/E) = (\$3.80)(22) = \$83.60$ per share

b. Step 3. $k_s = (D_1/P_0) + g$

$$= (\$2.28/\$83.69) + 0.06 = 0.0272 + 0.06 = 0.0872 = 8.72\%$$

10.4 Number of directors that can be elected with shares owned $= \dfrac{\left[\dfrac{\text{number of shares}}{\text{owned}} - 1\right] \times \left[\begin{array}{c}\text{directors to be}\\ \text{elected}\end{array} + 1\right]}{\text{total shares outstanding}}$

$$= \frac{(225,000 - 1)(7 + 1)}{1,000,000}$$

$$= \frac{1,799,992}{1,000,000}$$

$$= 1.8 \text{ or } 1 \text{ director}$$

10.5 Step 1. The present market price = (EPS)(P/E) = ($2.50)(10) = $25 per share

Step 2. Subscription price $= \dfrac{\text{funds to be raised}}{\text{number of additional shares}}$

$$= \frac{\$8,500,000}{400,000} = \$21.25 \text{ per share}$$

Step 3. Number of rights to buy one additional share $= \dfrac{\text{existing shares}}{\text{additional shares}}$

$$= \frac{\$2,000,000}{400,000} = 5 \text{ rights}$$

Step 4. The value of a right $= v_r = \dfrac{P_0 - P_s}{N + 1} = \dfrac{\$25.00 - \$21.25}{5 + 1} = \dfrac{\$3.75}{6}$

$$= \$0.625$$

Step 5. The ex rights price can be found by solving for P_x in the following equation:

$$v_r = \frac{P_x - P_s}{N}, \text{ or } P_x = N(v_r) + P_s = 5(\$0.625) + \$21.25 = \$24.375$$

An alternative approach not presented in the text is:
$P_x = P_0 - v_r = \$25.00 - \$0.625 = \$24.375$

10.6 a. Given $P_0 = \$44$, $P_s = \$32$, $N = 5$
Value of one right $= (P_0 - P_s)/(N + 1)$
$$= (\$44 - \$32)/(5 + 1) = \$2.0$$

b.   Value of one right, $v_r = (P_x - P_s)/N$

$$2 = (P_x - \$32)/5$$

$$P_x = \$42$$

Alternatively, using the equation in footnote 12,

$$P_x = (P_oN + P_s)/(N + 1) = [(\$44)(5) + \$32]/(5 + 1)$$

$$= \$42$$

c.   N = existing shares/additional shares

Additional shares = existing shares/N

$$= 100,000/5 = 20,000$$

10.7   Given the following:

$P_s = \$40$, $P_o = \$50$, $N = 4$

a. $v_r = (P_o - P_s)/(N + 1)$

$$= (50 - 40)/5 = \$2.0$$

b.   Number of shares existing before rights issue $= 4 \times 50,000 = 200,000$

Number of shares outstanding after issue $= 200,000 + 50,000 = 250,000$

c.   Value of one right $= P_o - P_x$

$$2 = 50 - P_x$$

Ex rights price $(P_x) = \$48$

or $P_x = [P_oN + P_s]/(N + 1)$

$$= [(\$50)(4) + \$40]/5 = 48$$

February 10–March 14: Market price = $50

March 15–April 16: Market price = $48

d.   You own 200 shares of ABC stock. Consider the following options:

i.   Exercise the rights: you therefore have 200 rights which entitle you to purchase 50 new shares at $40 each.

Buy 50 shares at $40 each: cost = $2,000

You now own 250 shares at $48 each $= \$48 \times 250 = \$12,000$

Net worth $= \$12,000 - \$2,000 = \$10,000$

Note: Your wealth before rights offering was $50 \times 200 = \$10,000$ (remains unchanged).

ii.   Sell the rights:

Proceeds from sale $= \$2 \times 200 = \$400$

Value of 200 shares $= 200 \times \$48 = \$9,600$

Net worth $= \$400 + \$9,600 = \$10,000$

iii.   If you allow the rights to expire your 200 shares will be worth $9,600 indicating a net loss of $400. This represents the loss from not selling the rights.

10.8   Given the following:

$P_s = \$5$, $N = 4$, $P_o = \$6$, and existing shares = 10 million

a.   N = existing shares/additional shares

4 = 10 million/additional shares

Additional shares = 10 million/4

$$= 2.5 \text{ million}$$

New funds raised $= 2.5 \text{ million} \times \$5 = \$12.5 \text{ million}$

b.   Four rights are needed to buy one new share.

c. $v_r = (P_o - P_s)/(N + 1)$

$$= (\$6 - \$5)/5 = \$0.20$$

d.   Noting that the value of one right $= P_o - P_x$

$$\$0.20 = \$6 - P_x$$

Ex rights price $= (P_x) = \$6 - \$0.20 = \$5.80$

or $P_x = [P_o N + P_s]/(N + 1)$

$$= [\$6(4) + \$5]/5$$

$$= \$5.80$$

e.   Given that $v_r = P_o - P_x$

when $v_r = 0$

$$P_o = P_x = \$5.00$$

Therefore the company's equity value must be $12.5 \times \$5 = \$62.5$ million or below before shareholders would be unwilling to take up their rights.

f.   Given $P_s = \$4.00$, $P_o = \$6.00$, and number of shares outstanding is 10 million. For Beaver Inc. to raise the required $12.5 million at $4 a share, the firm must issue $12.5/4 = 3.125$ million additional shares.

With 3.125 million additional shares to be issued,

$N = 10$ million$/3.125 = 3.2$ rights

Therefore, $v_r = (P_o - P_s)/(N + 1) = (\$6 - \$4)/4.2 = \$0.4762$

and $P_x = \$6 - \$0.4762 = \$5.5238$

Suppose you originally owned 100 shares of Beaver stock.

i.   If you decide to exercise your rights and buy Beaver shares at $4.00 per share:

Number of new shares purchased $= 100/3.2 = 31.25$

Buy 31.25 shares at $4.00: Cost $= \$125.00$

Value of 131.25 shares $= 131.25 \times \$5.5238$

$$= \$725.00$$

Net worth $= \$600$

ii.   If you decide to sell your rights

Proceeds $= 100 \,(\$0.4762) = \$47.62$

Value of shares $= 100 \,(\$5.5238) = \$552.38$

Net wealth $= \$600$, which is the same as before.

Chapter 11
Liability Management

How This Chapter Relates to the Rest of the Text

Chapter 10 discussed obtaining external funds and common stock. In Chapter 11, we examine two additional sources of long-term financing—bonds and preferred stock. Bonds trade based on their yield to maturity (Chapter 4) and are priced according to present values (Chapter 3). For both bonds and preferred stock, risk (Chapter 5) is an important determinant of price. Required returns on bonds and preferred stocks are important components of the opportunity cost of capital (Chapter 6) and the amount of debt a firm carries affects its capital structure (Chapters 12 and 13).

Topical Outline

I. Long-term debt.
    A. Reasons for issuing debt.
        1. Firms may deduct bond interest payments from pretax income; cash dividends on preferred stock and common stock are not tax-deductible.
        2. Under unexpected inflation, purchasing power is eroded and firms that have borrowed repay the debt in cheaper dollars.
        3. Firms might employ debt if they have a low level of debt usage compared to their industry.
        4. Firms might use debt if the sale of additional common stock would weaken the majority owner's control.
    B. The bond terms.
        1. All debt holders are guaranteed a prior claim to the firm's income over the common and preferred stockholders.
        2. The contract between the borrowing firm and the lender is called the bond indenture, which specifies the provisions of the bond.
        3. The prospectus, which is available through dealers, summarizes the bond indenture position.
    C. The role of the trustee.
        1. Since bonds are issued to many investors, a trustee is appointed to ease communication between the firm and the investors.
        2. The trustee sees that all the legal requirements for the bond indenture are met before issuance.
        3. The trustee monitors the issuing firm's performance to see that it meets the conditions of the indenture.
        4. The trustee takes action on behalf of the bondholders if the firm defaults on interest or principal payments.
    D. Security and seniority.
        1. Forms of secured debt, and their respective seniority.
            a. Mortgage bonds can be open- or closed-end; open-end provisions do not limit the amount of debt secured by the firm's assets, while closed-end provisions prohibit issuing further debt.
                i.   First mortgage bonds have prior claim on assets.
                ii. Second mortgage bonds are subordinate to first mortgage bonds.
            b. Equipment trust certificates frequently finance railroad cars, trucks, buses, and airplanes, giving formal ownership to the trustee.
                i.   The issuing firm provides a downpayment of 10 to 25 percent; when the loan is paid off, the title transfers to the firm.
                ii. Equipment trust certificates provide good security to the investor.
        2. Forms of unsecured debt and their respective seniority.
            a. Debentures are unsecured debt that are backed by the full faith and credit of the issuing corporation.
                i.   Large firms with excellent credit ratings can issue debentures.

      ii.   Debentures have a general claim on assets in the event of default; the claim is subordinate to those of bank loans, short-term debt, the government, and any mortgage bonds.

      iii.   Debenture restrictions frequently prohibit issuance of new debt containing a senior claim to assets.

      iv.   Subordinated debentures are inferior to other debentures and have claims or assets inferior to that of other debentures.

    b.   Income bonds pay interest only if the firm has sufficient earnings to do so.

E.   Provisions of the bond indenture.

    1.   The call provision allows the issuing firm to call the bond for redemption before its maturity date.

      a.   If interest rates fall sufficiently after a bond is issued, it is to the firm's benefit to call back the bond and reissue debt at a lower coupon rate.

      b.   Firms calling a bond must pay back the par value plus a call premium, which typically declines over time.

      c.   For many new issues, the call period begins five to ten years after the initial offering.

      d.   Callable bonds sometimes contain a nonrefundable provision so that the firm must wait a stated period of time before reissuing the debt at a lower coupon rate. This provision reduces the investors' call risk.

    2.   Extendible bond gives the bondholder the option to extend the maturity of the bond for an additional specified period of time, at the original interest rate.

      a.   Protects the bondholder from a sharp decline in the market rate of interest during the life of the bond.

      b.   Allows the investor to lock in the higher interest rate for a longer period of time.

    3.   Retractable bond allows the bondholder to redeem the bond on a specified date before the bond matures.

      a.   Protects the bondholder from an increase in interest rates after the bond is issued.

      b.   Allows the investor to take advantage of higher market rate of interest after the bond is issued.

      c.   Bonds are redeemed at par.

    4.   Sinking fund provisions require the firm to retire a given number of bonds at par value over a specified period of time.

      a.   If interest rates are high and bond prices are low, the firm buys the bonds in the open market.

      b.   If interest rates are low and bond prices are high, the firm calls the bonds by lottery.

      c.   Investors face call risk when they invest in bonds with sinking funds, but the sinking fund also decreases the risk that remaining bondholders will not be repaid.

      d.   Equipment trust certificates and other serial bonds are packages of bonds maturing in different years; the bonds are refunded at par when they mature.

    5.   Some bonds and preferred stock are convertible into shares of common stock.

      a.   The conversion price per share is stated on the bond or share of preferred stock.

      b.   Virtually all convertible bonds are convertible subordinated debentures.

      c.   The coupon rate on convertibles is typically less than for nonconvertibles.

      d.   The conversion price is set above the current market price of the stock when the bond is issued.

      e.   The firm has the ability to call the bonds at its discretion.

    6.   Other restrictive covenants.

      a.   Limited open-end and closed-end provisions stipulate the amount of additional mortgage debt that can be issued using the firm's existing assets as collateral.

      b.   Provisions also limit the payment of cash dividends, require the firm to maintain its property, limit the sale of assets, and limit sale and leaseback arrangements.

c. For private placements, and for bonds with a speculating grade rating (B and below), the lender often requires the firm to maintain minimum levels of net working capital and net worth.

II.   Financing with long-term debt.
   A.   Pricing and selling the issue.
      1.   The price of a bond is expressed as a percentage of its face value. For example, 99.5 percent of $1,000 is $995.
      2.   The market interest rate at the time the bond is issued determines its issuance price; if the market rate is above the coupon rate, the bonds are issued below par and vice versa.
      3.   Bonds pay interest semiannually and most often are fully registered so that interest and principal are sent directly to the registered owner.
      4.   Bearer bonds, which are becoming rare, have coupons which the owner clips to obtain the interest payments; the certificate itself is evidence of ownership.
      5.   Bonds are quoted net of accrued interest; the bond purchaser pays the purchase price plus interest that has accrued since the last coupon payment date.
      6.   The firm's net receipt from bond sales is reduced by the underwriting costs.
   B.   Bond ratings.
      1.   Bond ratings signify the probability of default on payment of both interest and principal.
      2.   Canadian Bond Rating Service and Dominion Bond Rating Service are two rating agencies; their ratings are described in Table 11.1.
         a.   AAA and AA (A++ and A+) rated bonds are of high quality, while A and BBB (A and B++) bonds are also investment grade; banks and institutions hold these top four grades of bonds.
         b.   BB and B (B+ and B) rated bonds are more speculative in respect to interest and principal payment, while bonds rated below B are either in default or have highly speculative characteristics.
      3.   Factors influencing the bond rating include the debt/equity ratio, the firm's competitive position, the firm's regulatory status, and special provisions of the bond itself.
      4.   Most bonds are rated B or above.
      5.   The higher the bond rating, the lower the risk of default, and the lower the required return.
      6.   Even long-term Government of Canada bonds have a risk premium over short-term Canadian treasury bills. As corporate bond rating decreases, the risk premium over treasury bills increases. The risk premium (yield spread) depends on the following:
         •   Default risk
         •   Interest rate risk, which is composed of price risk and reinvestment rate risk
         •   Call risk
         •   Liquidity risk
         The risk-free rate typically is the yield on government treasury bills with the same maturity as the bond.
      7.   Yield spreads or risk premiums among bond risk groups change over time depending upon the risk aversion of the investors.
      8.   Bond ratings are assigned before bonds are issued and are revised as necessary if changes occur in the perceived ability of the firm to pay interest and principal.
   C.   Term loans.
      1.   Term loans are used as an alternative to bond issues.
         a.   Usually used by small firms.
         b.   Issued by banks.
      2.   Loan amortization.
         a.   Determine the periodic payment needed to pay off loan.
         b.   An amortization schedule shows how much of each payment is principal and how much is interest.

D.   Debt financing and firm value.
1.   Public debt issues may adversely affect the price of common stock, but the magnitude of the effect is much smaller than for the issuance of new common stock.
2.   Bank borrowing may be regarded as good news because of the bank's ability to evaluate and monitor the borrowing firm.
E.   Financing in the 1990s.
1.   Deep discount and zero-coupon bonds.
a.   Deep discount bonds offer both coupon return and price appreciation. The coupon rate, however, is very small.
b.   Zero-coupon bonds are non-coupon-bearing bonds whose entire yield is realized over time in the form of price appreciation.
i.   The value of these bonds increases gradually over the bond's life; both the issuing firm and investor must impute and report interest for tax purposes each year.
ii.   Pension funds and other tax-exempt or lightly taxed institutions are the main investors in deep discount or zero-coupon bonds since they avoid the taxation on the implied interest income resulting from value appreciation.
iii.   Zero-coupon bonds are much more sensitive to changes in interest rates than are normal interest-bearing bonds. Zero-coupon bonds are exposed to only price risk and have no reinvestment rate risk.
2.   Junk bonds are those rated BB (B+) and below. Most are issued by firms with low credit ratings. While this is an established form of financing in the U.S., there is no established junk bond market in Canada.
3.   Variable rate bonds are bonds whose interest rate is tied to some short-term rate, such as the prime interest rate.
4.   Securitization takes place when assets are used as collateral for securities.

III.   Managing long-term debt.
A.   In bond refunding, a firm calls all of its old bonds at a fixed price and reissues new lower-coupon bonds to take advantage of lower interest rates. (Appendix 11A).
B.   Alternatives to bond refunding.
1.   The firm issues a public tender offer in an attempt to buy back outstanding bonds.
2.   The firm arranges a private market purchase from one or several institutional investors.
3.   Simultaneous tender and call—the firm makes a tender offer to buy back bonds at a slight premium while at the same time threatens to call the bonds through a "cash call" where the funds used to retire the bonds come from selling equity, selling assets, or internally generated funds, not from selling debt at a lower interest rate.
C.   Interest rate swaps: Separate interest payments and principal payments. Convert fixed-rate payments to floating-rate payments (and vice versa) by swapping interest payments with another party.
1.   Plain vanilla swap involves the same currency.
2.   For swap to be effective, one party must have a comparative advantage in the fixed-rate market but desires floating-rate financing, while the other party has a comparative advantage in the floating-rate market but desires a fixed-rate financing.
3.   Swap protects both parties from interest rate risk.

IV.   Pension plan liability.
A.   Most Canadian firms have pension plans that commit them to provide retirement benefits to employees. These obligations range from 1/4 to 3/4 of the firm's total liabilities.
B.   Employees covered by a pension plan have a claim against the firm's assets that are similar to bondholder claims.
C.   Types of pension plans.
1.   A defined benefit pension plan specifies either the level of benefits or the method of calculating them. Obligations can only be estimated since they are generally based on the level of future salaries.

2.   A defined contribution pension plan specifies the fixed contribution made to the pension fund on behalf of the employee.

    a.   The employee may also contribute to the fund.

    b.   Retirement income is based on contributions to the individual's account and investment returns earned.

D.   Other features of pension plans.

1.   Both corporate and personal contributions to pension funds are tax-deductible. Taxes are paid when an individual receives retirement benefits.

2.   Individuals are said to be vested if they have worked for a sufficient time to be qualified for pensions benefits.

3.   More and more pension plans are portable and can be transferred to a new employer's plan or a registered retirement savings plan (RRSP) when an employee changes jobs.

4.   There is increasing pressure from unions and employee associations to index benefits to inflation.

E.   Funding.

1.   The liabilities of a pension fund include payments to those currently retired and expected payments to current employees.

2.   The value of the assets of a pension fund include the market value of its portfolio plus the present value of expected contributions.

3.   To value a pension fund, many assumptions must be made. A change in any assumption can have a major effect on estimated value.

F.   Reporting requirements.

1.   If the value of assets is equal to the value of liabilities, the pension plan is fully funded. If assets exceed liabilities, the plan is overfunded.

2.   If a plan is underfunded, the unfunded liability must be funded within 15 years.

V.   Preferred stock.

A.   Characteristics of preferred stock.

1.   Preferred stock is extensively used by banks and public utility firms that want to reduce their debt/equity ratio; it is used to a lesser extent by other firms.

2.   Preferred stock generally has a par value, typically $25, $50, or $100, and is issued at a price close to this value.

3.   The market price on preferred stock fluctuates with market yields; as the market yields go up, the price goes down.

4.   If the firm does not have the money to pay cash dividends on preferred stock, it can skip the payment.

    a.   Unpaid dividends on preferred stock are called arrearages.

    b.   Most preferred stocks have cumulative cash dividends; all dividends in arrears must be paid before the common shareholders can receive cash dividends.

5.   Preferred stock has no fixed maturity date, but many recent issues make a provision for periodic repayment via a sinking fund.

6.   Virtually all preferred stock is callable at the option of the issuing firm.

7.   The claims of the preferred shareholder are junior to the claim of creditors, but senior to those of common shareholders.

8.   The use of preferred stock may result in restrictions on the firm's issuance of more senior securities, payment of cash dividends to common shareholders, and maintenance of a minimum level of common equity.

9.   Some preferred stock provides voting rights, especially if cash dividends are in arrearage.

B.   Advantages to the firm using preferred stock.

1.   Preferred stock dividends are generally fixed, so preferred stock provides financial leverage.

2.   Nonpayment of cash dividends to preferred shareholders does not throw the firm into default.

3.   Control of the firm generally remains in the hands of the common shareholders.

    C.   Adjustable rate preferred stock is a new security tying the dividend rate on the preferred stock to the bank prime rates, with upper and lower limits on the rates.

VI.   Long-term financing and financial distress.

    A.   Because of limited liability, shareholders are more inclined to bear risk than bondholders; if the firm is profitable, shareholders pay off bondholders and claim the rest. If the firm fails, shareholders walk away and bondholders may receive something.

    B.   Financial distress occurs when the firm has insufficient cash to meet current financial obligations.

        1.   Out-of-court options.

            a.   In an extension, creditors agree to accept delayed payments from the firm.

            b.   In a composition, creditors receive a pro rata settlement on their claims.

            c.   In an assignment, the firm voluntarily liquidates and pays off its creditors with the proceeds.

        2.   In-court options are covered in the Bankruptcy and Insolvency Act of 1992.

            a.   In a liquidation, the firm's assets are sold under the direction of the courts and the creditors are paid off with the proceeds on the basis of priority.

            b.   In a reorganization, the firm is restructured in terms of its businesses, creditors, and ownership, and is put back on its feet.

VII.   Appendix 11A: Refunding a bond or preferred stock issue.

    A.   Refunding is the issuance of new securities to replace an existing bond or preferred stock issue.

        1.   A firm occasionally calls and refunds an issue to get rid of overly restrictive provisions.

        2.   More often, a firm calls and refunds an issue because interest rates have fallen and the firm wants to issue securities at a lower yield.

    B.   Approach a refunding decision like a capital budgeting decision by calculating the net present value of the proposed refunding.

        1.   Find the after-tax initial outlay (ΔCF_0) associated with the refunding.

            a.   The call price on old bonds plus additional interest during the overlap period is an outflow.

            b.   The net proceeds from a new issue are an inflow, as are tax savings from tax-deductible expenses.

        2.   Find the incremental after-tax cash flows (ΔCF_t) resulting from the refunding.

            a.   The interest on the old bonds less the tax savings on the old bond's tax-deductible expenses is the cash outflow on the old bonds.

            b.   The interest on the new bonds less the tax savings on the new bond's tax-deductible expenses is the cash outflow on the new bonds.

            c.   The annual cash savings from the refunding (ΔCF_t) equals the cash outflow on the old bond less the cash outflow on the new bond.

        3.   Find the after-tax cost, k_i, of the new bond issue; multiply the coupon rate by $(1 - T)$.

        4.   Use the following formula to calculate the NPV:

$$NPV = \sum_{t=1}^{n} \frac{\Delta CF_t}{(1 + k_i)^t} - \Delta CF_0$$

        5.   Refund if the NPV is positive.

    C.   Preferred stock refinancing follows these same general steps; however, some differences, as noted in the text, exist.

Formulas

Accrued Interest on a Bond

    Accrued interest payments = (coupon percent) ($1,000) (number of days/365)

152   Chapter 11

Term Loan Amortization
$$PMT = \frac{PV_0}{PVA_{k,n}}$$

Price of a Zero-Coupon Bond
$$B_{0(\text{zero coupon})} = \text{par}\,(PV_{k,n})$$

Appendix 11A: Notation
ΔCF_t = incremental after-tax cash flows from refunding
k_i = after-tax cost of the new bond issue
ΔCF_0 = after-tax initial outlay for the refunding

NPV of proposed refunding
$$NPV = \sum_{t=1}^{n} \frac{\Delta CF_t}{(1 + k_i)^t} - \Delta CF_0$$

What to Look For

Chapter 11 continues our examination of the firm's sources of long-term capital. In this chapter you learn about long-term debt and preferred stock, which are fixed-income securities. As you will notice, long-term debt or bonds are the main feature of the chapter, since bonds are more widely issued and occur in more varied forms than preferred stock.

The Various Forms of Corporate Bonds
Corporate bonds vary in their collateral, their seniority, their various restrictions, their riskiness, and their return.

Seniority of debt
If a college grants tuition aid on a seniority basis, the students who have been with the college the longest or who are at the higher levels receive tuition grants first. If the tuition grant money runs out before all applicants receive aid, so be it. Similarly, a seniority system is established setting out the order in which claims are paid if the firm liquidates its assets. A firm that does not make its interest payments is in default. It must pay the interest on debt, restructure its debt to allow for repayment, or go into liquidation proceedings. If the firm must liquidate its holdings, the provisions of each security's claims show its seniority. According to the Bankruptcy and Insolvency Act, creditors, bondholders, and preferred stockholders have a prior claim (on a relative basis) on assets before common stockholders. As we discuss the collateral status of various bond issues, we will discuss their respective seniority.

Collateral of bonds and their respective seniority
Secured bonds backed by mortgages to specific assets of the firm are called first mortgage bonds and second mortgage bonds. First mortgage bonds have a prior claim to assets in the event of a default, while second mortgage bonds have a subordinate claim. Open-end provisions allow the firm to pledge the same asset for additional debt. Closed-end provisions prohibit this additional pledging.

Equipment trust certificates give the trustee formal ownership to the specific assets being financed. Since the trustee holds the title, these securities provide excellent collateral for their purchasers.

Unsecured bonds are debentures, subordinated debentures, or income bonds. These are backed by the full faith and credit of the issuing corporation. Debentures are often issued by firms with excellent credit ratings. The claims of debentures come after those of bank loans, short-term debt, the government, and any mortgage bonds. Subordinated debentures have even more junior claims to assets. Income bonds require interest to be paid only if it is earned. For the firm, this arrangement is somewhat similar to preferred stock, except that the interest is a tax-deductible expense, whereas cash dividend payments are not tax-deductible.

Restrictions on issuing debt

Restrictions on issuing debt help reduce the riskiness of the debt issue for the investor. Therefore, the more risky the firm or the characteristics of the debt issue, the more restrictive will be the covenants. For example, privately placed issues may be more risky than public issues. The lender often requires the borrowing firm to maintain a minimum level of net working capital and a minimum net worth. These restrictions help ensure that the lender will receive interest payments and that the firm will be able to repay the principal.

Restrictive bond covenants also include restrictions on the payment of cash dividends, prohibitions against issuing additional senior debt, and limitations on the sale of the firm's assets. Again, these restrictions help reduce the investor's risk of not receiving payment of interest and principal. These restrictions can, and sometimes do, impede the borrowing firm's ability to operate. In such cases, the borrowing firm attempts to modify the indenture or call the issue.

Bond risk and bond ratings

We introduced issue-specific and default risk in Chapter 2. Issue-specific risk concerns the type of bond and the indenture. A bond with good collateral, like a sinking fund, and reasonably good covenants has less issue-specific risk than a subordinated debenture with no sinking fund or restrictive covenants. Call provisions introduce call risk into the debt issue; the nonrefundable provision included in a bond's indenture will help to minimize call risk. Sinking funds introduce call risk into the debt issue, but also increase the probability that the issue will eventually be retired. Extendible and retractable features of bonds offer investors protection from decreases and increases in market interest rates.

Firms that have stable or growing positive cash flow and a history of meeting their obligations in a timely fashion have low default risk. Firms that often have cash flow deficits and pay creditors late or default on their obligations have relatively high default risk.

Investors require a lower return from less risky firms and bond issues. It is in the firm's best interest, then, to maintain a good credit rating in order to minimize its financing costs. Typically, debt issues require a bond rating prior to their issuance. Two major rating agencies are the Canadian Bond Rating Service and the Dominion Bond Rating Service. The text discusses their ratings. Firms, especially small firms, use term loans as an alternative to issuing bonds.

The return on bonds

The bond's rating goes hand in hand with its required rate of return. The riskier the bond, the higher its required yield. Although the coupon on a bond stays fixed over the bond's life (except for variable rate bonds), the required yield changes over time as the level of inflation, risk, and investors' attitudes change. With increases in expected inflation, the required rate of return on bonds of all quality ratings increases. In addition, the yield difference or risk premium between bonds of different qualities narrows or widens over time. We call this yield difference the yield spread. The more risk averse investors become, the wider the yield spread, since investors require a greater reward for taking on additional risk. Conversely, as investors become less risk averse, the yield spread narrows.

Deep discount bonds and zero-coupon bonds have a yield that relies on a low purchase or issuance price. These bonds provide some or all of their return in the form of bond value appreciation. Deep discount bonds have a low coupon rate but provide a higher yield through a deep discount issuance price. Zero-coupon bonds carry no coupon rate and are deeply discounted to provide a large value appreciation yield over the life of the bond.

Pension plan liabilities

Most Canadian firms offer pension plans that commit the firm to making payments to employees after retirement. In many ways, pension plans are similar to long-term debt in that someone (in this case employees) have a prior claim on the firm's assets. Proper liability management requires consideration of all the firm's liabilities, including pension plans.

There are two forms of pension plans. In a defined benefits plan, either the retirement benefits or the means of calculating them are specified. For example, your pension plan may guarantee retirement benefits of 70 percent of your average salary over your last five years of employment. In a defined contribution plan, a specified percentage of your salary is contributed each pay period. Your retirement benefit will depend on how much has been contributed and how well the pension fund has performed.

A defined benefits plan is the most common of the two. Firms are required to calculate the value of the fund's assets and liabilities, and if liabilities exceed assets, the firm must make up the difference, known as the unfunded liability, within 15 years. The firm is responsible for this unfunded liability even if it ceases operations.

Preferred Stock

Preferred stock is most frequently employed by banks and public utilities that must temper their debt/equity ratios. Preferred stock, except for variable rate issues, provides a fixed return to investors. Like debt, the required return on preferred stock varies as the structure of interest rates changes. As the required yield falls, the market price of outstanding preferred stock rises. Firms need not pay cash dividends on preferred stock unless they have sufficient cash flows. Dividends in arrears typically must be paid before cash dividends on common stock can be paid. Finally, in the case of default, the preferred shareholder has a claim junior to creditors but senior to common shareholders.

Long-Term Financing and Financial Distress

A firm in financial distress faces either out-of-court or in-court settlement of its financial obligations. Extensions, compositions, and assignments are methods by which creditors and the firm can agree out of court to handle the firm's financial obligations. In-court options take the form of reorganization or liquidation. With voluntary bankruptcy, the firm itself sees that liquidation is inevitable, files for bankruptcy, and obtains protection from creditors.

In an involuntary bankruptcy, one or more creditors files a petition for a receiving order against a debtor. The court then appoints a licensed trustee to oversee the liquidation and the proceeds from the liquidation are paid to creditors according to a priority schedule.

An alternative to liquidation is reorganization, which is instituted by the insolvent firm. The courts allow for reorganization so long as the plan is fair, equitable, and feasible. If the creditors are at least as well off as under liquidation, the firm should be reconstituted.

In any reorganization or involuntary liquidation, the creditors' viewpoint is the guide, not that of the stockholders. So the best way to maximize shareholder value is to avoid financial distress through good financial planning and management.

Appendix 11A: Refunding a Bond or Preferred Stock Issue

In a refunding, the firm issues new bonds or preferred stock to replace an existing issue. Although refunding can be motivated by a desire to eliminate restrictive covenants, it is primarily done to lower the cost of financing to the issuing firm. If, for instance, the coupon rate on new debt is substantially less than the rate on existing debt, it may be to the firm's benefit to refund the issue.

The decision to refund is simply a time value of money problem and is approached in the same manner as a replacement capital budgeting decision. If the present value of the after-tax savings is greater than the cost of refunding, it is in the shareholders' best interest to refund the issue.

Completion Questions

11.1   _____ securities obligate the firm to pay a fixed annual return for financing.

11.2   In contrast to the tax treatment of cash dividends on common stock and preferred stock, the interest on debt is a _____ expense for the firm.

11.3   The _____ is the contract between the firm and the lender. It spells out the interest payment schedule, the term of the bond, and the maturity value. In addition, it may include _____ _____ to help protect the bond investors.

11.4   _____ are bonds which have primary claim on specific assets in the event of a default by the firm.

11.5   _____ are backed by the full faith and credit of the issuing corporation, and have no specific assets pledged as collateral.

11.6   The right to redeem a bond before it matures is called a _____ . In redeeming the bond early, the firm must pay an amount _____ the par value of the bond. This extra amount, the _____ , declines over time.

11.7   A firm's indenture might contain a _____ provision requiring the firm to retire a given number of bonds over a specified time period.

11.8   If a firm is retiring debt for its sinking fund, it will buy the debt _____ _____ if the interest rates are high and the bond price is low. Otherwise, the firm will retire the same issue at par value using a _____ .

11.9   The restrictive covenants for private placements may be _____ than those for public issues, since the lending institution is the sole purchaser of the issue and wants to maximize the value of its claim.

11.10   The greatest percentage of large bond issues are underwritten and are _____ , recording the ownership of the bond.

11.11   Purchasers of bonds pay the price of the bond plus any _____ . The issuer of a bond receives less than $1,000 per bond due to the _____ involved.

11.12   _____ reflect the probability of payment of both interest and principal. The higher the rating, the _____ the required return on the bond.

11.13   A difference in required yield exists between bonds of different quality ratings, AAA and AA, for example. This difference is called the _____ . As investors become more risk averse, this difference _____ , since investors want to be rewarded for taking on additional risk.

11.14   _____ -specific conditions can result in the lowering of a bond's rating. If a firm's executives do not improve the quality rating of the firm's debt, the next long-term financing may be _____ costly. In addition, the increased riskiness of the firm's debt may increase the firm's stock _____ , resulting in a reduced market value of the stock.

11.15   Bonds which are issued at a low price and which carry no coupon are called _____ bonds.

11.16   Unpaid cash dividends on preferred stocks are called _____ . With _____ preferred stock, these unpaid dividends must be paid before common stockholders can receive _____ .

11.17   _____ is a situation in which the firm cannot meet its current obligations with available cash sources.

11.18   In a _____ pension plan, either retirement benefits or the means to calculate them, is specified.

11.19   The difference between the value of pension fund assets and liabilites is called the _____ . If the pension fund is underfunded, the firm has _____ years to fully fund the plan.

Problems

11.1   Halifax Public Power, Ltd. has an abbreviated balance sheet as follows (in millions):

Current assets	$15	Current liabilities	$ 6
Net long-term assets	70	Long-term debt (12% coupon)	24
Total assets	$85	Stockholders' equity	55
		Total liabilities and stockholders' equity	$85

The firm has earnings after taxes (EAT) of $7 million and is subject to a marginal corporate tax rate of 30 percent. The company wishes to issue new long-term debt at 8 percent to increase its base of net fixed assets. The present debt, however, carries several restrictive covenants as follows:

a.   Interest coverage (EBIT/I) must be at least 4.

b.   The ratio of net long-term assets to long-term debt must be at least 2.

c.   The total debt to equity ratio must remain below 0.80.
How much additional debt can the firm issue? (Assume there are no interest costs associated with current liabilities.)

11.2   Halburton Home Construction has outstanding a 15 percent bond issue with 8 years left until maturity. The bonds have a face value of $1,000, pay interest annually, and have a provision that will allow them to be called with a premium of $50 per bond. The company is considering two options.

Option A: Call the bonds and replace them with new 13 percent coupon bonds also with 8 years to maturity. The firm will incur no transactions costs. These bonds will sell at par.

Option B: Repurchase present bonds in the open market and replace them with the above new issue. The purchase in the open market results in a transaction cost of 1 percent of the market price.

Should the firm repurchase or call the bonds?

11.3   Abecrombie Limited, a wholesale importer, is in the process of issuing $6,000,000 of 12 percent coupon debt with a maturity of 5 years. A sinking fund must be established to retire 60 percent of the issue prior to maturity. Assuming the bonds are retired at par and the tax rate is 35 percent, how large must the annual sinking fund payments be if the firm wishes to retire the bonds in equal installments over 4 years starting one year from now? What will be the annual after-tax cash outflow for each of the 5 years?

11.4   Arvin Custom Clothiers has just borrowed $150,000. The loan has an annual interest rate of 9 percent and requires five equal payments with the first payment made one year from today. Calculate the annual loan payment and develop a loan amortization schedule for Arvin.

11.5   Blackstone Enterprises wishes to raise $12.4 million through the issuance of new preferred stock. The stock will have a par value of $50 per share and a 9.3 percent cash dividend. The existing preferred stock, which has a dividend of $3.00 per share, sells for $20 per share. Assuming that the required return on the new preferred stock is the same as that on the old, how many shares of preferred stock will have to be issued? (Ignore flotation costs.)

11.6   Eskimo Outfitters has a defined benefits pension plan available to its employees. The market value of the fund's assets is $16 million, and the value of expected future contributions is $31 million. The fund has estimated the value of payments to current retirees at $18 million and the value of future payments to be $37 million. What is the fund's unfunded liability?

11A.1   Lacey Carpet Manufacturers is considering the refunding of its present $50,000,000 issue of oustanding bonds. The bonds, which were issued 5 years ago with a coupon rate of 15 percent, have a remaining term to maturity of 15 years but can be called at face value with a premium of 1 year's interest. The flotation costs of the original issue were $600,000. These costs were amortized over five years. The bonds will be replaced with $50,000,000 of 13.5 percent coupon rate bonds, which will be issued at par. The flotation costs of these new bonds, which will mature in 15 years, are expected to be $960,000. To ensure that funds will be available when needed, there will be a one month overlap, and net proceeds from the new issue will be invested at 8 percent. Lacey's tax rate is 30 percent. Should the firm refund its existing debt?

Answers to Completion Questions

11.1   Fixed income
11.2   tax-deductible
11.3   indenture; restrictive provisions
11.4   First mortgage bonds
11.5   Debentures
11.6   call provision; greater than; call premium

11.7   sinking fund

11.8   on the open market; lottery

11.9   more onerous (or burdensome)

11.10   fully registered

11.11   accrued interest; underwriting costs

11.12   Bond ratings; lower

11.13   yield spread; widens

11.14   Firm; more; beta

11.15   zero-coupon

11.16   arrearages; cumulative; cash dividends

11.17   Financial distress

11.18   defined benefits

11.19   unfunded liability; 15

Solutions to Problems

11.1   **Step 1.**   Starting with covenant A, find the maximum amount of debt the firm can issue and have an interest coverage ratio of at least 4.

Since EAT = EBT(1 − T)

$$EBT = \frac{EAT}{1 - T} = \frac{\$7,000,000}{1 - 0.30} = \$10,000,000$$

Step 2.   EBIT = EBT + I

= \$10,000,000 + \$24,000,000 (0.12) = \$12,880,000

Step 3.   If times interest earned must be greater than or equal to 4,

EBIT/I ≥ 4, so I must be less than or equal to EBIT/4

$$I \leq \frac{EBIT}{4} \leq \frac{12.88}{4} \leq \$3.22 \text{ million}$$

The firm can increase its interest expense by \$0.34 million (\$3.22 million − \$2.88 million) which means it can issue (\$0.34/0.08) = \$4.25 million of additional debt without violating covenant A.

Step 4.   Covenant B: $\dfrac{\text{net long-term assets}}{\text{long-term debt}} = \dfrac{70}{24} = 2.91667$

since any new debt (X) will be used to purchase net long-term assets, according to covenant B.

$$\frac{70 + W}{24 + W} \leq 2 \qquad\qquad 70 + W = 2(24 + W)$$

$$70 + W = 48 + 2W$$

$$W = \$22 \text{ million}$$

The firm could issue \$22 million in debt and not violate covenant B.

Step 5.   Covenant C: $\dfrac{\text{total debt}}{\text{total equity}} = \dfrac{30}{55} = 0.54545$

Since $\dfrac{\text{total debt}}{\text{total equity}} \leq 0.80$, $\dfrac{\text{total debt}}{55} \leq 0.80$

Total debt ≤ 44

The firm could issue up to (44 − 30) = \$14 million in new debt without violating covenant C.

The binding covenant is A; the firm can issue only \$4.25 million in new debt.

11.2   Step 1.   Option A

The cost per bond of recalling = face value + premium

$$= \$1,000 + \$50 = \$1,050 \text{ per bond}$$

Step 2.   Option B

To figure out the cost of repurchasing the bonds, we need to know the market price. Since the 13 percent coupon bonds will sell at par, the market rate of interest is 13 percent.

$$B_0 = \$150 \ (PVA_{13\%,8yr}) + \$1,000 \ (PV_{13\%,8yr})$$

$$B_0 = \$150 \ (4.799) + \$1,000 \ (0.376) = \$719.85 + \$376$$

$$= \$1,095.85$$

Step 3.   The transactions cost would be ($1,095.85)(0.01) = $10.96. The total cost of repurchasing the bond = $1,095.85 + $10.96 = $1,106.81. It is more expensive to repurchase than to call the bonds.

11.3   Step 1.   The firm needs to retire (0.60)($6,000,000) = $3,600,000 prior to maturity. Since the bonds mature in 5 years, the retirement must take place in only 4 years. So, Abecrombie should retire $3,600,000/4 = $900,000 per year.

Step 2.   The after-tax cash outflows:

Year	Bonds Outstanding	Interest (12%)	After-Tax Interest Expense [Interest $(1 - 0.35)$]	Sinking Fund Payment	=	Total
1	$6,000,000	$720,000	$468,000	$ 900,000		$1,368,000
2	5,100,000	612,000	397,800	900,000		1,297,800
3	4,200,000	504,000	327,600	900,000		1,227,600
4	3,300,000	396,000	257,400	900,000		1,157,400
5	2,400,000	288,000	187,200	2,400,000		2,587,200

11.4   Step 1.

$$PMT = \frac{\$150,000}{PVA_{9\%,5yr}} = \frac{\$150,000}{3.890} = \$38,560.41$$

Step 2.   Amortization Schedule

Year	Beginning Balance	+	Interest[a]	−	Payment[b]	=	Remaining Balance	Principal[c] Repayment
1	$150,000.00		$13,500.00		$38,560.41		$124,939.59	$ 25,060.41
2	124,939.59		11,244.56		38,560.41		97,623.74	27,315.85
3	97,623.74		8,786.14		38,560.41		67,849.47	29,774.27
4	67,849.47		6,106.45		38,560.41		35,395.51	32,453.96
5	35,395.51		3,185.60		38,581.11[d]		–0–	35,395.51
								$150,000.00

[a]Interest = 0.15 × balance

[b]Payment is calculated above

[c]Principal repayment = payment − interest

= beginning balance − remaining balance

[d]Due to rounding, the last payment must be different in order to completely pay off the loan: Last payment = beginning balance for year 5 + interest for year 5.

11.5   Step 1.   The yield on existing preferred is $3.00/$20 = 0.15 or 15%

Step 2.   The price of the new preferred $= D_{ps}/k_p$

Dividend = $50(0.093) = $4.65

Price   = $4.65/0.15 = $31 per share

Step 3.   Number of shares $= \dfrac{\text{total proceeds}}{\text{price per share}} = \dfrac{\$12,400,000}{\$31} = 400,000$ shares

11.6   Step 1.   Value of assets = market value of assets + value of expected future contributions

= $16 million + $31 million = $47 million

Step 2.   Value of liabilities = value of payments to present retirees + value of future payments

= $18 million + $37 million = $55 million

Step 3.   Unfunded liability = value of liabilities - value of assets

= $55 million - $47 million

= $8 million

The pension plan is underfunded by $8 million.

11.A1   Step 1.   Calculate the initial outlay:

Before taxes

Face value of existing debt	$50,000,000
Call premium (15% of $50,000,000)	7,500,000
Additional interest ($50,000,000 $\times$ 0.15 $\times$ 1/12)	625,000
Less: Net proceeds of new issue ($50,000,000 – $960,000)	-49,040,000
Less: Interest earned on net proceeds	
($49,040,000 $\times$ 0.08 $\times$ 1/12)	326,933
	8,758,067

Tax-deductible expenses

Unamortized flotation cost on old bond	0
Additional interest during overlap period	625,000
Present value of new issue flotation costs amortization	667,150
Less: Interest earned on net proceeds	326,933
Total tax-deductible expenses	$ 965,217
Tax savings ($965,217 $\times$ 0.30)	$ 289,565

Step 2.   Initial investment:

Before-tax outlay	$ 8,758,067
Less: Tax savings	289,565
Initial outlay, ΔCF_0	$ 8,468,502

Step 3.   Incremental savings:

Interest on old bonds (0.15 $\times$ $50,000,000)	$ 7,500,000
Tax savings ($7,500,000 $\times$ 0.30)	$ 2,250,000
After-tax cash outflow on old bond per year	$ 5,250,000
Interest on new bonds (0.135 $\times$ $50,000,000)	$ 6,750,000
Tax savings ($6,750,000 $\times$ 0.30)	$2,025,000
After-tax cash outflow on new bond per year	$ 4,725,000

Step 4. $\Delta CF_t = \$5,250,000 - \$4,725,000 = \$525,000$

Step 5.   Discount rate = 13.5% (1 − 0.30) = 9.45%, so
$PVA_{9.5\%,15yr}$ = 7.8509

$NPV = \Delta CF_t(PVA_{9.5\%,15yr}) - \Delta CF_0$

= \$525,000(7.8509) − \$8,468,502

= \$4,121,722.50 − \$8,468,502 = −\$4,346,779.50

Since the NPV is negative, the firm should not refund the bonds.

Chapter 12
Taxes and Capital Structure

How This Chapter Relates to the Rest of the Text

Chapters 10 and 11 examined the procedures for issuing bonds and common stock and Chapter 6 discussed how the cost of each long-term source of funds affects the firm's cost of capital. In this chapter, we discuss the firm's capital structure and how debt affects the firm's value. The risk (Chapter 5) of a firm's common stock is related to how much debt financing is used. The business risk of the firm is primarily a function of the firm's past capital budgeting decisions (Chapters 7–9).

Topical Outline

I. Introduction.
    A.   Prior to this chapter, we assumed the firm's capital structure was given.
    B.   The issue in capital structure is: Does how we slice the pie affect its size? That is, does the value of the firm change as we change its financing proportions? The answers are complex and controversial.
    C.   Once the capital structure is determined, the opportunity cost of capital can be estimated, and capital budgeting decisions can be made.

II. Risk and capital structure.
    A.   Long-term sources of funds make up the firm's capital structure.
        1.   Long-term sources include common stock, preferred stock, debt, leases, and internally generated funds.
        2.   The chapter looks at what proportion measured by the market value of each of these sources the firm should use.
    B.   Business risk.
        1.   Business risk is the relative dispersion or variability in the firm's expected EBIT.
        2.   The coefficient of variation measures the relative variability of the firm's EBIT.
        3.   Business risk is primarily caused by the nature of the firm's operations.
            a.   The more sensitive the firm's sales are to general economic fluctuations, the higher the business risk.
            b.   The smaller the firm and its share of the market, the higher the business risk.
            c.   The higher the proportion of fixed versus variable operating costs, the higher the operating leverage and the greater the business risk.
            d.   The more uncertain the input prices for the firm's products, the greater the business risk.
            e.   The greater the firm's ability to adjust output prices, the lower the business risk.
        4.   Business risk is a direct function of the firm's accumulated investment (capital budgeting) decisions.
            a.   Capital budgeting decisions affect the nature of the firm's business as well as the composition of its assets.
            b.   Cyclical industries, such as steel, have greater business risk than less cyclical industries, such as the grocery industry.
        5.   Business risk has a major impact on how much financial risk a firm is able to undertake.
    C.   Financial risk.
        1.   Financial risk is a result of the firm's long-term financing decisions.
        2.   Financial risk refers to
            a.   The increased variability of earnings available to the firm's common stockholders due to its debt obligations.
            b.   The increased probability of financial distress borne by the firm's stockholders if financial leverage is employed.
        3.   The primary sources of financial leverage are debt, leases, sinking fund, and preferred stock. Chapter 12 focuses only on debt.

4. The coefficient of variation of earnings per share (EPS) is higher when more debt is employed, signifying an increase in relative variability and an increase in financial risk.

D. Impact on the value of the firm is more important than impact on EPS.

III. The development of capital structure theory.

A. Assumptions.

1. Only two types of securities are used—long-term debt and common stock.

2. The firm is not expected to grow, so we can value common stock with the no-growth dividend model. Earnings are expected to stay at the same level forever.

3. All earnings are assumed to be paid out in cash dividends, so the market price can be written $P_0 = EPS/k$, while the total market value of the firm, S, can be calculated by $S = E/k_s$ since the present value of growth opportunities is zero.

4. No taxes, no transactions costs, and perfect markets. This means no risk of default.

B. The no-tax case: If the firm pays no corporate taxes, what effect does debt financing have on the value of the firm?

1. For example, an all-equity firm chooses between issuing more common stock or new debt to pay for a capital investment.

a. If common stock is used, the firm will still be all-equity financed, so its total market value will be the present value of the future perpetual dividend stream: $V = S = D/k_s$.

b. If the firm uses debt rather than common stock, the apparent value of the firm seems higher than if the firm uses all equity, but that appears so because the change in risk has not been taken into account. The cost of equity, k_s, increases.

2. Modigliani and Miller (MM) suggest that the value of the firm actually does not change when using debt under a no-tax assumption.

a. MM assumptions.

i. Perfect capital markets.

ii. All debt is risk-free.

iii. All firms can be grouped into risk classes based on variance in EBIT.

iv. Homogeneous expectations.

b. Proposition I: The market value of any firm is independent of its capital structure and is found by capitalizing EBIT at the appropriate discount rate for an all-equity firm, k_s^U

c. Proposition II: The cost of equity for a levered firm, k_s^L, is equal to k_s^U plus a risk premium:

$$k_s^L = k_s^U + (k_s^U - k_b)\frac{B}{S_L}$$

d. Propositions I and II hold because individuals can replicate (or undo) anything the firm does; there is no advantage in having the corporation issue debt.

e. See Figure 12.3 for Modigliani and Miller's position; as financial leverage increases, the value of the firm and the opportunity cost of capital remain constant.

3. The MM no-tax model tells us where to look to determine whether capital structure choices affect firm value. It tells us that we need to look at taxes, transactions costs, and the capital investment policies of the firm.

C. The MM model with corporate taxes. Assume T = 30 percent.

1. Since the common stock price results from capitalizing the expected income by the required rate of return, the value of the all-equity firm would be lower since the earnings would decline by 30 percent due to taxes.

2. If the firm funds a capital project with debt, any additional earnings are split among the original number of shares. The interest payments on debt are tax-deductible.

a. The firm's common stock market price will increase due to the addition of debt.

   b.   In spite of the increase in risk due to debt usage, the presence of corporate taxes subsidizes the use of debt, increasing the value of the firm (S + B) by the amount B × T, and decreasing the firm's opportunity cost of capital.

   3.   Proposition I (adjusted for taxes): $V_L = V_U + TB$

   4.   Proposition II (adjusted for taxes):

   $$k_s^L = k_s^U + (k_s^U - k_b)(1 - T)\frac{B}{S}$$

D.   Personal taxes and the value of the firm.

   1.   While corporations have the benefit of deducting interest payments for tax purposes, investors pay taxes on interest earned.

       a.   With personal taxes,

       $$V_L = V_U + \left[1 - \frac{(1 - T)(1 - T_{ps})}{(1 - T_{pb})} \right] B$$

       b.   There is no optimal capital structure for individual firms.

       c.   There may be an equilibrium optimal amount of aggregate debt for the entire economy.

E.   Other tax impacts

   1.   Modigliani and Miller's, and Miller's theories ignore nondebt tax shields such as depreciation. DeAngelo and Masulis show that the tradeoff between interest tax shields and nondebt tax shields leads to an optimal capital structure that is less than 100 percent debt.

   2.   Since individual investors face different marginal tax rates, bondholder clienteles, based on different personal marginal tax rates, will have an impact on the level of debt used to maximize firm value.

   3.   Due to different maturity structures of corporate debt, firms can have a variety of different mixes of capital structures and debt maturities that are consistent with maximizing firm value.

IV.   Setting the debt/equity ratio.

A.   EPS-EBIT analysis.

   1.   Different financing decisions will have differing impacts on EPS; the effects of several alternatives can be found by EPS-EBIT analysis.

       a.   By finding EBIT*, one finds the EBIT at which one would be indifferent between the two financing alternatives.

       b.   This known crossover (or indifferent) EBIT is found by solving the following equation for EBIT*:

       $$\frac{(EBIT^* - I_1)(1 - T) - D_{ps1}}{N_1} = \frac{(EBIT^* - I_2)(1 - T) - D_{ps2}}{N_2}$$

       c.   One should also consider the effects of debt usage on the capitalization rate; as risk increases, will the required rate of return increase and the common stock market price decrease?

B.   Other tools to help select the target capital structure.

   1.   Coverage ratios help ascertain whether the firm can cover additional interest payments that result from the use of debt.

   2.   Lender requirements may impose certain performance standards that must be met before assets can be sold, cash dividends can be paid, and so on.

   3.   Some firms tie their capital structure decision to the bond rating they want to maintain.

   4.   A cash-flow analysis of how the firm might fare in a severe recession will indicate the firm's ability to take on debt.

V.   Guidelines for setting debt/equity ratios.

A.   Firms with high amounts of business risk use less debt. Business risk is related to the types of assets employed.

B.   Although interest expenses from debt reduce taxes, firms need to consider their future expected tax liabilities as well. If it is unlikely that the firm can take advantage of tax shields in the future, use less debt.

C.   Firms need to maintain some financial slack in order to take advantage of new positive NPV projects.

VI.   Appendix 12A: Operating, financial, and total leverage.

A.   Operating leverage.

1.   Operating leverage arises if the firm experiences fixed operating costs for such things as labour, rent, and the like; variable operating expenses do not provide operating leverage.

2.   Operating leverage is the responsiveness of the firm's earnings before interest and taxes (EBIT) to fluctuations in sales.

3.   The greater the leverage, the greater the responsiveness of EBIT to a given change in sales:

$$\text{Degree of operating leverage (DOL) from base sales level} = \text{DOL} = \frac{\text{percentage change in EBIT}}{\text{percentage change in sales}}$$

$$= \frac{\Delta \text{EBIT}/\text{EBIT}}{\Delta \text{sales}/\text{sales}} \text{ or DOL} = \frac{\text{sales} - \text{variable costs}}{\text{EBIT}}$$

4.   As the firm's sales increase, if all else stays the same, the degree of operating leverage declines (see Table 12A.1).

B.   Financial leverage.

1.   Financial leverage is the responsiveness of the firm's earnings per share to fluctuation in EBIT.

2.   The greater the financial leverage, the greater the responsiveness of EPS to changes in EBIT.

$$\text{Degree of financial leverage (DFL) from base level EBIT} = \text{DFL} = \frac{\text{percentage change in EPS}}{\text{percentage change in EBIT}}$$

$$= \frac{\Delta \text{EPS}/\text{EPS}}{\Delta \text{EBIT}/\text{EBIT}} \text{ or DFL} = \frac{\text{EBIT}}{\text{EBIT} - \text{Interest}}$$

C.   Combining operating and financial leverage.

1.   With combined leverage, even small changes in sales can have a large impact on EPS.

$$\text{Degree of combined leverage (DCL) from base level sales} = \text{DCL} = \frac{\text{percentage change in EPS}}{\text{percentage change in sales}}$$

$$= \frac{\Delta \text{EPS}/\text{EPS}}{\Delta \text{sales}/\text{sales}}$$

$$\text{or DCL} = \frac{\text{sales} - \text{variable costs}}{\text{EBIT} - \text{Interest}}$$

$$\text{or DCL} = (\text{DOL})(\text{DFL})$$

2.   With both operating and financial leverage, the change in sales affects the change in EBIT, which magnifies the change in EPS.

Formulas

Notation

D_1	= the expected constant amount of cash dividend
P_0	= current common stock price
k_s	= required return on equity
k_s^U	= required return on equity for an all-equity firm
k_s^L	= required return on equity in the levered firm
EPS	= earnings per share

EBIT = earnings before interest and taxes

$\overline{\text{EBIT}}$ = expected earnings before interest and taxes

EBIT* = the unknown crossover point in EBIT

I_1, I_2 = the annual total interest charges under two financing plans

N_1, N_2 = number of shares of common stock outstanding under two financing plans

D_{ps1}, D_{ps2} = preferred stock cash dividends under two financing plans

P/E = firm's price/earnings ratio

k_i = after-tax cost of debt

k_b = before-tax cost of debt

V_U = market value of the unlevered firm

V_L = market value of the levered firm

S_L = market value of stock for the levered firm

S_U = market value of stock for the unlevered firm

B = market value of debt

T = firm's marginal tax rate

T_{ps} = personal tax rate on stock income

T_{pb} = personal tax rate on bond income

G_L = gain from leverage

PV = present value

DOL = degree of operating leverage

DFL = degree of financial leverage

DCL = degree of combined leverage

Expected EBIT

$$\overline{\text{EBIT}} = \sum_{i-1}^{n} P_i(\text{EBIT}_i)$$

Standard Deviation of Expected EBIT

$$= \left[\sum_{i-1}^{n} P_i (\text{EBIT}_i - \overline{\text{EBIT}})^2 \right]^{0.5}$$

Coefficient of Variation of Expected EBIT

$$CV = \frac{\text{standard deviation}}{\overline{\text{EBIT}}}$$

Crossover EBIT, EBIT*

$$\frac{(\text{EBIT}^* - I_1)(1 - T) - D_{ps1}}{N_1} = \frac{(\text{EBIT}^* - I_2)(1 - T) - D_{ps2}}{N_2}$$

Expected Market Price

$$P_0 = (P/E)(EPS)$$

Earnings per Share

$$EPS = \frac{(\text{EBIT} - \text{interest} - \text{taxes} - \text{cash dividends on preferred stock})}{\text{number of shares of common stock outstanding}}$$

After-Tax Cost of Debt (k_i)

$$k_i = k_b(1 - T)$$

Valuation Approach When Dividends Are Constant
$$P_0 = D_1/k_s$$

Valuation Approach Where All Earnings Are Paid in Dividends and No Growth Opportunity Is Expected
$$P_0 = EPS/k_s, \text{ or } S[\text{total firm value}] = E[\text{earnings in perpetuity}]/k_s$$

The Modigliani–Miller Model Without Taxes
The value of an unlevered firm
$$V_U = EBIT/k_s^U$$
The value of a levered firm (Proposition I)
$$V_L = S_L + B = EBIT/k_s^U = V_U$$
The required return on equity (Proposition II)
$$k_s^L = k_s^U + (k_s^U - k_b)\frac{B}{S_L}$$

k_s^L = (earnings available to shareholders)/(market value of stock)
The opportunity cost of capital
$$\text{Opportunity cost of capital} = k_s^L[S_L/(S_L + B)] + k_i[B/(S_L + B)]$$

The Modigliani–Miller Model With Corporate Taxes
The value of an unlevered firm
$$V_U = EBIT (1 - T)/k_s^U$$
The value of a levered firm
$$V_L = V_U + TB$$
The value of stock in a levered firm (Proposition I adjusted for taxes)
$$S_L = V_L - B$$
The required return on equity (Proposition II adjusted for taxes)
$$k_s^L = k_s^U + (k_s^U - k_b) (1 - T) \frac{B}{S_L}$$

The gain from leverage
$$G_L = TB$$

The Value of a Firm with Corporate and Personal Taxes
$$V_L = V_U + \left[1 - \frac{(1 - T) (1 - T_{ps})}{(1 - T_{pb})} \right]B$$

The gain from leverage
$$G_L = \left[1 - \frac{(1 - T) (1 - T_{ps})}{(1 - T_{pb})} \right]B$$

Appendix 12A
Degree of operating leverage (DOL) from the base level sales
$$DOL = \frac{\text{percentage change in EBIT}}{\text{percentage change in sales}} = \frac{\Delta EBIT/EBIT}{\Delta sales/sales}$$
$$= \frac{\text{sales} - \text{variable costs}}{EBIT}$$

Degree of financial leverage (DFL) from the base level EBIT

$$DFL = \frac{\text{percentage change in EPS}}{\text{percentage change in EBIT}} = \frac{\Delta EPS/EPS}{\Delta EBIT/EBIT} = \frac{EBIT}{EBIT - interest}$$

Degree of combined leverage (DCL) from the base level sales

$$DCL = \frac{\text{percentage change in EPS}}{\text{percentage change in sales}} = \frac{\Delta EPS/EPS}{\Delta sales/sales}$$

$$= \frac{\text{sales} - \text{variable costs}}{EBIT - interest} = (DOL)(DFL)$$

What to Look For

Again in Chapter 12, we see that financial management is both an art and a science. There is no single obvious optimum combination of debt, equity, and preferred stock, but skillful managers using the proper tools can determine the appropriate capital structure for their firm. Chapter 12 discusses the theory of capital structure and the tools for selecting a capital structure.

Capital Structures

The use of debt introduces financial leverage. The interest payments on debt are tax-deductible, and act as a tax shield to decrease taxable earnings. In comparison to the payment of an equal dollar amount of cash dividends, interest payments increase the earnings available for distribution to common shareholders. Thus, debt used in place of common stock in prudent amounts can increase earnings per share.

Financial leverage

Interest payments on debt represent a fixed cost that must be paid no matter what the revenues of the firm are. This fixed-cost nature of interest payments increases the variability of EPS with changes in EBIT and increases the firm's likelihood of financial distress. We call this variability financial leverage. As long as the return on total assets exceeds the interest rate of debt (and risk has not increased too much), financial leverage is beneficial. That is, up to a point, debt usage increases the value of the firm.

Operating leverage

Fixed operating costs introduce operating leverage to the firm. The higher the level of fixed operating costs, the more variable the firm's EBIT is to changes in sales. Appendix 12A lists equations for calculation of the degrees of operating, financial, and combined leverage. When both operating and financial leverage are combined, even small changes in sales will have a major impact on EPS. Figure 12.A1 depicts this magnified effect on EPS due to combined leverage.

Business and financial risk

Although business and financial risk are not synonomous with operating and financial leverage, they are interrelated. Firms that have the following characteristics tend to have more variable EBIT and higher business risk: (1) higher operating leverage due to higher fixed operating costs versus variable operating costs; (2) small market share; (3) greater sensitivity to changes in economic conditions; (4) little control of input prices for its products; and (5) an inability to pass on the effects of inflation to customers. The level of business risk will have a major impact on the amount of financial risk the firm can undertake.

Financial risk, on the other hand, is a result of the firm's long-term financing decisions. It refers to the increased variability in earnings available to the firm's common stockholders and the increased probability of financial distress as the firm employs financial leverage. Financial risk is a result of employing financial leverage, and business risk is partially the result of employing operating leverage.

The Effect of Taxes on Optimal Capital Structure

In the absence of taxes, capital structure does not affect the value of the firm, assuming there is no probability of costly bankruptcy. If we use the dividend valuation model and suppose that dividends will be perpetual, then the value of a share of common stock is the discounted value of this perpetual stream of cash dividends. If we add stock to this all-equity firm in order to fund capital projects, the value of common shares is unaffected. However, when we add taxes to our valuation model, the earnings available to common stockholders (our perpetual dividend stream) will be reduced by that amount of taxes. Thus, the value of each share of common stock is lower than the nontaxed shares.

The use of debt

Now consider the same previously all-equity firm if it chooses to use debt rather than equity to fund its capital projects. Remember, if the firm uses debt rather than increase the number of common shares outstanding, the perpetual dividend stream is divided by the original number of common shares rather than a larger number. If the perpetual dividend stream from the new project is higher than the previous dividend stream, the original common stockholders enjoy higher dividends.

Let's first consider the no-tax case. Debt usage increases the riskiness of the firm's cash flows. Modigliani and Miller (MM) suggest that if no taxes existed, the required return on the common stock would increase with an increase in debt usage, so any benefit of debt financing would be exactly offset by an increase in the cost of equity. As such, adding debt to a firm's capital structure does not affect value at all. The importance of the MM no-tax model is that it reveals what factors might make a difference when firms determine their capital structure. They are taxes, transactions costs, and the firm's capital investment policy. This chapter addresses the effect of taxes on the capital structure decision while the next chapter considers the remaining two factors.

Corporate and personal taxes

We will now add corporate taxes to our analysis. We noted above that interest payments are tax-deductible and shield some income from taxes. So the earnings available for distribution are higher when the firm pays interest rather than cash dividends on common stock for new financing. Thus, the value of the firm will increase by the present value of the tax shield provided by this debt. If the debt is perpetual,

$$\text{Present value of the debt tax shield} = \frac{(\text{expected interest payment}) (\text{corporate tax rate})}{\text{expected rate of return on debt}}$$

$$= \frac{k_b B (T)}{k_b} = B (T)$$

If the manager's goal is to maximize the value of the firm, he or she would choose the largest amount of debt possible and the firm's optimal capital structure would be almost 100 percent debt!

A factor that limits the use of debt is personal taxation. Corporations gain a tax benefit when they issue bonds; interest payments are tax-deductible. But, bondholders pay a penalty since interest income is taxable, and at a rate higher than stock income. According to Miller, bondholders will require higher returns on bonds to compensate for the additional tax, and in equilibrium, the gain to corporations is exactly offset by the loss to bondholders. Consequently, there are no additional gains to be made from issuing more debt.

Other tax impacts

Firms have means other than debt to shield their income from taxes. Once nondebt tax shields, such as depreciation, are considered, the probability that the firm will be able to use all of its interest tax shield decreases. Thus the existence of nondebt tax shields means that the firm has to trade off their use against the use of interest tax shields. The result is an optimal capital structure that is less than 100 percent debt, but more than zero debt.

The existence of different individual marginal tax rates results in bondholder tax clienteles that impact on the firm's value maximizing level of debt. Likewise, the use of debt with different maturities may result in different value maximizing capital structures.

EPS-EBIT analysis

EPS-EBIT analysis is a tool to help managers analyze the effects of various financing packages on EPS. Since financial risk increases with debt usage, we want to look at the EBIT at which the alternative financing methods produce the same dollar EPS. At this EBIT*, the firm would be indifferent between the two methods. Once the financial manager has calculated EBIT*, the probability distribution of the firm's EBIT can help assess the risk–return tradeoff. While EPS is important, increased use of debt may raise the required return on equity, and thus, this debt usage could decrease the value of the firm. The analysis must always focus on maximizing the value of the firm—not simply on maximizing EPS.

Completion Questions

12.1   The firm's _____ affects how much financial risk it can undertake.

12.2   Firms whose sales fluctuate more with changes in economic conditions have _____ business risk than those whose sales fluctuate less.

12.3   The _____ measures the relative variability of the firm's expected EBIT or EPS.

12.4   The higher the proportion of fixed costs to variable costs, the greater the _____.

12.5   Financial risk refers to _____ in earnings available to common stockholders and the increased probability of _____ as the firm employs more financial leverage.

12.6   The coefficient of variation of the firm's EPS will _____ as a firm employs more debt in its capital structure.

12.7   If there were no taxes, and if an all-equity firm financed new projects with more equity, then according to Modigliani and Miller, the market price per share of the stock would _____.

12.8   If there were no taxes, Modigliani and Miller argue that the required return on a firm's common stock would _____ as the firm begins to use debt.

12.9   If taxes exist in the MM world, the market price of a firm's common stock _____ when more debt financing is employed. As the firm increases its usage of debt, the total value of the firm will _____ as a result of the tax deductibility of interest.

Problems

12.1   North Bay Resorts, an all-equity firm, is planning a $20 million expansion of its hotel complex. The expansion will be financed by the issuance of 400,000 shares of common stock at $50 per share or a bond issue carrying an interest rate of 12 percent. The firm presently has 600,000 shares of common stock outstanding. The firm has a 30 percent marginal tax rate.

North Bay has spent considerable time determining the effects of the expansion. According to its financial analysts, the following scenarios seem likely.

EBIT if the company chooses *not* to expand:

Probability	0.10	0.30	0.40	0.20
EBIT (in millions)	$1	$1.5	$2.0	$3.5

EBIT if the company expands:

Probability	0.10	0.30	0.40	0.20
EBIT (in millions)	$5	$6	$7	$9

a.   Does North Bay face more business risk before or after the acceptance of the project?

b.   Determine EPS if (1) the company does not expand; (2) the company expands using only equity financing; and (3) the company finances the expansion with 12 percent debt. Compare the degrees of financial risk under each scenario.

12.2   National Glass Company has EBIT of $150 million, outstanding equity with a market value of $800 million, and 10 percent coupon perpetual debt worth $200 million.

    a.   Suppose an MM world existed without taxes. What would be the cost of equity capital, k_s^L? What would be the firm's opportunity cost of capital?

    b.   The firm decides to issue an additional $100 million in debt and repurchase $100 million in common stock. How have the k_s^L and the firm's opportunity cost of capital changed?

    c.   Suppose now that corporations are subject to a tax rate of 30 percent and that k_s for a firm with no debt is equal to the opportunity cost of capital in (a). What is the value of National Glass if it has no debt?

    d.   Using k_s^L from (a), determine the market value of equity and the opportunity cost of capital if the firm now issues $200 million in debt.

    e.   Finally, using k_s^L from (b), now determine the opportunity cost of capital if the firm has $300 million of debt. What does the difference between opportunity cost of capital in (d) and (e) suggest about the optimal capital structure?

12.3   Air West is an unlevered firm with an equilibrium market value of $9 million. The firm wishes to issue $5 million in 10 percent coupon perpetual debt. An analyst has estimated that their marginal shareholder faces a personal tax rate of 25 percent, and the marginal bondholder faces a personal tax rate of 30 percent. If Air West's tax rate is 40 percent, what is the value of the levered firm?

12.4   Recently an unlevered firm, with 1 million shares outstanding and EBIT of $4 million forever, became levered by issuing 8 percent coupon long-term bonds and using the proceeds to repurchase some of the shares. The current market value of the levered firm is $24 million. With no debt, shareholders required a return of 12 percent. Assume the existence of an MM world and that the corporate tax rate is 40 percent.

    a.   i   Calculate the change in the value of the firm after leveraging.

           ii.   What accounts for the change in value?

           iii.   How much in debt was raised through issue of bonds?

    b.   Calculate the share price before and after the firm became levered.

    c.   Determine the cost of equity (k_s^L) and the opportunity cost of capital of the levered firm.

12.5   ABC Corporation is currently assessing its capital structure. It is financed entirely with equity, of which 1,000 shares are outstanding. At the present capital structure, investors require 20 percent return on the firm's common stock. ABC pays all earnings as dividends (no growth opportunities) to common share-holders and the expected EBIT is $3,000 in perpetuity. Assume T = 0 and no personal taxes.

    a.   i.   Compute value of the firm.

           ii.   Compute market price per share.

           iii.   What is the firm's opportunity cost of capital?

    b.   Suppose the president of the company proposes to issue $7,500 of debt at the coupon rate of 10 percent and use the proceeds to repurchase shares of ABC. Discuss the effect on

           i.   The value of the firm.

           ii.   The value of equity.

           iii.   The price per share.

           iv. k_s^L and the opportunity cost of capital of the firm.

    c.   Assume the corporate tax rate is 40 percent and MM assumptions hold (i.e., no risk of bankruptcy). What would the market value and the opportunity cost of capital of the firm be with the presence of $7,500 debt at 10 percent coupon interest?

    d.   Suppose that returns to equity holders are taxed at the rate of 20 percent. The recipients of interest are in the 30 percent personal income tax bracket and the corporate tax rate is 40 percent at 10 percent coupon interest.

i.   Calculate the market value of the firm with $7,500 debt.
ii. Calculate the market value of the firm if, instead, the recipients of interest on debt are in the 20 percent income tax bracket.
iii. Calculate the market value of the firm if, instead, the recipients of interest on debt are in the 15 percent income tax bracket.

(The following information pertains to problems 12.6 through 12.9. These problems integrate concepts taught in Chapters 7–12.)

Reynolds Manufacturing has an opportunity to invest in a project with an initial capital cost of $600,000. The project is expected to generate before-tax operating cash flows of $250,000 for five years. Resale value is expected to be zero. Capital cost allowance is figured on a straight-line basis over five years (ignoring the half-year rule) and the firm has a marginal corporate tax rate of 40 percent.

The company's current (market value) capital structure consists of $20 million of equity and $10 million of debt. The firm considers this capital structure to be optimal. The contemplated project has the same risk attributes as the existing firm, so the firm's capital structure and beta will be used to evaluate the project.

12.6   Reynold's debt consists of 12,500 bonds with a par value of $1,000 each, a coupon rate of 8 percent, and a maturity date of 2550. (With this maturity date, the bond can be treated as a perpetuity.) Calculate the after-tax cost of debt.

12.7   Currently, the expected return on the market is estimated to be 18 percent, while the risk-free rate is 8 percent. The common stock beta is 1.3. What is the firm's opportunity cost of capital?

12.8   Calculate the project's NPV. Should the project be accepted?

12.9   How much debt should be issued for Reynolds to maintain its optimal capital structure?

12.10 Air Yukon has decided to purchase two new airplanes to allow it to expand its charter service. In order to finance this $800,000 expenditure, the company is considering three financing plans:
   Plan A   Issue common stock at $40 per share. This plan will increase the number of outstanding shares of common stock to 120,000 shares.
   Plan B   Issue 12 percent preferred stock only.
   Plan C   Issue 12 percent coupon rate bonds only.
   The firm presently has no preferred stock but has interest expenses of $44,000 per year; its tax rate is 35 percent. What is the crossover EBIT (EBIT*) between plans A and B, and between plans A and C?

12A.1 Tidwell Industries, Ltd., is a manufacturer of housing and furniture located in Haleyville, Manitoba. According to a recent announcement, its income statement for the nine months ending September 30, 1997, is as follows:

Income Statement
January 1 to September 30, 1997
(units of $1,000)

Sales	$ 147,477
Less: Variable costs	125,986
Revenues before fixed costs	21,491
Less: Fixed costs	14,400
EBIT	7,091
Less: Interest	1,509
Taxable income	5,582
Less: Taxes	2,395
Net income	$ 3,187
Its EPS is	$ 0.99

Calculate the degrees of operating, financial, and combined leverage.

12.A2   ACL Limited has 500,000 shares outstanding and earnings per share of $4.20. Its current capital structure is made up of the following:

Debt (10% coupon rate) = $4 million
Common stock (500,000 shares) = $6 million
Retained earnings = $2 million

The variable operating costs are $320,000 and the fixed operating costs amount to $250,000. The shares of ACL are currently trading at $20 a share. This firm wants to raise an additional $2.4 million and is considering the following alternatives:

A.   Sell $2.4 million worth of bonds, face value $1,000, that would carry a 14 percent coupon rate.
B.   Sell $2.4 million worth of new shares that would net the firm $16 per share.
C.   Raise 40 percent from selling new bonds with 12 percent coupon rate and the remainder from new equity that would net the company $16 per share.

Assume ACL's marginal tax rate is 40 percent and that under new financing, sales are expected to increase from $3.5 million to $4.75 million. With the additional investment, the firm's fixed costs are expected to stay the same while the variable operating costs are expected to increase to $400,000.

a.   Under the current capital structure compute the following for ACL:
   i.   the degree of operating leverage (DOL).
   ii.   the degree of financial leverage (DFL).
   iii. the degree of combined leverage (DCL).
b.   Compute ACL's degree of financial leverage under each financing alternative.
c.   Compute ACL's earnings per share (EPS) under each financing alternative. Which financing option would you choose and why? Any reservations?
d.   What level of EBIT would yield the same EPS for alternatives A and B? What EPS corresponds to this level of EBIT?
e.   What level of EBIT would yield the same EPS for alternatives A and C? What EPS corresponds to this level of EBIT?
f.   Determine the minimum level of EBIT the firm would have to earn under each alternative in order to be able to meet interest payments on debt.

Answers to Completion Questions

12.1   level of business risk
12.2   more
12.3   coefficient of variation
12.4   operating leverage
12.5   the increased variability; financial distress

12.6   increase
12.7   be unaffected
12.8   increase
12.9   increases; increase

Solutions to Problems

12.1   a.   Step 1.   If the company chooses not to accept the project:
Expected EBIT = 0.10 ($1 million) + 0.30 ($1.5 million) +

0.40 ($2 million) + 0.20 ($3.5 million) = $2.05 million

Step 2.   Standard deviation = $[0.10 (\$1 - \$2.05)^2 + 0.30 (\$1.5 - \$2.05)^2$

$+ 0.40 (\$2.0 - \$2.05)^2 + 0.20 (\$3.5 - \$2.05)^2]^{0.5}$

$= [\$0.6225]^{0.5} = \$0.79$ million

Coefficient of variation = $0.79/$2.05 = 0.3854

Step 3.   If the company expands:
Expected EBIT = 0.10 ($5 million) + 0.30 ($6 million) +

0.40 ($7 million) + 0.20 ($9 million) = $6.90 million

Step 4.   Standard deviation = $[0.10 (\$5 - \$6.90)^2 + 0.30 (\$6 - \$6.90)^2$

$+ 0.40 (\$7 - \$6.90)^2 + 0.20 (\$9 - \$6.90)^2]^{0.5}$

$= [\$1.49]^{0.5} = \$1.22$ million

Coefficient of variation = $1.22/$6.90 = 0.1768
The company will have less business risk if it accepts the expansion project.

b.   Step 5.   Assuming the company does not expand:

$$\overline{EAT} = \overline{EBIT} (1 - T)$$

$$= \$2.05 (1 - 0.30) = \$1.435 \text{ million}$$

$$\overline{EPS} = \overline{EAT} / 600,000$$

$$= \$1.435 \text{ million} / 600,000 = \$2.392$$

As mentioned in the text, the variability in EPS under all-equity financing is the same as business risk; therefore, the coefficient of variation = 0.3854.

Step 6.   Assuming the firm expands using equity financing:

$$\overline{EAT} = \overline{EBIT} (1 - T)$$

$$= \$6.90 (1 - 0.30) = \$4.83 \text{ million}$$

$$\overline{EPS} = \overline{EAT} / 1,000,000$$

$$= \$4.83 \text{ million} / 1,000,000 = \$4.83$$

Again, since the project is still all-equity financed, the coefficient of variation of 0.1768 [from (a)] is still relevant.

Step 7.   Assuming the project is financed with debt: Interest = ($20 million)(0.12) = $2.4 million.

Probability	0.10	0.30	0.40	0.20
EBIT (in millions)	$5.00	$6.00	$7.00	$9.00
Less: Interest	2.40	2.40	2.40	2.40
EBT	2.60	3.60	4.60	6.60
Less: Tax (at 30%)	0.78	1.08	1.38	1.98
EAT	$1.82	$2.52	$3.22	$4.62
EPS (EAT/600,000)	$3.03	$4.20	$5.37	$7.70

Step 8.   Expected EPS   = 0.10 ($3.03) + 0.30 ($4.20) + 0.40 ($5.37) + 0.20 ($7.70)

= $5.25

Standard deviation = [0.10 ($3.03 − $5.25)^2 + 0.30 ($4.20 − $5.25)^2

+ 0.40 ($5.37 − $5.25)^2 + 0.20 ($7.70 − $5.25)^2]$^{0.5}$

= [$2.03]$^{0.5}$ = $1.42

Coefficient of variation = $1.42/$5.25 = 0.2705

The level of financial risk (as indicated by the coefficient of variation of EPS) is greater if the project is financed with debt rather than equity, but because of the reduction in business risk caused by the expansion, risk is still less than if the firm chose not to expand.

12.2   a.   Step 1.   Cash available to equity holders = EBIT − interest
= $150 − $200 (0.10) = $150 − $20 = $130 million
k_s^L = $130/$800 = 0.1625 = 16.25%

Step 2.   Opportunity cost of capital = ($800/$1,000) (16.25%) + ($200/$1,000) (10%)

= 13% + 2% = 15%

b.   Step 3.   Cash available to equity holders = EBIT − interest
= $150 − ($300) (0.10) = $120 million
k_s^L = $120/$700 = 17.14%

Step 4.   Opportunity cost of capital = ($300/$1,000) (10%) + ($700/$1,000) (17.14%)
= 3% + 12% = 15%

Although k_s^L has increased, the opportunity cost of capital remains constant.

c.   Step 5.   EAT = EBIT(1 − T) = $150(1 − 0.30) = $105 million

Step 6. V_U = EAT/k_s^U = $105/0.15 = $700 million

d.   Step 7. $V_L = \dfrac{(EBIT - interest)\,(1 - T)}{k_s^L}$

$= \dfrac{[\$150 - 0.10(\$200)]\,(1 - 0.30)}{0.1625} = \dfrac{\$130(0.70)}{0.1625}$

= $560 million

Step 8. Opportunity cost of capital $= k_b(1 - T)W_{debt} + k_s^L W_{common\ equity}$

$$= 10\%(1 - 0.30)\left[\frac{\$200}{\$560 + \$200}\right]$$

$$+ (16.25\%)\left[\frac{\$560}{\$560 + \$200}\right]$$

$$= 1.84\% + 11.97\% = 13.81\%$$

Step 9. $V_L = \dfrac{[\$150 - 0.10\ (\$300)]\ (1 - 0.30)}{0.1714} = \$490$ million

Step 10. Opportunity cost of capital $= 10\%(1 - 0.30)(\$300/\$790) + 17.14\%(\$490/\$790)$

$$= 2.66\% + 10.63\% = 13.29\%$$

The opportunity cost of capital falls as more and more debt is issued. According to MM, the firm should finance itself with virtually 100 percent debt, since that will maximize the value of the firm.

12.3 $V_L = V_U + \left[1 - \dfrac{(1 - T)\ (1 - T_{ps})}{(1 - T_{pb})}\right]B$

$$= \$9,000,000 + \left[1 - \frac{(1 - 0.40)\ (1 - 0.25)}{(1 - 0.30)}\right]\$5,000,000$$

$$= \$9,000,000 + \left[1 - \frac{(0.60)\ (0.75)}{(0.70)}\right]\$5,000,000$$

$$= \$9,000,000 + [1 - 0.6429]\ \$5,000,000$$

$$= \$9,000,000 + \$1,785,714 = \$10,785,714$$

12.4   EBIT $= \$4$ million, $V_L = \$24$ million, $k_s^U = 12\%$, $T = 40\%$

  a. i. First, calculate the value of unlevered firm.
Cash flow to shareholders of unlevered firm $= \$4$ million $(0.6) = \$2.4$ million
$V_U = \$2.4$ million$/0.12 = \$20$ million
Next, use the MM equation with corporate taxes:
$V_L = V_U + TB$
$\$24$ million $= \$20$ million $+ TB$
$TB = \$4$ million
Increase in value is $\$4$ million.

     ii. The increase is accounted for by the present value of the tax shield from the use of debt.

     iii. $(0.4)\ (B) = \$4$ million
$B = \$10$ million
$\$10$ million debt was raised.

  b. i. Before the firm became levered:
Value of equity $= \$20$ million
Number of shares outstanding $= 1$ million
Market price $= \$20$ million$/1$ million $= \$20.00$

    ii.   After the firm became levered: If the $10 million debt raised is used to repurchase the shares at $20 a share, then the number of shares repurchased is 500,000 ($10 million/$20).

Value of the levered firm = $24 million

Value of debt = $10 million

Value of equity of levered firm = $14 million

Share price = $14 million/(1 million – 0.5 million) = $28.00

However, it is not likely that shares will be repurchased at $20 a share if the market price immediately after repurchase will rise to $28. For the market to be in equilibrium, shares will have to be repurchased at $24 a share and the share price after the firm became levered will still be $24.

    c.   Cost of equity of levered firm:

Cash flow to shareholders= [$4 million – 0.8($10 million)](0.6)

$$= \$1.92 \text{ million}$$

Cost of equity k_s^L = $1.92 million/$14 million = 13.714%

Opportunity cost of capital = $(8\%)(0.6)(\$10 \text{ million}/\$24 \text{ million})$

$$+ (13.714\%)(\$14 \text{ million}/\$24 \text{ million})$$

$$= 8 + 2 = 10\%$$

12.5   a.   Since ABC is unlevered, debt = 0 and interest = 0.

    i.   Cash flow to shareholders = $3,000

V_U = $3,000/0.2 = $15,000

    ii.   Market price per share = $15,000/1,000 = $15

    iii.   Opportunity cost of capital = 20% (For unlevered firm, opportunity cost of capital = k_s^U)

    b.   With $7,500 debt at 10% coupon rate, interest = $750. If shares are repurchased at $15 each, the total number of shares repurchased will be 500.

    i.   Value of the firm will remain the same = $15,000, with no taxes.

    ii.   Value of equity = $15,000 – $7,500 = $7,500

    iii.   Price per share = $7,500/500 = $15, which remains the same.

    iv.   Cash flow to shareholders = $3,000 – $750 = $2,250

k_s^L = $2,250/$7,500 = 30%

Opportunity cost of capital = ($7,500/$15,000) (10%) + ($7,500/$15,000) (30%)

$$= 20\% \text{ (the same)}$$

    c.   First we need to calculate the value of the unlevered firm in the presence of corporate taxes.

    i.   Cash flow to shareholders = $3,000 × 0.6 = $1,800

V_U = $1,800/0.2 = $9,000

    ii.   Value of the levered firm with $7,500 debt:

$V_L = V_U + TB$

V_L = $9,000 + 0.4 × $7,500 = $12,000

The value of the levered firm would be $12,000.

To calculate the opportunity cost of capital, we need to determine the cost of equity of the levered firm.

Cash flow to shareholders = ($3,000 – $750) × 0.6 = $1,350

Value of equity of levered firm = $4,500 ($12,000 – $7,500)

k_s^L = $1,350/$4,500 = 30%

Opportunity cost of capital = (10%)(0.6)($7,500/$12,000) + (30%)($4,500/$12,000)

$$= 3.75 + 11.25 = 15\%$$

Or using Equation 12.13:

$$\text{Opportunity cost of capital} = 0.20\left(1 - \left[0.40\left(\frac{\$7,500}{\$12,000}\right)\right]\right)$$

$$= 15\%$$

d. Given $T_{ps} = 20\%$, $T_{pb} = 30\%$, and $T = 40\%$

   i. With \$7,500 debt at 10%

   $V_U = \$9,000$

   $$V_L = V_U + \left[1 - \frac{(1 - T)(1 - T_{ps})}{(1 - T_{pb})}\right]B$$

   $V_L = \$9,000 + [1 - (0.6)(0.8)/(0.7)]\,\$7,500$

   $V_L = \$9,000 + \$2,357 = \$11,357$

   Equity financing is more appealing to debt financing.

   ii. Given $T_{ps} = 20\%$, $T_{pb} = 20\%$, and $T = 40\%$

   $V_L = \$9,000 + [1 - (0.6)(0.8)/(0.8)]\,\$7,500$

   $V_L = \$9,000 + \$3,000 = \$12,000$

   This is the same value as the MM with corporate taxes.

   iii. Given $T_{ps} = 20\%$, $T_{pb} = 15\%$, and $T = 40\%$

   $V_L = \$9,000 + [1 - (0.6)(0.8)/(0.85)]\,\$7,500$

   $V_L = \$9,000 + \$3,265 = \$12,265$

   Debt financing is more appealing than equity financing.

12.6 Step 1. Bond price = \$10,000,000/12,500 = \$800

   Step 2. $k_b = \$80/\$800 = 10\%$

   Step 3. $k_i = k_b(1 - T) = 10\%(1 - 0.40) = 6\%$

12.7 Step 1. $k_s^L = k_{RF} + \beta\,(k_M - k_{RF}) = 8\% + 1.3(18\% - 8\%) = 21\%$

   Step 2. Opportunity cost of capital $= k_i W_{debt} + k_s W_{common\ equity}$

   $$= (6\%)\,(0.333) + (21\%)\,(0.667) = 16\%$$

12.8 Step 1. $CF_t = \$250,000\,(1 - 0.40) + (\$600,000/5)\,(0.40) = \$198,000$

   Step 2. $NPV = CF_t(PVA_{16\%,5yr}) - \$600,000 = \$198,000(3.274) - \$600,000$

   $$= \$48,252$$

   Accept the project since it has a positive NPV.

12.9 Step 1. Note that the amount of debt to be issued should be determined by first examining the increase in the market value that will result from accepting the project. The increase in the market value will be greater than the cost of the project, since the NPV is positive. The increase in market value will be \$600,000 + \$48,252, the present value of the cash flows associated with the project, assuming the market is efficient.

   Step 2. Amount of debt that should be issued equals the change in market value times the targeted amount of debt in the capital structure:

   New debt = (\$648,252)(0.333) = \$215,868

12.10 Step 1. If the new stock is issued, the resulting number of shares will be 120,000. Since the issue increases the number of shares outstanding by \$800,000/\$40 = 20,000, the present number of shares is 120,000 − 20,000 = 100,000.

Step 2.   The crossover EBIT is determined by

$$\frac{(EBIT^* - I_1)(1 - T) - D_{ps1}}{N_1} = \frac{(EBIT^* - I_2)(1 - T) - D_{ps2}}{N_2}$$

Under plan A, $D_{ps1} = 0$
Under plan B, $D_{ps2} = \$800,000(0.12) = \$96,000$

$$\frac{(EBIT^* - \$44,000)(1 - 0.35) - 0}{120,000} = \frac{(EBIT^* - \$44,000)(1 - 0.35) - \$96,000}{100,000}$$

$$\frac{(0.65)(EBIT^*) - \$28,600}{120,000} = \frac{(0.65)(EBIT^*) - \$28,600 - \$96,000}{100,000}$$

$$65,000\ EBIT^* - \$2,860,000,000 = 78,000\ EBIT^* - \$14,952,000,000$$

$$13,000\ EBIT^* = \$12,092,000,000$$

$$EBIT^* = \$12,092,000,000 / 13,000 = \$930,153.85$$

If EBIT is less than \$930,153.85, equity financing will generate a higher EPS.

Step 3.   Plans A and C
Plan C will result in an increase in interest expense of (\$800,000)(0.12) = \$96,000, so interest will be \$140,000.

$$D_{ps1} = D_{ps2} = 0$$

$$\frac{(EBIT^* - \$44,000)(1 - 0.35)}{120,000} = \frac{(EBIT^* - \$140,000)(1 - 0.35)}{100,000}$$

$$\frac{(0.65)(EBIT^*) - \$28,600}{\$120,000} = \frac{(0.65)(EBIT^*) - \$91,000}{100,000}$$

$$65,000\ EBIT^* - \$2,860,000,000 = 78,000\ EBIT^* - \$10,920,000,000$$

$$13,000\ EBIT^* = \$8,060,000,000$$

$$EBIT^* = \$8,060,000,000 / 13,000 = \$620,000$$

Equity financing leads to a higher EPS if EBIT is less than \$620,000.

12A.1   Step 1. $DOL = \dfrac{sales - variable\ costs}{EBIT} = \dfrac{\$147,477 - \$125,986}{\$7,091} = \dfrac{\$21,491}{\$7,091}$

= 3.03 times

Step 2. $DFL = \dfrac{EBIT}{EBIT - interest} = \dfrac{\$7,091}{\$7,091 - \$1,509} = \dfrac{\$7,091}{\$5,582} = 1.27$ times

Step 3. $DCL = (DOL)(DFL) = (3.03)(1.27) = 3.85$ times; or

$DCL = \dfrac{sales - variable\ costs}{EBIT - interest} = \dfrac{\$147,477 - \$125,986}{\$7,091 - \$1,509} = \dfrac{\$21,491}{\$5,582}$

= 3.85 times

12A.2   ACL currently has $4 million debt at 10 percent coupon interest. Current interest payments amount to $400,000 per year.

Variable costs (VC) = $320,000
Fixed costs (FC) = $250,000
Sales = $3.8 million

a.   i. $\text{DOL} = \dfrac{\text{sales} - \text{variable cost}}{\text{EBIT}} = (\text{EBIT} + \text{FC})/\text{EBIT}$

EBIT = sales − VC − FC

= $3.8 million − $320,000 − $250,000 = $3.23 million

DOL = ($3.23 million + $0.250 million)/$3.23 million = 1.08

ii.   DFL = EBIT/(EBIT − interest) = $3.23 million/($3.23 million − $0.4 million) = 1.141

iii.   DCL = DOL × DFL = 1.08 × 1.141 = 1.233

b.   With 100% debt:

Increase in interest payments = 0.14 × $2.4 million = $0.336 million
Total interest = $0.4 million + $0.336 million = $0.736 million
EBIT = $4.75 million − $0.4 million − $0.25 million = $4.1 million
DFL = 4.1 million/(4.1 million − 0.736) = 1.219
Financial leverage increases from 1.141 to 1.219.

With 100% equity financing, DFL = 1.141 (the same).

With 40% debt at 12% and 60% equity:

Increase in interest on debt = 0.12 × $0.96 = $0.1152 million
Total interest = $0.5152 million
Number of shares issued = $1.44 million/$16 = 90,000
DFL = $4.1 million/($4.1 million − $0.5152) = 1.144
Financial leverage increases from 1.141 to 1.144.

c.   Earnings per share under each financing scheme.

Under 100% debt financing:

EBIT = $4.1 million
Interest = $0.736 million
EBT = $3.364 million
EAT = $2.0184 million
Number of shares = 500,000
EPS = $4.0368

Under 100% equity financing:

EBIT = $4.1 million
Interest = $0.4 million
EAT = $2.22 million
Number of shares = 500,000 + $2.4 million/$16 = 650,000
EPS = $2.22 million/0.65 million = $3.415

Under 40% debt and 60% equity:

EBIT = $4.1 million
Interest = $0.5152 million
EAT = $2.15088 million
EPS = $2.15088 million/0.59 million = $3.646

Based on EPS, you would choose alternative C. However, this does not take into consideration the risk factors.

d.   To calculate the level of EBIT that achieves the same EPS for any two alternatives, determine the equation for EPS under each alternative and then set the two equations equal.

Alternative A.   100% debt financing

$$EPS_{debt} = (EBIT - \$0.736 \text{ million})/0.5 \text{ million}$$

Alternative B: 100% equity financing

$$EPS_{equity} = (EBIT - \$0.4 \text{ million})/0.65 \text{ million}$$

Equating the two, we have

$$(EBIT - \$0.736 \text{ million})/0.5 \text{ million} = (EBIT - \$0.4 \text{ million})/0.65 \text{ million}$$
$$1.3(EBIT - \$0.736 \text{ million}) = (EBIT - \$0.4 \text{ million})$$
$$0.3EBIT = \$0.5568 \text{ million}$$
$$EBIT = \$1.856 \text{ million}$$

When EBIT = $1.856 million, both debt and equity financing provide the same level of EPS.

$$EPS_{debt} = (\$1.856 \text{ million} - \$0.4 \text{ million})/0.65 \text{ million} = \$2.24$$
$$EPS_{equity} = (\$1.856 \text{ million} - \$0.736 \text{ million})/0.5 \text{ million} = \$2.24$$

e. $EPS_{40\% \text{ debt},60\% \text{ equity}} = (EBIT - \$0.5152)/0.59 \text{ million}$

$EPS_{debt} = (EBIT - \$0.736 \text{ million})/0.5 \text{ million}$

Equating the two alternatives, we have

$$(EBIT - \$0.736 \text{ million})/0.5 \text{ million} = (EBIT - \$0.5152)/0.59$$
$$1.18(EBIT - \$0.736 \text{ million}) = (EBIT - \$0.5152)$$
$$0.18EBIT = \$0.35328 \text{ million}$$
$$EBIT = \$1.962667 \text{ million}$$

The corresponding EPS is given as

$$EPS = (\$1.962667 \text{ million} - \$0.736 \text{ million})/0.5 \text{ million}$$
$$EPS = \$2.45$$

f.   Under alternative A: 100% debt financing, to break even,

$$EBIT - \$0.736 \text{ million} = 0$$
$$EBIT = \$0.736 \text{ million}$$

Under alternative B: 100% equity financing, to break even,

$$EBIT - \$0.4 \text{ million} = 0$$
$$EBIT = \$0.4 \text{ million}$$

Under alternative C: 40% debt and 60% equity, to break even,

$$EBIT - \$0.5152 \text{ million} = 0$$
$$EBIT = \$0.5152 \text{ million}$$

Chapter 13
The Dynamics of the Capital Structure Decision

In Chapter 12, we showed that under MM assumptions of no taxes and no transactions costs, the value of the firm is independent of its capital structure. That is, the value of the firm is a function of its investment decisions and not its financing decisions. In the presence of corporate taxes, the government provides a subsidy to the firm in the form of tax shield from interest expense. The optimal capital structure is almost 100 percent debt. With personal taxes, the value of the firm increases with more debt but by less than the increase with corporate taxes only. The optimal capital structure depends on the relationship between the personal tax on equity income and that on interest income. Transactions costs, other than taxes, include financial distress costs and agency costs, which are the main focus of Chapter 13.

Topical Outline

I.   The costs of financial distress.
        Financial distress occurs when the firm has difficulty in honouring obligations to its creditors. Sometimes this is temporary and shortlived, and sometimes it appears to be permanent. When permanent, it induces direct and indirect costs to the firm.
        A.   Direct costs are a result of the limited liability feature of corporations.
                1.   If the value of the firm's assets are less than the value of its debts at maturity, the shareholders are able to walk away from the firm, turning it over to the creditors.
                2.   The direct costs associated with this transaction are bankruptcy costs, including fees for lawyers, accountants, and court-appointed administrators.
        B.   Indirect costs are opportunity costs arising from situations such as the following:
                1.   Management may opt for high-risk projects in place of low-risk projects even though the high-risk projects have negative NPVs.
                2.   New positive NPV investments may be passed. This may be due to difficulty in raising capital externally or to management's decision to pass this investment if they believe that the likely gains are going to be captured by bondholders. This leads to underinvestment.
                3.   Suppliers may tighten their credit terms for security.
                4.   Management may be less lenient in dealing with employee contracts. This may lead to employee dissatisfaction, reduced productivity, and work stoppage. These are called operational and managerial inefficiencies.
                5.   Lenders may charge higher rates to reflect the increased risk.
                6.   Creditors may use the terms in the protective covenants to restrict the firm's operations.
II.   Agency costs.
        A.   These costs arise from two sources:
                1.   Conflicts between shareholders and management often lead to agency costs of equity.
                        a.   Unless a firm's equity is completely owned by managers, the managers have an incentive to consume perquisites. This agency cost increases as external equity increases.
                2.   Conflicts between shareholders and bondholders often lead to agency costs of debt.
                        a.   Since the claims of bondholders are fixed, equityholders have an incentive to invest in more risky projects. Bondholders demand restrictive covenants and monitoring to guard these agency costs.
                3.   Since some forms of agency costs increase with equity and some with debt, there must be an optimal capital structure.
                4.   Given financial distress costs (FD) and agency costs (AC),
                        $$V_L = V_U + TB - PV(FD) - PV(AC).$$
III.   Signalling.
        A.   Managers may use capital structure changes to signal their expectations about the firm's future prospects.
                1.   Debt signals better future prospects.
                2.   Under signalling theory, capital structure is an ongoing, dynamic process.

B.   Under the pecking order theory, managers try to maintain a target capital structure.
1.   Internal financing is preferred because of lack of flotation costs or lack of submission to market disciplinary forces.
2.   Managers develop a target dividend payout ratio and avoid sudden changes in dividends.
3.   When firms have excess cash, they build up cash balances, pay down debt, or buy back stock. If cash is less than needed, the firm draws down its cash balances.
4.   External financing is a last resort; if external financing is needed, debt is preferred to new equity.

IV.   Factors to be considered in making capital structure decisions.
A.   Asset uniqueness. When principal assets of the firm are intangible or physical in nature.
1.   Firms whose principal assets are intangible in nature are exposed to much higher costs of financial distress and tend to carry less debt.
2.   Firms with physical assets tend to carry more debt relative to those with intangible assets.
B.   Protective covenants. These are prohibitions on the actions of the firm to alleviate some of the divergent interests between bondholders and shareholders. These may include:
1.   Restrictions on dividend payments.
2.   Restrictions on pledging of assets as collateral for loans or issuance of additional debt. Firms may prefer to issue subordinated bonds or convertible bonds.
3.   Restrictions on disposition of assets.
4.   Restrictions on mergers.
C.   Growth opportunities. Studies have confirmed that firms with more growth opportunities tend to carry less debt. Such firms do not want to hamper their ability to secure additional capital as the need arises.
D.   Economic conditions. Firms tend to raise more equity than debt in times of good economic conditions.

What to Look For

Chapter 12 discussed one factor (taxes) out of the three revealed by the MM no-tax case as causing capital structure decisions to impact on firm value. In this chapter, we focus on the two remaining factors—transactions costs and the firm's investment decision.

Transactions Costs
The two primary transactions costs are financial distress costs and agency costs.

Financial distress costs
As the firm adds more debt, it becomes riskier. With more debt come larger interest payments, and the likelihood that the firm cannot make its interest payments increases. Since bankruptcy is costly, investors will demand higher returns in compensation for possible losses due to financial distress. These financial distress costs can effectively limit the amount of debt a firm is willing to issue. Furthermore, they may lead to risk shifting by providing incentives for management to accept a riskier project even though it may have a negative net present value. For example, suppose a firm under financial distress has the following market-value–based balance sheet:

Assets		Liabilities	
Cash	$150,000	Debt	$180,000
Other assets	40,000	Equity	10,000

The debt matures in one year for $250,000. The firm has identified two investment opportunities, labelled A and B, each requiring $140,000 and having a one-year payoff available. The first project, A, has a 25 percent chance of having $300,000 cash flow and 75 percent chance of having a $80,000 cash flow at the end of the year. The second project has a 60 percent chance of receiving $200,000 and a 40 percent chance of receiving $140,000 at the end of the year. Assume the opportunity cost of capital is 20 percent.

a.   What is the NPV of each project?
        Project A:
                $E(CF_A) = 0.25(\$300,000) + 0.75(\$80,000)$
                        $= \$75,000 + \$60,000$
                        $= \$135,000$
                $NPV_A = -\$140,000 + \$135,000/1.2 = -\$27,500$
        Project B:
                $E(CF_B) = 0.6(\$200,000) + 0.4(\$140,000)$
                        $= \$120,000 + \$56,000$
                        $= \$176,000$
                $NPV_B = -\$140,000 + \$176,000/1.2 = \$6,667$
b.   What is the standard deviation of the cash flows for each project?
        Project A:
                $\sigma^2_A = 0.25(\$300,000 - \$135,000)^2 + 0.75(\$80,000 - \$135,000)^2$
                        $= \$6,806.25 \times 10^6 + \$2,268.75 \times 10^6 = \$9,075 \times 10^6$
                $\sigma_A = \$95,263$
        Project B:
                $\sigma^2_B = 0.6(\$200,000 - \$176,000)^2 + 0.4(\$140,000 - \$176,000)^2$
                        $= \$345.6 \times 10^6 + \$518.4 \times 10^6 = \$864 \times 10^6$
                $\sigma_B = \$29,394$
c.   If you are a shareholder, which project would you prefer?
        As a shareholder, I would prefer project A (high-risk project) since, if it suceeds, it will generate enough cash inflow to pay off the debt and still realize a benefit. Note that project A has a negative NPV.
d.   As a bondholder, which project would you prefer?
        As a bondholder, I would prefer project B (low risk) since the gain from the project will accrue only to bondholders.

On the other hand, an underinvestment problem will occur if debt claims are so high that more debt financing cannot be raised and current equityholders are unwilling to finance positive NPV projects. They are unwilling to invest more because virtually all of the benefits derived from the project will go to the bondholders when the shareholders are forced to walk away from the firm at the maturity of the bonds.

Agency costs
Agency problems also serve to limit the amount of debt a firm issues. For instance, shareholders (principals) hire managers (agents) to operate the company. While managers supposedly act to maximize the value of the firm, they may choose to maximize their own benefits. If a firm has many outside shareholders, managers may try to maximize their own wealth by demanding high wages or consuming excessive perquisites. This agency cost makes debt the preferred method of financing.

Debt leads to other agency problems as well. Since the amount of money owed to bondholders is fixed, shareholders prefer more risky projects because they have a greater likelihood of being profitable for the shareholders. This is another form of risk shifting that would be accentuated if both financial distress and agency problems were present. Because of this, bondholders typically demand restrictive covenants and monitoring devices when they buy debt.

With financial distress and agency costs, the value of the levered firm is
        $V_L = V_U + PV(\text{Tax shield from debt}) - PV(\text{Financial distress costs}) - PV(\text{Agency costs}).$

With financial distress and agency costs, optional capital structure is somewhere between 0 percent debt and 100 percent debt. The rationale is as follows: For moderate amounts of debt, the benefits from the use of debt (the relatively low cost of debt and tax shield from interest expense) dominate any costs of using debt, thus making further debt financing more desirable. At a certain level of debt financing, the benefits from the use of debt are just offset by the costs of financial distress and agency, and the value of the firm is maximized. Beyond this amount of offset by the costs of financial distress and agency, and the value of the firm is maximized. Beyond this amount of debt, a dollar increase in debt financing increases financial distress and agency costs by more than it increases the benefits from the use of debt. The optimal capital structure is therefore less than 100 percent debt financing.

Impact of Capital Investment Decisions

The investment decision of the firm may affect the choice of debt or equity, and hence capital structure. The issuance of new debt may signal to investors that managers expect future prospects to be better and, therefore, may be perceived as "good news." Managers may have an order of preference (a "pecking order") in which they raise new funds. Finally, issuing equity may indicate that managers think that the firm's stock is overpriced. All these explanations are plausible.

Other Factors

Many other factors may influence a firm's capital structure decision. Some of these are:

Asset uniqueness

Firms with assets that can be easily sold if the firm is forced to liquidate can carry more debt than firms that have highly specialized or intangible assets.

Growth options

Firms with substantial future growth prospects need as much financial slack and flexibility as possible in order to move quickly to take advantage of new investment opportunities. As a result, such firms tend to have less debt in their capital structure.

Product or input market factors

Firms that produce general purpose products may use high levels of debt since, if they are forced to liquidate, their inventories have a high resale value. On the other hand, firms that use the same technology as the vast majority of firms in an industry may use less debt since it would be difficult to sell this technology to others in the industry.

Economic conditions

Firms tend to use more equity financing when an economic expansion is under way, since high-quality projects are harder to find and lower-quality projects are more likely to be financed by equity.

Corporate control

A firm that finds itself to be an unwanted takeover target may increase its debt level, which should cause its stock price to increase, thus making it less attractive as a takeover target.

Completion Questions

13.1   _____, including legal fees and disruption of the firm's operations, can decrease the value of the firm.

13.2   Underinvestment and risk shifting result in _____ financial distress costs.

13.3   In addition to financial distress costs, _____ also serve to limit the amount of debt use by a firm.

13.4   Managers may use the choice of new debt equity to _____ to investors their changes in expectations about future prospects.

13.5   Firms with highly specialized assets will use _____ equity in their capital structure.

13.6   Firms with many future growth opportunities need a high degree of _____ and _____.

13.7   Under the pecking order theory, managers prefer internally generated funds because of lack of _____ and lack of submission to the forces of _____.

13.8   During a time of economic expansion, firms tend to use more _____.

13.9   Firms more concerned about maintaining ownership control may tend to issue _____ debt than those who are not so concerned.

Problems

13.1   Halifax Beaver Ltd. has been going through financial distress for quite some time. On its balance sheet, the asset side indicates cash and marketable securities valued at $280,000. The liability side indicates debt totalling $350,000 due in one year. Management of the firm has identified two investment opportunities. Project A costs $280,000. If undertaken, this project has a 40 percent chance of generating an expected cash flow of $500,000 and a 60 percent chance of generating an expected cash flow of $180,000 by year end. Project B, which requires an initial investment of $200,000, has a 20 percent chance of generating an expected cash flow of $320,000 and an 80 percent chance of generating an expected cash flow of $250,000 by year end. Due to the riskiness of Beaver Ltd., its cost of capital is estimated to be 25 percent.
   a.   For each project, compute the expected cash flow and the total risk (variability) of the cash flow.
   b.   As a shareholder of Beaver Ltd., which project would you choose and why?
   c.   As a bondholder of Beaver Ltd., which project would you choose and why?

13.2   ACL Ltd., a levered firm, has 100,000 shares outstanding and an EBIT of $2 million. Its debt has a face value of $10 million and the cost of debt is 15 percent. Management of ACL is concerned about the high cost of the firm's debt and is considering issuing $4.5 million in equity and using the proceeds to retire some of its debt. When this restructuring occurs, the cost of the remaining debt will decrease to 10 percent and the cost of equity will also decrease from 20 percent to 12 percent. The firm's tax rate is 40 percent.
   a.   What is the current market value of the firm?
   b.   What effect will the decrease in debt have on the value of the firm and its opportunity cost of capital?
   c.   Determine the per share price of ACL after restructuring, given that the shares are issued at $15 per share.
   d.   What is the per share price of ACL if the shares are issued at $10 per share?

13.3   ABX Enterprises is in the process of determining its target capital structure. Currently ABX is unlevered and has 1 million shares outstanding and EBIT of $6 million. Manangement is seriously considering issuing debt and using the proceeds to repurchase some of its shares in the open market. The risk-free rate is 4 percent and the average return on the TSE 300 index is 12 percent. Assume ABX pays out all earnings as cash dividends and the firm's tax rate is 40 percent. An investment dealer for the firm has estimated the before-tax costs of debt and the firm's systematic risk (beta) for various levels of debt as follows:

Proportion of Debt (%)	Beta	Before-Tax Cost of Debt (%)
0	0.8	8
20	0.9	9
40	1.05	9.5
60	1.35	11.7
75	1.60	13.8

   a.   Discuss the impact of the various proportions of debt on the firm's overall opportunity cost of capital and market value.
   b.   If shares are repurchased at $34.62 per share, what would be the impact on the firm's share price?
   c.   What should ABX's target capital structure be? Give an intuitive explanation to your anwer.

Answers to Completion Questions

13.1   Financial distress costs
13.2   indirect
13.3   agency costs (problems)
13.4   signal
13.5   more
13.6   financial slack; flexibility
13.7   flotation costs; market discipline
13.8   equity
13.9   more

Solutions to Problems

13.1   a.   Project A:
E(cash flow) = $0.4 \times \$500,000 + 0.6 \times \$180,000$
$= \$200,000 + \$108,000 = \$308,000$
$\sigma_A^2 = 0.4 \times (\$500,000 - \$308,000)^2 + 0.6 \times (\$180,000 - \$308,000)^2$
$= \$14,745.60 \times 10^6 + \$9,830.4 \times 10^6$
$= \$24,576 \times 10^6$
$\sigma_A = \$156,767$

Project B:
E(cash flow) = $0.2 \times \$320,000 + 0.8 \times \$250,000$
$= \$64,000 + \$200,000 = \$264,000$
$\sigma_B^2 = 0.2 \times (\$320,000 - \$264,000)^2 + 0.8 \times (\$250,000 - \$264,000)^2$
$= \$583.2 \times 10^6 + \$156.8 \times 10^6$
$= \$740 \times 10^6$
$\sigma_B = \$27,203$

b.   First compute the NPV for each project.
Project A:
$NPV_A = \$308,000/1.25 - \$280,000$
$= -\$33,600$
Project B:
$NPV_B = \$264,000/1.25 - \$200,000$
$= \$11,200$
As a shareholder, I would prefer project A even though it is riskier and has a negative NPV. This is because if the $500,000 flow occurs, the firm can pay off the debt and the shareholders take the rest.

c.   As a bondholder, I would prefer project B with less risk and a positive NPV.

13.2   a.   EBIT = $2 million
Interest = $0.15 \times \$10$ million = $1.5 million
$S_L = [(\$2 \text{ million} - \$1.5 \text{ million}) \times 0.6]/0.2 = \$1.5$ million
B = $10 million
Therefore, $V_L = \$1.5$ million + $10 million = $11.5 million

b. When $4.5 million debt is retired, the remaining debt would be $5.5 million and cost of debt would be 10 percent.

Interest = $0.1 \times \$5.5$ million = $0.55 million

S_L = [($2 million − 0.55 million) × 0.6]/0.12 = $7.25 million

B = $5.5 million

V_L = $7.25 million + $5.5 million = $12.75 million

The value of the firm will increase to $12.75 million, indicating an increase of $1.25 million.

Before restructuring:

Opportunity cost of capital = ($10/$11.5) × 15% × 0.6 + ($1.5/$11.5) × 20%

= 7.83% + 2.61% = 10.44%

After restructuring:

Opportunity cost of capital = ($5.5/$12.75) × 10% × 0.6 + ($7.25/$12.75) × 12%

= 2.59% + 6.82% = 9.41%

The decrease in debt will increase the value of the firm and decrease the opportunity cost of capital.

c. Number of shares issued = $4.5 million/$15 = 300,000

After restructuring, the number of shares outstanding would be 400,000 (100,000 + 300,000).

Price per share = $7.25 million/0.4 million = $18.13

Since the share price before restructuring was $15 per share ($1.5 million/100,000), the restructuring increases the share price by $3.13.

d. Number of shares issued = $4.5 million/$10 = 450,000

After restructuring, the number of shares outstanding would be 550,000.

Price per share = $7.25 million/0.55 million = $13.18

Share price decreases by $1.82 to $13.18.

13.3 a. Step 1. Determine the cost of equity for each proportion of debt using the SML:

$k_s = k_{RF} + \beta_s(k_m - k_{RF})$

Step 2. Determine the opportunity cost of capital of the firm for each proportion of debt.

Opportunity cost of capital = $W_{debt} \times k_b(1 - t) + W_{equity} \times k_s$

Step 3. Determine the value of the firm using the formula

$V_L = EBIT(1 - t)/(\text{opportunity cost of capital})$

The final solution is given in the table below (given tax rate = 40%).

Proportion of Debt	Beta	k_b	k_s	Opportunity Cost of Capital	Value of Firm
0	0.8	8	10.4	10.4	$34,615,385
0.2	0.9	9	11.2	10.04	35,856,574
0.4	1.05	9.5	12.4	9.72	37,037,037
0.6	1.35	11.7	14.8	10.13	35,538,006
0.75	1.60	13.8	16.8	10.41	34,582,133

The opportunity cost of capital is minimized where the proportion of debt is 40 percent. This also corresponds to the highest market value of the firm.

b. Given that shares are repurchased at $34.62 per share:

i. When debt = 0 and 1 million shares outstanding

V_U = $34,615,385

Share price = $34.62

      ii.   When debt = 20%

V_L = \$35,856,574

Debt = 0.2 × \$35,856,574 = \$7,171,315

Equity = \$28,685,259

Number of shares repurchased = \$7,171,315/\$34.62 = 207,144

Number of shares outstanding = 792,856

Share price = \$28,685,259/792,856 = \$36.18

      iii.   When debt = 40%

V_L = \$37,037,037

Debt = 0.4 × \$37,037,037 = \$14,814,815

Equity = \$22,222,222

Number of shares repurchased = \$14,814,815/\$34.62 = 427,926

Number of shares outstanding = 572,074

Share price = \$22,222,222/572,074 = \$38.85

      iv.   When debt = 60%

V_L = \$35,538,006

Debt = 0.6 × \$35,538,006 = \$21,322,804

Equity = \$14,215,202

Number of shares repurchased = \$21,322,804/\$34.62 = 615,910

Number of shares outstanding = 384,090

Share price = \$14,215,202/384,090 = \$37.01

      v.   When debt = 75%

V_L = \$34,582,133

Debt = 0.75 × \$34,582,133 = \$25,936,600

Equity = \$8,645,533

Number of shares repurchased = \$25,936,600/\$34.62 = 749,180

Number of shares outstanding = 250,820

Share price = \$8,645,533/250,820 = \$34.47

Share price is maximized when debt = 40%. This corresponds to the minimum opportunity cost of capital and the highest value for the firm.

    c.   ABX's target capital structure should be 40 percent debt and 60 percent equity. This is where the value of the firm is maximized.

Chapter 14
Dividend Policy

How This Chapter Relates to the Rest of the Text

Cash dividends are the basis for common stock valuation (Chapter 4). In this chapter, we examine dividend policy and its link between the capital budget (Chapters 7–9) and the firm's required return (Chapter 6). The chapter also discusses the advantages and disadvantages of changing the dividend policy, stock splits and dividends, and stock repurchases, as well as the effects of each on stock prices (Chapter 10).

Topical Outline

I.   Dividends and financing.
    A.   The firm's cash dividend policy results in a decision simultaneously to issue cash dividends and not to reinvest the cash in the firm.
    B.   The cash dividend policy affects the firm's cash budget as well as its long-run financing plan.
        1.   Over two-thirds of a firm's total funds for investment are generated internally.
        2.   Firms that pay cash dividends have less internally generated funds available for other uses such as investment.
    C.   In practice, firms pay out a substantial portion of their earnings in the form of cash dividends in both good and bad times.
        1.   Firms that do not pay high cash dividends rely substantially less on external financing for their ongoing needs.
        2.   Many firms attempt to increase cash dividends at a rate that at least equals the rate of inflation.
II.   Does dividend policy matter? The irrelevance arguments.
    A.   Miller and Modigliani's irrelevance argument.
        1.   MM assume:
            a.   Perfect capital markets — no taxes, brokerage fees, or flotation costs.
            b.   The capital structure is fixed — all external financing comes from issuing new equity.
            c.   The firm's investment policy is fixed — it has already accepted all positive NPV projects. They conclude that the firm's cash dividend policy does not affect the value of the firm nor does it matter to the firm's current shareholders.
        2.   Firm value is maximized by accepting all projects with positive NPVs.
        3.   The MM argument provides the frame of reference for considering what factor might cause cash dividends to affect firm value.
    B.   The residual theory of dividends.
        1.   The firm can determine its cash dividend policy after looking at its optimal cash budget and its target capital structure. Dividends are paid only if there is internally generated cash left over.
        2.   The residual theory of dividends suggests that investors are as well or better off when the firm reinvests internally generated funds in opportunities whose returns equal or exceed the investors' returns on alternative investments.
            a.   Determine the optimal capital budget, accepting all projects with a positive net present value.
            b.   Determine the amount of common equity needed to finance new investments while maintaining the firm's capital structure; if the capital structure is 70 percent equity, the investments will be 70 percent financed with equity.
            c.   Use internally generated funds to supply this equity whenever possible, issuing common stock for the shortfall.
            d.   Pay cash dividends only after funding capital investments according to the target capital structure.
        3.   Like the MM argument, residual dividend policy suggests that cash dividends do not affect the value of the firm, and that the value of the firm does not change even though the timing of dividend payments may change.

III.   Why do firms pay cash dividends?
    A.   Taxes and the firm's cash dividend policy.
        1.   Some corporate cash flow is taxed twice, once at the corporate level and again at the personal level since dividends are taxed.
        2.   Individuals are taxed on wages, salaries, dividends, interest, and capital gains.
            a.   Federal income tax rates are progressive. Currently there are three tax brackets; up to $29,590 is 17%, $29,590 to $59,180 is 26%, $59,180 and over is 29%.
            b.   Provincial taxes (except in Quebec) are from 45% to 69% of the federal tax liability.
        3.   Capital gains are taxed at 3/4 of the individual's marginal tax rate.
        4.   Common shareholders have a choice of when to pay taxes if the returns come from capital gains instead of cash dividends.
        5.   Because of the dual taxation of dividends and to offset the tax advantage of receiving capital gains, tax laws allow individuals to employ a gross-up (25% of dividends) and tax credit (13.33% of taxable dividends) system.
        6.   For Canadian corporations, dividend income earned from investments in other Canadian corporations is not taxed whereas capital gains are taxed at 3/4 of the firm's marginal tax rate. Thus, corporations prefer to receive dividends.
    B.   Dividends, cash flow, and growth options.
        1.   Firms with more growth opportunities channel more of their cash flows to finance growth and, therefore, pay less dividends.
        2.   Firms with more growth opportunities can tolerate more restrictions on dividends in bond covenants and, therefore, should pay out less of their cash flows as dividends.
    C.   Signalling.
        1.   Dividends may signal unique information about the future prospects of the firm.
            a.   High dividend payout may indicate high future cash flows for the firm; the market may bid the price of the stock up reflecting these cash flows.
    D.   Some further arguments for the influence of dividend policy.
        1.   Investors as a whole might prefer high-dividend-payout firms.
            a.   Returns from investing in common stock come from cash dividends and capital gains. Capital gains are considered riskier than cash dividends since an investor may not realize the gains at all. Therefore, a high-dividend payout may make some of the return more certain.
                i.   Investment in a high-payout firm may be perceived as less risky.
                ii.   The required return of the high-payout (less risky) firm is lower and its price is higher than that of the low-payout firm.
            b.   Some investors may prefer certain current income from dividends rather than the less certain capital gains.
        2.   Investors as a whole might prefer low-payout firms.
            a.   Flotation costs make funding with internally generated funds less expensive than funding with newly issued securities.
            b.   Brokerage costs make selling stock to provide current income more costly for the investor.
IV.   Is there an optimal dividend policy?
    A.   The clientele effect: Some investors prefer high-payout firms while others prefer low-payout firms.
        1.   Investors with low incomes and high current income needs would favour high-payout firms.
        2.   Once the dividend policy is established, some investors will buy the stock, and the dividend policy will not affect the market price unless the policy is subsequently changed.
    B.   Other factors in the dividend decision.
        1.   Stable firms have fewer investment opportunities than newer, fast-growing firms, so they have higher payout policies.

      2.   Firms with a shortage of cash will often restrict cash dividends, but firms with a cash surplus will often pay high dividends to avoid being a tempting takeover candidate.

      3.   More stable firms are in a better position to pay high cash dividends, since they can plan for the future with more certainty than highly cyclical firms.

      4.   Small firms, with limited access to equity markets, pay lower cash dividends.

      5.   Firms concerned about maintaining ownership control will prefer to fund new capital investment with internally generated funds rather than issue new common stock.

   C.   Constraints inhibiting the firm's ability to pay cash dividends.

      1.   Contractual restrictions require that firms withhold payment of cash dividends on common stock until preferred stockholders have received their dividends.

      2.   Incorporation laws typically prohibit firms from paying cash dividends if the firms' liabilities exceed their assets, if the dividend would be paid from the firms' invested capital, or if the dividend exceeds retained earnings.

V.   Dividend policy in practice.

   A.   Firms act as though dividend policy is an important decision.

      1.   Firms try to maintain stable and increasing cash dividends over time, avoiding a reduction in cash dividends if at all possible.

      2.   Most firms use a smoothed residual dividend policy, setting a target dividend payout ratio and a target capital structure ratio after funding the capital budget; they increase the dollar amount if it seems it can be maintained.

   B.   Dividend payout policies differ depending on the primary industry in which the firm is located and sometimes vary within the industry.

   C.   Increases and decreases in cash dividends depend somewhat on the economy and how it affects earnings and the availability of internally generated funds.

   D.   Firms that do not want to increase cash dividends permanently may pay an "extra" dividend in a good year.

VI.   Dividend payment procedures.

   A.   Cash dividends are normally paid quarterly.

   B.   Procedures:

      1.   The board of directors meets and issues a statement declaring the next quarter's dividends (date declared).

      2.   An arbitrary date, the ex-dividend date (which is the second business day preceding the record date), is established to determine who is entitled to the dividend payment.

      3.   The record date is the date that stockholder books are closed in order to determine the current stockholders.

      4.   The payment date is the date the firm actually mails the dividend cheques to the stockholders.

   C.   Because the ex-dividend date determines who is entitled to the next cash dividend, the market price of the stock drops, on average, by the amount of the quarterly dividend on the ex-dividend date.

   D.   Dividend reinvestment plans involve reinvesting in additional new or existing shares of the common stock.

      1.   In buying existing shares, a trust company acts as trustee, accumulating funds from all stockholders who take the option, and purchases (for a small transaction cost) shares in the open market.

      2.   In buying new shares, investors often enjoy a 3 to 5 percent reduction in the stock's current market price, and firms enjoy expanded capital stock; many firms issue additional stock through dividend reinvestment plans.

   E.   Repurchasing stock.

      1.   Methods.

          a.   Tender offer to all the firm's stockholders.

          b.   Purchase of the stock on the secondary market.

          c.   Agreement with a small group of the firm's major investors to buy their shares.

2.   Effect of repurchasing stock.
    a.   The EPS should increase and result in a higher market price per outstanding share of common stock.
    b.   Stockholders not selling their shares back to the firm will enjoy a capital gain if the repurchase increases the stock price.
3.   Advantages of repurchasing.
    a.   Repurchase can be used to effect a large-scale change in the firm's capital structure.
    b.   If the firm has an excess of cash but does not want to increase cash dividends, it can increase the investors' return without creating an expectation of higher future dividends.
    c.   The firm can reduce future cash dividend requirements, or increase cash dividends per share on the remaining shares, without creating a continuing incremental cash drain.
    d.   From the stockholder's point of view, capital gains are treated more favourably than cash dividends for tax purposes.
4.   Disadvantages of repurchasing.
    a.   Firms that repurchase substantial amounts of stock rather than invest in capital projects generally have poorer growth and investment opportunities than those that do not repurchase large amounts.
    b.   The provincial securities commissions may raise questions about the intention of the stock repurchase, or the share repurchase may not qualify the investor for a capital gain.

VII.   Stock splits and dividends are methods of issuing more shares.
    A.   Effects of stock split or stock dividend: Increase the number of shares per investor, decreasing each share's value respectively.
        1.   No change in firm's total assets, liabilities, stockholders' equity, earnings, cash dividends, or total market value.
        2.   Drop in per share earnings, cash dividends, and common stock market price, and a corresponding increase in the number of shares outstanding.
    B.   Difference between stock splits and stock dividends.
        1.   Stock splits and stock dividends have the same effect from an economic standpoint.
        2.   Accounting treatment of stock splits and stock dividends.
            a.   With a stock split, the number of shares is increased.
            b.   In a stock dividend:
                i.   A transfer is made from the retained earnings account to the common stock accounts.
                ii.   The transfer size depends upon the size of the stock dividend and the stock's current market price.
        3.   Stock splits and stock dividends have no economic effect on the stockholders.
        4.   Reasons for declaring stock splits and stock dividends.
            a.   Some firms view it as an extension of their cash dividend policy.
            b.   Many firms believe their shares have an optimal trading price, contrary to market efficiency.
            c.   Firms use stock splits or stock dividends to communicate extra information about their future cash flows.
            d.   Firms may "conserve cash" by declaring a stock dividend rather than a cash dividend.

Formulas

Notation

P_0 = market price of a share of stock at time 0

k_s = cost of equity capital

g = expected compound percentage growth rate in cash dividends

<u>Basic Valuation Framework</u>

$$P_0 = D_1/(k_s - g)$$

<u>Effect of a Stock Repurchase</u>

Current EPS = total earnings/number of shares outstanding

Current P/E = market price per share/EPS

EPS after repurchase = total earnings/decreased number of shares

Expected market price after repurchase = (current P/E)(new EPS)

What to Look For

In Chapters 12 and 13, we examined the firm's capital structure decision. We noted that firms act as if they have a target capital structure that maximizes firm value. In Chapter 14, we look at cash dividend policy and its relationship to capital structure and market value.

<u>Dividend Policy and the Capital Structure</u>

Maintaining the capital structure is not simple. Each time the firm decides to issue cash dividends, it is making a capital structure decision. Any earnings used as dividends are unavailable for reinvestment in the firm in the form of internally generated capital. So the firm must either curtail capital investments or fund projects with additional externally generated capital.

<u>Dividend Policy and the Value of the Firm</u>

Miller and Modigliani's irrelevance argument

With frictionless capital markets (i.e., no taxes, brokerage fees, or flotation costs) MM demonstrate that, if a firm's capital structure and capital investment decisions are fixed, its dividend decision will not impact on firm value. Firm value is maximized by accepting all projects with positive NPVs, not by the size of its dividend payment.

Residual theory of dividends

The residual theory of dividends states that investors will be as well or better off if the firm invests internally generated funds in capital projects whose returns exceed that available to its common stockholders. The firm would maintain its target capital structure and fund these projects with as much internally generated equity as is needed to meet the equity requirements.

The earnings remaining after this investment would be distributed as cash dividends. If the year's earnings fell short of the equity requirement for capital funding, the firm would issue common stock to cover the shortfall. Similar to the MM argument, the residual theory suggests that the value of the firm is unaffected by the pattern of cash dividends, as long as projects yield a higher rate of return than that available to the firm's common shareholders.

Individual and corporate taxes

In Canada, personal tax rates are progressive; that is, the higher your income, the higher the percentage of tax paid. There are personal income taxes at both the federal and the provincial levels. In all provinces except Quebec, provincial taxes "piggyback" on federal taxes. This means that the provincial tax is a percentage (which varies across provinces) of the federal taxes paid.

Consider, for example, the case of Ms. Eleanor McClellan who lives in Alberta. She had $45,000 in income in 1996. According to Table 14.2 in the book, her federal tax would be $5,030 on the first $29,590 of income and 26% on the remainder, or $5,030 + ($45,000 − $29,590)(0.26) = $9,036.60. Her provincial tax bill, since she lives in Alberta, is 45.5% of her federal tax bill, or $9,036.60(0.455) + $4,111.65. Ms. McClellan must pay $9,036.60 + $4,111.65 = $13,148.25 in income taxes.

Income from investments is also taxed at the personal level. Net capital gains, for instance, are taxed at 3/4 of the personal tax rate. Dividend and interest income is also taxed, but there are some complications. Because corporate income is taxed, taxing dividends amounts to dual taxation. Because of this, the Canadian tax system provides for a gross-up and tax credit system. To see how this works, suppose Ms. McClellan has $6,000 in dividend income. She would calculate her taxes as follows:

Dividends	$6,000.00
Add: Gross-up (25%)	1,500.00
Taxable dividends	7,500.00
Federal tax (0.26 × $7,500)	1,950.00
Less: Dividend tax credit (0.1333 × $7,500)	999.75
Federal tax payable	950.25
Add: Alberta tax ($950.25 × 0.455)	432.36
Total tax liability	$1,382.61

As you can see, the gross-up and tax credit systems lower the effective tax rate on dividends and partially correct for dual taxation of corporate income.

Dividends received by a Canadian corporation from another Canadian corporation are tax exempt. On the other hand, any capital gains earned by a corporation are taxed at 3/4 of the firm's marginal tax rate. Thus, firms have a preference for dividend income as opposed to capital gains.

Growth options and signalling
Firms with significant future growth opportunities will use more of their internally generated cash flows to finance these opportunities and, therefore, will pay less cash dividends. On the other hand, a firm may increase its cash dividend to signal an improvement in its future prospects (cash flows).

Preferences of dividend payout levels
Most empirical testing lends some support to the idea of the clientele effect of dividend payout levels. Investors with low current income and high needs for current income will favour high-payout firms. The text discusses other reasons investors may prefer one payout level or another. No consensus exists, however, on whether dividend policy by itself affects the value of the firm's common stock.

Dividend Policy in Practice
In general, firms use a smoothed residual dividend policy. They maintain a stable or increasing dividend and often attempt to increase it to match inflation. Firms are reluctant to decrease the cash dollar dividend per share. In a good year, they sometimes declare extra dividends rather than permanently increase the dividend. Faster-growing firms have more investment opportunities and pay smaller dividends than mature firms. Firms whose management wants to maintain ownership control tend to pay lower dividends, since they use internally generated equity rather than issue more common stock.

Dividends can be an opportunity for the firm to obtain new equity capital. That is, if common shareholders participate in dividend reinvestment plans that invest in new shares rather than outstanding shares of the firm's stock, the equity capital base of the firm can expand without the cost of underwriting. Such plans are popular with many firms.

Stock Repurchases
In addition to paying dividends, firms occasionally repurchase their stock. From the firm's standpoint, repurchases have several advantages; the firm can provide stockholders with cash without adjusting its dividend policy, reduce future cash dividend requirements, and effect large changes in its capital structure. Repurchasing is also used as a means of attempting to fend off unwanted corporate suitors.

What Are Stock Splits and Stock Dividends?
Stock splits and stock dividends are issuances of additional shares of common stock on a *pro rata* basis to the existing shareholders. Neither process affects the stockholder's wealth. The text discusses the accounting of stock splits and stock dividends, as well as reasons why firms declare them.

Completion Questions

14.1 The cash dividend decision involves a decision simultaneously to pay dividends and not to _____.

14.2 If firms do not pay cash dividends, they would not have to rely as much on _____ to finance their capital expenditures.

14.3 Investors may be as well or better off if the firm _____ internally generated funds, as long as these funds yield a return that _____ the return available to common shareholders on alternative investments.

14.4 In determining how much common equity the firm needs for financing new projects, the firm should maintain its _____.

14.5 If internally generated funds fall short of the equity needed for new projects, the firm will _____.

14.6 The residual theory of dividends suggests that dividend policy _____ the value of the firm.

14.7 Under a progressive tax system, individuals with _____ face _____ tax rates.

14.8 Individual taxes on dividends are based on a _____ and _____ system.

14.9 For a corporation, dividend income from _____ companies is taxable, while dividend income from _____ companies is tax exempt.

14.10 The payment of high current dividends can resolve _____. The current market price for firms with high payout ratios may be _____ as a result of this resolution.

14.11 An increase in the firm's dividend payout ratio may be viewed as an indication of _____ of the firm.

14.12 The tax treatment of _____ versus dividend income for taxpaying investors creates a bias toward _____ payout firms.

14.13 According to the clientele effect, the low-income investor needing current income prefers a _____ payout firm. Once the clientele and dividend policy are established, the dividend policy _____ the value of the firm's stock.

14.14 In practice, firms prefer to pay _____ dividends. They are reluctant to _____ the level of dividends.

14.15 On the ex-dividend date, the market price of the firm's common stock generally _____.

Problems

14.1 Main Line Railroad, Ltd., has a target capital structure of 60 percent debt and 40 percent equity. The company currently has available to it $2,000,000 in cash earnings available for cash dividends or reinvestment. It is considering five capital expenditures, each with a 10-year life. The projects are summarized below:

Project	CF_0 (in thousands)	CF_{1-10} (in thousands)
A	$1,000	$254.91
B	2,000	560.07
C	3,000	597.73
D	500	107.32
E	500	115.23

The railroad follows a residual dividend policy. If Main Line's opportunity cost of capital is 16 percent, what should be its dividend payout ratio?

14.2 Mr. Ralph Zeigler lives in British Columbia. In 1996, Mr. Zeigler had wage earnings of $25,000, dividend income of $3,000, and interest income of $2,000. What is Mr. Zeigler's total tax liability?

14.3   Sandburg Manufacturing has earnings available for distribution to shareholders of $500,000 in cash, which
it may pay out or reinvest. The firm is considering three options.

    Alternative 1:   A cash dividend. The firm has a 75 percent dividend payout ratio.
    Alternative 2:   A 3-for-2 stock split.
    Alternative 3:   A 50 percent stock dividend.

The shareholders' equity portion of the balance sheet presently looks like this:

    Common stock (1 million shares outstanding, no par) $ 9,000,000
    Retained earnings   10,000,000
        Total shareholders' equity $19,000,000

How would the shareholders' equity portion of the balance sheet look under each of these three alternatives
assuming the stock is selling for $10 per share?

14.4   Baron Realty has 100,000 shares of common stock outstanding with a market price of $50 per share. The
firm normally distributes 60 percent of its earnings as cash dividends; however, this year, the firm wishes
to use its $540,000 in earnings to repurchase 10,000 shares at $54 per share from a dissident shareholder.
Assuming that the P/E ratio remains constant, are the remaining shareholders better or worse off after the
repurchase? (Ignore any tax effects.)

Answers to Completion Questions

14.1   reinvest these funds in the firm
14.2   external financing
14.3   retains and reinvests; equals or exceeds
14.4   target capital structure
14.5   issue new common stock
14.6   does not affect
14.7   higher (lower); higher (lower)
14.8   gross-up; tax credit
14.9   foreign-owned; Canadian
14.10   investor uncertainty; bid up
14.11   the future profitability
14.12   capital gains; low
14.13   high; does not directly influence
14.14   stable or increasing; reduce
14.15   decreases by the amount of the cash dividend per share

Solutions to Problems

14.1   Step 1.   Solve for the internal rate of return on each of the projects to determine which ones should be
accepted. Since the projects are annuities, the IRR can be solved for by finding k, such that

$$CF_t(PVA_{k\%,10yr}) - CF_0 = 0$$

    or $PVA_{k\%,10yr} = (CF0/Cft)(CF_0/CF_t)$

    Project A $PVA_{k\%,10yr} = (\$1,000/\$254.91) = 3.923$ The IRR = 22%
    Project B $PVA_{k\%,10yr} = (\$2,000/\$560.07) = 3.571$ The IRR = 25%
    Project C $PVA_{k\%,10yr} = (\$3,000/\$597.73) = 5.019$ The IRR = 15%
    Project D $PVA_{k\%,10yr} = (\$500/\$107.32) = 4.659$ The IRR = 17%
    Project E $PVA_{k\%,10yr} = (\$500/\$115.23) = 4.339$ The IRR = 19%

    Step 2.   The firm should choose projects with IRRs greater than 16 percent. Those projects are A, B,
D, and E.

    Total $CF_0 = \$1,000 + \$2,000 + \$500 + \$500 = \$4,000$ or $4 million

Step 3.　　Amount financed by equity = (proportion of equity)(total CF_0) = (0.40)($4,000,000) = $1,600,000. Since the firm has $2,000,000 in earnings, in order to maintain its target capital structure, it should retain $1,600,000 and pay the residual $400,000 ($2,000,000 − $1,600,000) as dividends. The dividend payout ratio is ($400,000/$2,000,000) = 0.20.

14.2

Wages		$25,000.00
Interest income		2,000.00
Dividends received	$3,000.00	
Gross-up (25%)	750.00	
Taxable dividends		3,750.00
Taxable income		30,750.00

Federal tax:
　　$5,030 + ($30,750 − $29,590)(0.26) =　5,331.60
Less: Dividend tax credit ($3,750 × 0.1333)　　499.88
　　Total federal tax　　　　　　　　　　　　4,831.72
Provincial tax ($4,831.72 × 0.5215)　　　　　2,536.65
　　　　Total taxes　　　　　　　　　　　$7,368.37

14.3　Step 1.　Alternative 1:　The firm would pay total cash dividends of ($500,000)(0.75) = $375,000 and retain $500,000 − $375,000 = $125,000. New retained earnings would be $10,000,000 + $125,000 = $10,125,000. So,

Common stock (1 million shares, no par)	$ 9,000,000
Retained earnings	10,125,000
Total shareholders' equity	$19,125,000

Step 2.　Alternative 2:　Under a stock split, only the number of shares outstanding is adjusted. If no cash dividends are paid, retained earnings will increase by $500,000; the new net worth portion of the balance sheet will be as follows:

Common stock (1.5 million shares, no par)	$ 9,000,000
Retained earnings	10,500,000
Total shareholders' equity	$19,500,000

Step 3.　Alternative 3:　Under a stock dividend, the number of shares outstanding increases and the common stock account is increased by the market value of the new shares. Shares outstanding = 1,000,000 × 1.5 = 1,500,000. The increase in shares is 1,500,000 − 1,000,000 = 500,000. The market value of the new shares is $10 × 500,000 = $5,000,000 and the common stock account becomes $9,000,000 + $5,000,000 = $14,000,000. Since no cash dividend will be paid, retained earnings are $10,000,000 + $500,000 − $5,000,000 = $5,500,000. So,

Common stock (1.5 million shares, no par)	$14,000,000
Retained earnings	5,500,000
Total shareholders' equity	$19,500,000

14.4　Step 1.　EPS = $540,000/100,000 = $5.40 per share
　　　　　P/E = $50/5.40 = 9.26

$$\text{New EPS} = \frac{\$540,000}{100,000 - 10,000} = \$6 \text{ per share}$$

New price = (P/E)(EPS) = (9.26)($6) = $55.56 per share
Investors will realize an increase in value of $55.56 − $50 = $5.56 per share.

Step 2.   The alternative is to receive a cash dividend of

$$\frac{(\$540,000)(0.60)}{100,000} = \$3.24 \text{ per share}$$

The shareholders will be better off with the repurchase since the increase in price ($5.56) is greater than $5.40, which is the sum of the dividend ($3.24) and the increase in the share price from earnings retained ($2.16).

Chapter 15
Leasing

How This Chapter Relates to the Rest of the Text

To this point, we have assumed that when a firm found a profitable investment (Chapters 7–9), it raised funds either internally or externally (Chapters 10 and 11) and purchased the asset. An alternative method of acquiring the asset is through leasing. Leasing is similar to debt financing (Chapter 11). Cash flow and taxes (Chapter 8) form the basis for lease analysis. Conceptually, the net present value of leasing (NPV_{lease}) is an application of the net present value techniques employed in the replacement capital budgeting decision (Chapter 8). The discount rate employed is the after-tax cost of debt.

Topical Outline

I.   Leasing and the firm.
   A.   Who provides lease financing?
      1.   Some manufacturers, such as railway or airplane manufacturers, use leasing as part of their regular sales effort.
      2.   Firms such as chartered banks, investment leasing companies, subsidiaries of other firms, and commercial finance companies also provide lease financing.
   B.   Types of leases.
      1.   The operating lease is short-term and generally cancellable.
         a.   Often used with relatively inexpensive assets such as office machines and cars.
         b.   The lessor generally services the equipment and pays any insurance and property taxes; this lease is often called a service lease.
         c.   Large service leases should undergo in-depth financial analysis before the lessee signs the agreement.
      2.   Finance leases are noncancellable long-term contracts between the lessor, who owns the asset, and the lessee, who agrees to lease the asset for a specified period of time.
         a.   Finance leases are a form of long-term financing similar to borrowing, and the cash flow consequences are also similar to borrowing.
         b.   The lessee agrees to provide for maintenance, insurance coverage, and property taxes related to the asset leased.
      3.   Sale and leaseback arrangements occur when an asset owner decides to sell the asset to another party and lease it back.
         a.   The firm desires to raise capital by selling an asset, usually real estate, but wishes to maintain use of the asset for some period of time.
         b.   The financial analysis of sale and leaseback arrangements versus borrowing resembles the analysis of other finance leases analyzed later.
      4.   Leveraged leases involve three parties: the lender, the lessor, and the lessee.
   C.   Tax considerations.
      1.   Lease payments are a tax-deductible expense for the lessee.
      2.   The lessor takes the capital cost allowance for the asset.
      3.   Revenue Canada considers lease-options to be sales (and thus not tax-deductible) if
         a.   Title to the asset automatically transfers to the lessee after a prespecified amount of time.
         b.   The lessee is required to buy the asset.
         c.   The lessee is required to guarantee that it or a third party will pay an option price to the lessor.
         d.   The lessee is able to purchase the asset at a price substantially below its market value.
      4.   Some sale and leaseback agreements are classified as secured loan agreements by Revenue Canada.

    D.   Accounting for leases.
        1.   Capital leases exist if the lease
            a.   Transfers ownership of the property to the lessee by the end of the lease term or provides the lessee with an option to purchase the asset at a bargain price.
            b.   Has a lease term equal to 75 percent or more of the estimated life of the property.
            c.   The present value of the lease payments is equal to or greater than 90 percent of the value of the asset.
        2.   Capital leases must be capitalized on the firm's financial statements.
            a.   The present value of the lease payments must be entered as a liability on the firm's balance sheet.
            b.   A corresponding entry to value the asset must be made on the balance sheet.
            c.   This asset is amortized over the useful life of the asset or the lease term, resulting in a reduction in reported income, with corresponding reductions on the liability side each year.
        3.   Operating leases for accounting purposes are those that do not meet the above conditions, and that need not appear on the balance sheet; instead, they show up in footnotes to the financial statements.

II.   How are lease rates set by the lessor?
    A.   The lessor wants to set a rate that provides it with a satisfactory risk-adjusted return.
    B.   The lessor focuses on
        1.   The after-tax required return on debt-type investments (k_i).
        2.   The marginal tax rate (T).
        3.   The cost of the leased asset (CLA_0).
        4.   The CCA class and the prescribed CCA rate (d).
    C.   To determine the proper lease rate:
        1.   Determine the tax benefits from owning the asset and depreciation.
        2.   Calculate the present value of benefits:

$$\text{Present value of benefits} = \left[\frac{T \times d \times CLA_0}{k_i + d} \right] \times \left[\frac{1 + 0.5k_i}{1 + k_i} \right]$$

        3.   Determine the amount to be recovered from lease payments.

$$\text{Net amount recovered from lease payments} = CLA_0 - \text{Present value of benefits}$$

        4.   The after-tax lease payment (ATL) is found by solving

$$\text{Net amount recoverable from lease payments} = ATL\ (PVA_{k\%,\ n\ yr})\ (1 + k_i)$$

        5.   The required lease payment is

$$L = \frac{ATL}{(1 - T)}$$

III.   To lease or not to lease?
    A.   Good reasons for leasing.
        1.   Tax implications.
            a.   Lessees may often benefit from leasing if they have a lower marginal tax rate than the lessor, and the lessor passes these savings on to the lessee in the form of reduced lease payments.
            b.   The CCA benefits are worth more to the lessor than the lessee if the lessor has a higher tax rate.
        2.   Leases provide flexibility and convenience.
            a.   With an operating lease, the lessor secures, sets up, and maintains the assets.
            b.   It is preferable to lease certain types of assets under a service lease than to buy them.

3. Some leases often contain an option to cancel.
   a. This option is valuable and enhances the desirability of a lease.
   b. Lessors charge a higher lease rate as compensation for this option.
4. Other factors.
   a. Many leases are set at a fixed rate.
   b. It is becoming more common for lessors to provide maintenance, insurance, and other services.
   c. Leasing offers an element of protection for firms with international operations.

B. Dubious reasons for leasing.
1. Conservation of working capital.
   a. Leases do not provide 100 percent financing, since they require a prepayment.
   b. Although smaller firms might need to rely on leases for financing, larger firms generally can secure about the same amount of financing from leasing as from the capital markets.
2. Increase the firm's borrowing capacity.
   a. The firm can obtain more long-term funding by combining leasing and borrowing.
   b. This assumes that bankers, lenders, and capital markets do not recognize that leasing places a financial obligation on the firm, just as borrowing does.
3. Avoiding restrictions is a weak and perhaps invalid reason to lease.

C. The ultimate test of a lease proposal is to determine whether the value of the firm is maximized by leasing or by borrowing.

IV. Evaluation of finance leases.
A. What decision are we concerned with?
1. Our capital budgeting treatment assumed the asset will be purchased if the NPV is positive.
2. If leasing is a possibility, another step must be added to the capital budgeting analysis to determine whether the asset should be leased or purchased.
   a. Calculate the net present value of leasing (NPV_{lease}).
   b. If the NPV_{lease} is positive, the firm should acquire the asset by leasing rather than by purchasing.
   c. NPV (capital budgeting) and NPV_{lease} decisions interact.
      i. If the NPV is negative, the asset might still be leased if favourable lease terms more than completely offset the negative NPV.
      ii. If the NPV is negative, the asset should not be leased if the NPV_{lease} does not offset the negative NPV.

B. Why compare leasing with borrowing?
1. Leasing imposes the same kind of financial commitment that borrowing does.
2. We want to neutralize the risk between the two alternatives.
   a. Establish an equivalent borrowing amount that, in terms of the after-tax cash flows, is the same in each future period as the after-tax lease cash flows.
   b. Employ the after-tax borrowing rate of the firm as the relevant discount rate to accomplish this.

C. Financial lease evaluation using the NPV_{lease} approach.
1. Major elements of the NPV_{lease} approach.
   a. Lease payments (L) made periodically on an after-tax basis, with the first payment at $t_0 = 0$, are an annuity due.
   b. The capital cost allowance (CCA) over the life of the lease; the tax shield from the CCA is foregone when leasing.
   c. The cost of the asset (CLA_0) if purchased.

2.   Formula:

$$\text{NPV}_{\text{lease}} = \text{cost of buying the asset} - \begin{array}{c}\text{explicit and opportunity costs}\\\text{of leasing the asset}\end{array}$$

$$= \text{CLA}_0 - \left\{ \left[\sum_{t=1}^{n} \frac{L_t (1-T)}{(1+k_i)^t} \right] (1+k_i) + \left[\frac{T \times d \times \text{CLA}_0}{k_i + d} \right] \times \left[\frac{1 + 0.5 k_i}{1 + k_i} \right] \right\}$$

a. $\text{NPV}_{\text{lease}}$ = cost of asset – [present value of the after-tax annuity due + discounted present value of foregone CCA tax shield].

b.   If the cost of leasing is less than the cost of purchasing the asset, the firm should lease rather than purchase.

D.   Two frequently incurred complications if the asset is purchased.

1.   Annual incremental operating costs (O_t).

2.   Resale value of the asset (RV_n when it is disposed of.

3.   The formula becomes

$$\text{NPV}_{\text{lease}} = \text{CLA}_0 - \left\{ \left[\sum_{t=1}^{n} \frac{L_t(1-T)}{(1+k_i)^t} \right](1+k_i) + \left[\frac{T \times d \times \text{CLA}_0}{k_i + d} \right]\left[\frac{1 + 0.5 k_i}{1 + k_i} \right] \right.$$

$$\left. - \left[\frac{1}{(1+k_i)^n} \right]\left[\frac{T \times d \times RV_n}{k_i + d} \right] - \sum_{t=1}^{n} \frac{O_t(1-T)}{(1+k)^t} + \frac{RV_n}{(1+k)^n} \right\}$$

a.   The appropriate opportunity cost of capital for the asset in question, k, is used to find the present value of O_t and RV_n.

E.   The percentage annual cost of the lease can be found by solving the following formula for IRR:

$$\text{CLA}_0 - L_0(1-T) = \sum_{t=1}^{n-1} \frac{L_t(1-T)}{(1+\text{IRR})^t} + \frac{T \times d \times \text{CLA}_0}{\text{IRR} + d} \times \frac{1 + 0.5\,\text{IRR}}{1 + \text{IRR}}$$

Formulas

Notation

CLA   = cost of the asset (initial investment) if the asset is purchased
k_i = after-tax cost of debt
L_t = lease payment made for period t, starting at t = 0
k_b = before-tax cost of debt
k   = marginal cost of capital (or risk-adjusted required rate of return)
d   = CCA rate
O_t = incremental operating cost for period t if the asset is purchased
RV_n = resale value of the asset if purchased

Present Value of CCA Benefits

$$\text{Present value of CCA benefits} = \left[\frac{T \times d \times \text{CLA}_0}{k_i + d} \right] \times \left[\frac{1 + 0.5\,k_i}{1 + k_i} \right]$$

Net Amount Recoverable from Lease Payments

Net amount recoverable from lease payments = CLA_0 – present value of benefits

After-Tax Lease Payment

Solve the following for ATL.

$$\begin{array}{c}\text{Net recoverable from}\\\text{lease payments}\end{array} = \text{ATL} \, (\text{PVA}_{k\%, \, n \, yr}) \, (1 + k_i)$$

Lease Payment

$$L = \frac{ATC}{(1 - T)}$$

Net Present Value of Leasing

$$NAL = CLA_0 - \left\{ \left[\sum_{t=1}^{n} \frac{L_t(1-T)}{(1+k_i)^t} \right](1+k_i) + \left[\frac{T \times d \times CLA_0}{k_i + d} \right] \times \left[\frac{1 + 0.5k_i}{1 + k_i} \right] \right\}$$

What to Look For

Leasing is a debt-like form of financing. It sounds like a good way to finance assets off the balance sheet. The hitch is that capital leases must appear on the firm's balance sheet, and the lease payments are as legal an obligation for the firm as debt payments. In fact, leases have the same cash flow effects on the firm as borrowing.

Perspectives on Leasing

The tax perspective and the accounting perspective on leasing differ somewhat. These differences are reflected in the different terminology Revenue Canada and the accountant use for leases. From the tax perspective, two types of leases exist. The first is the finance lease, defined as a long-term noncancellable contract between the lessor, who owns the asset, and the lessee, who agrees to lease it for a specified period of time. Revenue Canada analyzes finance leases carefully to insure that the lease payment is actually rent rather than payments made to purchase the asset. The text lists the types of contracts that Revenue Canada considers to be sales and whose payments are not tax-deductible. All other leases, from the tax perspective, are considered operating leases.

Accountants classify leases in two categories. The first is the capital lease, defined under CICA 3065. Capital leases must be capitalized on the firm's balance sheet. That is, the lessee must set up asset and liability accounts on the balance sheet reflecting the present value of the lease payments. The firm amortizes the asset over the asset's useful life, reducing the net income and the liability correspondingly each year. For accountants, the second type of lease is the operating lease, which need not appear on the firm's balance sheet. The important point to remember is that a capital lease for accounting purposes may not be a financial lease for tax purposes, and vice versa.

We can also view leases from the perspective of the lessor and the lessee. From the lessor's point of view, there are sales-type leases, direct financing leases, leveraged leases, and operating leases (shorter-term, generally cancellable leases that do not fit in the other categories). From the lessee's viewpoint, there are two types of leases, financial leases and operating leases (which are all leases other than financial leases). From either perspective, lease valuation employs the net present value techniques discussed in Chapters 7–9.

The Lease-or-Buy Decision

Debt and lease obligations have the same cash flow effects on the firm, but these obligations are valued differently since taxes, bankruptcy costs, and transactions costs exist. Consider just the effect of capital cost allowance (CCA) on the lease-or-buy decision. If the firm's marginal tax rate is 40 percent, a purchased asset provides a CCA tax shield of 40 percent times the annual CCA. This tax shield, in effect, reduces the annual cash outflow for the purchase (or borrowing) decision, making purchasing more attractive.

When the firm is operating at a profit, the potential lessee weighs the after-tax cash flows and opportunity cost of leasing against the cost of the asset if purchased. As we noted above, the chief opportunity cost of leasing is the foregone CCA tax shield. In making this NPV_{lease} calculation, discount all the value to the present with the firm's after-tax borrowing rate. If the NPV_{lease} is positive, the firm should lease the asset. Otherwise, the firm should buy the asset (assuming the NPV (capital budgeting) is positive).

Completion Questions

15.1   An _____ lease is a lease that is short term and generally cancellable. The _____ is responsible for the maintenance of the leased asset under this type of lease.

15.2   The cash flow consequences of leasing resemble those of _____.

15.3   Since lease payments are an expense of the lessee in doing business, they are _____.

15.4   If a firm has a _____ lease, the firm must capitalize the lease obligation on its financial statements. _____ leases appear in footnotes to the firm's financial statements.

15.5   In order to decide whether to lease or purchase an asset, the firm calculates the _____.

15.6   To calculate the CCA tax shield of borrowing, multiply the _____ times the marginal tax rate. When entering into a lease, the lessee incurs an opportunity cost equal to this tax shield. The lower the firm's _____, the lower this opportunity cost.

15.7   The relevant discount rate in the net present value of leasing calculation is the _____.

15.8   In a _____ , the owner of an asset decides to sell it to another party and lease it back.

15.9   Unless a lease is _____ apart from tax consequences, it cannot be considered a financial lease.

Problems

15.1   Canadian Aircraft has been approached about a five-year lease for a new small airplane. The plane costs $1,500,000 and has a CCA rate of 25 percent. If $k_i = 8$ percent, and $T = 30$ percent, what lease rate should Canadian set?

15.2   After a capital budgeting process, Amalgamated Plastics Company has decided to acquire a plastic moulding machine. If purchased, the firm would be able to depreciate its $350,000 cost at a CCA rate of 20 percent. McMillin has offered to lease the same machine to Amalgamated for $80,000 a year for the five years, with the lease payments being made in advance. Should the moulding machine be leased if the firm's before-tax cost of debt is 15 percent and its marginal tax rate is 40 percent?

15.3   Acme Freightways has recently purchased three forklifts for $450,000. The company intends to depreciate them at a CCA rate of 30 percent to a zero salvage value. The company has the opportunity to sell the forklifts to a leasing company for $450,000 and lease them back for five years with the annual lease payments made in advance. If Acme's tax rate is 25 percent and the before-tax cost of debt is 16 percent, what is the maximum lease payment it would be willing to make?

Answers to Completion Questions

15.1   operating; lessor
15.2   borrowing, or debt
15.3   tax-deductible
15.4   capital; Operating
15.5   net present value of leasing, or NPV_{lease}
15.6   CCA; marginal tax rate
15.7   after-tax cost of borrowing
15.8   sale and leaseback
15.9   economically justified

Solutions to Problems

15.1   Step 1.   Determine the present value of benefits.

$$\text{Present value of benefits} = \left[\frac{T \times d \times CLA_0}{k_i + d}\right] \times \left[\frac{1 + 0.5k_i}{1 + k_i}\right]$$

$$= \frac{0.30 \times 0.25 \times \$1,500,000}{0.08 + 0.25} \times \frac{1 + 0.5 \times 0.08}{1.08}$$

$$= \frac{\$112,500}{0.33} \times \frac{1.04}{1.08}$$

$$= \$328,282.83$$

Step 2.   Amount to be recovered from lease payments:
$\$1,500,000 - \$328,282.83 = \$1,171,717.17$

Step 3.   After-tax lease payment:

$$\begin{array}{l}\text{Amount to be recovered} \\ \text{from lease payments}\end{array} = ATL \times (PVA_{k_i\%, \, n \, yr}) \, (1 + k_i)$$

$$\$1,171,717.17 = ATL \times PVA_{8\%, 5 \, yr}$$

$$= ATL \, (3.993) \, (1.08)$$

$$4.312 ATL = \$1,171,717.17$$

$$ATL = \frac{\$1,171,717.17}{4.312} = \$271,734.04$$

$$L = \frac{ATL}{(1 - T)} = \frac{\$271,734.04}{(1 - 0.30)} = \frac{\$271,734.04}{0.70} = \$388,191.48$$

15.2   Step 1. $NPV_{lease} = CLA_0 - \left\{\left[\sum_{t=1}^{n} \frac{L_t \, (1 - T)}{(1 + k_i)^t}\right] (1 + k_i) + \left[\frac{T \times d \times CLA_0}{k_i + d}\right] \times \left[\frac{1 + 0.5k_i}{1 + k_i}\right]\right\}$

From the problem, $CLA_0 = \$350,000$

$$\begin{array}{ll} L & = \$80,000 \\ T & = 0.40 \\ k_i & = k_b(1 - T) = 15\%(1 - 0.40) = 9\% \\ d & = 0.20 \\ n & = 5 \end{array}$$

Step 2.   So, $NPV_{lease} = \$350,000 - [\$80,000 \, (1 - 0.40)(PVA_{9\%, \, 5yr})(1 + 0.09)$

$$+ \left[\frac{0.40 \times 0.20 \times \$350,000}{0.09 + 0.20}\right] \times \left[\frac{1 + 0.5 \times 0.09}{1 + 0.09}\right]]$$

$$= \$350,000 - \left[\$48,000(3.890)(1.09) + \left[\frac{\$28,000}{0.29}\right] \times \left[\frac{1.045}{1.09}\right]\right]$$

$$= \$350,000 - (\$203,524.80 + \$92,565.64)$$

$$= \$350,000 - \$296,090.44 = \$53,909.56$$

Since the NPV_{lease} is greater than zero, the firm should lease the machine.

15.3   Step 1.   Set the $NPV_{lease} = 0$

$$0 = CLA_0 - \left\{ \left[\sum_{t=1}^{n} \frac{L_t(1-T)}{(1+k_i)^t} \right] (1 + k_i) + \left[\frac{T \times d \times CLA_0}{k_i + d} \right] \times \left[\frac{1 + 0.5k_i}{1 + k_i} \right] \right\}$$

$CLA_0 = \$450,000$

$k_i = 16\%(1 - 0.25) = 12\%$

$d = 0.30$

$n = 5$

Step 2.   So, $0 = \$450,000 - \left[L (1 - 0.25)(PVA_{12\%, 5 yr}) (1 + 0.12) \right.$

$$\left. + \left[\frac{0.25 \times 0.30 \times \$450,000}{0.12 + 0.30} \right] \times \left[\frac{1 + 0.50 \times 0.12}{1 + 0.12} \right] \right]$$

$0 = \$450,000 - \left[0.75L(3.605)(1.12) + (\$80,857.14) \times (0.9463) \right]$

$0 = \$450,000 - (3.028L + \$76,041.96)$

$3.028L = \$373,958.04$

$L = \$373,958.04/3.028 = \$123,500.01$ per year

Chapter 16
Mergers and Corporate Restructuring

How This Chapter Relates to the Rest of the Text

In Chapters 7–9, we saw how firms expand through investing in new projects. Another method of growth is through merger with or acquisition of another company. The decision to merge is simply an extension of the capital budgeting process. The firm considers the cash flows associated with the merger, their timing (Chapter 3), and riskiness (Chapter 5) and calculates a value (Chapter 4). The appropriate opportunity cost of capital is the target firm's market-determined opportunity cost of capital (Chapter 6). Merger and acquisition possibilities should be considered in financial and strategic planning (Chapter 26). In a corporate restructuring, the firm adds bonds to its capital structure to take advantage of the disciplining role of debt and to make the firm less attractive as a takeover candidate. Additional debt affects the firm's opportunity cost of capital (Chapter 6), and capital structure (Chapters 12 and 13). Divestiture is the opposite of a merger; the firm sells an asset or division. The divestiture decision is another example of capital budgeting (Chapters 7–9).

Topical Outline

I.   Introduction.
     A.   Firms can grow not only internally, but also by acquiring other firms.
          1.   A firm might acquire a division or part of the assets of another firm.
          2.   A firm might acquire an entire firm or all of its assets.
     B.   In the market for corporate control, management teams vie for the right to acquire and manage corporate activities and assets.
     C.   The focus of the text is the standpoint of the bidding firm rather than the target company.
II.   Reasons for merging.
     A.   Sensible reasons.
          1.   Increased economic performance.
               a.   Economies of scale may result when the combined firm has sufficient size to drive down its expenses.
               b.   Economies may result from vertical integration by ensuring the continous flow from raw material acquisition to production, distribution, and sale.
               c.   Merged firms may be able to take advantage of overlapping areas of expertise.
               d.   An additional benefit of mergers is market protection.
               e.   In achieving economies, the firm attempts to obtain synergistic benefits; the whole is worth more than the parts.
          2.   Mergers may create increased economies by removing inefficient management and providing a fresh viewpoint in the management of the acquired firm.
          3.   Tax considerations.
               a.   The bidding firm with past losses would acquire a profitable target firm.
               b.   The profitable bidding firm would acquire a target firm with past losses.
               c.   Tax benefits may be due to the write-up of assets to a new tax basis; this increases depreciation for tax purposes, and hence, cash flow.
               d.   The combined firm may have a greater debt capacity, increasing interest expense and lowering taxes. Increased debt also provides managerial incentives to create operating efficiency.
     B.   Dubious reasons for acquisitions.
          1.   Diversification: Diversification does not really benefit the stockholder, since individuals can diversify their own portfolios.
          2.   Growth for growth's sake does not produce anything of value unless it is accompanied by economies or tax benefits.
          3.   Earnings per share increases which result immediately from acquisition do not maximize the value of the firm unless they are accompanied by economies or tax benefits.

III.   Deciding whether to merge.
    A.   A merger is a capital budgeting decision; use NPVs.
        1.   NPV = benefits – costs.
           a.   Benefits = change in value + value of the target firm, i.e. Δ value + value$_B$.
        2.   Costs = price paid.
        3.   For the NPV to be positive, the bidding firm must be able to realize economic or tax benefits not available to the target firm.
    B.   Calculating benefits.
        1.   Value$_T$ is simply the market value of the target's outstanding securities.
        2.   Incremental benefits are the present value of the incremental cash flows, i.e.,

$$\Delta \text{value} = \sum_{t=1}^{n} \frac{\Delta CF_t}{(1+k)^t}$$

           a. Δafter-tax operating cash flows = $\Delta CFBT_t(1-T) + \Delta CCA_t(T)$.
           b..   Include additional outlays for new equipment or working capital.
           c.   If a target firm's assets are sold for an amount different than their value as an ongoing concern, ΔCF_t is affected.
           d. $\Delta CF_t = \Delta CFBT_t(1-T) + \Delta CCA_t(T) - \Delta$investment in long-term assets and net working capital $\pm$ after-tax gains or loss on the disposition of some of the target firm's assets.
    C.   Cost equals the value of cash or securities used in the exchange.
        1.   In a cash transaction, the value of the combined firm equals the value of the bidding firm + NPV. All net benefits go to the bidding firm's stockholders.
        2.   When common stock is used, gains are shared since the target firm's stockholders end up owning part of the combined firm.
           a.   Proportion of the firm owned by the target firm's shareholders:
               W = shares held by target firm's former shareholders ÷ total shares outstanding after the merger
           b.   Cost with stock = W(value$_{BT}$).
    D.   Exchange ratio = market value of cash and/or securities offered by the bidding firm ÷ market value of target firm's stock.
        1.   Often, a higher exchange ratio is required for cash mergers.
    E.   How to avoid mistakes in mergers.
        1.   Rely on market values; in a reasonably efficient market, the best estimate of the target firm's worth is its market price.
        2.   Concentrate on incremental cash flows from the proposed acquisition.
        3.   Use an opportunity cost of capital appropriate for the riskiness of the incremental cash flows.
        4.   Consider transactions costs in your analysis.
        5.   Be critical; avoid overpaying, especially in a bidding war. The firm may be better off if it loses.
        6.   Consider the form of financing.
    F.   Who benefits from mergers?
        1.   Most mergers involve a premium paid over the target firm's premerger market value, so the target's stockholders benefit.
        2.   Empirical evidence does not show that stockholders of the bidding firm receive much benefit.
        3.   Investment bankers and others who offer merger valuation services benefit.
    G.   Free cash flow and mergers.
        1.   Free cash flow is the cash flow above that needed to finance all positive NPV projects.
        2.   Firms with high free cash flow and poor investment opportunities decrease their shareholders' wealth by merging.
IV.   Mechanics of a merger.
    A.   Form of the acquisition.

1. Statutory amalgamation occurs when two or more firms combine to form a completely new firm, leaving no target or bidding firm.
2. A merger occurs through the acquisition of the target firm's stock.
3. The bidding firm can acquire the assets of the target firm, and the target firm can dissolve after paying its liabilities and distributing the net proceeds to its shareholders.
4. A holding company can acquire complete or partial control over another company.

B. Tax implications.
1. With a taxable transaction, the target's shareholders must treat the acquisition as a sale for tax purposes, and declare capital gains or losses.
2. If the merger meets the requirement for a tax-free transaction, the target's shareholders experience capital gains or losses only when they sell the new stock at some later date.

C. Accounting treatments.
1. Pooling of interests.
   a. Balance sheet treatment of a pooling of interests is a simple adding together of the two balance sheets.
   b. Income statement effects.
      i. The pooling of interests is a transfer of assets at their current depreciated book value.
      ii. Earnings per share may or may not change depending on the total earnings and postmerger number of shares outstanding.
2. Purchase.
   a. Balance sheet effects: The assets acquired are revalued to indicate the actual purchase price paid for the target firm, possibly creating goodwill.
   b. Income statement effects.
      i. Assets are revalued to reflect the value of the merger, so more depreciation is often charged off in future years than in pooling of interests, and goodwill is often created.
      ii. As a result, earnings per share tends to decrease.

V. Defensive tactics for fending off takeovers.
A. Preoffer defences.
1. General preoffer defences.
   a. Private companies are almost invulnerable to takeovers.
   b. Blocking stakes are holdings of more than 50 percent of the outstanding shares held by an individual or close-knit group.
   c. Employee stock ownership plans (ESOPs) have been used to place large amounts of stocks with a group that is less likely to sell the firm.
   d. Some firms are unlikely takeover candidates because of size or political reasons.
   e. Strong stock prices fend off many suitors.
2. Shark repellant charter amendments.
   a. Staggered board of directors.
   b. Some charters require approval of 62 2/3 percent to 80 percent of the shareholders before a merger can be affected.
   c. Fair price amendments prohibit two-tiered bids.
3. Other pretakeover defences.
   a. Dual class recapitalization gives one class of shareholders control over the firm.
   b. Poison pills provide shareholders with the right to purchase additional shares or sell existing shares to the target at attractive prices, if a bidder acquires a certain percentage of outstanding shares.

B. Post-offer defences.
1. Litigation.
2. Asset restructuring involves purchasing other assets, making another merger, or selling off the

firm's "crown jewels" to make it unattractive to the bidder.

3. Liability restructuring involves issuing new shares to a "white squire" or levering up the firm.

4. Under a standstill agreement, the bidder agrees not to increase its stock holding of the target for a specified time period.

C. Targeted repurchases (greenmail) involve the repurchase of shares, held by an unfriendly suitor, at a premium over their current market value.

D. Golden parachutes are supplemental compensation packages for the target firm's management. These packages are paid in the case of takeover and resignation by management.

VI. Corporate restructuring.

A. There is increased recognition that corporate "fit" and maximizing NPV are the most important aspects of maximizing the value of the firm.

B. Debt disciplines managers.

1. With high amounts of debt (and interest expense), managers are forced to concentrate on cash flow instead of accounting earnings.

2. Because debt is unforgiving, managers must pay closer attention to the firm's operations.

3. Debt makes the firm less attractive as a takeover candidate.

C. In a leveraging up operation, the firm issues debt and buys back shares of common stock, drastically increasing its ratio of total debt to total assets.

D. Many firms are going private; outstanding common stock is purchased by a small group of owners.

1. In a management buyout, the top management of the firm, typically with an outside partner, buys the firm and turns it into a privately held company.

2. In a leveraged buyout (LBO), the purchase is financed by borrowing. Often, the borrowing is in the form of junk bonds.

E. Restructuring can also involve changing the legal structure of the business from a corporation to a limited partnership.

F. Firms may voluntarily restructure in order to become more competitive.

G. Firms sometimes restructure through a spinoff by distributing shares of the spinoff portion of the firm to current shareholders.

VII. Deciding to divest.

A. Estimate the operating after-tax cash flows associated with the decision including any complementary or substitute effects with other aspects of the firm.

B. Determine k, the division's opportunity cost of capital.

C. Calculate the present value of the CFs.

D. Determine the NPV of keeping the division by subtracting the market value of the division's associated liabilities from the present value of the CFs:

$$NPV = \sum_{t=1}^{n} \frac{CF_t}{(1 + k)^t} - B$$

E. If the NPV is less than the after-tax divestiture proceeds (DP), sell the division.

F. The divestiture proceeds (DP) may vary.

1. If the bidding firm also acquires both the assets and the liabilities of the division, the after-tax amount received by the seller is DP.

2. If the seller retains the liabilities of the division, DP = after-tax divestiture proceeds $- B_0$.

G. The divestiture decision is the opposite of capital budgeting and merger decisions; the firm divests if the benefits do not exceed the foregone divestiture opportunity.

H. This analysis is useful for any kind of asset divestiture decision, but is typically used only for fairly large projects or divisions.

Formulas

<u>Notation</u>

$Value_B$ = value of the bidding firm

$Value_T$ = value of the target firm

$Value_{BT}$ = value of the combined firm

ΔCF_t = change in cash flows in period t

B = current market value of debt associated with the assets

DP = after-tax divestiture proceeds

k = opportunity cost of capital

<u>Net Present Value of a Merger</u>

NPV = benefits − costs

Benefits = $\Delta value + value_T$

Costs = price paid in cash or stock

<u>Incremental Gains</u>

$$\Delta value = \sum_{t=1}^{n} \frac{\Delta CF_t}{(1 + k)^t}$$

<u>Incremental Cash Flows</u>

$\Delta CF_t = \Delta CFBT_t(1 - T) + \Delta CCA_t(T) - \Delta$investment in long-term assets and net working capital $\pm$ after-tax gains or loss on the disposition of some of the target firm's assets

<u>Proportion of the Combined Firm Held by the Target Firm's Shareholders</u>

W = shares held by the target firm's former shareholders ÷ total shares outstanding after the merger

<u>True Cost of a Merger Involving Stock</u>

True cost with stock = $W(value_{BT})$

<u>Exchange Ratio</u>

$$Exchange\ ratio = \frac{market\ value\ of\ cash\ and/or\ securities\ offered\ by\ the\ bidding\ firm}{market\ value\ of\ target\ firm's\ stock}$$

<u>Divestiture</u>

Net present value of keeping assets:

$$NPV = \sum_{t=1}^{n} \frac{CF_t}{(1 + k)^t} - B$$

Divestiture proceeds when the seller retains the liabilities:

DP = after-tax divestiture proceeds − B

What to Look For

The firm plans to build on its strengths through growth. Any kind of growth the firm pursues should maximize the value of the firm. This rule applies not only to internal growth in capital budgeting projects, but also to external growth through mergers. The text discusses how firms evaluate merger proposals from the bidding firm's point of view.

Good and Poor Motives for Merging

Merger decisions should make shareholders better off. Wise merger decisions are those made to pursue an increase in the firm's value through synergistic effects. Such synergistic mergers produce a merged firm whose value is greater than the sum of the two individual firm's values. Synergism can occur only when the bidding firm obtains either economies or tax benefits unavailable except through the merger. Economies can result from vertical or horizontal integration, and through economies of scale. Tax savings can result if either the target firm or the bidding firm has unused tax losses that the other can use to offset taxable income.

Some firms choose poor reasons to merge. They might merge in order to diversify and reduce risk. However, there is no evidence that this increases the value of the firm for its shareholders. In efficient capital markets, shareholders can diversify more cheaply and efficiently on their own. In addition, firms merge in order to keep growing. But if the merger is not accompanied by economies or tax benefits, it does not increase the value of the firm. A nonsynergistic merger sometimes produces the illusion of an immediate earnings per share increase. But this increase is a mathematical phenomenon and does not reflect increased value, since such a merger does not involve tax benefits or economies. Thus, an increase in EPS is not, in and of itself, a good reason to pursue a merger.

Pricing the Target Firm

Merger decisions are like capital budgeting decisions. The only difference is that the growth is from acquiring an external project or firm rather than developing an entity within the firm. In deciding whether to proceed with a merger proposal, the bidding firm weighs the value of the merger after taking account of the cost of acquisition. The gain from the proposed acquisition is the maximum price the bidding firm should offer to pay for the target firm. In this net present value calculation, the bidding firm takes into account expected cash inflows and outflows from the merger.

The least the bidding firm can offer for the target firm is the target firm's premerger market value. Usually, the bidding firm offers the target firm some premium over market value. The greater the synergism the bidding firm expects to experience with the merger, the higher the premium it is willing to pay. If several firms are competing for a single target firm, their different offering prices somewhat reflect the synergism each expects to experience, or how much the merger is worth to them. The bidding firm should remember, however, that the expected synergism might not occur if the firm has trouble integrating the new firm (or division) into its ongoing operations.

Who Benefits from Mergers?

The premium offered over the target firm's premerger value makes the target shareholders better off with the merger than without it. The economy and the shareholders of the bidding firm may or may not benefit from mergers, however. No new products or services are produced. They just change hands. If the merger eliminates inefficient management, then the economy as a whole might gain.

The Basics of Mergers

Mergers can occur in any of four ways: (1) the statutory amalgamation or combination of two or more firms; (2) the acquisition of the target firm's stock, perhaps through a tender offer; (3) the acquisition of only the assets of the target firm; (4) the gain of partial control of the firm by a holding company.

The second type of merger, the acquisition, can be a tax-free or taxable transaction for the target firm's shareholders. If the transaction results in an exchange of stock for cash, the shareholders must declare capital gains or losses. If the transaction is tax-free, they report capital gains or losses only when they sell the new stock later on and pay taxes at that time.

Not every merger attempt is friendly. If a target firm wants to ward off an unfriendly tender offer, the target might try to find a friendly merger partner (a "white squire") or give its chief executives "golden parachutes." In any defensive tactic, the target firm should keep the shareholders' interests in mind. Sometimes merger tactics and golden parachutes can harm rather than help the target firm and its shareholders.

Divestiture

The firm's goal is to maximize the value of the firm. Sometimes it is best if the firm sells a division or some assets which either do not fit or have a low profitability. In contrast to the acquisition decision, the divestiture decision requires the firm to decide how much to ask for the assets or division. The firm should not divest if the after-tax proceeds from the divestiture will not exceed the NPV of the expected cash flows from the assets if retained.

As noted in Chapter 9, the appropriate discount rate for the NPV calculation depends upon the riskiness of the asset's cash flows. The riskier the cash flows, the higher the discount rate and the lower the NPV. Note that the divestiture decision is exactly the opposite of the capital budgeting decision. The firm divests the assets if the discounted cash flows do not exceed the expected after-tax proceeds from the divestment. Financial distress, or the inability to meet current financial obligations, can force firms to involuntarily divest assets.

Completion Questions

16.1   Waves of merger activity typically are related to _____ and general economic activity.

16.2   Increased _____ may result from a merger. In firms with large fixed costs, these economies would be _____. In firms hoping to achieve a continuous flow from acquisition of raw materials through ultimate sale, the economies would be the result of _____ _____.

16.3   _____ refers to the idea that the sum of two firms is worth more than the individual firms.

16.4   When a profitable firm acquires a target firm having tax losses, the rationale for the merger is to receive the _____ benefit.

16.5   From the bidding firm's point of view, the decision to acquire a target firm is a _____ _____ decision.

16.6   For a positive net present value to exist, the bidding firm must achieve _____ or _____ not available to the target firm.

16.7   Postmerger EPS is _____ to the merger decision. When the focus is on postmerger EPS rather than NPV, the decision can be _____.

16.8   A _____ is an offer by the bidding firm directly to the target firm's stockholders.

16.9   A _____ occurs when two or more firms combine to form a completely new firm.

16.10 If a merger transaction qualifies as a tax-free transaction, the target firm's shareholders realize their capital gains or loss _____ _____.

16.11 When firms account for the merger as a _____, the individual balance sheet accounts are simply added together. When it is a _____, the assets are revalued and goodwill may be recorded.

16.12 A _____ is a special employment package that protects certain key executives if their firm is acquired in a merger.

16.13 The issue involved in divestiture is the opposite of the issue involved in _____.

16.14 If the net present value of keeping the assets exceeds the net proceeds expected from the divestiture, the firm should _____ the assets.

Problems

16.1   Cougar Aluminum is considering a potential merger with Anderson Mining Company. Anderson presently has 1,000,000 shares of common stock outstanding trading at $10 per share. Cougar has estimated the following incremental cash flows from the merger:

Year	ΔCFBT	ΔCCA	ΔInvestment
1	$100,000	$100,000	$300,000
2	200,000	100,000	100,000
3	300,000	100,000	
4	400,000	100,000	
5	500,000	100,000	
6–10	600,000	100,000	

Anderson has agreed to sell the shares for $11.00 per share. If Cougar's tax rate is 40%, and k = 16%, should they merge?

16.2   Benson Industries is thinking of acquiring Vantage Corporation via an all stock sweep. Information for both firms is as follows:

Firm	Stock Price	Shares
Benson	$50	5,000,000
Vantage	$10	2,000,000

ΔValue is estimated to be $5,000,000. Benson intends to exchange one share of Benson for each five shares of Vantage. What will be the price per share of Benson after the merger?

16.3   Millhouse Manufacturing recently acquired Spencer Industries by exchanging four shares of Millhouse for five shares of Spencer. Information on the two firms prior to the merger is listed below:

	Millhouse	Spencer
Total earnings	$200,000	$600,000
Number of shares	100,000	150,000
Price	$15	$12

What is the EPS for Millhouse before and after the merger?

16.4   The president of Mervin Toys has suggested the divestiture of the company's plastic model division. Next year's CFs are expected to be $2 million, and because of the mature nature of the business, these cash flows are expected to grow at only 1 percent per year. The appropriate opportunity cost of capital is 11 percent, and the division now has $12 million in debt. What is the minimum divestiture price the firm would be willing to accept?

16.5   Jacobson Luggage, Ltd., is unhappy with the performance of its designer luggage division. Full capacity has been reached, which means that the firm can only expect CFs of $600,000 per year, with no growth prospects. A proposal to expand the plant has been put forth. The expansion will require investments of $2.5 million per year for the next two years, during which time the CFs will remain as above. After that (starting in year 3), CFs will be able to grow at a rate of 10 percent per year. The division presently has $2 million in debt, and no new debt will be added should the company expand. A competitor has offered to pay Jacobson $5 million (after-tax) for the division. If the discount rate is 15 percent, what should Jacobson do?

Answers to Completion Questions

16.1   stock market prices
16.2   economies; economies of scale; vertical integration
16.3   Synergism
16.4   tax
16.5   capital budgeting
16.6   increased economies; tax benefits
16.7   irrelevant; wrong
16.8   tender offer
16.9   statutory amalgamation
16.10   at a later date when they sell the new stock
16.11   pooling of interests; purchase
16.12   golden parachute
16.13   capital budgeting (or mergers)
16.14   retain

Solutions to Problems

16.1   Step 1.   Calculate ΔCF_t (units of $1,000).

Year	ΔCFBT	ΔCCA	ΔCFBT$(1 - T)$	$+ \Delta$CCA(T)	$-$	Inv	$=$	ΔCF_t
1	100	100	60	40		300		−200
2	200	100	120	40		100		60
3	300	100	180	40				220
4	400	100	240	40				280
5	500	100	300	40				340
6–10	600	100	360	40				400

Step 2.   Calculate Δvalue.

$$\Delta\text{value} = \sum_{t=1}^{n} \frac{CF_t}{(1 + k)^t}$$

$$= -\$200 \, (PV_{16\%,1\ yr}) + \$60 \, (PV_{16\%,2\ yr}) + \$220 \, (PV_{16\%,3\ yr})$$

$$+ \$280 \, (PV_{16\%,4\ yr}) + \$340 \, (PV_{16\%,5\ yr})$$

$$+ \$400 \, (PVA_{16\%,5\ yr}) \, (PV_{16\%,5\ yr})$$

$$= -\$200 \, (0.862) + \$60 \, (0.743) + \$220 \, (0.641) + \$280 \, (0.552)$$

$$+ \$340 \, (0.476) + \$400 \, (3.274) \, (0.476)$$

$$= -\$172.40 + \$44.58 + \$141.02 + \$154.56 + \$161.84 + \$623.37$$

$$= \$952.97 \text{ or } \$952,970$$

Step 3.   Benefits = value$_T$ + Δvalue

$$= \$10(1,000,000) + \$952,970$$

$$= \$10,952,970$$

Step 4.   NPV   = benefits − costs

$$= \$10,952,970 - \$11(1,000,000)$$

$$= -\$47,030$$

Since the NPV is negative, the firms should not merge.

16.2 Step 1.   Number of new shares required = 2,000,000/5 = 400,000

Step 2.   Shares in combined firm = 5,000,000 + 400,000 = 5,400,000

Step 3. $\text{Value}_{BT} = \text{value}_B + \text{value}_T + \Delta\text{value}$

$= \$50(5,000,000) + \$10(2,000,000) + \$5,000,000$

$= \$250,000,000 + \$20,000,000 + \$5,000,000 + \$275,000,000$

Step 4. $\text{Price} = \dfrac{\text{value}_{BT}}{\text{shares}} = \dfrac{\$275,000,000}{5,400,000} = \$50.92$

16.3 Step 1. $\text{EPS before} = \dfrac{\text{total earnings}}{\text{number of shares}} = \dfrac{\$200,000}{100,000} = \$2 \text{ per share}$

Step 2.   Total new shares = 100,000 + 4/5(150,000) = 220,000

Step 3.   Postmerger EPS = [\$200,000 + \$600,000]/220,000 = \$3.64

16.4 Step 1.   The firm is indifferent if DP = NPV.

$$DP = \sum_{t=1}^{n} \frac{CF_t}{(1+k)^t} - B = \frac{\$2,000,000}{0.11 - 0.01} - \$12,000,000 = \$8,000,000$$

Step 2.   If Mervin Toys can get \$8,000,000 or more (after taxes) for the division, it should divest.

16.5 Step 1.   No expansion:

NPV = \$600,000/0.15 − \$2,000,000 = \$2,000,000. The net proceeds from divesting would be \$5 million − \$2 million in debt = \$3 million. Without the possibility of expanding the division, the decision would be to divest it since the net divestiture proceeds of \$3 million exceed the net present value of continuing to operate of \$2 million.

Step 2.   With expansion:

$\text{NPV} = (\$600,000 - \$2,500,000)(PV_{15\%, 1 \text{ yr}})$

$+ (\$600,000 - \$2,500,000) (PV_{15\%, 2 \text{ yr}})$

$+ [\$600,000 (1.10) / (0.15 - 0.10)] (PV_{15\%, 2 \text{ yr}}) - \$2,000,000$

$= -\$1,900,000 (0.870) - \$1,900,000 (0.756) + \$13,200,000 (0.756)$

$- \$2,000,000$

$= \$4,889,800$

Jacobson should proceed with the expansion since its value is greater than the net proceeds from divesting. The shareholders would receive only \$3 million from divestment since the \$2 million in debt must be paid off.

Chapter 17
International Financial Management

How This Chapter Relates to the Rest of the Text

To this point, we have concentrated on financial management within Canada. When operating internationally, our primary goal remains the same: maximize the value of the firm by focusing on cash flows (Chapter 3), risk (Chapter 5), and opportunity cost of capital. But, international operation carries with it several complications that affect capital budgeting (Chapters 7–9), capital structure (Chapters 12 and 13), and dividend issues (Chapter 14). The foreign markets also provide additional sources of short-term (Chapter 24) and long-term capital (Chapter 10). Funds may also be raised through leases (Chapter 15).

Topical Outline

I.   Financial management in an international context.
      A.   The goal of financial management remains the same: maximize the value of the firm.
      B.   Major reasons for locating operations in various countries.
            1.   Structural imperfections such as transportation costs and government restrictions.
            2.   Various product market imperfections such as unfamiliar products and economies of scale.
      C.   International strategies.
            1.   Invest in regional clusters around home country.
            2.   Invest in regional clusters elsewhere.
            3.   Raise capital wherever it is cheapest.
II.   Capital budgeting in an international context.
      A.   The basic steps of capital budgeting remain the same: identify the incremental after-tax cash flows, discount at an appropriate opportunity cost of capital, and accept projects with positive net present values.
      B.   The opportunity cost of capital.
            1.   Systematic risk and portfolio concerns.
                a.   Nondiversifiable risk (measured by beta, β) is a major determinant of the opportunity cost of equity capital.
                b.   The geographic diversification of multinationals may serve to reduce their nondiversifiable risk and, consequently, their opportunity cost of equity capital.
            2.   Expropriation and creditor risks.
                a.   International firms also face expropriation risk that may offset the benefits of geographic diversification.
                b.   Bankruptcy laws differ across countries. In many countries, creditors face more risk than in Canada and should demand a higher opportunity cost of capital.
                c.   It is impossible to state that the opportunity cost of capital for an international project should be higher than, lower than, or equal to that of a domestic project. Firms need to know the territory and to evaluate all possible legal, tax, and political factors to calculate the appropriate opportunity cost of capital.
      C.   Maximize net present values.
            1.   Calculate NPVs in terms of the foreign currency, using an appropriate local opportunity cost of capital.
                a.   Convert the NPV to dollars using the spot rate. Accept all projects with positive NPVs.
            2.   An alternative method is to convert cash flows to dollars and discount at a Canadian-based opportunity cost of capital.
                a.   Use the expected future spot rate to convert time t cash flows.
                b.   Calculate expected spot rates to convert future cash flows.

$$\text{i.} \quad \begin{array}{c} \text{Expected spot rate} \\ \text{at the end of year t} \end{array} = \begin{bmatrix} \text{spot} \\ \text{rate} \end{bmatrix} \begin{bmatrix} \text{inflation rate} \\ \text{differential} \end{bmatrix}$$

        c.   Discount at a dollar-denominated opportunity cost of capital.

        d.   Both methods of calculating net present values should provide the same NPV in terms of dollars.

    3.   Most Canadian firms convert cash flows to dollars to calculate NPVs.

  D.   Unremitted funds and tax considerations.

    1.   It may be difficult for parent companies to bring back funds from foreign subsidiaries.

        a.   Many countries are sensitive to exploitation and limit the ability of international firms to take funds out of host countries.

        b.   Taxes must be paid in foreign countries, and many countries also impose a withholding tax on remitted funds.

        c.   Taxes may also have to be paid in Canada; if so, the firm receives a foreign tax credit.

    2.   The amount of tax paid in Canada on foreign profits depends on the following:

        a.   How the funds are remitted to the parent.

        b.   Whether the foreign investment is a branch or an affiliate.

        c.   Whether the host country has a tax treaty with Canada or not.

    3.   For unincorporated foreign branches.

        a.   A branch tax is imposed by the host country on branch cash flows.

        b.   The cash flows are taxed in Canada whether or not they are remitted to the parent.

        c.   The parent is eligible for a foreign tax credit equal to the branch tax.

    4.   For a foreign affiliate that is at least 10-percent owned by the parent.

        a.   Cash flows are subject to Canadian tax only when they are remitted to parent.

        b.   Remitted cash flows are subject to a withholding tax by the host country.

        c.   If the host country is a treaty country, the remitted cash flows are considered to be dividends from another Canadian corporation and, consequently, are tax exempt; however, the parent does not receive a foreign tax credit.

        d.   If no tax treaty exists, the dividends are fully taxable in Canada in the year that they are remitted to the parent and a tax credit is taken.

    5.   For a foreign affiliate that is less that 10-percent owned.

        a.   Any cash flows remitted to the parent are fully taxable and a tax credit is allowed.

  E.   Evaluating acquisitions outside the bidder's home country.

    1.   A merger or acquisition outside the bidder's home country is just another capital budgeting decison complicated by exchange rates and can be handled by one of the approaches previously discussed in this section.

  F.   International investment strategy.

    1.   Requires developing the corporate skills and vision necessary to capitalize on world-wide opportunities while dealing effectively with various risks through

        a.   An ability to transfer domestic expertise to other countries.

        b.   A solid understanding of the market that the firm wishes to enter.

        c.   Continuous monitoring of the investment and its future prospects.

        d.   A commitment to consider the international dimension of all investment decisions.

III.   Capital structure and dividend issues.

  A.   World-wide capital structure and dividend policy should not be piecemeal decisons; world-wide issues need to be considered in order to maximize firm value.

  B.   Capital structure considerations.

    1.   Implicit or explicit guarantees of subsidiary debt by the parent firm makes the parent's overall capital structure the primary concern.

    2.   The multinational parent's objective is to raise funds in the most cost-effective manner at the subsidiary level and then make adjustments at the firm level.

    3.   Because of exchange controls and tax effects, multinational firms often use debt rather than equity to finance their investment in a subsidiary.

C. Dividend policy.
    1. Cash dividends are the most important means of transferring funds to the parent.
    2. To ensure that subsidiaries are contributing their appropriate share to the parent's cash dividend policy and to provide the multinational firm with a rationale for dealing with exchange or currency controls of different nations, subsidiaries are often required to pay dividends to the parent at a rate at least equal to the rate the parent pays to its shareholders.

IV. International financing issues.
    A. Many firms are turning to the international bond market for long-term debt capital.
    B. The international bond market involves Eurobonds and foreign bonds.
        1. The Eurobond is underwritten by an international syndicate and sold primarily in countries other than that in which the issue is denominated.
            a. Most Eurobonds pay interest once a year, reducing Eurobond yields in comparison to bonds issued in Canada, which pay interest semiannually.
            b. Most Eurobonds are issued in bearer form, rather than being fully registered.
            c. Almost all Eurodollar bonds are listed on one or more recognized financial exchange.
        2. A foreign bond is one issued by a foreign borrower, but underwritten, sold, and denominated in one country.
    C. In financing capital investments abroad, multinational companies typically invest a small amount of equity and raise the remainder of the funds.
        1. Raise funds by borrowing in Canada.
            a. The borrower is exposed to exchange risk.
        2. Raise funds by borrowing in the country where the project is located.
            a. This procedure provides a direct hedge against exchange risk.
        3. Raise funds where interest rates are most favourable.
    D. Leasing is another financing decision that allows the multinational to gain flexibility, defer or avoid taxes, and safeguard assets by limiting the ownership of assets by subsidiaries in unstable countries.

V. International accounting issues.
    A. Reporting of financial results of foreign operations.
        1. Under CICA 1650, foreign operations are classified as integrated or self-sustaining.
        2. An integrated subsidiary is financially or operationally interdependent with the parent company. Monetary balance sheet items are reported at market value and are translated into Canadian dollars at the exchange rate prevailing on the last day of the fiscal year. Nonmonetary items are converted into Canadian dollars at the exchange rate prevailing when the items were acquired. Revenues and expenses are generally translated at the year's average exchange rate.
        3. Self-sustaining foreign subsidiaries are financially and operationally independent of the parent firm. For these subsidiaries, balance sheet items are translated at the current exchange rate and income statement items at the average annual rate.
        4. This makes the analysis of accounting statements of multinationals more difficult, since assets and equity fluctuate with exchange rates.

VI. Foreign exchange issues.
    A. Firms face a variety of risks, including risk caused by the continuous changes in the rate of exchange of one currency for another currency.
    B. Three types of foreign exchange exposure.
        1. Translation exposure refers to the accounting treatment arising from fluctuations in exchange rates; it does not affect the economic value of the firm.
        2. Transaction exposure refers to the impact of exchanging one currency for another when the rate of exchange between the currencies changes from the time the transaction occurs until it is settled.
        3. Economic exposure refers to the impact of foreign exchange exposure that directly affects the cash flows and, thus, the long-run value of the firm.

VII.   Operating, investment, and financing approaches to hedging exchange rate risk.

    A.   Firms normally use a number of different approaches to deal with part, or all, of their transaction or economic exchange rate risk exposure.

        1.   Invoicing in the home currency can eliminate any transaction-based foreign exchange problem.

        2.   Pay early (leading) or late (lagging) depending on the weakness or strength of the two currencies.

        3.   Set up a separate subsidiary, or reinvoicing centre, to be responsible for all interfirm transfers.

        4.   Locate subsidiaries in the countries where the final goods or services are to be sold.

        5.   Acquire financing in the country where it will be used.

VIII.   Hedging using forward contracts.

    A.   If hedged, the exchange risk is said to be covered; if unhedged, it is said to be open.

    B.   To hedge a future receipt of funds, sell a foreign exchange forward contract for the same date as the future receipt.

    C.   To hedge a future payment of funds, buy a foreign exchange forward contract with the same maturity date as the future payment.

    D.   Any gain or loss from the hedge exactly offsets the loss or gain from the foreign exchange exposure.

    E.   Other considerations.

        1.   Because of credit risk, the use of forwards is restricted to institutions, corporations, and governments with easy access to sufficient lines of credit to back them up.

IX.   Hedging using futures contracts.

    A.   Futures contracts are similar to forward contracts except they are standardized as to size and maturity date and trade on organized exchanges.

    B.   If we stand to lose as a foreign currency weakens (strengthens) relative to the home currency, we would sell (buy) futures contracts to offset some or all of the expected loss in value.

        1.   A perfect hedge can be obtained if a futures contract matches the firm's needs in terms of size and maturity.

        2.   The use of futures for hedging, while generally not perfect, is widespread.

    C.   Other considerations.

        1.   Because the size and maturity of a futures contract rarely matches the firm's needs exactly, perfect hedges are not possible.

        2.   Cross-hedging is often required because the currency needed to be hedged against does not have a traded futures contract.

X.   Hedging using swaps.

    A.   In a plain vanilla currency swap, two firms agree to exchange principal amounts denominated in different currencies at the beginning of the swap period and agree on the type of interest rate (fixed or floating) that each will be responsible for; at the end of the swap period, they re-exchange the original principal.

    B.   A parallel (or back-to-back) loan involves two firms in separate countries arranging to borrow in each other's currency for a specific period of time, exchanging principal and interest payments, and at the agreed termination date returning the principal.

    C.   A currency swap involves a domestic firm raising funds in Canada while the foreign firm raises an equivalent amount in its currency; the firms agree to swap the initial principal and interest payments for a specified period of time and then reswap the principal at the end of the agreed period.

Formulas

Net Present Value

$$NPV = \sum_{t=1}^{n} \frac{CF_t}{(1 + k)^t} - CF_0$$

Expected Spot Rate

Expected spot rate
at the end of year t = (spot rate) (inflation rate differential)

What to Look For

In the past 30 years, economies of various countries have become more and more integrated; for example, Japanese automobile manufacturers, either alone or in concert with U.S. companies, own and operate manufacturing facilities in the United States. Canadian corporations now own or operate facilities in virtually all corners of the globe. Many of the financial decision-making tools we have discussed are applicable to international situations, but additional factors must be discussed.

Although the goal of international financial management is still to maximize the value of the firm, it is complicated by the fact that transactions are conducted in more than one currency. Canadian companies doing business in Malaysia are likely to be paid in ringgits, in India, rupees, or in Denmark, krone. Like any commodity, foreign currencies trade, and their prices, relative to the Canadian dollar, fluctuate. This fluctuation, called exchange rate risk, can be eliminated by good financial management.

Capital Budgeting in an International Context

Firms may benefit from geographic diversification because markets or economic cycles in different countries are not in perfect sychronization. Therefore, a firm can accomplish something through international diversification that it cannot achieve through further domestic investments. It can decrease its nondiversifiable risk (as measured by beta, β) and, consequently, its opportunity cost of equity.

However, the benefits of geographic diversification may be offset, since not all economies and governments are as stable as Canada's. Firms venturing into less developed countries face expropriation risk; the host country may take over or demand part of the enterprise, resulting in a loss to the parent company. This risk is real, and must be accounted for in determining the opportunity cost of capital. Bankruptcy laws also differ across countries and need to be considered in reaching appropriate decisions. There is no substitute for understanding the economic and political climate in which the foreign subsidiary operates.

Traditional capital budgeting approaches can be used to make capital budgeting decisions, so long as we consider the additional risk associated with international operations. Suppose that Westfall Limited is considering a capital budgeting project for their British subsidiary, York Industries Limited. If the project was undertaken in Canada, Westfall would use an opportunity cost of capital of 16 percent. The cash flows from the project (in pounds) are as follows:

Year	CF
0	−45,000
1	10,000
2	12,000
3	15,000
4	18,000
5	20,000

We can calculate the NPV in two ways. First, let's leave the cash flows in the local currency (in this case, pounds). A question immediately arises; is the 16 percent opportunity cost of capital appropriate for this project? To answer this, we need to determine what the risk premium on this project is. Recall that the opportunity cost of capital for the project must satisfy the equation:

$$1 + \text{opportunity cost of capital} = (1 + \text{risk-free rate}) (1 + \text{risk premium})$$

If the risk-free rate in Canada is 7.5 percent, the risk premium is

$$1 + \text{risk premium} = 1.16/1.075$$
$$= 1.07907$$
$$\text{Risk premium} = 0.07907 \text{ or } 7.907\%$$

Using this risk premium, we can solve for the opportunity cost of capital in Britain. If the British risk-free rate is 9.5 percent, the required return is

$$1 + \text{opportunity cost of capital} = (1.095) (1.07907)$$
$$= 1.1816$$
$$\text{Opportunity cost of capital} = 0.1816 \text{ or } 18.16\%$$

Using this opportunity cost of capital, we can calculate the NPV of the project.

$$\text{NPV} = \frac{10,000}{(1.1816)^1} + \frac{12,000}{(1.1816)^2} + \frac{15,000}{(1.1816)^3} + \frac{18,000}{(1.1816)^4} + \frac{20,000}{(1.1816)^5} - 45,000$$
$$= -932.41 \text{ pounds}$$

Given an exchange rate of 0.44292 pounds per dollar, the NPV in dollars is −932.41/0.44292 = −$2,105.14. The project is unacceptable. You should note that if you had not adjusted the opportunity cost of capital and used 16 percent as the discount rate, the net present value would be 1,612.01 pounds ($3,639.51) and you would have made the wrong decision.

A second approach is to convert cash flows to dollars and use a domestic discount rate to calculate net present value. To do so, we must forecast expected spot rates. The expected spot rate is simply the current spot rate times the inflation rate differential. If we assume that the real rate of interest is 2 percent in both Great Britain and Canada, using the risk-free rates, the rate of inflation in Canada is 7.5% − 2% = 5.5%, and in Great Britain, 9.5% − 2% = 7.5%. The expected spot rate at the end of year 1 is $(0.44292)(1.075^1/1.055^1) = 0.4513$. At the end of year 2, the expected spot rate is $(0.44292)(1.075^2/1.055^2) = 0.4599$, and so on. Given all of the expected spot rates, we can convert the cash flows from pounds to dollars.

	Year					
	0	1	2	3	4	5
1. Cash flow in pounds	−45,000	10,000	12,000	15,000	18,000	20,000
2. Expected spot rates	0.44292	0.4513	0.4599	0.4686	0.4775	0.4865
3. Cash flows in dollars (1/2)	−$101,598	$22,158	$26,093	$32,010	$37,696	$41,110

At 16 percent, the NPV of the above cash flows is −$2,205.30. Theoretically, it should be identical to that of the first method. Most Canadian companies convert cash flows to dollars before calculating present values.

A discussion of international capital budgeting would not be complete without mention of how funds generated by foreign operations are taxed. To this point, we have assumed that the Canadian firm can bring back (remit) the cash flows to Canada. Many nations provide barriers to such a remittance. These barriers include controls on exchange or taxes on remittance. Firms must also pay taxes in the foreign countries and sometimes in Canada, in which case the foreign taxes result in a tax credit. Taxes, of course, reduce cash flows and make projects less attractive.

The amount of taxes paid on funds generated by and/or remitted by the foreign operation to Canada depends on three factors:

1. How the funds are remitted.
2. Whether the foreign investment is a branch or an affiliate.
3. Whether or not the host country has a tax treaty with Canada.

Capital Structure and Dividend Issues

Capital structure and dividend policies are complicated by the number of subsidiaries and the many different laws, tax considerations, and government regulations faced by international firms.

In setting a foreign subsidiary's capital structure, the objective is to minimize capital cost and to have the multinational parent viewed as responsible by the host country. Afterward, the multinational can manage its capital structure on a global basis to maximize the value of the firm.

A subsidiary's dividend policy should reflect the parent's dividend policy and the cash needs of the subsidiary. High-growth and low-growth subsidiaries have different needs for funds. Although a high-growth subsidiary has a high demand for funds to foster its growth, it may be required to declare a dividend even though it is not remitted. This establishes the principle that dividends are a necessary cash flow associated with doing business.

International Financing Issues

Many firms raise their long-term debt capital in the international bond market, either through Eurobonds or foreign bonds. In addition, a multinational firm typically invests only a part of the proceeds (in the form of equity) in a foreign operation and finances the rest of it by borrowing. There are three general approaches to financing. First, the firm can borrow in Canada and export the funds. Since the debt is denominated in dollars, the borrower is exposed to considerable exchange rate risk. The second approach is to borrow in the country where the project is located; this shifts exchange rate risk to the lender. The third alternative is to find the cheapest source of financing. In this approach, the parent should consider exchange rate risk. Furthermore, multinational firms are also turning to leasing to gain flexibility and to safeguard assets in unstable countries.

Hedging Foreign Exchange Risk

Because foreign exchange rates fluctuate over time, multinational corporations face foreign exchange exposure in three different forms:

1. Translation exposure is purely an accounting phenomenon that does not have any effect on the economic value of the firm.
2. Transaction exposure is caused when foreign exchange rates fluctuate from the time the transaction occurs until it is settled.
3. Economic exposure reflects the direct impact that foreign exchange exposure has on cash flows and, thus, on the long-run value of the firm.

Multinational corporations can hedge against foreign exchange risk through their operating, investment, and financing activites by

1. Invoicing in the home currency.
2. Leading and lagging.
3. Using reinvoicing centres.
4. Locating investments where sales occur.
5. Acquiring financing in the country where it will be used.

They may also eliminate foreign exchange rate risk by using foreign exchange forward contracts. The buyer of a forward currency contract agrees to trade dollars for a foreign currency at a rate decided upon today while the seller agrees to trade the currency for dollars. For example, suppose Consolidated Manufacturing agrees to sell equipment to Knessel Industries. Knessel agrees to pay 3.5 million marks for the equipment in 90 days. Consolidated is exposed to exchange risk; if exchange rates vary, Consolidated could receive fewer dollars than expected. They can eliminate this risk by selling a 90-day forward contract on 3.5 million marks. This will ensure that they can trade marks at a rate of $0.8452 per mark and receive 3,500,000($0.8452) = $2,958,200 in the transaction, irrespective of spot rates 90 days from now.

There are other methods by which firms can construct at least partial hedges against exchange rate risk. For instance, a firm may hedge downside risk by buying or selling foreign exchange futures contracts. The company may also hedge foreign exchange risk by using currency swaps and parallel loans.

Operating a foreign enterprise is complex; you must consider local customs and the local economy and take into account various sources of international risk. There are also accounting complications that arise from foreign operations. Managers need to consider all of these facets before deciding whether or not to engage in an international project.

Completion Questions

17.1   _____ risk is the risk that a host country will take over all or part of an enterprise.

17.2   Bankruptcy laws differ across countries, exposing Canadian borrowers in foreign countries to _____ risk.

17.3   Some countries restrict _____ of funds and make it difficult for Canadian firms to bring profits back to Canada.

17.4   The expected spot rate is equal to the current spot rate times the _____.

17.5   _____ is the risk that exchange rates will fluctuate and adversely affect cash flows.

17.6   Managers can eliminate some or all exchange rate risk by _____.

17.7   A firm expecting a payment in a foreign currency in the future can hedge by _____ a forward contract.

Problems

17.1   Ontario Gardeners is considering a joint venture with Netherlands Tulip Co. The cost of the project is 100,000 Dutch guilders and cash flows (after taxes) are forecasted to be:

Year	Cash Flows (in guilders)
0	–100,000
1	30,000
2	35,000
3	40,000
4	40,000

Ontario Gardeners would use an opportunity cost of capital of 19 percent. The current spot rate is 0.7505 guilders per dollar. The Canadian risk-free rate is 9.5 percent, while the risk-free rate in the Netherlands is 5.4 percent. Both countries have a real rate of interest of 3 percent. Should the above project be accepted?

17.2   Toronto Fashions is considering setting up a foreign affiliate in Paris. Toronto Fashions will own 90 percent of the shares of Paris Designs. The venture will cost Toronto Fashions 68,000 francs and promises the following cash flows (before all taxes):

Year	1	2	3	4
CF (in francs)	15,000	20,000	30,000	50,000

The corporate tax rate in France is 45 percent, and remittances are subject to a withholding tax of 12 percent. The Canadian tax rate is 40 percent. The current spot rate is 3.9919 francs per dollar, the French inflation rate is expected to be 5 percent, and the Canadian rate is expected to be 7 percent. Toronto Fashions believes that, domestically, this project should have an opportunity cost of capital of 15 percent. Should Toronto Fashions participate in the joint venture?

Answers to Completion Questions

17.1 Expropriation
17.2 creditor
17.3 remittance
17.4 inflation rate differential
17.5 Exchange rate risk
17.6 hedging
17.7 selling

Solutions to Problems

17.1 Step 1.   Calculate the expected spot rates.

Inflation rate – Canada = 9.5% – 3% = 6.5%

Inflation rate – Netherlands = 5.4% – 3% = 2.4%

$$\text{Expected spot rate} = \begin{bmatrix} \text{current} \\ \text{spot rate} \end{bmatrix} \begin{bmatrix} \text{expected} \\ \text{inflation differential} \end{bmatrix}$$

Year 1 expected spot rate $= 0.7505 \left[\dfrac{1.024^1}{1.065^1} \right] = 0.7216$

Year 2 expected spot rate $= 0.7505 \left[\dfrac{1.024^2}{1.065^2} \right] = 0.6938$

Year 3 expected spot rate $= 0.7505 \left[\dfrac{1.024^3}{1.065^3} \right] = 0.6671$

Year 4 expected spot rate $= 0.7505 \left[\dfrac{1.024^4}{1.065^4} \right] = 0.6414$

Step 2.

	Year				
	0	1	2	3	4
Cash flows (in guilders)	−100,000	30,000	35,000	40,000	40,000
Expected spot rate	0.7505	0.7216	0.6938	0.6671	0.6414
Cash flows in dollars (1/2)	−133,245	41,574	50,447	59,961	62,364

Step 3.   NPV $= \$41,574(PV_{19\%,1yr}) + \$50,447(PV_{19\%,2yr})$

$+ \$59,961(PV_{19\%,3yr}) + \$62,364(PV_{19\%,4yr}) - \$133,245$

$= \$41,574(0.840) + \$50,447(0.706) + \$59,961(0.593)$

$+ \$62,364(0.499) - \$133,245$

$= \$34,922.16 + \$35,615.58 + 35,556.87 + \$31,119.64 - \$133,245$

$= \$3,969.02$

Yes, the project should be accepted since the NPV is positive.

17.2   Step 1.   Calculate the expected spot rates.

$$\text{Expected spot rate} = \begin{bmatrix} \text{current} \\ \text{spot rate} \end{bmatrix}\begin{bmatrix} \text{expected} \\ \text{inflation differential} \end{bmatrix}$$

$$\text{Year 1 expected spot rate} = 3.9919\left[\frac{1.05^1}{1.07^1}\right] = 3.9173$$

$$\text{Year 2 expected spot rate} = 3.9919\left[\frac{1.05^2}{1.07^2}\right] = 3.8441$$

$$\text{Year 3 expected spot rate} = 3.9919\left[\frac{1.05^3}{1.07^3}\right] = 3.7722$$

$$\text{Year 4 expected spot rate} = 3.9919\left[\frac{1.05^4}{1.07^4}\right] = 3.7017$$

Step 2.   Following Table 17.1:

	Year				
	0	1	2	3	4
1. Cash flow before taxes, in francs	−68,000	15,000	20,000	30,000	50,000
2. French corporate tax (1 × 0.45)		−6,750	−9,000	−13,500	−22,500
3. Cash flow available for remittance to parent (1 − 2)		8,250	11,000	16,500	27,500
4. Tax withheld at 12% (3 × 0.12)		−990	−1,320	−1,980	−3,300
5. Remittance after French taxes, in francs (3 − 4)		7,260	9,680	14,520	24,200
6. Forecasted spot rate (from step 1)	3.9919	3.9173	3.8441	3.7722	3.7017
7. Remittance received by parent in dollars (5/6)	−17,034	1,853	2,518	3,849	6,538
8. Canadian corporate tax		0	0	0	0
9. Foreign tax credit		0	0	0	0
10. Cash flow in dollars, CF (7 − 8 + 9)	−17,034	1,853	2,518	3,849	6,538

Step 3.   Calculate NPV.

$$\begin{aligned}
\text{NPV} &= \$1,853(\text{PV}_{15\%,1yr}) + \$2,518(\text{PV}_{15\%,1yr}) \\
&\quad + \$3,849(\text{PV}_{15\%,3yr}) + \$6,538(\text{PV}_{15\%,4yr}) - \$17,034 \\
&= \$1,853(0.870) + \$2,518(0.756) + \$3,849(0.658) \\
&\quad + \$6,538(0.572) - \$17,034 \\
&= \$1,612.11 + \$1,903.61 + \$2,532.64 + \$3,739.74 - \$17,034 \\
&= -\$7,245.90
\end{aligned}$$

Since the NPV is negative, the project should not be accepted.

Chapter 18
Options

How This Chapter Relates to the Rest of the Text

Options are contracts that give the owner the right, but not the obligation, to buy or sell assets at a fixed price over a specified period of time. Many aspects of financial management, such as warrants attached to bonds (Chapter 20), rights offerings (Chapter 10), options to buy other firms and merge (Chapter 16), and capital budgeting (Chapters 7–9) have options embedded in them. Good financial management requires that the firm understand options and their requirements.

Topical Outline

I.   Some definitions of option terms.
    A.   A call option provides the owner the right, but not the obligation, to buy the underlying asset at a specified price (the exercise or strike price) over some time period.
    B.   A put option provides the owner the right, but not the obligation, to sell the underlying asset at a specified price over some time period.
    C.   The act of purchasing or selling the underlying asset is called exercising the option.
    D.   The maturity (exercise) date is when the option expires. After expiration, the option is worthless.
    E.   An American option can be exercised anytime up to and including the expiration date; a European option can be exercised only on the expiration date. The right to early exercise of an American option makes it at least as valuable as a European one with similar features.
    F.   An option contract is written on 100 shares, but option prices are quoted on a per share basis.
    G.   The option contract specifies the underlying security, the exercise price, and the expiration date.
    H.   Options are classified into a particular expiration cycle: namely, January, February, March cycles, etc. The expiration date refers to the Saturday following the third Friday of the expiration month.

II.   The option premium represents the cost to purchase an option.
    A.   An option premium consists of intrinsic value and time value.
    B.   The intrinsic value of a European option is its value at times other than the expiration date.
        1.   For a call option, intrinsic value is positive if stock price is greater than the exercise price; otherwise, it is zero (since the option will not be exercised).
        2.   For a put option, intrinsic value is positive if stock price is below the exercise price; otherwise, it is zero (since the option will not be exercised).
    C.   The difference between the option premium and the intrinsic value is the time value of the option, which reflects the time remaining for the option to expire and the uncertainty about whether at expiration the price of the stock will be above or below the exercise price. At the expiration, the time value of an option is zero and the option price is determined solely by the intrinsic value.

III.   In-the-money, at-the-money, and out-of-the-money options.
    A.   An option is in-the-money if its intrinsic value is positive.
        1.   For a call option, the stock price must be greater than the exercise price.
        2.   For a put option, the stock price must be below the exercise price.
    B.   An option is at-the-money if the stock price is exactly equal to the exercise price. Here the intrinsic value is zero, since the option will not be exercised.
    C.   An option is out-of-the-money if the stock price is below the exercise price (for a call option) or the stock price is above the exercise price (for a put option). Here also, the intrinsic value is zero since the option will not be exercised.

IV.   A.   Binomial option pricing model. This is based on the law of one price, which states that equivalent securities or portfolios should sell for the same price. The two methods are (1) replicating portfolio approach and (2) risk-neutral approach.
        1.   Replicating portfolio approach.
            a.   Determine the hedge ratio for the call option.

      b.   Construct a portfolio consisting of a share of the stock and borrowing that replicates the payoff.

      c.   Equate today's value of the portfolio and the call.

  2.   Risk-neutral approach. In this approach, we assume the expected return on the stock equals the risk-free rate.

      a.   Determine the probability of an upward/downward movement in stock price.

      b.   Compute the expected value of the call option.

      c.   Compute the present value of expected value of option using the risk-free rate as the discount rate.

B.   Valuing European call options: basic determinants of call option value.

  1.   Everything else being equal, the higher the exercise price (X), the lower the value of the call option.

  2.   The longer the time to expiration (t), the higher the call option value, other things being equal.

  3.   The value of the call option is positively related to the risk-free rate of interest (k_{RF}).

  4.   Other things being equal, the higher the stock price (P_0), the higher the value of a call option.

  5.   The greater the variability (standard deviation) of the underlying asset (σ), the higher the value of a call option.

C.   Valuing European call options: the Black–Scholes option pricing model.

  1.   Terms:

      a. V_c = the value of the call option

      b. P_0 = the current stock price

      c.   X = the exercise price

      d.   t = time to expiration

      e. k_{RF} = the risk-free rate of interest in decimal form

      f. σ = the stock's standard deviation

      g.   e = 2.71828

      h.   ln() = the natural logarithm

      i.   N(d) = the probability from a standard normal distribution that a variable will be less than or equal to d

  2.   The model:

$$V_c = P_0 N(d_1) - \frac{X}{e^{k_{RF}t}} N(d_2)$$

$$\text{where } d_1 = \frac{\ln(P_0/X) + (k_{RF} + 0.5\sigma^2)\,t}{\sigma(t)^{0.5}}$$

$$d_2 = d_1 - \sigma(t)^{0.5}$$

      a.   Calculate d_1 and d_2.

      b.   Look up the values for $N(d_1)$ and $N(d_2)$ in Table B.5.

      c.   Using $N(d_1)$ and $N(d_2)$, compute the value of the call option, V_c.

  3.   Assumptions in the Black–Scholes option pricing model.

      a.   No taxes or transactions costs.

      b. k_{RF} is constant over the option's life.

      c.   The stock market operates continually.

      d.   The stock price is continuous; there are no sudden jumps in price.

      e.   The stock pays no cash dividends.

      f.   The option can only be exercised at expiration (European-style option).

      g.   Short selling is allowed.

      h.   The distribution of returns is log-normal.

    4.   In spite of the restrictive assumptions, the Black–Scholes model is a good predictor of actual option prices.

  D.   A short-cut approach to valuing call options.

    1.   Calculate the standard deviation times the square root of time.

    2.   Calculate the market price divided by the present value of the exercise price.

    3.   Using the two values, determine the factor using Table B.6.

    4.   Multiply the tabled factor by the share price to determine the value of a call.

  E.   When dividends are declared and known to be paid at a certain date, the stock price falls by the present value of the dividends to be received.

$$P_0{}^* = P_0 - PV(\text{Dividends})$$

The adjusted price $P_0{}^*$ is then employed in the Black–Scholes valuation formula.

V.   Valuing put options.

  A.   A put option is an option to sell the underlying asset at a specified price.

  B.   Put–call parity: The value of a call plus the present value of the exercise price equals the value of a put plus the value of the stock.

Formula for calculating the value of a put option:

$$V_p = V_c + X/e^{k_{RF}t} - P_0$$

  C.   Use Table B.7 to calculate put values using the short-cut method.

Formulas

Notation

P_0 = the price of the underlying asset

X = the exercise price of the option

t = time to expiration

σ = the standard deviation of the underlying asset

k_{RF} = the continuously compounded risk-free rate

e = 2.71828

$\ln()$ = the natural logarithm of the number in the brackets

$N(d)$ = the probability from a cumulative standard normal distribution that a random number will be less than or equal to d.

Black–Scholes Option Pricing Model

$$V_c = P_0 N(d_1) - \frac{X}{e^{k_{RF}t}} N(d_2)$$

$$d_1 = \frac{\ln(P_0/X) + (k_{RF} + 0.5\sigma^2)\, t}{\sigma(t)^{0.5}}$$

$$d_2 = d_1 - \sigma(t)^{0.5}$$

Value of a Put Option

$$V_p = V_c + X/e^{k_{RF}t} - P_0$$

What to Look For

Central to informed financial management is a sound understanding of the various financial instruments available to financial managers through the financial markets. Chapter 18 introduces options, a group of financial instruments known generally as derivative securities. The use of options has increased dramatically in recent years.

Briefly, an option is a contract between two parties—the buyer who has a long position and the writer or seller who has a short position. The buyer has the right, but not the obligation, to exercise his/her part of the contract (i.e., to buy or sell an asset at a specified price over some specified time period). If the buyer exercises the option, the writer has the obligation to fulfill his/her part of the contract. The right of the buyer carries a price, called the option premium, which he/she pays to the writer. The maximum an option buyer can lose is the premium paid for the option. This makes an option a limited liability instrument for the buyer. The same can not be said for the seller of options, whose losses can be significant. Consequently, the current widespread use of options mandates that financial managers have a solid understanding of how to value options and what factors affect their value.

Call Options
A call option gives the option owner the right, but not the obligation, to purchase the underlying asset at a fixed price over some time period. The owner of a May $55 call option on Hewlett-Packard stock has the right to purchase 100 shares of Hewlett-Packard stock at $55 per share ($5,500 total) up until the end of May, irrespective of the market price of the stock. If H-P is trading for $58 per share when the option expires, the owner of the call will exercise the option and buy the stock for $55 per share, $3 less than the market price. Buying a call option is a bet that the market price of the stock will rise above the exercise price before expiration.

Put Options
The owner of a put option has the right, but not the obligation, to sell an asset at a specified price over some period of time. For example, suppose your firm buys a fleet of trucks. The truck dealer agrees to buy the trucks back at the end of three years for $10,000 each. Your firm owns a put option. If, three years from now, the value of a truck falls below $10,000, your firm still has the right to sell the trucks for that price. The owner of a put option is wagering that the market price of an asset will fall below the exercise price.

Factors Affecting Call Option Values
In an important paper, Fischer Black and Myron Scholes developed a model for calculating call options. The model shows that a call option's value is related to five factors. Let's examine how each factor affects value while holding the others constant.

Exercise price
The higher the exercise price, the lower the value of a call option. Imagine two options, one with an exercise price of $10 and one with an exercise price of $100. If the stock is trading today for $25, and the option expires in one week, it is quite likely that, at expiration, the stock will be worth more than $10 but less than $100 per share. Thus, the option with the lower exercise price will be worth more since its owner will make a profit.

Time to expiration
Imagine two call options on the same stock, both with exercise prices of $25 per share. The first option expires in one month, the second in six months. If the stock is trading for $20 per share, it would need to increase in value by at least $5 per share (25 percent) for the option to be exercised. It is more likely that the stock price will increase by that amount over six months than over one month. The longer the term to expiration, the higher the value of the call option.

The risk-free rate of interest
The value of a call option must be at least today's stock price less the present value of the exercise price. As the risk-free rate rises, the present value of the exercise price falls and the value of the call option increases.

Stock price
The profit from investing in call options is the difference between the stock price and the exercise price. The higher the stock price, the larger the profit. Thus, call option values are positively related to the stock price.

Standard deviation of the stock
The more variable the stock price is, the higher the value of the call option. The higher the variability in stock prices, the more likely it is that the stock price will be above the exercise price at maturity.

Using Binomial Option Pricing
Consider a one-year option on ABX stock currently priced at $42 a share, exercise price $40. Two possible outcomes of ABX stock at year end are $60 or $30. The risk-free rate is 8 percent. What is the price of an ABX call option?

1.   a.   The replicating portfolio approach:
           If the stock price at year end is $30, the call price = 0 and if it is $60, the call price = $20.
           Hedge Ratio (HR) = ($20 − 0)/($60 − $30)
                           = 20/30 = 2/3

           We now consider a portfolio consisting of one share of the stock and borrowing $27.78 (30/1.08) at 8 percent interest. The payoff to this portfolio at year end is as follows:

	$P_1 = 30$	$P_1 = 60$
Value of stock	$30	$60
Repay loan	−30	−30
Total	0	30

           We observe that at year end, the payoff to this portfolio is exactly 3/2 that of the call option.

           Cost of the portfolio = P_0 − $27.78

                           = $42 − $27.78
                           = $14.22
           Therefore, $(3/2) V_c$ = $14.22
                      V_c = $9.48
           The value of the call is $9.48.
           Or using Equation 18.2 in the text,
             V_c = $42(2/3) − $27.78(2/3)
                = $9.48

      b.   Alternatively, to create a riskless portfolio, we could purchase two shares of ABX and write three calls. The payoffs to the portfolio at expiration are as follows:

	$P_1 = 30$	$P_1 = 60$
Buy 2 shares	$60	$120
Write 3 calls	0	−60
Total	60	60

           Thus, a portfolio of two shares and three calls written is perfectly hedged (riskless), with a payoff of $60 regardless of stock price.

(Today's) Value of such portfolio $= 2P_0 - 3V_c$

Thus $2P_0 - 3V_c = 60/1.08$
$84 - 3V_c = 55.556$
$V_c = \$9.48$

c.   The risk-neutral approach:
If the stock price falls from \$42 to \$30, the return on the stock will be −0.2857, and if it rises to \$60, the return will be 0.4286.

Let W denote probability that the stock price rises, and $1 - W$, the probability that it falls at expiration. Thus, the expected return on the stock is given as

Expected return $= W(0.4286) + (1 - W)(-0.2857)$

In a risk-neutral approach, the expected return on the stock equals the risk-free rate.

$0.08 = 0.4286W + (1 - W)(-0.2857)$
$0.3657 = 0.7143W$
$W = 0.5120$ and $1 - W = 0.4880$

Expected call price given the probabilities of upward/downward movement in stock price becomes:
Expected call price $= 0.5120(\$20) + 0.4880(0)$
$= \$10.2394$
Today's value of the call, $V_c = \$10.2394/1.08$
$= \$9.48$

2.   Determine the corresponding price for ABX put option. Using the put–call parity relationship given as
$V_c + PV(X) = V_P + P_0$
$V_P = \$9.48 + \$40/1.08 - \$42$
$= \$4.52$

Using the Black–Scholes Option Pricing Model

The Black–Scholes option pricing model looks (and is) very complex, but with the help of a good calculator and Table B.5 in your text, we can use the model to value call options. The Black–Scholes model is

$$V_c = P_0 N(d_1) - \frac{X}{e^{k_{RF}t}} N(d_2)$$

$$d_1 = \frac{\ln(P_0/X) + (k_{RF} + 0.5\sigma^2)t}{\sigma(t)^{0.5}}$$

$$d_2 = d_1 - \sigma(t)^{0.5}$$

Suppose we wish to calculate the value of a call option on Westland Ltd.'s common stock. The exercise price is \$75 per share and the stock price is \$71 per share. The option expires in three months (25 percent of one year), the risk-free rate is 10 percent per year, and $\sigma = 36\%$. What is the value of the call option?

First, calculate d_1 and d_2.

$$d_1 = \frac{\ln(P_0/X) + (k_{RF} + 0.5\sigma^2)\, t}{\sigma(t)^{0.5}}$$

$$= \frac{\ln(71/75) + [0.10 + 0.5(0.36)^2]\,(0.25)}{(0.36)(0.25)^{0.5}}$$

$$= \frac{-0.0548 + (0.1648)(0.25)}{(0.36)(0.50)}$$

$$= -0.076 \approx -0.08$$

$$d_2 = d_1 - \sigma(t)^{0.5}$$

$$= -0.0756 - 0.36(0.25)^{0.5}$$

$$= -0.226 \approx -0.23$$

Now, look up the closest tabled value for $N(d_1)$ and $N(d_2)$ in Table B.5 in the text. For $d_1 = -0.08$ and $d_2 = -0.23$, we find that $N(d_1) = 0.468$, and $N(d_2) = 0.409$.

Next, use the Black–Scholes formula to solve for the value of a call.

$$V_c = P_0 N(d_1) - \frac{X}{e^{k_{RF}t}} N(d_2)$$

$$= \$71\,(0.468) + \frac{\$75}{e^{0.10\,(0.25)}}\,(0.409)$$

$$= \$33.23 + \frac{\$75}{e^{0.025}}\,(0.409)$$

$$= \$33.23 - \$29.92$$

$$= \$3.31$$

An individual purchasing this call option would pay \$3.31 per share or \$331.00 (\$3.31 × 100 shares) for it.

Calculating option values using the Black–Scholes model can be quite complex. The text discusses a short-cut approach using Table B.6 to estimate call option values. Although the answers using this approach are not precise, they are easier to compute.

Valuing Put Options

Puts are options to sell. Put values can be calculated by taking advantage of put–call parity. The value of a put is

$$V_p = V_c + \frac{X}{e^{k_{RF}t}} - P_0$$

A put option on the above stock with the same exercise price and expiration date can be valued as:

$$V_p = \$3.31 + \frac{\$75}{e^{0.10\,(0.25)}} - \$71$$

$$= \$3.31 + \$73.15 - \$71$$

$$= \$5.46$$

An investor will be willing to pay \$5.46 per share for the right to sell this stock at \$75 per share in three months. Again, there is a short-cut method using Table B.7 to estimate put values.

Completion Questions

18.1   A _____ option is the right to buy an asset at a specific price over some time period.

18.2   A put option is the right to _____ an asset at a specific price over some period of time.

18.3   The _____ is the cost to purchase the option.

18.4   Call option values are inversely related to the _____.

18.5   The _____ price of an option is the stated purchase or sale price.

18.6   A call option is _____ when the stock price is greater than the exercise price.

18.7   A put option is out-of-the-money if the _____ is greater than the _____.

18.8   _____ options can only be exercised on the expiration date, while _____ options can be exercised up to and including the expiration date.

18.9   A call option is a bet that the asset will _____ in price while a put option is a bet that the asset will _____ in price.

18.10   In the _____, there are only two possible outcomes for the stock price at the end of the year.

18.11   The _____ is the spread of the option price divided by the spread of the stock price.

18.12   In the risk-neutral approach, the expected return on the stock is set equal to the _____ _____.

18.13   The _____ is used when there are many possible outcomes for the stock price.

Problems

18.1   Imagine that you are a portfolio manager establishing a one-year program. The portfolio you manage is currently worth $20 million, and you believe that by year end the portfolio will either increase in value by 20 percent or decrease in value by 10 percent. T-bills currently pay 8 percent per year continuously compounded, and you guarantee a minimum return of 5 percent on the portfolio. Suppose call and put index options containing the same assets as your portfolio exist.
   a.   What is the hedge ratio for the call option?
   b.   i.   What is the value of the call option today (t = 0)? the put option today (t = 0)?
         ii.   Would you exercise the call or put early? Why or why not?

18.2   A stock is currently $40. It is known that at the end of 3 months it will be either $36 or $46. The risk-free rate of interest with quarterly compounding is 8.25 percent per year. There exists both a 3-month European call and put option on the stock, each with an exercise price of $40.
   a.   Use the risk-neutral (binomial) method to price the call.
   b.   Use the risk-neutral (binomial) method to price the put.

18.3   Nordik Sports' common stock is selling for $16 per share. Using the Black–Scholes option pricing model, calculate the value of a call option and a put option with six months to maturity and an exercise price of $20 per share assuming $\sigma = 0.40$ and $k_{RF} = 0.12$.

18.4   The common stock of Edmonton Electrical Supply is presently selling for $69 per share. Using the tables, approximate the value of a three-month call option and a three-month put option with an exercise price of $75, assuming $k_{RF} = 0.08$ and $\sigma = 0.30$.

18.5   The stock of IBM currently sells for $62.75 and pays no dividends. A call option on IBM stock with exercise price of $60 expires in 87 days. You estimate the volatility of IBM stock returns to be 0.48.
   a.   Given that an IBM call is priced at $7.04 and the put at $4.05, what is the implicit rate of interest contained in these values?
   b.   Given that the T-bill rate is 6.5 percent, what is the theoretically correct (equilibrium) value of an IBM call?
   c.   Determine the equilibrium price of an IBM put option with 87 days to expiration and exercise price of $60.
   d.   How sensitive are the IBM call and put options to changes in the stock price?

Answers to Completion Questions

18.1   call
18.2   sell
18.3   option premium
18.4   exercise price
18.5   exercise
18.6   in-the-money
18.7   stock price; exercise price
18.8   European; American
18.9   increase; decrease
18.10 binomial option pricing model
18.11 hedge ratio
18.12 risk-free rate
18.13 Black-Scholes option pricing model

Solutions to Problems

18.1   a.   Step 1.   The portfolio value at t = 1 will be
                      $20 million (1.20) = $24 million or
                      $20 million (0.90) = $18 million

            Step 2.   The exercise price at t = 1 will be
                      $20 million (1.05) = $21 million

            Step 3.   The possible values of the call option are

	Portfolio = $24 million	Portfolio = $18 million
V_c	$3 million	$0

            Step 4.   Hedge ratio $= \dfrac{\text{spread of option price}}{\text{spread of portfolio price}}$

                      $= \dfrac{\$3 \text{ million} - \$0}{\$24 \text{ million} - \$18 \text{ million}} = \dfrac{1}{2}$

b.   i.   Step 1.   Present value of loan = $18 million / 1.08 = $16.67 million

Step 2. V_c = (portfolio price)(hedge ratio) − (present value of loan)(hedge ratio)
= $20 million(1/2) − $16.67 million(1/2) = $1.665 million

Step 3. V_p = $1.665 million + $21 million/1.08 − $20 million
= $1.109 million

ii.   The exercise price, X, is $21 million and the stock price is $20 million. The call will not be exercised early since it is out-of-the-money. The put is in-the-money. However, if exercised, its exercise value is $1.00 million, which is less than V_p($1.109 million). The put will not be exercised early.

18.2   a.   Step 1.   The possible increase in value is $(46/40) - 1 = 15$ percent. The possible decrease in value is $(36/40) - 1 = -10$ percent.

Step 2.   The expected return is 8.25 percent, so the probability of an upward movement, W, is

$$0.0825 = W(0.15) + (1 - W)(-0.10)$$
$$0.0825 = 0.15W - 0.10 + 0.10W$$
$$W = 0.1825/25 = 0.73$$
$$1 - W = 0.27$$

Step 3.   Expected value$_1$ = 0.73($6) + 0.27($0)
= $4.38

The present value of the call is
V_c = $4.38/1.0206 = $4.29

b. V_p = $4.29 + $40/1.0206 − $40 = $3.48

18.3   Step 1. $d_1 = \dfrac{\ln (P_0/X) + (k_{RF} + 0.5\sigma^2)\, t}{\sigma(t)^{0.5}}$

$= \dfrac{\ln (16/20) + \left[0.12 + 0.5\,(0.40)^2\right]\, 6/12}{(0.40)(0.5)^{0.5}}$

$= \dfrac{-0.2231 + 0.10}{0.2828}$

$= -0.44$

Step 2. $d_2 = -0.44 - 0.40(0.5)^{0.5}$

$= -0.44 - 0.28$

$= -0.72$

Step 3.   Calculate $N(d_1)$ and $N(d_2)$:

$N(d_1) = N(-0.44) = 0.330$

$N(d_2) = N(-0.72) = 0.236$

Step 4. $V_c = P_0 N(d_1) - \dfrac{X}{e^{k_{RF}t}} N(d_2)$

$= \$16\,(0.330) - \dfrac{\$20}{e^{0.12\,(0.5)}}\,(0.236)$

$= \$5.28 - \$18.84\,(0.236)$

$= \$5.28 - \$4.45$

$= \$0.83$

Step 5. $V_p = V_c + \dfrac{X}{e^{k_{RF}t}} - P_0$

$= \$0.83 + \dfrac{\$20}{e^{0.12\,(0.5)}} - \$16$

$= \$0.83 + \$18.84 - \$16$

$= \$3.67$

18.4   Step 1.   Calculate the standard deviation times the square root of time.

$\sigma(t)^{0.5} = 0.3(3/12)^{0.5} = 0.3(0.25)^{0.5} = 0.15$

Step 2.   Calculate the market price divided by the present value of the exercise price.

$\dfrac{P_0}{X/e^{k_{RF}t}} = \dfrac{\$69}{\$75/e^{0.08(0.25)}} = \dfrac{\$69}{\$73.51} = 0.94$

Step 3.   Using Table B.6 and the two values calculated above, find the tabled factor for a call option and multiply it by the share price.
Tabled factor = 0.035

$V_c = 0.035(\$69)$

$= \$2.42$

Step 4.   Using Table B.7 and the two values calculated above, find the tabled factor for a put option and multiply it by the share price.
Tabled factor = 0.099

$V_p = 0.099(\$69)$

$= \$6.83$

18.5   Given the following information:
$P_0 = \$62.75$, $X = \$60$, $t = 87/365 = 0.2384$ and $\sigma = 0.48$

a.
$$V_c + \frac{X}{e^{k_{RF}t}} = P_0 + V_p$$

$$\$7.04 + \frac{\$60}{e^{k_{RF}(0.2384)}} = \$62.75 + \$4.05$$

$$\frac{\$60}{e^{k_{RF}(0.2384)}} = \$59.76$$

$$\frac{1}{e^{k_{RF}(0.2384)}} = 0.996$$

$$e^{k_{RF}(0.2384)} = 1.00402$$

Taking the natural log of both sides, we obtain the following:
$$k_{RF} \times 0.2384 = 0.004008$$
$$k_{RF} = 1.68\%$$

b.   Given $k_{RF} = 0.065$:

Step 1.   Calculate the values of d_1 and d_2.

$$d_1 = \frac{\ln(\$62.75/\$60) + [0.065 + 0.5(0.48)^2]0.2384}{0.48(0.2384)^{0.5}}$$

$$= \frac{0.0448 + 0.0430}{0.2344} = 0.3745$$

$$d_2 = 0.3745 - 0.48(0.2384)^{0.5}$$

$$= 0.3745 - 0.2344 = 0.1401$$

Step 2.   Compute $N(d_1)$ and $N(d_2)$ using Table B.5.
The closest tabled values are
$$N(d_1) = N(0.37) = 0.644$$
$$N(d_2) = N(0.14) = 0.556$$

Step 3.   Use the Black–Scholes option pricing formula.

$$V_c = \$62.75(0.644) - \frac{\$60}{e^{(0.065)(0.2384)}}(0.556)$$

$$= \$40.41 - \$32.85 = \$7.56$$

c.
$$V_p = V_c + \frac{X}{e^{k_{RF}t}} - P_0$$

$$= \$7.56 + \frac{\$60}{e^{(0.065)(0.2384)}} - \$62.75$$

$$= \$7.56 + \$59.08 - \$62.75 = \$3.89$$

d. Note that delta of IBM call option, $N(d_1)$, is 0.6460 and that of IBM put option, $N(d_1) - 1$, is −0.3540. If the IBM stock price increases by $1.00, the call price will increase by $0.6460, while the put price will decrease by $0.3540.

Chapter 19
Option Applications in Financial Management

How This Chapter Relates to the Rest of the Text

In Chapter 18, we examined the characteristics of call and put options. In this chapter, we express the relationship between common stock and the firm in terms of options. The concepts developed in Chapter 18 allow us to expand the traditional NPV model for evaluating capital investments, which was presented in Chapters 7 and 8, by recognizing that embedded or hidden options exist in all capital investment decisions. This enables us to develop a strategic NPV. Options are also used as an effective means of hedging interest and foreign exchange risks.

Topical Outline

I.   Valuing the firm using the option pricing model.
    A.   Common stock in a levered firm is similar to a call option.
        1.   The face value of debt is the exercise price.
        2.   Stockholders can exercise the option by paying off the bondholders.
    B.   Stockholders also own a put option (or option to default).
    C.   The value of the stock plus the value of riskless bonds equals the value of the right to default plus the market value of the firm's assets.
    D.   Use the option pricing model to calculate the value of the stock (a call option), using the value of the firm's assets as the stock price.
    E.   Use the put–call parity relationship to calculate the value of the option to default.

II.   Options in capital investment.
    A.   An example of a call option is an option to purchase another firm.
    B.   The acceptance of a capital budgeting project often carries with it an option for future investment.
    C.   When a capital investment decision can be deferred, a call option exists.
    D.   The option to abandon a capital investment is a put option.
    E.   Guarantees are also put options.
    F.   If a capital expenditure contains an option, the option value must be considered in calculating the strategic net present value of the expenditure.

III.   Uses of options.
    A.   Interest rate risk management.
        1.   Investment companies use options on fixed income securities to speculate on movements in interest rates. For example, if investors expect future spot rates of interest to drop substantially, and hence the prices of government bonds to rise, they will purchase a call option on government bonds. If investors expect future spot rates of interest to rise, they will purchase a put option on government bonds.
        2.   Interest rate cap. This is a call option on a floating interest rate. It is employed by businesses (borrowers) to place a ceiling on the amount of interest paid on a floating rate loan.
        3.   Interest rate floor. This is a put option on a floating interest rate. It is employed by financial institutions (lenders) to protect themselves against a falling interest rate. It sets limits on how low the interest rate can fall.
        4.   Interest rate collar. This is a combination of a cap and a floor.
    B.   Hedging against exchange rate fluctuations.
        1.   The purchase of call options on a foreign currency offers protection to Canadian businesses that import goods and services to foreign countries and make payment in the foreign currency.
        2.   Buying put options on a foreign currency offers protection to Canadian businesses that export goods and services abroad and receive payment in foreign currencies.
        3.   In the currency options market, the exchange rates are quoted in terms of U.S. dollars.

Formulas

<u>Notation</u>

Default option	= value of the option to default
V	= market value of the firm's assets
S	= market value of stock
B(riskless)	= value of riskless bonds
M	= face value of bonds
B	= value of risky debt

<u>Valuing the Firm</u>

$$B(\text{riskless}) = M/e^{k_{RF}t}$$

$$S = VN(d_1) - \frac{X}{e^{k_{RF}t}} N(d_2)$$

$$d_1 = \frac{\ln(V/M) + \left[k_{RF} + 0.5\sigma^2\right] t}{\sigma(t)^{0.5}}$$

$$d_2 = d_1 - \sigma(t)^{0.5}$$

Default option $= S + B(\text{riskless}) - V$

$B = V - S = B(\text{riskless}) - \text{default option}$

What to Look For

Many decisions made by financial managers contain options. An option is simply a contract that gives the owner the right, but not the obligation, to buy or sell an asset at a specific price over some specified time period. For instance, a firm may purchase a piece of manufacturing equipment from a supplier and the supplier may agree to sell additional equipment at the same price for the next year. This option has value; correct decision making requires that managers understand what affects option values and how they are calculated.

<u>Valuing the Firm Using Option Pricing</u>

Option pricing is useful in determining where stock values come from. Consider a typical firm. The firm owns assets that generate cash flows. The firm is financed in part by common stock and in part by debt. The presence of debt in a firm's capital structure leads to two options.

First, common stock can be viewed as a call option. If the firm does well, shareholders have the right to buy the firm's assets from the bondholders for a fixed price (the face value of debt). From the put–call parity relationship,

$$V_c = P_0 - \frac{X}{e^{k_{RF}t}} + V_p$$

We can see that the owners of the stock also own a put option. In this case, the put option is the right to default on debt if the firm does poorly. Because of limited liability, shareholders can lose only their investment; they cannot be held liable for the firm's debt. This default option is valuable to shareholders. In other words,

$$\text{Value of stock} = \begin{array}{c}\text{value of the}\\\text{firm's assets}\end{array} - \begin{array}{c}\text{value of}\\\text{riskless bonds}\end{array} + \begin{array}{c}\text{default}\\\text{options}\end{array}$$

If we know the various factors necessary to use the option pricing model, we can use it to calculate the value of the firm's stocks and bonds. The model can also provide insights into the sources of conflict between shareholders and bondholders.

Options in Financial Management

Most people think of options traded on major exchanges when the topic is mentioned. However, options are present in many of the firm's activities. For example, a firm may engage in a contract to purchase shares in another firm for a fixed price, or a supplier may agree to sell goods at a contracted price. Capital budgeting projects often contain implied options since they may lead to future projects or the firm may be able to defer projects until some later date. The value of each of these call options must be considered in order to make appropriate decisions.

Put options also exist for the firm. The option to sell an existing asset at a specified price and abandon a project is a put option. Suppose a firm is considering a project with a cost of \$1,000,000 and a PV of cash flows of \$940,000. The NPV of the project is \$940,000 − \$1,000,000 = −\$60,000, which is negative. But, suppose the firm has the option to abandon the project at the end of one year and sell the assets for \$800,000. The risk-free rate is 10 percent, and $\sigma = 0.60$. The put option's value must be considered before the decision can be made. Using the three-step short-cut:

$$\sigma(t)^{0.5} = 0.60(1)^{0.5} = 0.60$$

$$\frac{P_0}{X/e^{k_{RF}t}} = \frac{\$940,000}{\$800,000/e^{0.10\,(1)}} = 1.30$$

From Table B.7, the factor is 0.112, so the value of the put option is 0.112(940,000) = \$105,280. The strategic NPV of the project, including the option value, is −\$60,000 + \$105,280 = \$45,280, which is positive. Failure to include the option value would have led to an incorrect decision.

Hedging Interest Rate and Foreign Exchange Rate Risks with Options

Financial managers can use futures options to hedge against increases or decreases in interest rates or to contain a floating interest rate within specific bounds. An interest rate cap offers protection to a borrower by placing a ceiling on the interest cost for variable interest rate debt, while an interest rate floor gives a lender protection against an interest rate decline. An interest rate collar combines both an interest rate cap and floor.

A weakening foreign exchange rate can be hedged against by purchasing currency options. For example, an importer who must pay for goods with a foreign currency can hedge against a weakening domestic currency by purchasing a foreign exchange call option. An exporter faced with a similar situation can hedge by purchasing a foreign exchange put option.

Completion Questions

19.1   Common stock in a firm can be considered a _____ option since the shareholders can buy the firm's assets from the bondholders by paying the _____.

19.2   Shareholders own a put option since they can _____ on the firm's debt.

19.3   The value of risky debt is actually the difference between _____ and _____
_____.

19.4   Capital budgeting projects often contain _____ since they can lead to future investments.

19.5   _____ is the original NPV plus the value of the option.

19.6   The ability to _____ a capital investment is a call option.

19.7   The decision to _____ a project and sell the assets is really a put option.

19.8   A guarantee is an example of a _____ option.

19.9   An _____ puts a ceiling on the cost of variable rate debt.

19.10   Currency options can be used to hedge against _____.

Problems

19.1   LaBarge Garden Products has a total market value of \$10 million and 10-year zero-coupon bonds with a face value of \$3 million. If $k_{RF} = 9\%$, and the annual standard deviation of the firm's value is 0.80, what is the value of the default option on the bonds using the Black–Scholes option pricing model?

For problems 19.2 to 19.4, approximate the option values using the factors in Tables B.6 and B.7.

19.2   Mideast Semiconductor is considering a merger with one of its major competitors, Computer Components Limited. CCL has offered to sell a 90-day option with an exercise price of $120 per share. If $k_{RF} = 11$ percent, $\sigma = 0.40$, and CCL's stock price is currently $94 per share, how much should Mideast be willing to pay for options on the 2 million shares of CCL outstanding?

19.3   Manitoba Adhesives is considering the purchase of Canadian Glue's contact cement division. Forecasted cash flows after tax are

Year	CF
1	$200,000
2	400,000
3	500,000
4	600,000
5	600,000

Canadian Glue is trying to get rid of the division and has offered to guarantee CFs of $450,000 per year. Manitoba Adhesives believes the CFs should be discounted at 20 percent, $k_{RF} = 7$ percent, and $\sigma = 0.80$. What is the maximum price Manitoba Adhesives should be willing to pay for this division? (Assume continuous compounding in calculating the PV of the CFs.)

19.4   Exact Precision Tools is considering the purchase of a computerized manufacturing machine. The present value in year 0 of the cash flows after year 1 is $775,000, and the company has the option of abandoning the machine after 1 year and selling the equipment for $500,000. If $k_{RF} = 12$ percent, and $\sigma = 0.55$, what is the value of the option to abandon?

Answers to Completion Questions

19.1   call; face value of debt
19.2   default
19.3   riskless debt; the default option
19.4   call options
19.5   Strategic NPV
19.6   defer
19.7   abandon
19.8   put
19.9   interest rate cap
19.10   foreign exchange risk

Solutions to Problems

19.1   Step 1.   The value of the bonds if risk free, B(riskless),

$$B(riskless) = (face value)/e^{k_{RF}t}$$

$$= \frac{\$3,000,000}{e^{0.09 \times 10}} = \$1,219,708.98$$

Step 2.   Use the Black–Scholes model to calculate the value of the stock (S).

$$d_1 = \frac{\ln (V/\text{face value of bonds}) + \left[k_{RF} + 0.5(\sigma)^2\right] t}{\sigma(t)^{0.5}}$$

$$= \frac{\ln (\$10,000,000/\$3,000,000) + \left[0.09 + 0.5 (0.8)^2\right] \times 10}{0.8(10)^{0.5}}$$

$$= \frac{1.2040 + 4.10}{2.5298}$$

$$= 2.0966$$

$$d_1 \approx 2.10$$

$$d_2 = d_1 - \sigma(t)^{0.5}$$

$$= 2.0966 - 0.8(10)^{0.5}$$

$$= -0.4332$$

$$d_2 \approx -0.43$$

From Table B.5, $N(d_1) = 0.982$
$N(d_2) = 0.334$

Step 3. $S = V \times N(d_1) - \dfrac{\text{face value of bond}}{e^{k_{RF}t}}$

$$= \$10,000,000 (0.982) - \frac{\$3,000,000}{e^{0.09 \times 10}} (0.334)$$

$$= \$9,820,000 - \$407,382.80$$

$$= \$9,412,617.20$$

Step 4. $V = B + S$
$B = V - S$
$\quad = \$10,000,000 - \$9,412,617.20$
$\quad = \$587,832.80$
$B = B(\text{riskless}) - \text{default}$
$\text{Default} = B(\text{riskless}) - B$
$\qquad = \$1,219,708.98 - \$587,382.80$
$\qquad = \$632,326.18$

19.2   Step 1. $\sigma(t)^{0.5} = 0.40(90/365)^{0.5} = 0.20$

Step 2. $\dfrac{P_0}{X/e^{k_{RF}t}} = \dfrac{\$94}{\$120/e^{0.11 \, (90/365)}} = \dfrac{\$94}{\$116.7889} = 0.80$

Step 3.   From Table B.6, the tabled factor = 0.0148, so
$V_c = 0.015(\$94)$
$\quad = \$1.41$

Step 4.   For options on 2 million shares, Mideast should pay
$2,000,000(\$1.41) = \$2,820,000$

19.3   Step 1.

Year	CF	Present Value of CFs at 20%	
1	$200,000	$200,000/e^{0.07(1)}$ =	$ 186,478.76
2	400,000	$400,000/e^{0.07(2)}$ =	347,743.29
3	500,000	$500,000/e^{0.07(3)}$ =	405,292.12
4	600,000	$600,000/e^{0.07(4)}$ =	453,470.24
5	600,000	$600,000/e^{0.07(5)}$ =	422,812.85
		Total PV of CFs	$1,815,797.26

Step 2.   Calculate the factors needed to use Table B.7 to value the put options, rounding the factors to the closest tabled values.

Year	$\sigma(t)^{0.5}$	$\dfrac{P_0}{X/e^{k_{RF}t}}$
1	$0.80(1)^{0.5} = 0.80$	$\dfrac{186,478.76}{450,000/e^{0.07(1)}} = 0.44 \approx 0.45$
2	$0.80(2)^{0.5} = 1.13 \approx 1.15$	$\dfrac{347,743.29}{450,000/e^{0.07(2)}} = 0.89 \approx 0.90$
3	$0.80(3)^{0.5} = 1.39 \approx 1.40$	$\dfrac{405,292.12}{450,000/e^{0.07(3)}} = 1.11 \approx 1.12$
4	$0.80(4)^{0.5} = 1.60 \approx 1.50$	$\dfrac{453,470.24}{450,000/e^{0.07(4)}} = 1.33 \approx 1.35$
5	$0.80(5)^{0.5} = 1.79 \approx 1.75$	$\dfrac{422,812.85}{450,000/e^{0.07(5)}} = 1.33 \approx 1.35$

Step 3.

Year	Tabled Factor	×	P_0	=	Value of the Put
1	1.317		$186,478.76		$245,592.53
2	0.516		$347,743.29		$179,435.54
3	0.436		$405,292.12		$176,707.36
4	0.354		$453,470.24		$160,528.47
5	0.415		$422,812.85		$175,467.33
			Total value of the puts	=	$937,731.23

Step 4.   Maximum price = PV of CF + value of put option
= $1,815,797.26 + $937,731.23
= $2,753,528.49

19.4   Step 1. $\sigma(t)^{0.5} = 0.55 (1)^{0.5} = 0.55$

Step 2. $\dfrac{P_0}{X/e^{k_{RF}t}} = \dfrac{\$775,000}{\$500,000/e^{0.12(1)}} = 1.75$

Step 3.   From Table B.7, the factor = 0.033, so
Value of option to abandon = 0.033($775,000)
= $25,575.00

Chapter 20
Warrants and Convertibles

How This Chapter Relates to the Rest of the Text

Warrants are call options issued by the firm whose common shares serve as the underlying security. They are usually issued in conjunction with other securities such as debt. Convertibles are securities that can be converted into shares of the same company at the option of the holder but under stated terms. Warrants and convertibles can be viewed as call options with longer expiration dates than stock options. The valuation of warrants and convertibles requires an understanding of options (Chapters 18–19), valuation of stocks and bonds (Chapter 4), capital budgeting (Chapters 7–9), and rights offering (Chapter 10).

Topical Outline

I.   Warrants.
    A.   Warrants are usually issued with debt to induce investors to buy the firm's debt at a lower coupon interest than would otherwise be required.
        1.   Warrants, once issued, may be detached from the bond and sold separately.
        2.   Unlike options, warrants are created by the firm issuing the stock.
        3.   The holder of warrants receives no dividends or voting rights.
        4.   Warrants are protected against stock split and stock dividends.
        5.   If warrants are exercised, the number of outstanding shares of the company increases. This will likely cause a dilution of the wealth of existing shareholders.
    B.   When warrants are issued initially, the firm attaches them to new bond issues and markets these bonds with coupon interest substantially below the market rate. The company also has to specify the exercise price and expiration of the warrants attached to the bond issue. Once the bonds have been sold, the warrants may be detached and sold separately. The binomial and the Black–Scholes option pricing techniques can be employed to value warrants anytime prior to expiration.
    C.   In valuing warrants, one has to bear in mind that warrants affect the firm in the following ways:
        1.   The proceeds from the issue and sale of warrants accrue directly to the firm. The effect of this on the share price must be recognized.
        2.   Warrants are exercised only when the underlying firm's share price exceeds the exercise value. Therefore, when warrants are exercised, the number of shares outstanding increases, causing a dilution of the wealth of existing shareholders.
        3.   Like a call option, the value of a warrant is determined by the following:
            a.   The current price of the stock (P_0).
            b.   The exercise price (X).
            c.   The time remaining to expiration (t).
            d.   The risk-free rate (k_{RF}).
            e.   The variability of the underlying asset (σ).
        4.   Use the Black–Scholes option pricing formula to value warrants.
            a.   Before using the formula, you need to adjust the stock price for any known cash dividends to be paid on the stock.
            b.   Since the number of shares outstanding increases when warrants are exercised, you have to adjust the call price for dilution effect.
II.   Convertibles.
    A.   Convertible bonds can be exchanged for the shares of the same company at the option of the holder and under specified terms. These terms are:
        1.   Conversion ratio (CR): This ratio determines the number of shares the bondholder receives when conversion occurs.
        2.   Conversion value (CV): This value determines the effective price paid for the common stock of the underlying company when conversion occurs.

B. Over time, as interest rates change, the price of a nonconvertible bond with the same risk characteristics and maturity as the convertible bond also changes (to reflect the changing market conditions). The market value of such nonconvertible bonds is called "straight-bond value." The holder of a convertible bond has two options, namely:

1. Hold the bond as nonconvertible and continue to receive coupon payments until the maturity date.
2. Convert the bond into common shares of the company and sell them immediately.

   Conversion value (CV) = Conversion ratio (CR) × Stock price (P_0)

C. Issues.

1. Most convertibles are callable. When called for redemption, the firm has 30 days in which to either convert the bond into common stock or surrender the bond for the call price.
2. Most convertible bonds are subordinated to other long-term debt of the firm.
3. Convertibles offer investors opportunities for capital gains to be realized at a future date. For this reason, investors are prepared to accept a lower coupon rate on convertible bonds.
4. Convertibles are a good source of equity financing, especially for firms whose stock price is temporarily depressed but is likely to rise from its current level in the future.
5. When a bond is converted into common stock,
   a. The number of shares outstanding increases.
   b. Interest payments are reduced.
   c. Capital structure of the firm changes and so does financial leverage.

D. Value before maturity.

1. The market price of the bond (convertible) is typically above the floor price of the bond.

   Market price > Floor price

   or   Market price > Max{CV, SBV}

2. Since the holder of a convertible bond has the option to hold the bond until it matures, when the price of a convertible bond is below that of a straight bond (nonconvertible), investors will buy the convertible and hold it as nonconvertible. If the price of the convertible is below the conversion value, investors would buy the bond, convert it immediately, and make a riskless profit.

What to Look For

Warrants are long-term call options. A warrant gives the holder the right to purchase the shares of stock of a firm at a specific price. This right exists up to and including a specified date. Each warrant specifies the number of shares that the holder can buy if exercised.

Issuing Warrants

The firm initially attaches warrants to bond issues, marketing these bonds with coupon interest substantially below the market rate.

For example, suppose the current market rate of interest is 13 percent, so that if a firm issues 20-year straight bonds at par, it will have to pay 13 percent coupon interest. Suppose the firm decides to attach warrants to these bonds and market them at 10 percent coupon interest for $1,000 each. Then the value of the straight bonds (SB) with 10 percent coupon is

$$SB = 100 \, PVA_{13\%, 20yrs} + 1,000/(1.13)^{20} = \$789.50$$

Since the straight bonds with warrants sell for $1,000 each, the value of the warrants is $1,000 − $789.50 = $210.50. In this case, if the company attaches 15 warrants to each bond, then the value of each warrant is $14.03.

Exercising Warrants

When warrants are exercised, the wealth of existing shareholders is diluted, because the number of shares outstanding increases.

Suppose ABC, with $1 million shares outstanding and share price of $32, plans to issue 100,000 warrants at $12.50 a share. These warrants, with an exercise price of $40, expire in 4 years. The risk-free rate is 6, and the volatility of the returns on ABC's common stock is estimated to be 0.6.

Calculate the value of each warrant.

i.   When warrants are issued, the proceeds of $1,250,000 accrue to the firm.

$$\text{Adjusted share price } P_0 = (\$32 \text{ million} + \$1.25 \text{ million})/1 \text{ million}$$
$$= \$33.25$$

ii.   Given $\sigma = 0.6$, $k_{RF} = 6\%$, $t = 4$ years, $P_0 = \$33.25$ and $X = \$40$:

$$d_1 = [\ln(\$33.25/\$40) + (0.06)(4) + 0.5(0.6)^2(4)]/[(0.6)(4)^{0.5}]$$
$$= 0.7752/1.2 = 0.646 \approx 0.65$$
$$d_2 = d_1 - \sigma(t)^{0.5} = -0.554 \approx -0.55$$
$$N(d_1) = 0.742, \ N(d_2) = 0.291$$
$$V_c = \$33.25(0.742) - \$40e^{-0.24}(0.291)$$
$$= \$24.67 - \$9.16 = \$15.51$$

iii. Bearing in mind that when warrants are exercised the number of shares outstanding increases from $1 million to $1.10 million (i.e., by 10 percent):

Value of a warrant = $15.51/1.1 = $14.10

Convertibles

Suppose you own $10 million worth of IBM convertible bonds, carrying 10 percent coupon and maturing in 12 years. The bonds may be exchanged for 25 shares of IBM stock. The current market price of IBM stock is $47. IBM nonconvertible bonds, with 10 percent coupon and maturing in 12 years, are priced to yield 8 percent in the market today.

Note: Number of bond certificates = $10 million/1,000 = 10,000

a.   Conversion ratio = 25 shares, and conversion price = $1,000/25 = $40

b.   Since stock price is $47,

Conversion value = 25 × $47 = $1,175

c.   Noting that the straight bond value (SBV) is the value of a nonconvertible bond with the same risk, coupon, and maturity as the convertible bond:

$$\text{SBV} = 100 \ \text{PVA}_{8\%,12yr} + 1,000/(1.08)^{12} = \$1,151$$

d.   Floor price represents the minimum price at which the bondholder will sell the convertible bond in the market.

$$\text{Floor price} = \text{Max}\{\text{CV, SBV}\}$$
$$= \text{Max}\{1,175, 1,151\}$$
$$= \$1,175$$

Therefore, the minimum price of the convertible bond, given prevailing market conditions, is $1,175.

Suppose this same convertible bond is callable at a premium of 12 percent. Then the call price is $1,120. When called for redemption, the holder of the convertible bond has the following options:

a.   Surrender the bonds for $1,120 each.

b.   Convert each bond into 25 common shares of IBM and sell the shares immediately for $1,175 per bond converted.

Still, the bond will be converted when called.

Price of Convertibles

Suppose a firm wants to issue a 12-year convertible, par value $1,000, coupon rate 7.5 percent. This bond is callable after 6 years. Similar bonds without conversion are priced to yield 10 percent in the market.

a. $SBV = 75PVA_{10\%,12yr} + \$1,000/(1.1)^{12}$

                 $= 75(6.814) + 318.63$

                 $= \$829.68$

If the convertible bond is sold at par ($1,000), then the conversion premium = $170.32.

b.   Note $P_0 = 32$, CR = 25, CV = 800

Assume this convertible bond is callable at $1,075 anytime after 6 years. Your estimate of the growth rate in the company's shares is 8 percent; the current market price of common stock is $32, and CR = 25.

     i. $P = \$32(1.08)^6 = \$50.78$

     ii. $CV = 25 \times \$50.78 = \$1,269.50$

     iii.   If converted in year 6:

             $\$1,000 = 75[(1 - (1 + k)^{-6})]/k + \$1,269.50/(1 + k)^6$

             $IRR = k = 11\%$

         (You may buy the stock hoping the price will increase and you will gain from it.)

Completion Questions

20.1   Warrants are long-term _____ issued by a firm.

20.2   When issued, warrants are usually attached to _____.

20.3   Unlike ordinary call options, when warrants are exercised the number of outstanding shares of common stock _____.

20.4   Once the bonds are sold, the warrants may be _____ and _____.

20.5   When valuing warrants, the presence of _____ must be recognized.

20.6   Convertible securities can be converted into _____ of the issuing firm at the discretion of the _____.

20.7   Two important aspects of a convertible are its _____ and _____ _____.

20.8   Most convertibles are _____ and _____ to other long-term debt.

20.9   When a convertible bond is converted, the number of shares outstanding _____, and _____ are reduced.

20.10   Warrants and convertibles are similar to call options with _____ than stock options.

Problems

20.1   Bulldog Lock Company is issuing debt with warrants attached. Each warrant enables the owner to purchase a share of common stock at $35 per share in 8 years. The stock is presently trading for $20 per share, the risk-free rate is 7 percent, and $\sigma = 0.30$. Use the short-cut method and Table B.6 to determine the value of a warrant.

20.2   Suppose a firm wants to issue a 20-year bond, par value $1,000, with warrants. The current market rate of interest is 13 percent, so that if straight bonds are issued at par, a coupon interest of 13 percent would be required. Suppose the firm decides to attach 20 warrants to each bond and market these bonds with a coupon interest of 10 percent at par. Each warrant would entitle the holder to buy one share of common stock for $38 and expires in 6 years. The company's stock is currently trading for $30. Determine the value of each warrant.

20.3   Suppose a firm currently has 90,000 shares of common stock and 10,000 warrants outstanding. A warrant-holder can purchase one share at $31.50 for each warrant held. The current market price of the company's stock is $40 a share. Calculate the loss for old shareholders if warrants are exercised.

20.4   Consider a 4.75 percent convertible subordinated debenture that matures in 8 years, with conversion price of $47 and callable at $1,027.50. The market price of the convertible is 91 percent of the face value and that of common stock is $41.50. Assume the value of the bond in the absence of a conversion feature is 65 percent of the face value.
   a.   What is the conversion ratio (CR)?
   b.   What is the conversion value (CV)?
   c.   At what level of stock price is the CV equal to the straight bond value (SBV)?
   d.   How much is the holder of a convertible paying for the option to buy one share of the common stock?
   e.   By how much should the common stock price rise to justify conversion?

Answers to Completion Questions

20.1   call options
20.2   bonds
20.3   increases
20.4   detached; sold separately
20.5   dilution
20.6   shares (common shares); investor
20.7   conversion ratio; conversion value
20.8   callable; subordinated
20.9   increases; interest payments
20.10   longer expiration dates

Solutions to Problems

20.1   Step 1.   Calculate

$$\sigma(t)^{0.5} = 0.30(8)^{0.5}$$
$$= 0.30 \ (2.8284)$$
$$= 0.85$$

Step 2.   Calculate

$$\frac{P_0}{X/e^{k_{RF} t}} = \frac{\$20}{\$35/e^{0.07 \, (8)}}$$

$$= \frac{\$20}{\$35/1.7507}$$

$$= \frac{\$20}{\$19.9923}$$

$$= 1.00$$

Step 3.   Using Table B.6 and the two values above, look up the tabled factor and multiply it by the share price.

Tabled factor $= 0.329$
Value of a warrant $= 0.329 \ (\$20)$
$= \$6.58$

20.2   Step 1.   Determine the market price of a 20-year 10-percent coupon bond, given that the current market yield is 13 percent.

Price $= 100PVA_{13\%,20yr} + \$1,000/(1.13)^{20}$

$= \$702.475 + \$86.782$

$= \$789.26$

Step 2.   Since this bond with 20 warrants attached is sold at par:

Total value of warrants $= \$1000 - \$789.26$

$= \$210.74$

Value of each warrant $= \$210.74/20 = \$10.54$

20.3   Step 1.   Current market value of equity $= \$40 \times 90,000$

$= \$3,600,000$

Step 2.   If warrants are exercised, equity increases by \$315,000 ($\$31.50 \times 10,000$), and

Share price $= \$3,915,000/100,000 = \$39.15$

Step 3.   Gain by new shareholders $= 10,000(\$39.15 - \$31.50)$

$= \$76,500$

Loss by old shareholders $= 90,000(\$40 - \$39.15)$

$= \$76,500$

20.4   a.   Conversion ratio (CR) $= \$1,000/\$47 = 21.28$

b.   Conversion value (CV) $= 21.28 \times \$41.50 = \$883.92$

c.   SBV $= 0.65 \times \$1,000 = \$650$

$21.28P_0 = \$650$

$P_0 = \$30.55$

d.   Value of convertible $= 0.91(\$1,000)$

$= \$910$

Conversion premium per share $= (\$910 - \$650)/21.28 = \$12.22$

e.   Stock price should rise by $\$47/\$41.50 - 1 = 13\%$ to justify conversion.

Chapter 21
Short-Term Financial Management Policy

How This Chapter Relates to the Rest of the Text

While the emphasis to this point has been on long-term decisions, much of the manager's time is spent making decisions that affect day-to-day operations. Chapter 21 begins the discussion of managing current assets and liabilities. The components of short-term assets and liabilities (or working capital)—cash and marketable securities (Chapter 22), accounts receivable and inventories (Chapter 23), and short-term financing (Chapter 24)—are analyzed in greater detail in later chapters. As in earlier chapters, the concepts of cash flow and risk and return (Chapter 5) are important components of our analysis.

Topical Outline

I.   Short-term assets and liabilities.
    A.   Current assets and current liabilities comprise a large portion of a firm's total assets and total liabilities.
        1.   Inventories and accounts receivable are the largest current asset investments; accounts payable are the largest current liability or source of short-term funds.
        2.   Current assets and liabilities tend to be volatile within single years and over business cycles.
    B.   Short-term financial management decisions.
        1.   Manage the collection of funds from customers and the disbursement of funds to suppliers.
        2.   Cash concentration.
        3.   Liquidity management.
        4.   Bank relations.
        5.   Receivables management.
        6.   Inventory management.
    C.   Why do firms have short-term assets and liabilities?
        1.   Transactions costs.
        2.   Time delays.
        3.   Financial distress costs.
    D.   The importance of short-term assets and liabilities.
        1.   The size and volatility of short-term assets and liabilities makes working capital management a key function in a manager's day-to-day activities.
        2.   As sales grow, firms must increase both inventories and accounts payable; accounts receivable will also increase.
        3.   The health of a firm is apparent from its short-term asset and liability accounts; financial problems show up first in these accounts.
        4.   Effective short-term asset and liability management can mean the difference between survival and bankruptcy for smaller firms, since a large percentage of their assets and liabilities are current.
    E.   The goal of short-term asset and liability management is to maximize the value of the firm by effective working capital management that increases the level of future cash flows or decreases their risk.
II.   Liquidity and the cash cycle.
    A.   Ongoing liquidity refers to the inflows and outflows of cash through the firm during the course of the business.
        1.   Cash conversion cycle is the net time interval between actual cash expenditures on the productive resources and the ultimate recovery of cash: operating cycle less days payable.

        a.   The cash cycle: Increases in purchases, inventories, or receivables serve to decrease liquidity, and vice versa.

            i.   As raw materials are purchased, current liabilities increase through accounts payable.

            ii.   Firm pays for accounts payable.

            iii.   Raw materials are converted into finished goods in production process.

            iv.   Finished goods inventory is sold for cash or credit.

            v.   Credit sales (accounts receivable) are collected, resulting in cash.

        b.   Days sales outstanding is the number of days it takes to collect credit sales.

    2.   The operating cycle is the sum of the days sales outstanding and the days inventory.

    3.   Days payable = 365/payables turnover.

  B.   Ratios of the cash conversion cycle.

    1.   Receivable turnover = sales/accounts receivable.

    2.   Inventory turnover = cost of goods sold/inventory.

    3.   Payables turnover = (cost of goods sold + general, selling, and administrative expenses)/(accounts payable + salaries, benefits, and payroll taxes payable).

    4.   Conversion periods = 365/the above turnover ratios.

  C.   Use the above ratios to compute the cash conversion cycle, as in Table 21.1.

    1.   The cash conversion cycle is useful for analyzing a firm's liquidity over time.

    2.   This cycle can pick up information hidden by other liquidity measurements.

  D.   Financial slack is the backup liquidity that allows a firm to adjust to unforeseen cash demands.

III.   Strategy for current asset and current liability management.

  A.   Current assets.

    1.   Factors affecting the level of current assets.

        a.   Nature of the firm's business.

        b.   Size of the firm.

        c.   Rate of increase (decrease) in sales.

        d.   Stability of the firm's sales.

    2.   Aggressive versus conservative management.

        a.   Figure 21.3 shows the difference between aggressive and conservative asset management.

        b.   Level of current assets: aggressive—level is lower.

        c.   Cash conversion cycle: aggressive—cycle is shorter.

        d.   Expense and revenue levels: aggressive—lower expense levels leading to higher EBIT.

        e.   Risk and return vary together.

            i.   Aggressive asset positions have greater risks of running out of cash and the possibility of lost sales due to lower inventory.

            ii.   Aggressive asset positions may lead to greater EBIT.

  B.   Current liabilities.

    1.   Factors affecting the level of current liabilities: type of firm and desired flexibility.

    2.   Aggressive versus conservative management.

        a.   Figure 21.4 shows the differences between aggressive and conservative liability management.

        b.   Level of current liabilities: aggressive—level is higher.

        c.   Cash conversion cycle: aggressive—cycle is shorter.

        d.   Interest costs.

            i.   Term structure of interest rates: interest costs for various maturities of debt.

            ii.   Yield curve: visualizes the term structure of interest rates. (See Chapter 2, which shows shifts of yield curve over time.)

            iii.   Corporate borrowing costs include a risk premium over the cost of government borrowing.

      e. Risk and return.

         i. Aggressive: There is substantial interest-rate risk associated with large amounts of short-term debt, since this debt must be refinanced frequently, and short-term rates can fluctuate widely.

         ii. Aggressive: Greater returns are possible by reducing the cash conversion cycle and financing at short-term rates, which are generally lower than long-term rates.

C. The management of short-term assets and liabilities.

    1. The matching principle.

      a. Aggressive: Match a low level of current assets with a low level of current liabilities.

      b. Conservative: Match a high level of current assets with a high level of current liabilities.

      c. Moderate: Match a moderate current asset position with a moderate current liabilities position.

      d. Generally, a firm should establish a target for its working capital position that takes into account its appropriate current asset and current liabilities positions.

    2. Recognizing and dealing with liquidity problems.

      a. Signs of liquidity problems.

         i. Unexpected buildup of inventories.

         ii. Increase in level of outstanding accounts receivable.

         iii. Decline in the daily or weekly cash inflows.

         iv. Increased costs that the firm is unable to pass on to customers.

         v. Decline in the firm's net working capital, or an increase in its debt ratio.

      b. Steps toward the solution of liquidity problems.

         i. Control and reduce inventory investment.

         ii. Re-examine and tighten credit standards.

         iii. Increase the short-term or long-term debt, or issue equity.

         iv. Control overhead and increase concentration on effective asset management.

         v. Lay off employees.

         vi. Reduce planned long-term capital expenditures.

         vii. Reduce or eliminate cash dividends.

    3. Providing for financial slack.

      a. Lines of credit.

      b. Marketable securities portfolio.

Formulas

Cash conversion cycle = operating cycle − days payable

Operating cycle = days sales outstanding + days inventory

Receivables turnover = sales/accounts receivable

Inventory turnover = cost of goods sold/inventory

Payables turnover = (cost of goods sold + general, selling, and administrative expenses)/(accounts payable + salaries, benefits, and payroll taxes payable)

Days sales outstanding = 365/receivables turnover

Days inventory = 365/inventory turnover

Days payable = 365/payables turnover

Total before-tax interest cost = short-term (ST) interest + long-term (LT) interest
$$= (ST \text{ rate} \times \$ST \text{ debt}) + (LT \text{ rate} \times \$LT \text{ debt})$$

What to Look For

In Parts Three and Four we considered long-term investment and financing decisions. While these aspects of financial management are very important, it is equally important to understand the management of current assets and current liabilities—the firm's working capital. This chapter considers the underlying aspects of the firm's working capital levels, while later chapters in this section examine the management of each of the components of working capital. Since firms must carefully manage their current assets and current liabilities to ensure continued operation, knowledge of these techniques will help managers identify problems and develop appropriate financial plans and strategies as discussed in Part Eight.

Managing Short-Term Assets and Liabilities

Short-term asset and liability levels
Chapter 21 focuses on the policies underlying a firm's short-term asset and liability levels. For example, accounts receivable result from the firm's credit policy. The more lenient the policy, the higher the level of accounts receivable. Accounts payable result from the firm's policy for trade credit financing. If the firm's policy is to take advantage of cash discounts for early payment, its level of accounts payable will be lower than it would be if the firm paid for trade credit on or after the date it is due. If the firm is loose in its inventory control, its inventory levels may be higher than if it used a tighter inventory management policy. The policies themselves are not good or bad. However, the goal of short-term asset and liability management is to find policies that maximize the value of the firm.

Liquidity and the cash cycle
Since there is cash flowing into and out of the firm, the levels of the current asset and current liability accounts vary daily. The cash cycle involves investment in inventory, accounts receivable, and the spontaneous financing supporting this investment. The cycle completes itself as trade credit is paid from sales revenues and credit sales are collected.

Unless the firm is going out of business, this cash cycle is ongoing and the firm operates simultaneously at many points within the cycle. For example, the credit manager might be collecting accounts receivable while a salesperson is accepting a credit sale. At the same time, the inventory manager is purchasing more inventory on trade credit, and the controller is seeing that the credit is repaid in a timely fashion. This continuous cycle of cash is called ongoing liquidity. The firm may also maintain financial slack in order to cover unforeseen circumstances, such as a bulk-ordering opportunity or financial emergency.

Although the cash cycle is ongoing, we can measure its average length at any point in time. To do this, we calculate the cash conversion cycle, the time from cash investment in productive resources to recovery of the cash:

$$\text{Cash conversion cycle} = \text{operating cycle} - \text{payable deferral period}$$

$$= \frac{\text{days sales}}{\text{outstanding}} + \frac{\text{days}}{\text{inventory}} - \frac{\text{days}}{\text{payable}}$$

$$= \frac{365}{(\text{sales}/\text{accounts receivable})} + \frac{365}{(\text{cost of goods sold}/\text{inventory})}$$

$$- \frac{365}{(\text{cost of goods sold} + \text{administrative expenses}/\text{accounts payable} + \text{salaries, benefits, and payroll taxes payable})}$$

The days sales outstanding, days inventory, and days payable are major components of the cash cycle. These measures help pinpoint increases or decreases in a firm's ongoing liquidity. Table 21.1 compares the liquidity ratios and turnover ratios to the cash conversion cycle.

<u>Aggressive Versus Conservative Policies</u>
A manager can choose from a spectrum of current asset and current liability policies that range from conservative to aggressive. It may be appropriate for managers to match conservative short-term asset management policies with aggressive short-term liability management policies and vice versa. The reason for this suggestion is that managers often attempt to match the life of the financing to the life of the assets funded. If a firm has an aggressive current asset position, it will have a relatively low level of current assets. So it should be funding with mostly long-term rather than short-term financing. This matched approach, however, will give a more moderate return and more moderate risk exposure than that of the firm using both aggressive asset and aggressive liability policies.

Current asset policies
Low current asset levels indicate an aggressive policy. If the managers attempt to shorten the cash conversion cycle, they will reduce their investment in current assets to a minimum. Such a policy will increase the return of the firm, since these current assets work harder and faster to return assets to cash. But this policy will also increase the risk that the firm will have insufficient liquidity in times of emergency. In addition, since inventory and accounts receivable are kept low, those carrying costs are lower, but the firm risks lost sales due to insufficient inventory and unreasonably tight credit management.

Current liability policies
High current liability levels indicate aggressive current liability management. Again, the manager is attempting to shorten the cash conversion cycle. The financing costs of this policy are comparatively lower than those of the conservative policy *if* short-term interest rates are lower than long-term rates. (We can discover whether short-term rates are higher or lower than long-term rates by looking at the term structure of interest rates. Look at the yields on short-term securities versus the yields on long-term securities of equal risk.) Aggressive current liability policies, however, are more risky since firms face two possibilities: (1) The short-term lenders might not agree to extend the necessary credit on an ongoing basis; (2) The cost of funds changes each time the firm returns for new credit arrangements. With short-term credit, the firm seeks new credit and interest terms more frequently, producing greater uncertainty about financing costs.

Aggressive and conservative policies are neither good nor bad per se. Managers must consider the objective of maximizing the market value of the firm when adopting short-term asset and liability policies. The policy should be re-evaluated if they see unexpected buildups in current assets, declines in cash inflows, increases in costs that cannot be passed on to consumers, or a decline in net working capital.

Completion Questions

21.1   _____ refers to the firm's current assets minus its current liabilities.

21.2   In a percentage breakdown of retail firms' current assets and current liabilities, the largest current asset investment is in _____ while the largest current liability is _____.

21.3   A firm that maintains _____ can adjust rapidly to unforeseen cash demands and has backup sources for raising cash.

21.4   _____ is the net time interval that elapses between the actual cash investment in productive resources and the ultimate recovery of cash.

21.5   The operating cycle is the time between the purchase of inventory and the receipt for sale of finished goods. It is the sum of the _____ plus the days sales outstanding.

21.6   The days payable measures how long the firm _____.

21.7   As the cash conversion cycle lengthens, the firm's liquidity _____.

21.8   In matching, a firm should match its short-term investments with _____ financing.

21.9   A firm holding low levels of current assets is using an _____ asset management approach, while a firm holding low levels of current liabilities is using a _____ liability management approach.

21.10   Aggressive current asset management _____ a firm's liquidity, since the firm does not have as large a portion of its assets tied up in accounts receivable and inventories.

21.11 An unexpected buildup in inventories, or an increase in the firm's level of outstanding accounts receivable, may be a sign of _____.

21.12 The manager has discovered an increase in the firm's level of accounts receivable. A corrective measure would be to re-examine the firm's _____.

Problems

21.1 Michaelson's Paint Store has annual sales of $912,500. Michaelson's grants credit on sales, the average accounts receivable balance is $50,000, and the store keeps $139,000 in inventory on hand. Cost of goods sold amounts to 60 percent of sales. General and administrative expenses are $12,000. Accounts payable are $10,000, and salaries, benefits, and payroll taxes due are $50,000. What is Michaelson's cash conversion cycle?

21.2 Edict Computers, Ltd., of Hamilton, Ontario, was formed in February 1980. The company designs, manufactures, and markets computers for a variety of scientific and engineering applications.
The following information is from its most recent annual report (in units of $1,000):

	1996	1995
Sales	$18,009	$3,400
Cost of goods sold	8,047	2,244
Cost of goods sold + general, selling, and administrative expenses	14,889	5,133
Accounts receivable	4,360	1,680
Inventory	5,692	1,029
Accounts payable + salaries, benefits, and payroll taxes payable	5,039	1,024

How has Edict's cash conversion cycle changed from 1995 to 1996?

21.3 Canadian Foods Ltd. is a manufacturer of packaged "gourmet" foods. At present, the book value of the stockholders' equity is $50 million. The firm also has $30 million of long-term debt and long-term assets of $70 million. The following are forecasts of the firm's current asset needs for the next two years (in millions of dollars):

Year 1	Quarter 1	$21
	2	24
	3	35
	4	30
Year 2	Quarter 1	25
	2	29
	3	40
	4	36

Payables and accruals average 40 percent of current assets.

a. Determine the amount of short-term borrowing needed per quarter to complete the financing of current assets.

b. The interest rate on long-term bonds is 12 percent; on short-term borrowing, it is 10 percent. Suppose Canadian Foods reduced long-term debt by $10 million and matched current assets with current liabilities. How much interest would it save over the two years?

21.4   Maylock Cosmetics is considering two working capital management policies, one aggressive and one conservative. Net income is expected to vary under each plan and is also expected to vary with economic conditions. Maylock estimates that there is a 25 percent probability of a growing economy, a 50 percent probability of a normal economy, and a 25 percent probability of a recession. Net income forecasts for each plan are as follows:

	Growing Economy	Normal Economy	Recession
Probability	0.25	0.50	0.25
Net income; aggressive plan	$184,000	$120,000	$92,000
Net income; conservative plan	$120,000	$ 96,000	$72,000

The firm has 20,000 shares of common stock outstanding. The more risky policy, as measured by the coefficient of variation in EPS, is expected to have a P/E ratio of 8 times. The other policy is expected to have a P/E ratio of 12. Which working capital policy should Maylock Cosmetics undertake?

Answers to Completion Questions

21.1   Net working capital
21.2   inventories; accounts payable
21.3   financial slack
21.4   The cash conversion cycle
21.5   days inventory
21.6   is receiving credit from others
21.7   worsens
21.8   short-term
21.9   aggressive; conservative
21.10   increases
21.11   deteriorating liquidity
21.12   credit granting policy

Solutions to Problems

21.1   Step 1.   Receivables turnover $= \dfrac{\$912,500}{\$50,000} = 18.250$ times

Step 2.   Inventory turnover $= \dfrac{\$912,500 \ (0.60)}{\$139,000} = 3.939$ times

Step 3.   Payables turnover $= \dfrac{\$912,500 \ (0.60) + \$12,000}{\$10,000 + \$50,000} = 9.325$ times

Step 4.   Days sales outstanding $= 365/18.25 = 20.00$ days
Days inventory $= 365/3.939 = 92.66$ days
Days payable $= 365/9.325 = 39.14$ days

Step 5.   Cash conversion cycle $= 20.00$ days $+ 92.66$ days $- 39.14$ days
$= 73.52$ days

21.2   Step 1.   Receivables turnover $= \dfrac{\text{sales}}{\text{accounts receivable}}$

Receivables turnover$_{1996}$ $= \dfrac{\$18,009}{\$4,360} = 4.131$ times

Receivables turnover$_{1995}$ $= \dfrac{\$3,400}{\$1,680} = 2.024$ times

Step 2.   Inventory turnover $= \dfrac{\text{cost of goods sold}}{\text{inventory}}$

Inventory turnover$_{1996}$ $= \dfrac{\$8,047}{\$5,692} = 1.414$ times

Inventory turnover$_{1995}$ $= \dfrac{\$2,244}{\$1,029} = 2.181$ times

Step 3.   Payables turnover   = (cost of goods sold + general, selling, and administrative expenses)/(accounts payable + salaries, benefits, and taxes payable)

Payables turnover$_{1996}$ $= \dfrac{\$14,889}{\$\ 5,039} = 2.955$ times

Payables turnover$_{1995}$ $= \dfrac{\$5,133}{\$1,024} = 5.013$ times

Step 4.   Operating cycle   = days sales outstanding + days inventory
Days inventory   = 365 days/inventory turnover

Days inventory$_{1996}$ $= \dfrac{365 \text{ days}}{1.414} = 258.13$ days

Days inventory$_{1995}$ $= \dfrac{365 \text{ days}}{2.181} = 167.35$ days

Step 5.   Days sales outstanding $= \dfrac{365 \text{ days}}{\text{receivables turnover}}$

Days sales outstanding$_{1996}$ $= \dfrac{365 \text{ days}}{4.131} = 88.36$ days

Days sales outstanding$_{1995}$ $= \dfrac{365 \text{ days}}{2.024} = 180.34$ days

Step 6.   Operating cycle 1996 = 88.36 days + 258.13 days = 346.49 days
Operating cycle 1995 = 180.34 days + 167.35 days = 347.69 days

Step 7.   Cash conversion cycle = operating cycle – days payable

Days payable $= \dfrac{365 \text{ days}}{\text{payables turnover}}$

Days payable$_{1996}$ $= \dfrac{365 \text{ days}}{2.955} = 123.52$ days

Days payable$_{1995}$ $= \dfrac{365 \text{ days}}{5.013} = 72.81$ days

Step 8.   Cash conversion cycle$_{1996}$ = 346.49 days – 123.52 days = 222.97 days
Cash conversion cycle$_{1995}$ = 347.69 days – 72.81 days = 274.88 days

The cash conversion cycle was shortened by approximately 52 days primarily due to the extension of the days payable.

21.3   a.   Step 1.   The amount of long-term funding available to finance current assets is Stockholders' equity + long-term debt − long-term assets = $50 million + $30 million − $70 million = $10 million

Step 2.   The cash flow needs are (in millions)

	Current Assets −	Long-Term Sources −	Payables + Accruals (40% of Current Assets) =	Short-Term Borrowing
Year 1				
Quarter 1	$21	$10	$ 8.4	$ 2.6
2	24	10	9.6	4.4
3	35	10	14.0	11.0
4	30	10	12.0	8.0
Year 2				
Quarter 1	25	10	10.0	5.0
2	29	10	11.6	7.4
3	40	10	16.0	14.0
4	36	10	14.4	11.6

b.   Step 3.   Under the present scenario, the interest expenses are
Long-term debt: ($30 million)(0.12)(2 yr) = $7.2 million
Short-term debt:

	Short-Term Borrowing ×	Interest Rate (0.10/4) =	Interest
Year 1			
Quarter 1	$ 2.6	0.025	$0.065
2	4.4	0.025	0.110
3	11.0	0.025	0.275
4	8.0	0.025	0.200
Year 2			
Quarter 1	5.0	0.025	0.125
2	7.4	0.025	0.185
3	14.0	0.025	0.350
4	11.6	0.025	0.290

Interest on short-term debt = $1.600 million
Total interest is $8.800 million ($7.2 million + $1.6 million).

Step 4.   If the firm reduces long-term debt by $10 million, it will have to borrow an additional $10 million per quarter short-term debt at 10 percent.

Long-term debt: ($20 million)(0.12)(2 yr) = $4.8 million

Short-term debt:

Year 1			
Quarter 1	$12.6	0.025	$0.315
2	14.4	0.025	0.360
3	21.0	0.025	0.525
4	18.0	0.025	0.450
Year 2			
Quarter 1	15.0	0.025	0.375
2	17.4	0.025	0.435
3	24.0	0.025	0.600
4	21.6	0.025	0.540

Interest on short-term debt = $3.600 million

Total interest is $8.4 million ($4.8 million + $3.6 million). Total interest expense has been reduced by $8.8 million − $8.4 million = $0.4 million or $400,000.

Step 5.   An alternative short solution is to take the difference in interest rates times the amount borrowed. Thus, 12% − 10% = 2% savings. $10 million reduction in long-term debt × 2% = $200,000 per year, or $400,000 over the two years.

21.4   Step 1. $EPS = \dfrac{\text{Net income}}{\text{Number of shares}}$, so

	Growing Economy	Normal Economy	Recession
Probability	0.25	0.50	0.25
Aggressive EPS	9.2	6.0	4.6
Conservative EPS	6.0	4.8	3.6

Step 2.   Agressive Policy:

E(EPS) = 0.25 (9.2) + 0.50 (6) + 0.25 (4.6)

= 2.30 + 3.00 + 1.15 = $6.45

σ_{EPS} = [0.25 (9.2 − 6.45)^2 + 0.50 (6.0 − 6.45)^2 + 0.25 (4.6 + 6.45)^2]$^{0.5}$

= [0.25 (2.75)^2 + 0.50 (−0.45)^2 + 0.25 (−1.85)^2]$^{0.5}$

= [0.25 (7.5625) + 0.50 (0.2025) + 0.25 (3.4225)]$^{0.5}$

= [1.890625 + 0.101250 + 0.855625]$^{0.5}$

= [2.8475]$^{0.5}$ = $1.687

Step 3. $CV = \dfrac{\sigma_{EPS}}{E\,(EPS)} = \dfrac{\$1.687}{\$6.45} = 0.262$

Step 4.   Conservative Policy:

E(EPS) = 0.25 (6.0) + 0.50 (4.8) + 0.25 (3.6)

= 1.5 + 2.4 + 0.9 = $4.80

= 4.8

σ_{EPS} = [0.25 (6 − 4.8)^2 + 0.50 (4.8 − 4.8)^2 + 0.25 (3.6 + 4.8)^2]$^{0.5}$

= [0.25 (1.2)^2 + 0.50 (0)^2 + 0.25 (−1.2)^2]$^{0.5}$

= [0.25 (1.44) + 0.25 (1.44)]$^{0.5}$

= [0.36 + 0.36]$^{0.5}$

= [0.72]$^{0.5}$ = $0.849

Step 5. $CV = \dfrac{\sigma_{EPS}}{E\,(EPS)} = \dfrac{\$0.849}{\$4.800} = 0.177$

Since the aggressive policy is more risky, its P/E ratio is 8; the conservative policy is 12.

Step 6.   Price = E(EPS) × P/E ratio, so

Under the aggressive policy, $P_0 = \$6.45 \times 8 = \$51.60$

Under the conservative policy, $P_0 = \$4.80 \times 12 = \$57.60$

Maylock should implement the conservative policy, since it will yield a higher stock price.

Chapter 22
Cash and Marketable Securities

How This Chapter Relates to the Rest of the Text

Chapter 22 examines the management of cash and marketable securities, an important component of short-term assets and liabilities (Chapter 21). Additional components, accounts receivable and inventory (Chapter 23) and short-term financing (Chapter 24), will be discussed later. Cash and marketable security analysis involves the study of cash flows, and risk and return (Chapter 5). Due to the short time involved, discounting techniques (Chapter 3) are typically ignored. Marketable securities share many features with long-term bonds (Chapter 11).

Topical Outline

I.   The cash management function.
  A.   Reasons for holding cash.
    1.   Transactions purposes: Cash is necessary to meet requirements such as monthly bill payments, tax payments, cash dividend payments, and salaries.
    2.   Hedging against uncertainty: Marketable securities and lines of credit provide financial slack for unexpected cash needs.
    3.   Flexibility: Liquidity is useful for weathering bad times when credit is tight and also facilitates taking advantage of unforeseen opportunities.
    4.   Compensating balance agreements: In order to obtain lines of credit and other bank services, firms often agree that a compensating balance be left in a chequing account.
  B.   Risk and return.
    1.   Returns earned from holding liquid assets.
      a.   Investment in marketable securities results in interest income that can make an important contribution to the firm's profitability.
      b.   Liquidity allows firms to take advantage of cash discounts offered by suppliers.
      c.   Savings on purchases can result if firms have sufficient liquidity to take advantage of special sale prices.
      d.   Their credit rating improves, lowering the risk and thus the associated borrowing costs, if firms increase their liquidity to reasonable levels.
    2.   Risks from holding too little cash.
      a.   Problems may occur in paying bills; bill payment may have to be deferred, capital spending curtailed, expensive short-term financing obtained, and growth options bypassed.
      b.   In the extreme, firms may be forced to liquidate or file for bankruptcy.
    3.   The risk-expected return tradeoff involves firms holding adequate cash so they can meet their obligations, but holding cash does not then allow them to secure the higher returns earned by investing their funds in long-term assets.
II.   Cash management techniques.
  A.   Paper-based versus electronic payment systems.
    1.   Cheques are the main means of making noncash payments in North America.
    2.   The giro system, used in Europe, operates on a basis of direct deposit and credits.
  B.   A goal of the cash gathering system is to speed collections (to the level at which the increased benefits equal the increased costs of the system).
    1.   Float is the time that elapses from the writing of a cheque until the recipient receives the funds and can draw upon them (when it has "good funds").
      a.   Mail float is the length of time it takes a firm to receive a cheque after it is mailed by a customer.
      b.   Processing float is the time that elapses until the selling firm deposits the cheque; firms can reduce this float first.
      c.   Transit float is the time required for the cheque to clear through the banking system.

2.   Decentralized collections in various points in the country can reduce mail float.
    a.   Local offices of a major firm can collect payments to deposit in a local branch of the firm's bank.
    b.   Customers can mail payments to lockboxes—post-office boxes in specified cities; a bank picks up the payments several times a day for clearance.
    c.   Managers must weigh the costs of using these systems versus the benefits of reduced mail float.
3.   Banking network for use with collection by lockboxes or local offices.
    a.   Lockbox: A regional bank branch maintains the lockbox, forwards the funds to the concentration (or central) branch, and sends the supporting documents to the firm.
    b.   Local offices: A local bank branch receives the funds from the local office and forwards them to the firm's central concentration branch.
4.   Other collection approaches include special couriers and preauthorized cheques from customers.
5.   Analysis of cash-gathering techniques involves weighing the increased benefits (ΔB) of the system against the increased costs (ΔC).

$$\Delta B = (\Delta t)(TS)(I_{daily})(1 - T)$$

where Δt = float change time
TS = size of transaction
I_{daily} = daily interest rate

    a.   If the change in costs exceeds the change in benefits, the firm should not change the system—$\Delta C > \Delta B$—and vice versa. If the change in benefits equals the change in costs, the firm is indifferent to the change. This is simply another NPV decision since $\Delta B - \Delta C = NPV$.
    b.   Lockbox per-day benefits include increased efficiency and reduced float, which can be calculated with the equation above. The costs include the bank fee charged either directly or through a compensating balance agreement.
    c.   To convert per-day figures to per-year figures, convert daily volume to a yearly basis by multiplying TS by 365, or the daily interest rate (I_{daily}) to a yearly interest rate by multiplying it by 365.
    d.   To decide between the present method and an alternative, determine the incremental costs, and then determine how much you would have to decrease float time (t), the interest rate (I_{daily}), or the average transaction size (TS) to be indifferent between the two methods.

B.   A goal of the cash disbursement system is to control and slow down the outflow of cash without hurting the firm's credit rating.
1.   Controlled disbursing takes advantage of transit float.
    a.   Judge the usefulness of this system with the cost-benefit equation above.
    b.   The branch banking system presents little opportunity to extend transit float.
    c.   Controlled dispersing may create ill will among suppliers and is only suited to large, nationwide firms.
2.   Zero-balance accounts at the central concentration branch allow all the firm's divisions to draw on individual zero-balance disbursing accounts, creating negative balances that are restored to zero by the firm's positive balance master account at the central branch. Excess cash balances do not build up.
3.   Other disbursement approaches include centralized payables and timing of cheque payments.
4.   Again, the incremental costs and benefits of the disbursement management system should be weighed.

C.   Interactions between cash gathering and cash disbursing.
1.   Managers must take into account the joint effects and costs of cash disbursement and gathering systems.
2.   Firms should select the best mix of disbursement and collection services for them, given the wide variety of cash management techniques offered by the financial services industry.

       D.   International aspects include concentration banking, international transfer, international lockboxes, intracompany netting, and timing according to anticipated exchange rate fluctuations.

III.   Advances in payment and information systems.

       A.   Electronic payment systems, or electronic funds transfer (EFT), such as debit cards, replace cheques with an electronic payment system.

          1.   Eliminates accounts receivable and provides virtually immediate use of cash.

          2.   Essentially eliminates float.

       B.   Electronic data interchange (EDI).

          1.   EDI affects everything from the ordering and manufacturing cycle to the flow of documents related to shipment and payment.

IV.   Determining the daily cash balance: How much should be kept?

       A.   The approach.

          1.   Prepare cash budget on monthly basis, breaking down inflows and outflows.

          2.   Identify the timing of the major inflows and outflows for the month so you can estimate when daily transfers into and out of the marketable securities portfolio will be necessary.

          3.   Use modelling to predict routine inflows and outflows in order to detect cash surpluses and cash needs.

          4.   Compare the actual outflows and inflows with those predicted, to evaluate the planning procedure and to fine-tune it.

          5.   Evaluate the value of a change by comparing incremental benefits and incremental costs: $\Delta B = (\Delta t)(TS)(I_{daily})(1 - T) = \Delta C$.

V.   Models for determining the target cash balance.

       A.   The Miller–Orr model has upper and lower control limits that, if exceeded, require adjustments in the firm's cash balance.

          1.   Assumptions:

              a.   Daily cash flows are random and cannot be predicted.

              b.   Transfers to and from marketable securities are instantaneous.

              c.   Seasonal and cyclical trends are not considered.

              d.   The costs of buying and selling marketable securities are fixed.

              e.   The term structure is flat and constant.

          2.   The target cash balance (Z) is

$$Z = \left[\frac{3F\sigma^2}{4k_{daily}} \right]^{1/3} + L$$

              where σ^2 is the variance of the net daily cash flows, k_{daily} is the daily opportunity cost of holding cash, and L is the lower control limit.

          3.   The upper control limit is $H = 3Z - 2L$.

          4.   The average cash balance is $(4Z - L)/3$.

          5.   If the upper control limit is exceeded, the firm should buy marketable securities and reduce cash to the target cash balance; if the lower control limit is exceeded, the firm should sell marketable securities sufficient to attain Z.

       B.   The Stone model is similar to the Miller–Orr model except that it places more emphasis on managing cash balances rather than determining optimal transaction size.

          1.   The upper and lower control limits do not automatically trigger a transaction.

          2.   If an outer control limit is exceeded, look at the expected cash flows over the next few days.

          3.   If, during the "look ahead" period, the cash balance is expected to move inside the inner control limits, do not make a transaction.

          4.   The firm buys or sells securities to retain the target cash balance if the cash balance is not expected to move inside the inner control limits during the "look ahead" period.

VI.   The marketable securities portfolio.

       A.   Short-term investment alternatives include treasury bills, commercial paper, negotiable certificates of deposit, bankers' acceptances, Eurodollars, repurchase agreements, and sales finance paper.

B. Managing the marketable securities portfolio.
    1. The firm's risk-return posture determines the specific composition of the marketable securities portfolio after taking into consideration the interaction of risk, liquidity, maturity, and yield.
    2. Funds that are not likely to be needed will be invested in longer-term (6 months to 1 year) instruments.
    3. Funds that represent very temporary excess cash are invested in repurchase agreements or other short-term investments.
    4. Stock and bonds are not generally part of the marketable securities portfolio.
C. Selection criteria for choosing among marketable securities.
    1. General economic conditions change, as do monetary and fiscal policies. These changes affect the level of interest rates.
        a. As market interest rates go up, bond prices go down, providing opportunities to gain through purchasing and to lose through selling at these low prices; this creates uncertainty or risk.
        b. The bond equivalent yield on Government of Canada treasury bills is the investors' expected return as a percent of the face value of the security.

$$k_{BE} = \left(\frac{P_M - P_0}{P_0}\right)\left(\frac{365}{n}\right)$$

    2. Some marketable securities are not routinely redeemable before maturity, and some have a limited secondary market.
    3. Firms match their need for funds with the maturity of the securities they invest in.
    4. The expected yield on market securities, balanced by the risk, is the criterion for selection.

Formulas

Evaluation of Cash Gathering Techniques

ΔB = incremental benefits
ΔC = incremental costs
Δt = time in days that float is changed
TS = size of the transaction
I_{daily} = daily interest rate
ΔB = $(\Delta t)(TS)(I_{daily})$
T = tax rate

Attempt to find the ΔC that will make $\Delta B = \Delta C$, and thus make the firm indifferent; i.e., where $\Delta C = \Delta B = (\Delta t)(TS)(I_{daily})(1 - T)$.

Relationship Between Daily and Annual Interest

$$\text{Daily interest rate} = \frac{\text{annual interest rate}}{365}$$

Relationship Between Daily Transaction Size and Annual Transaction Size

Annual TS = (daily TS) (365)
Annual ΔB = (annual TS)(daily interest rate I_{daily})
        or (daily TS)(daily interest rate I_{daily})(365)

Miller–Orr Model

Z = target cash balance

L = lower control limit

H = upper control limit

σ^2 = variance of net daily cash flow

k_{daily} = opportunity cost of holding cash on a daily basis

Z = $[3F\sigma^2/4k_{daily}]^{1/3} + L$

H = $3Z - 2L$

Average cash balance = $(4Z - L)/3$

Bond Equivalent Yield

$$k_{BE} = \left[\frac{P_M - P_0}{P_0} \right] \left[\frac{365}{n} \right]$$

k_{BE} = bond equivalent yield

P_M = the maturity value of the treasury bill

P_0 = the discounted price

n = the number of days until maturity

What to Look For

Chapter 22 begins the in-depth study of short-term asset management by focusing on the most liquid assets—cash and marketable securities.

As you recall, the left side (asset side) of the balance sheet shows investment in the firm. The right side (liabilities and stockholders' equity) of the balance sheet shows the funding sources for these investments. As noted in the preceding chapter, we may want to match the maturity of the financing source with the life or recovery period of the asset financed. All financing sources involve a cost. In order to maximize the value of the firm, the return on all assets, including current assets like cash, must exceed their cost.

Why Hold Cash?

If cash itself earns no rate of return, why hold cash? Cash can provide the necessary financial slack for the firm to take advantage of discounts. For example, suppose a firm purchases $20 million of material from a supplier. The supplier informs the firm that if they pay cash for the goods, they will be eligible for a 5 percent discount. Firms with sufficient cash on hand to pay immediately could save $20 million × (0.05) = $1 million per year. As you can see, keeping cash to take advantage of cash discounts can easily pay for itself. Cash budgeting, discussed in Chapter 26, can help managers fine-tune the cash management system so they can free sufficient cash during the cash conversion cycle to meet such payments.

Financial slack in the form of cash reserves may also allow managers to purchase items at sale prices. If the sale price is low enough, the savings provide a return in excess of the cost of holding the cash. In emergency situtations, cash is often essential to avoid costly delays. This financial slack can also be served by a line of credit (Chapter 24) or a marketable securities portfolio, which we discuss later. In any case, the return from holding liquid assets should exceed the cost of holding these assets, since the objective of cash management is to maximize the value of the firm.

Cash Management and the Cash Conversion Cycle

In cash management, we meet this value-maximizing objective most efficiently by slowing payments and speeding collections. Recall the discussion of the cash conversion cycle in Chapter 21. In doing business, the firm buys raw materials or inventory with cash or on trade credit. The operating cycle begins at this point. The firm sells its inventory for cash or on credit. As the firm collects on the credit sales, the cash is generated to pay off the trade credit, completing the cash conversion cycle. Thus, the cash conversion cycle is

$$\frac{\text{Days sales}}{\text{outstanding}} + \frac{\text{days}}{\text{inventory}} - \frac{\text{days}}{\text{payable}}$$

By speeding collections and delaying disbursements, firms attempt to shorten the days sales outstanding and lengthen the days payable. The result is a shorter cash conversion cycle. The goal of cash management techniques, then, is to speed collections and slow payments without hurting the firm's credit rating and without having the incremental costs exceed the incremental benefits.

Methods of Speeding Collections

The text focuses on several methods of speeding cash collections or shortening float time, including lockboxes, local office collection, and bank transfer mechanisms. The analysis of these techniques involves weighing the increased costs versus the increased benefits in terms of reduced float time (t), and daily interest return (I_{daily}) on the increased liquidity. For example, suppose Manitoba Industries has no collections speeding system. It is considering lockboxes at a cost of $35 per day or local office collection at a cost of $30 per day.

Assume that the average payment is $780, with 75 cheque payments a day. If the company uses lockboxes, the reduced float time is 2 days; it is 1.50 days with the local office collection. To calculate the change in benefits for these two systems, we will use a daily basis. We will adjust our interest rate by dividing by 365. The firm faces a tax rate of 40 percent. The total TS is calculated by multiplying the number of transfers or transactions per day times the average size. The incremental benefits are

ΔB = reduced float time (Δt) $\times$ transaction size (TS) $\times$ interest rate (I_{daily}) $\times$ (1 − T)

Lockbox: $\Delta B = (2 \text{ days})(\$780 \times 75)(0.12/365 \text{ days})(1 − 0.4) = \$23.08$. The costs are $\$35(1 − 0.40) = \$21$, so benefits exceed costs by $\$23.08 − \$21 = \$2.08$.

Local collection: $\Delta B = (1.50 \text{ days})(\$780 \times 75)(0.12/365 \text{ days})(1 − 0.40) = \$17.31$. The costs are $\$30(1 − 0.40) = \$18$, so costs exceed benefits by $\$18 − \$17.31 = \$0.69$.

The lockbox option is most attractive, since its incremental benefits exceed its incremental costs while the local collection has costs exceeding benefits.

To make the local collection system pay its way, Manitoba Industries could increase its number of transactions. Thus:

$\Delta C = \$30 (1 − 0.40) = \Delta B = (1.50 \text{ days}) (\$780 \times \text{TS}) (0.12/365 \text{ days})(1 − 0.40)$

$\$18 = \$0.230796\text{TS}$

$\text{TS} = 77.99$ or 78 transactions per day.

If the number of transactions increased by three per day, Manitoba Industries would be indifferent between its present system and the local collection system.

Cash Management Models

Managing a firm's cash balance can be difficult. The text discusses two models of cash management. The appropriateness of each model depends on how well the assumptions match the reality of the firm's cash flows.

The Miller–Orr model assumes that daily cash flows are random. In this model, the firm has a target cash balance (Z) and upper (H) and lower (L) control limits. The cash balance is allowed to fluctuate within the control limits. If, however, the cash balance moves outside the limits, the firm buys or sells marketable securities to attain the target cash balance.

The Stone model is like the Miller–Orr model, but emphasizes cash balance management rather than determining the optimal transaction size. In this model, if the upper or lower control limits are exceeded, the firm "looks ahead" to see what is expected to happen to the cash balance. If the balance reverts inside the inner control limits, the firm does nothing; otherwise, the firm buys or sells securities to re-attain the target cash balance. A problem with the Stone model is that it provides no guidance as to what the various limits should be. Managers must use their experience or some other management technique such as the Miller–Orr model to set them.

The Role of the Marketable Securities Portfolio

Once the cash budget and daily forecasting techniques have been used to determine the pattern of cash needs and surpluses, the marketable securities portfolio can both provide and absorb liquidity. On days the firm needs cash, the manager can liquidate holdings. On days where there is excess cash, the manager can purchase securities for the portfolio, keeping a minimum balance in demand deposits. The return on the marketable securities portfolio should exceed the costs of purchasing and holding these securities. Otherwise, the value of the firm will be reduced. In selecting among marketable securities for the portfolio, managers will want to layer the maturities of the securities, matching short-term expected cash surpluses with short-term instruments. See Table 22.1 for a description of the various short-term marketable securities and their characteristics.

The manager should also analyze the expected risk with respect to the economy, inflation, international conditions, and firm- or issue-specific conditions. As noted in Chapter 5, these risks increase the required return on securities. In choosing among corporate issues, managers must consider the financial ability of the corporation to pay interest and repay principal, since these cash flows are somewhat uncertain. The more uncertain the cash flows, the higher the required return. Managers ultimately should invest in the highest possible return, based on the risk-expected return posture of the firm that matches the firm's projected liquidity needs.

Completion Questions

22.1   _____ are short-term securities that the firm can hold temporarily and readily convert into _____.

22.2   Cash management techniques attempt to _____ collection float and _____ disbursement float.

22.3   _____ is the length of time from the writing of a cheque until the recipient can draw upon the funds. If the firm establishes an efficient internal management system to minimize the delay between payment receipt and payment deposit, the firm reduces _____.

22.4   In an effort to decrease the mail float, firms that do not have local offices can use a _____ arrangement. Customers mail payments to a _____ in a specified city for collection and clearance by a regional concentration branch.

22.5   Under a _____ procedure, customers authorize a firm to draw cheques directly on the customer's demand deposit account.

22.6   In order to assess the cost effectiveness of various cash management techniques, compare the incremental _____ with the _____. This technique can be conducted on either a per unit or total basis, on an annual or daily basis. To convert the annual interest rate to a daily interest rate, divide annual interest rate by _____.

22.7   With _____, divisions write cheques on individual disbursement accounts, creating negative balances; these negative balances are restored to zero by the firm's master account.

22.8   Excess cash left idle in a demand deposit account represents an _____ cost for the firm. In order to detemine the minimum necessary cash balance, the firm can prepare a _____ budget.

22.9   In a _____ budget, the firm breaks down the major cash inflows and outflows and identifies their _____ during the month. Thus, funds can be transferred at the appropriate times into and out of the _____ when needed.

22.10   As economic conditions decline and investors become more risk averse, the market rate of interest tends to _____, and the market price of outstanding debt _____.

22.11   _____ are promissory notes from a bank to repay a deposit.

22.12   _____ are time drafts issued by a business firm that have been accepted by a bank. Rather than paying interest, they are _____ when issued to yield a stated rate.

22.13   The sale of government securities by a securities dealer with a simultaneous agreement to repurchase them results in a _____.

22.14   In the Miller–Orr model, managers should sell marketable securities if the cash balance moves outside the
_____ control limit.

Problems

22.1   Stevenson Oil Limited allows its customers to purchase gasoline on credit if the balance is paid within 30
days. Presently, all cheques are mailed to the central office in Winnipeg. The average bill spends five days
in the mail and the Third Winnipeg Bank, which is the receiver of the cheques after processing, requires that
Stevenson leave the funds untouched for three days. Stevenson is considering a system of eight regional
lockboxes, each costing $100 per month before taxes. The lockbox system would cut mail float to two
days and transit float to one day. Presently, Stevenson receives 500 cheques per day, with the average
cheque being written for $45. If the annual interest rate is 14 percent, what will be the annual gain (or loss)
of the lockbox system, assuming the firm's tax rate is 40 percent?

22.2   Harris Industries has set up a controlled disbursing system with two out-of-town banks. The net benefit
after taxes (i.e., $\Delta B - \Delta C$) of the system to Harris is $40,000 per year. If Harris writes 300 cheques per day
with an average amount of $500, how many days of additional float will Harris obtain if the interest rate is
10 percent, the bank charges an additional $0.15 per cheque cleared, and Harris's tax rate is 40 percent?

22.3   Marion Francis is interested in purchasing a Government of Canada treasury bill for $9,800. The bill has a
$10,000 face value and matures in 100 days. Calculate the bond equivalent yield for Ms. Francis.

22.4   Mitchell Manufacturing has a variable daily cash flow with a daily standard deviation of $1,000. The cost of
transacting is $150 per transaction and the opportunity cost of holding cash is 12 percent annually. The
firm's minimum cash balance requirement is $5,000. Using the Miller–Orr model, calculate the target cash
balance, the upper control limit, and the average cash balance.

Answers to Completion Questions

22.1   Marketable securities; cash
22.2   reduce; increase
22.3   Float; the processing float
22.4   lockbox; post-office box
22.5   preauthorized cheques
22.6   costs; expected incremental benefits; 365
22.7   zero-balance accounts
22.8   opportunity; cash
22.9   cash; timing; marketable securities portfolio
22.10   increase; decreases
22.11   Negotiable certificates of deposit
22.12   Bankers' acceptances; discounted
22.13   repurchase agreement
22.14   lower

Solutions to Problems

22.1   Step 1.   Cost = (number of lockboxes)(monthly rent)(12 months)$(1 - T)$
                    = (8)($100)(12)$(1 - 0.40)$ = $5,760

        Step 2.   Total float under the present system = mail float + transit float
                    = 5 days + 3 days = 8 days
                    Total float under the lockbox system = 2 days + 1 day = 3 days
                    Float is reduced by 5 days.

        Step 3. ΔB = (days float changed)(365 × number of cheques per day × average cheque)
                    $(0.14/365)(1 - T)$
                    = (5)(365 × $500 × $45)$(0.14/365)(1 - 0.40)$ = $9,450

        Step 4. $\Delta B - \Delta C$ = $9,450 − $5,760 = $3,690. The lockbox system has incremental benefits of $3,690 per year greater than the incremental costs.

22.2   Step 1.   Net benefits = $\Delta B - \Delta C$
                    ΔC = (charge per cheque)(number of cheques)(365)$(1 - T)$
                    = ($0.15)(300)(365)$(1 - 0.40)$ = $9,855
                    $40,000 = \Delta B - $9,855, so ΔB = $30,145

        Step 2. $\Delta B = (\Delta t)[(300)($500)(365)](0.10/365)(1 - T)$
                    $30,145 = (\Delta t)($15,000)(1 - 0.40)$
                    Δt = 3.349 days

22.3 $k_{BE} = \left[\dfrac{P_M - P_0}{P_0}\right]\left[\dfrac{365}{n}\right]$

       $= \left[\dfrac{\$10,000 - \$9,800}{\$9,800}\right]\left[\dfrac{365}{100}\right]$

       $= \left[\dfrac{\$200}{\$9,800}\right]\left[\dfrac{365}{100}\right] = 0.07449$ or 7.449%

22.4   Step 1. $k_{daily} = (1.12)^{1/365} - 1 = 0.00031054$
                    $Z = [3F\sigma^2/4k_{daily}]^{1/3}$
                    = [3($150)($1,000)^2/4(0.00031054)] + $5,000
                    = $7,128.74 + $5,000
                    = $12,128.74
                    $H = 3Z - 2L$
                    = 3($12,128.74) − 2($5,000)
                    = $26,386.22

        Step 2.   Average balance = $(4Z - L)/3$
                    = [4($12,128.74) − $5,000]/3
                    = ($48,514.96 − $5,000)/3
                    = $43,514.96/3
                    = $14,504.99

Chapter 23
Accounts Receivable and Inventory

How This Chapter Relates to the Rest of the Text

This chapter extends the discussion of current asset and current liability management begun in Chapter 21 to accounts receivable. As in Chapter 22, this chapter concentrates on the management of current assets. Current liabilities, that is, sources of short-term financing, are discussed in Chapter 24. Decisions based on investments in receivables and inventory employ the concepts of cash flow, discounting (Chapter 3), and risk and return (Chapter 5).

Topical Outline

I.   Receivables, inventory, and the firm.
    A.   A firm that extends trade credit is establishing an account receivable, which is eventually paid in cash or becomes a bad debt loss.
    B.   The importance of receivables and inventory.
        1.   High levels of inventory and accounts receivable may help production and marketing efforts but require short-term financing and may reduce profits.
        2.   Large manufacturing and wholesale firms may hold 30 percent of total assets in accounts receivable and inventory.
        3.   Retail firms hold over 50 percent of total assets in receivables and inventory.
        4.   The size and type of the firm as well as its production process help determine the percent of total assets held in accounts receivable and inventory.
    C.   Size of accounts receivable is determined by total credit sales.
        1.   The state of the economy and aggressiveness of marketing efforts help determine the total sales level.
        2.   The credit terms, credit analysis, credit-granting decision, and collection policy help determine the level of credit sales.
II. Credit and collection management.
    A.   Terms and conditions of credit sales.
        1.   Domestic trade conditions.
            a.   Cash before delivery is the typical arrangement of payment for custom-made goods.
            b.   Cash on delivery (COD) is typical for risky or irregular deliveries.
            c.   Payment periods of 30 to 60 days, plus a discount for early payment, are typical for ordinary trade credit.
            d.   Payment agreements themselves include:
                i.   An open agreement: The invoice is the bill and contains the terms.
                ii.   A draft: The buyer agrees to pay a specified amount at a specific time to the bearer.
                iii. A sight draft: The customer pays the amount on presentation of the draft before receiving title to the goods.
                iv.   A time draft: The customer (trade acceptance) or the customer's bank (banker's acceptance) makes payment a certain number of days after accepting the draft; signature on the draft implies acceptance.
        2.   International sales include an order to pay, a bill of lading, and a letter of credit.
    B.   Credit analysis determines who will be granted credit and what the credit terms will be.
        1.   Sources of credit information.
            a.   Accounting statements help in judging the financial stability and cash-generating ability of the customer.
            b.   Dun & Bradstreet's Reference Book provides credit ratings for 3 million firms.
            c.   In addition, banks, trade associations, and firms evaluate the creditworthiness of potential customers.
        2.   Risk class determination.
            a.   Classify potential customers by risk class.

b. Determine credit policy for each risk class.
c. Review risk status of customers at least once a year.
d. Many firms use a credit scoring model to determine the risk of a customer.

C. The credit decision.
   1. The basic model considers the net present value of expected cash inflows and cash outflows from credit sales.
      a. Calculate the after-tax cash flows for credit sales (CF):
         $$CF = [(\text{cash inflows}) - (\text{cash outflows})](1 - T)$$
      b. Choose a discount rate appropriate to the riskiness of the cash flows.
      c. Discount the cash flows to their net present value (NPV):

      $$NPV = \sum_{t-1}^{n} \frac{CF_t}{(1 + k)^t} - CF_0 = \frac{CF_t}{k} - CF_0$$

      (If we assume the cash flows go into infinity)

   2. Making the credit decision.
      a. Determine the initial investment in accounts receivable (CF_0):
         $$CF_0 = (VC)(S)(DSO/365\text{days})$$
      b. Determine the cash flows (CF_t):
         $$CF_t = [S(1 - VC) - S(BD) - CD](1 - T)$$
      c. Determine the NPV. If positive, grant credit.

D. Collection policy.
   1. Managing collections.
      a. Days sales outstanding (DSO) hides individual differences among customers; changes in both receivables and sales levels outside of the month the sales are made affect DSO.
      b. Payments pattern approach.
         i. Considers customers' varying payment patterns by focusing on the percent paid relative to the month of sale.
         ii. Exercise control on accounts receivable by focusing on deviations from the projected pattern.
   2. Analysis of changes in collection policy.
      a. Determine the incremental initial investment (ΔCF_0):

      $$\Delta CF_0 = \frac{\text{initial investment}}{\text{new (N)}} - \frac{\text{initial investment}}{\text{old (O)}}$$

      $$= [(VC_N)(S_N)(DSO_N/365)] - [(VC_O)(S_O)(DSO_O/365)]$$

      b. Evaluate incremental after-tax cash flow (ΔCF_t):

      $$\Delta CF_t = \frac{\text{after-tax cash flow}}{\text{new (N)}} - \frac{\text{after-tax cash flow}}{\text{old (O)}}$$

      $$= [(S_N)(1 - VC_N) - S_N(BD_N) - CD_N](1 - T)$$

      $$- [S_O(1 - VC_O) - S_O(BD_O) - CD_O](1 - T)$$

      c. Calculate NPV:

      $$NPV = \frac{\Delta CF_t}{k} - \Delta CF_0$$

      d. k is the opportunity cost of capital given the riskiness of the expected cash flows.
      e. Make a policy change only if NPV is positive, since the goal of accounts receivable management is to maximize the value of the firm.
      f. A similar approach compares the NPV of the new policy with that of the old: if $NPV_{new} > NPV_{old}$, change policies.

III. Inventory management.
   A. Types of inventory include raw materials, work-in-process, and finished goods.

1. Manufacturers hold all three types of inventory.
2. Retail and wholesale firms hold finished goods inventory.
3. Service firms have no inventory except supplies.

B. Benefits of inventory investment include:
1. Firms can take advantage of quantity discounts and add to existing inventory.
2. Firms can avoid stock outages.
3. Firms can offer a full line of products for marketing purposes.
4. Inventory speculation is possible; during times of inflation, add to existing inventory.

C. Costs of inventory investment.
1. Carrying costs include storage, spoilage, property taxes, and insurance.
2. Ordering costs include clerical and shipping costs.
3. Costs of stock outages are lost sales.

D. Three approaches for inventory management are the "just-in-time" approach, the economic order quantity (EOQ) (see Appendix 23A), and the ABC method.

E. Analysis of inventory investment.
1. An investment in current assets, although it often accompanies a long-term asset investment, also results from a change in policy.
2. Calculate the NPV of the expected incremental cash inflows and cash outflows due to the increased inventory investment, discounting at an opportunity cost of capital appropriate to the riskiness of the cash flows.
3. Pay attention to the important inventory items while using management-by-exception for other items.

F. Interaction of accounts receivable and inventory decisions.
1. Cost and benefit trade-offs exist between them, with varying consequences for the firm.
2. Develop and evaluate inventory and receivables policies on a joint basis.

IV. Appendix 23A: The economic order quantity (EOQ) model.

A. The basic inventory decision is based on carrying costs (C), ordering costs (O), and annual sales (S).
1. Carrying costs = (average inventory)(carrying costs)
$$= (Q/2)C = QC/2$$
2. Ordering costs = (sales/order size)(ordering costs)
$$= (S/Q)O = SO/Q$$
3. Total costs = carrying costs + ordering costs
$$= QC/2 + SO/Q$$
4. Maximize the firm's value by minimizing the total costs.

B. EOQ model.
$$EOQ = (2SO/C)^{0.5}$$

C. Quantity discounts.
1. Savings from quantity discount = (discount per unit)(number of units, S)
2. Additional carrying costs:
Additional costs = $Q'C/2 - [(EOQ)(C)]/2$, where Q' = new order quantity
3. Additional savings in ordering costs:
Additional savings = $SO/EOQ - SO/Q'$

D. EOQ assumptions are uniform demand and constant carrying and ordering costs; modify EOQ to deal with variations.

E. Safety stocks should be added only to the point where additional carrying costs equal benefits from avoiding stock outages.

Formulas

<u>Notation</u>

CF	= cash flow after taxes
CF_0	= initial investment in accounts receivable or inventory
CF_t	= after-tax cash inflow in each time period
k	= appropriate after-tax risk-adjusted opportunity cost of capital
n	= number of time periods
NPV	= net present value
VC	= variable cash outflow of producing and selling the goods as a percentage of cash inflows
BD	= bad debts as a percentage of sales
T	= firm's marginal tax rate
DSO	= days sales outstanding
ΔCF_0	= incremental initial investment
ΔCF_t	= incremental after-tax cash inflows
S	= cash inflows (sales) expected each period
CD	= additional credit department cash outflow
N	= subscript for new cash flows resulting from new collection policy
O	= subscript for old cash flows from old credit policy

<u>The Basic Model</u>

$$CF = (\text{cash inflows} - \text{cash outflows}) (1 - T)$$

$$NPV = \sum_{t-1}^{n} \frac{CF_t}{(1 + k)^t} - CF_0 = \frac{CF_t}{k} - CF_0 \text{ (assuming cash flows are perpetual)}$$

<u>Credit Decision Making</u>

$$CF_0 = (VC)\,(S)\,(DSO/365)$$

$$CF_t = [S\,(1 - VC) - S\,(BD) - CD]\,(1-T)$$

$$NPV = \frac{CF_t}{k} - CF_0$$

<u>Evaluating a Change in Collection Policy</u>

$$\Delta CF_0 = \text{New initial investment} - \text{old initial investment}$$

$$= [(VC_N)\,(S_N)\,(DSO_N/365)] - [(VC_O)\,(S_O)\,(DSO_O/365)]$$

$$\Delta CF_t = \text{New incremental cash flow} - \text{old incremental cash flow}$$

$$= [S_N\,(1 - VC_N) - S_N(BD_N) - CD_N]\,(1 - T) - [S_O\,(1 - VC_O) - S_O(BD_O) - CD_O](1 - T)$$

$$NPV = \frac{\Delta CF_t}{k} - \Delta CF_0$$

Appendix 23A

Notation

EOQ = economic order quantity
C = carrying cost in dollars per unit of inventory
O = ordering costs in dollars per order
Q = order quantity expressed in units
S = sales per year in units
Q′ = new order size

Carrying costs

$(Q/2)C = QC/2$

Ordering costs

$(S/Q)O = SO/Q.$

Total costs

Carrying costs + ordering costs $= QC/2 + SO/Q$

Economic order quantity

$EOQ = (2SO/C)^{0.5}$

Savings from quantity discounts

Savings = (discount per unit)(number of units, S)

Additional carrying costs for using quantity discount

Additional costs $= Q′C/2 - [(EOQ)(C)]/2$

Savings in ordering costs

Savings in costs $= SO/EOQ - SO/Q′$

What to Look For

Chapter 23 focuses on managing investments in accounts receivable and inventories. These investments are commonly financed by revolving lines of credit, commercial paper, and trade credit. "Permanent" investments in receivables and inventories are often financed with long-term financing sources. The goal is to earn more on these investments than the firm pays in financing them.

The Cash Conversion Cycle and Current Asset Management

Let's return again to the cash conversion cycle (Chapter 21). The days inventory is the time between the purchase of inventory and its cash or credit sale. The days sales outstanding is the time between credit sales and the collection of these receivables. To maximize the value of the firm, managers should speed up cash inflows, taking into account the increased costs and risks. Managers want to shorten both the days sales outstanding and the days inventory. In Chapter 22, we discussed shortening the days sales outstanding by reducing float. In Chapter 23, we talk about how to reduce the days sales outstanding and the days inventory by selecting and managing the credit and inventory policies. The optimal credit policy will produce the maximum credit sales net of bad debt losses and collection costs. Achieving such a policy is difficult, but it can be done by following the steps outlined below.

Analyzing and Establishing a Credit and Collections Policy

Credit policy
In choosing and implementing a credit policy, the manager should (1) determine the creditworthiness of potential credit customers; (2) rank customers by credit risk; (3) calculate the expected cash flows of each risk class; and (4) provide credit to those customers for which the net present value of the expected cash flows is positive.

We will demonstrate steps 3 and 4 for two risk classes assuming a corporate tax rate of 30 percent.

Risk Class	Opportunity Cost of Capital (k)	Variable Costs as a Percentage of Sales (VC)	Days Sales Outstanding (DSO)	Sales (S)	Bad Debts as a Percentage of Sales (BD)	Additional Collection Department Cash Out-flows (CD)
A	16%	82%	60 days	$200,000	3%	$ 8,000
E	28%	82%	120 days	$240,000	6%	$12,000

Class A:

$$CF_0 = (VC)\ (S)\ (DSO/365)$$

$$= (0.82)\ (\$200,000)\ (60/365) = \$26,958.90$$

$$CF_t = [S\ (1 - VC) - S\ (BD) - CD]\ (1 - T)$$

$$= [\$200,000\ (1 - 0.82) - \$200,000\ (0.03) - \$8,000]\ (1 - 0.30)$$

$$= \$15,400$$

$$NPV = \frac{CF_t}{k} - CF_0 = \frac{\$15,400}{0.16} - \$26,958.90 = \$69,291.10$$

Since the NPV is positive, credit should be granted to customers in risk class A.

Class E:

$$CF_0 = (0.82)\ (\$240,000)\ (120/365) = \$64,701.37$$

$$CF_t = [\$240,000\ (1 - 0.82) - \$240,000\ (0.6) - \$12,000]\ (1 - 0.30)$$

$$= \$11,760$$

$$NPV = \frac{\$11,760}{0.28} - \$64,701.37 = -\$22,701.37$$

Since the NPV is negative, the decision is not to grant credit to customers in risk class E, since it would reduce the value of the firm.

Collections policy
The credit policy, projections for bad debts, and total collection costs are only as good as the collections management. Lax collections management can increase collections costs and produce bad debt losses that far exceed estimates and can make all credit-granting activities unprofitable.

The payment pattern approach to collections management helps track the actual payment pattern experienced by the firm. It relates the accounts receivable to the month in which the sales are made. Although 20 percent of the accounts receivable are projected to be outstanding in the third month, 30 percent are still outstanding by this time period. This trend indicates the need to change the collection policy or modify credit risk classes.

In considering a change in collections policy, managers should calculate the net present value of the associated cash flow changes—ΔCF_0 and ΔCF_t. If the net present value is positive, the change will increase the value of the firm. As a manager, you can play with these variables and calculate the net present value under different credit policies. For example, you could considerably tighten up collections and decrease the days sales outstanding. If the new collection policy does not decrease sales excessively, the result will be a positive net present value, indicating the change should be undertaken.

Inventory Management

Inventories, like receivables, need management in order for the firm to meet the objective of value maximization. As we noted earlier, the days inventory is the period from inventory purchase to inventory sale. The lower the inventory level, the lower the carrying costs and the shorter the days inventory and cash conversion cycle. Lower inventory levels, however, increase the likelihood that the firm will lose sales through stock outages.

As you can see, the manager again weighs the benefits of inventory levels with the carrying costs, ordering costs, and costs of stock outages. The text briefly discusses two inventory management approaches, the just-in-time approach and the economic order quantity model. Production situations like those in Japan can easily be managed by the just-in-time approach, since the distance for transporting inventory is negligible. In Canada, however, some manufacturers may depend upon raw materials suppliers thousands of miles away.

In addition to choosing an inventory management approach, firms often must decide whether an actual increase in the level of inventory is wise. The manager calculates the expected cash flows and their net present value. Suppose Cagney Jeans Shop is considering increasing its inventory investment by $400,000. The expected increase in after-tax cash flows (CF_t) is $60,000 per year, net of storage costs. The inventory investment must return at least 18 percent to be worthwhile. The timeline below shows the cash flows. We will calculate the net present value of this inventory investment.

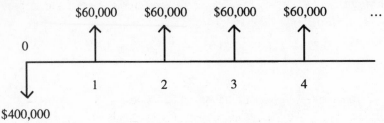

The NPV is ($60,000/0.18) – $400,000 = –$66,666.67. Cagney Jeans should not increase the inventory because the return is not satisfactory and will decrease the value of the firm.

Completion Questions

23.1   As the length of time increases before collection of accounts receivable, the firm's investment in receivables _____.

23.2   As an inducement to encourage early payment of trade credit, many firms offer a _____ _____.

23.3   In international trade, a _____ is the contract for shipment of goods and the title of those goods.

23.4   The backbone of any credit decision is the _____. Information necessary for this process comes from accounting statements, credit reports, banks, trade associations, and the company's own experiences.

23.5   In making a credit decision, managers may find it helpful to classify potential credit customers into _____.

23.6   In order to make the credit decision, the manager should find the net present value of the after-tax _____ _____. These flows would be the cash inflows from the credit sales less the _____ _____. Credit should be extended only if the net present value is _____.

23.7   The trouble with using the collection period to monitor collections is that it _____ _____. The _____ approach shows the percent of credit sales paid in the month of the sale, and in each subsequent month.

23.8 The incremental initial investment is the difference between the new initial investment and the _____.

23.9 A tighter collection policy might decrease the days sales outstanding, but it may also _____ _____.

23.10 For a manufacturing firm, the purpose of holding inventory is to _____ the acquisition of goods, the stages of production, and selling activities.

23.11 Costs of inventory investment include carrying costs, ordering costs, and costs of _____. The _____ decides the size of the inventory order to place in order to minimize all three costs.

23.12 Managers should consider the magnitude, _____, and _____ of the cash flows resulting from receivables and inventories investments.

Problems

23.1 Randleman Furnishing Ltd.'s credit terms are 2/15, net 30. Sales are $4,015,000 per year, half of which are credit. Some of the credit customers pay on the fifteenth day; the remainder pay on an average of the 35th day. If the days sales outstanding is 13.5 days, what proportion of the customers take the discount?

23.2 Parry Sound Manufacturing Ltd. presently makes all sales for cash. It is considering the development of a credit sales policy and has classified customers into three credit classes. The appropriate information follows:

Class	Opportunity Cost of Capital	Days Sales Outstanding (DSO)	Sales (in thousands)	Bad Debts	Additional Collection Department Cash Out-flows (CD) (in thousands)
1	14%	30 days	$3,000	2%	$150
2	18%	45 days	$4,000	6%	$150
3	25%	150 days	$5,000	15%	$300

Which, if any, class should be granted credit if the marginal tax rate is 30 percent and variable cash outflows are 70 percent of sales? (Assume a 365-day year.)

23.3 Mayo Medical Supply is considering a $1,000,000 investment in additional inventory to prevent having to turn away customers due to lack of goods. The loss in sales due to the shortage in inventory is estimated at $750,000 per year. Because of difficulty in inventory control, the company expects to lose an additional $50,000 (after tax) due to theft and spoilage if the new investment is made. Storage expenses are expected to increase by $10,000 per year. If variable cash outflows are 55 percent of sales, and the tax rate is 40 percent, should Mayo increase its inventory if its opportunity cost of capital is 16 percent?

23A.1 McMillian Industries has a projected demand for 22,500 units of inventory in the coming year. If the carrying cost is $2 per unit of inventory and the ordering costs are $100 per order, what is the EOQ?

23A.2 Miacom Electronics bases its inventory replenishment decision on an EOQ model. The ordering costs are $50, the storage costs are $0.40 per unit of inventory, and the EOQ is 2,000 units. If Miacom wishes to maintain a safety stock of 1,000 units and it takes 10 days to receive an order, what is the inventory level at which a reorder should be placed? (Assume a 365-day year.)

Answers to Completion Questions

23.1   increases
23.2   cash discount
23.3   bill of lading
23.4   credit analysis
23.5   risk classes
23.6   cash flows; cash outflows; positive
23.7   is affected by the sales level; payment pattern
23.8   old initial investment
23.9   reduce sales
23.10   uncouple
23.11   running short (or stock outages); economic order quantity model (EOQ)
23.12   timing; riskiness

Solutions to Problems

23.1   Step 1.   The days sales outstanding is the weighted average of the time to payment. Remember, for cash sales, there is no time until payment.

Step 2.   DSO = 0.5 (0 days) + W (15 days) + (0.5 − W) (35 days)

$13.5 = 0.5 (0) + W (15) + (0.5 − W) (35 \text{ days})$

$13.5 = 15W + 17.5 − 35W$

$20W = 4$

$W = 4/20 = 0.20$

20 percent of the customers take the discount.

23.2   Step 1.   Class 1
$CF_0 = (VC) (S) (DSO/365 \text{ days}) = (0.70) (\$3,000) (30/365) = \$172.60$

Step 2. $CF_t = [S (1 − VC) − S (BD) − CD] (1 − T)$

$= [\$3,000 (1 − 0.70) − \$3,000 (0.02) − \$150] (1 − 0.30)$

$= (\$900 − \$60 − \$150) (0.70) = \$483$

Step 3. $NPV = \dfrac{CF_t}{k} − CF_0 = \dfrac{\$483}{0.14} − \$172.60 = \$3,277.40$

Since NPV is greater than zero, credit should be granted to class 1.

Step 4.   Class 2
$CF_0 = (0.70) (\$4,000) (45/365) = \$345.21$

$CF_t = [\$4,000 (1 − 0.70) − \$4,000 (0.06) − \$150] (1 − 0.30)$

$= (\$1,200 − \$240 − \$150) (0.70) = \$567$

$NPV = \dfrac{\$567}{0.18} − \$345.21 = \$2,804.79$

Since NPV is positive, credit should be granted to class 2.

Step 5. Class 3

$$CF_0 = (0.70)(\$5,000)(150/365) = \$1,438.36$$

$$CF_t = [\$5,000(1 - 0.70) - \$5,000(0.15) - \$300](1 - 0.30)$$

$$= (\$1,500 - \$750 - \$300)(0.70) = \$315$$

$$NPV = \frac{\$315}{0.25} - \$1,438.36 = -\$178.36$$

Since NPV is negative, do not grant credit to class 3.

23.3 Step 1. $CF_t = [Sales (1 - VC) - storage\ cost](1 - T) - loss\ due\ to\ theft\ and\ spoilage$

$$= [\$750,000(1 - 0.55) - \$10,000](1 - 0.40) - \$50,000$$

$$= (\$337,500 - \$10,000)(0.60) - \$50,000 = \$146,500$$

Step 2. $NPV = \dfrac{CF_t}{k} - CF_0 = \dfrac{\$146,500}{0.16} - \$1,000,000 = -\$84,375$

No, the project has a negative NPV.

23.A1 $EOQ = \left(\dfrac{2SO}{C}\right)^{0.5} = \left(\dfrac{2(22,500)(\$100)}{\$2}\right)^{0.5} = (2,250,000)^{0.5} = 1,500$ units per order

23.A2 Step 1. Find total demand.

$$EOQ = \left(\frac{2SO}{C}\right)^{0.5}$$

$$2,000 = \left(\frac{2S(\$50)}{\$0.40}\right)^{0.5}$$

$$4,000,000 = \frac{2S(\$50)}{\$0.40}$$

$$S = \frac{\$0.40(4,000,000)}{2(\$50)} = \$16,000$$

Step 2. Sales per day $= \dfrac{\$16,000}{365} = 43.8$ units per day

Step 3. Reorder entry level = safety stock + (sales per day)(days to fill order)

$$= 1,000 + (43.8)(10\ days) = 1,438\ units$$

Chapter 24
Short-Term Financing

How This Chapter Relates to the Rest of the Text

Chapter 24 concludes the discussion of short-term financial management (Chapter 21) by considering current liabilities. The matching principle, which is the basis of current liability management, was discussed in Chapter 21. This chapter also discusses the costs of short-term financing, which are similar to the costs of long-term debt (Chapter 10). Current liabilities account for a substantial portion of total debt for many firms and hence affect the capital structure (Chapter 12).

Topical Outline

I.   Sources and importance of short-term financing.
    A.   Sources of short-term financing.
        1.   Trade credit results spontaneously when a firm purchases goods from another firm and does not pay immediately.
        2.   Short-term borrowings are negotiated with commercial banks, finance companies, and the like.
    B.   Size of short-term financing.
        1.   Accounts payable provide more short-term financing than do short-term borrowings.
        2.   Level of accounts payable and short-term borrowing depends upon firms and industries as well as economic conditions, business conditions, and company policy.
    C.   Calculation of the after-tax effective annual cost of short-term financing (calculated over the same time period).
        1.   Before-tax effective annual interest rate:

$$k_{\text{effective annual}} = \left(1 + \frac{\text{costs} - \text{benefits}}{\text{net amount of financing}}\right)^{m} - 1$$

        2.   After-tax effective annual cost, $k_i = k_{\text{effective annual}}(1 - T)$.
        3.   The effective annual interest rate adjusts the nominal (or stated) rate based on the frequency of compounding used.
        4.   The more frequent the compounding period, the higher the effective annual rate relative to the nominal rate.

II.   Accounts payable or trade credit is a spontaneous form of financing.
    A.   Level of accounts payable will increase with increased orders during the busy season, even if you pay accounts by the due date.
    B.   Calculation of before-tax effective annual cost of not taking cash discounts on trade credit.
        1.

$$k_{\text{effective annual}} = \left(\frac{\text{discount percent}}{100\% - \text{discount percent}}\right)^{365 / (\text{date paid} - \text{discount date})} - 1$$

        2.   In assessing the desirability of not taking the cash discount, both direct and indirect costs must be considered.
    C.   Advantages of trade credit: Readily available, free, flexible, not restrictive.

III.   Unsecured loans from bank loans or commercial paper are not spontaneous.
    A.   Bank loans or short-term notes payable have maturities of one year or less, often at a variable rate of interest.
        1.   Interest rates.
            a.   The prime rate is the basic interest charged by banks to their best customers; other customers pay some rate above prime.
           b.   The commercial paper rate is typically slightly less than the prime rate.
           c.   Short-term rates, such as the prime rate and the commercial paper rate, are volatile, changing with economic and business conditions.

2.   Types of bank loans.
    a.   Transaction loan is a loan for a specific purpose for which a promissory note is signed and a repayment schedule exists.
    b.   Line of credit is an agreement between a firm and a bank for the firm to borrow up to a dollar limit within a specified time period at a specific interest rate on the amounts borrowed.
        i.   Repayment must be made by the end of that period and the user often expects to maintain a compensating balance.
        ii. Can be informal, or can involve a commitment fee.
3.   The monitoring role of banks.
    a.   Banks have access to corporate information that is not publicly available, thus reducing any information asymmetry.
    b.   Benefits to the firm.
        i.   Reduces the likelihood of default and, therefore, reduces the cost of financial distress.
        ii. Lowers the direct cost of financing.
4.   Cost of bank loans depends upon the conditions attached to the agreement.
    a.   Regular interest is principal and interest paid at end of loan; calculate with a two-step procedure.
        i.   Determine interest paid:

$$\begin{bmatrix} \text{amount} \\ \text{borrowed} \end{bmatrix} \begin{bmatrix} \text{annual} \\ \text{interest rate} \end{bmatrix} \begin{bmatrix} \text{portion of year} \\ \text{borrowed for} \end{bmatrix}$$

        ii. Employ Equation 24.2 to determine $k_{\text{effective annual}}$:

$$k_{\text{effective annual}} = \left[1 + \frac{\text{interest}}{\text{principal}} \right]^m - 1$$

    b.   Discount interest is a loan from which the bank deducts the interest from the loan principal at the beginning of the loan.
        i.   The effective annual interest is greater than the stated interest.
        ii. Use the two-step procedure above to calculate the before-tax rate of interest.

$$k_{\text{effective annual}} = \left[1 + \frac{\text{interest}}{\text{principal} - \text{interest}} \right]^m - 1$$

    c.   Installment interest is paid periodically (monthly, etc.) along with principal repayment.
        i.   The total amount of interest is calculated and added to the original face value of the loan.
        ii. Principal is repaid along with interest, beginning at the end of the first period, and the borrower has use of about half the principal on average; so the effective annual interest rate is almost twice as high as the nominal rate.
        iii. Calculation of the approximate effective before-tax interest rate:

$$\text{Loan} = \text{payment } (\text{PVA}_{k_{\text{effective annual}}, n}) \text{ and solve for } k_{\text{effective annual}}$$

    d.   Variable rate loans have interest rates that may change over the life of the loan, and their cost can be calculated only after knowing the rates and the number of days those rates were in effect.
        i.   The two-step procedure works well for this calculation.
        ii. The effective annual rate will be somewhere within the range of the various rates paid.
    e.   Compensating balances sometimes are agreed to by customers.
        i.   If the compensating balance is less than the firm normally keeps in its demand deposit, this requirement does not influence the effective annual rate of interest on the loan.

ii.   If the compensating balance is more than the amount held in demand deposits by the firm, then the effective annual rate is greater than the stated rate, since those dollars otherwise could be invested or held in an interest-bearing account.

iii. Calculation of effective annual cost on a regular loan with compensating balance that is above the normal balance kept in the bank:

$$k_{\text{effective annual}} = \left[1 + \frac{\text{interest}}{\text{principal} - \text{compensating} \atop \text{balance} + \text{normal} \atop \text{balance}}\right]^m - 1$$

iv.   Calculation of effective annual cost on discounted loan with compensating balance:

$$k_{\text{effective annual}} = \left[1 + \frac{\text{interest}}{\text{principal} - \text{interest} - \text{compensating} \atop \text{balance} + \text{normal} \atop \text{balance}}\right]^m - 1$$

f.   Line of credit states an interest rate and often a commitment fee.

   i.   Determine commitment fee per loan period:
        (unused portion)(annual commitment fee)(portion of year)
        Do this calculation for each loan period.

   ii. Determine the per period interest cost:
        ($ loan)(annual interest rate)(number of days/365)

   iii.
$$k_{\text{effective annual}} = \left[1 + \frac{\text{total} \atop \text{commitment} + \text{interest} \atop \text{fees}}{\text{average net amount} \atop \text{of financing}}\right]^m - 1$$

B.   Commercial paper is a short-term unsecured promissory note sold by large firms to obtain financing.

1.   Nature and use.

   a.   Principal issuers include finance companies, bank holding companies, and large industrial firms.

   b.   Maturity is from a few days to one year or more; most maturities are 30, 60, or 90 days.

   c.   Sold through dealers or through direct placement.

   d.   Vary in riskiness and thus return, depending on issuer's cash flow.

2.   Cost tends to be one or two percentage points below the prime rate, depending upon economic and business conditions.

   a.   Sold at a discount to yield the stated rate at maturity.

   b.   Calculation of before-tax effective annual interest cost:

$$k_{\text{effective annual}} = \left[1 + \frac{\text{discount}}{\text{par value} - \text{discount}}\right]^m - 1$$

   c.   Commitment fee adds to the cost:
        Fee = ($ loan)(fee percent)(number of days/365)

   d.   Calculation of total before-tax effective annual cost:

$$k_{\text{effective annual}} = \left[1 + \frac{\text{discount} + \text{commitment fee}}{\text{par value} - \text{discount}}\right]^m - 1$$

IV.   Secured loans: Backed by accounts receivable and inventory.

A.   Financing with accounts receivable.

1.   Pledging accounts receivable.

   a.   Loan is a stated percent of all receivables pledged.

      i.   If all receivables are pledged, the lender has no control over quality.

      ii. If lender reviews specific invoices to choose which receivables can be pledged, the process is more costly, but lender can loan a larger amount on these receivables.

iii. Cost is a function of processing fee and annual interest charge.

(a) $\text{Interest} = \begin{bmatrix} \text{interest} \\ \text{percent} \end{bmatrix}\begin{bmatrix} \text{receivables} \\ \text{pledged} \end{bmatrix}\begin{bmatrix} \text{number of} \\ \text{days}/365 \end{bmatrix}$

(b) $\text{Processing fee} = \begin{bmatrix} \text{fee} \\ \text{percent} \end{bmatrix}\begin{bmatrix} \text{average} \\ \text{credit} \\ \text{sales} \end{bmatrix}\begin{bmatrix} \text{number of} \\ \text{days} \end{bmatrix}$

(c) Annual before-tax effective annual cost:

$$k_{\text{effective annual}} = \left[1 + \frac{\text{interest} + \text{processing fee}}{\text{principal}} \right]^{m} - 1$$

2. Factoring accounts receivable is the sale of accounts receivable to a bank or another firm engaged in factoring; it is often a continuous process.
   a. The amount of the loan is a stated percent of all receivables factored.
   b. Maturity factoring is the purchase of all receivables by the factor who pays the seller once a month for the receivables.
      i. Useful to substitute for credit and collections department.
      ii. Before-tax effective annual cost:

$$k_{\text{effective annual}} = \left[1 + \frac{\left(\begin{array}{c} \text{average} \\ \text{receivables} \end{array} \right)\left(\text{commission} \right) - \begin{array}{c} \text{cost} \\ \text{savings} \end{array}}{\text{average receivables}} \right]^{m} - 1$$

   c. In advance factoring, the factor makes a loan against receivables.
      i. Interest rate is usually 2 to 4 percent above prime; commissions are usually charged also.
      ii. Interest cost:
          (Interest rate)(receivables factored)(number of days/365)
      iii. Factoring commission:
          (Commission rate)(total receivables)
      iv. Before-tax effective annual cost:

$$k_{\text{effective annual}} = \left[1 + \frac{\text{interest} + \text{commission fee} - \begin{array}{c} \text{cost} \\ \text{savings} \end{array}}{\text{receivables factored}} \right]^{m} - 1$$

B. Financing with inventories is common.
   1. The borrowing firm can pledge all its inventories on a blanket lien to the bank.
   2. The trust receipt provides more protection for the lender and is common for larger ticket items like automobiles.
   3. Warehouse financing includes public (or terminal) warehousing on a third party's premises, and field warehousing on the borrower's premises.
      a. Cost consists of the processing fee or storage costs plus the interest costs.
      b. Field warehousing fee = (per diem fee)(number of days)
      c. $\text{Interest fee} = \begin{bmatrix} \text{interest} \\ \text{rate} \end{bmatrix}\begin{bmatrix} \text{inventory} \times \\ \text{pledge percent} \end{bmatrix}\begin{bmatrix} \text{number of} \\ \text{days}/365 \end{bmatrix}$
      d. Before-tax effective annual cost of field warehousing:

$$k_{\text{effective annual}} = \left[1 + \frac{\text{interest} + \text{warehousing fee}}{\text{principal}} \right]^{m} - 1$$

V. Choosing among short-term financing sources.
   A. Negotiated versus spontaneous.
   B. Match the position of the current assets with current liabilities—that is, match conservative with aggressive and vice versa.
   C. Consider the direct and indirect costs.
   D. Consider the availability of credit by various means at various times.

E.   Flexibility for the firm to pay off the loan, renew it, or increase it.
F.   Rank sources according to direct costs and then evaluate other factors, including less quantifiable or indirect costs.
G.   Firm should consider multiple sources of short-term financing, due to possible changes in financing needs.

Formulas

Basic Equation for Effective Annual Before-Tax Cost, $k_{effective\ annual}$

$k_{effective\ annual}$ = before-tax effective annual interest rate
m = number of compounding periods per year

$$k_{effective\ annual} = \left[1 + \frac{costs - benefits}{net\ amount\ of\ financing}\right]^m - 1$$

After-tax cost to the firm, $k_i = k_{effective\ annual}(1 - T)$

Effective Annual Versus Nominal Interest Rate

$$k_{effective\ annual} = \left(1 + \frac{k_{nominal}}{m}\right)^m - 1$$

Before-Tax Effective Annual Cost of Trade Credit

$$k_{effective\ annual} = \left[1 + \frac{discount\ percent}{100\% - discount\ percent}\right]^{365\ /\ (date\ paid\ -\ discount\ date)} - 1$$

Before-Tax Effective Annual Cost of Bank Loan with Regular Interest

Interest = (amount borrowed)(annual interest rate)(portion of year borrowed for)

$$k_{effective\ annual} = \left[1 + \frac{interest}{principal}\right]^m - 1$$

Before-Tax Effective Annual Cost of Discount Interest

$$k_{effective\ annual} = \left[1 + \frac{interest}{principal - interest}\right]^m - 1$$

Before-Tax Effective Annual Cost of Installment Interest

Loan = Payment $(PVA_{k_{effective\ annual}, n})$ and solve for $k_{effective\ annual}$

Before-Tax Effective Annual Cost of Variable Rate Loan

			Portion of Year
Amount Borrowed	×	Interest Rate	×	number of days/365)
$		%		days/365
$		%		days/365

The sum equals the interest cost and so on through the loan period.

$$k_{effective\ annual} = \left[1 + \frac{interest}{principal}\right]^m - 1$$

Before-Tax Effective Annual Cost of Regular Interest Loan with Compensating Balance

$$k_{\text{effective annual}} = \left[1 + \cfrac{\text{interest}}{\text{principal} - \substack{\text{compensating} \\ \text{balance}} + \substack{\text{normal} \\ \text{balance}}}\right]^m - 1$$

Before-Tax Effective Annual Cost of Discount Loan with Compensating Balance

$$k_{\text{effective annual}} = \left[1 + \cfrac{\text{interest}}{\text{principal} - \text{interest} - \substack{\text{compensating} \\ \text{balance}} + \substack{\text{normal} \\ \text{balance}}}\right]^m - 1$$

Before-Tax Effective Annual Cost for a Line of Credit

Loan Period	Commitment Fee Percent	×	Unused Portion	×	Portion of Year (number of days/365)
1	%		$		days/365
2	%		$		days/365

and so on over the life of the loan.

Interest cost per loan period = (interest percent)($ loan)(number of days per loan period/365)

Add together commitment fee + interest on a period by period basis.

$$k_{\text{effective annual}} = \left[1 + \frac{\text{total commitment fee} + \text{interest}}{\text{average amount of financing}}\right]^m - 1$$

Before-Tax Effective Annual Cost of Commercial Paper

$$k_{\text{effective annual}} = \left[1 + \frac{\text{discount} + \text{commitment fee}}{\text{par value} - \text{discount}}\right]^m - 1$$

Before-Tax Effective Annual Cost of Pledging Receivables

$$k_{\text{effective annual}} = \left[1 + \frac{\text{interest} + \text{processing fee}}{\text{principal}}\right]^m - 1$$

Before-Tax Effective Annual Cost of Maturity Factoring Receivables

$$k_{\text{effective annual}} = \left[1 + \frac{(\text{average receivables})(\text{commission}) - \text{cost savings}}{\text{average receivables}}\right]^m - 1$$

Before-Tax Effective Annual Cost of Advance Factoring

$$k_{\text{effective annual}} = \left[1 + \frac{\text{interest} + \text{commitment fee} - \text{cost savings}}{\text{receivables factored}}\right]^m - 1$$

Before-Tax Effective Annual Cost of Field Warehousing

$$k_{\text{effective annual}} = \left[1 + \frac{\text{interest} + \text{warehousing fee}}{\text{principal}}\right]^m - 1$$

What to Look For

Chapter 24, the mechanics of short-term financing, completes our study of short-term financial management. Short-term financing, which includes commercial paper, lines of credit, trade credit, and secured loans, covers current liabilities that fund investments in the current assets discussed in Chapters 22 and 23. All short-term financing entails a financing cost such as interest. Here we look at the advantages of and effective annual interest costs of financing alternatives.

Advantages of Various Short-Term Financing Alternatives

The majority of businesses in the Canada are small businesses. The key source of short-term financing for such firms is trade credit. Trade credit's advantages are that it is readily available and grows spontaneously with inventory purchases. In times of tight money, many small businesses cannot get bank loans, and so they rely on trade credit.

Commercial paper is a short-term security that is unsecured. Large firms with impeccable credit ratings can issue commercial paper. This security (1) can often be issued at a lower interest rate than many other short-term loans, and (2) permits a broad distribution of the security.

The terms of bank loans can vary widely, as can the cost. In choosing among financing sources, managers should look at the before-tax effective annual rate of interest. In the next section we will calculate the cost of short-term financing. Bank loans such as lines of credit provide flexibility and financial slack for firms. Therefore, bank loans are essential in the financing package of many firms. Secured loans are loans backed by such assets as accounts receivable and inventory. When a firm cannot obtain unsecured financing, it must seek a secured form.

Factoring of accounts receivable involves selling accounts receivable to the factor for a percentage of their dollar amount. Two key advantages of factoring are that the lender takes on the credit risk of the accounts receivable—that is, the borrower does not need to run a collections or credit department—and as the credit sales grow, the financing grows. Acting as the credit department, the factor can refuse to allow the borrower to grant credit to customers of questionable risk.

Pledging of accounts receivable involves using the receivables as a lien. The lender, however, does not take on the credit risks. The lender can refuse to lend on questionable receivables and has recourse to the borrower (the seller). Again, pledging is flexible since the financing grows with the credit sales. With both pledging and factoring, the manager should be careful to weigh the costs and benefits since the costs can be high.

Inventory financing includes a blanket inventory lien, trust receipts, and field warehousing financing. These methods provide flexible financing that grows with inventories. Field warehousing in particular can save the firm money in personnel and in inventory losses and damage. In addition, it is more convenient than trust receipts, which require receipts to be issued for specific goods, such as sacks of coffee beans. Trust receipts are most appropriate for bulky items like automobiles and trucks.

Cost of Short-Term Financing

Bank loans

The cost of bank loans varies widely depending upon the terms of the loan. We will work through a series of variations on a $10,000 2-month (60 day) loan to Jack's Sporting Goods with a nominal interest rate of 10 percent. The various loan terms are (1) regular interest; (2) discount interest; (3) installment interest; (4) compensating balance of $3,000, given that Jack's keeps a normal balance of $1,500; and (5) a $10,000 line of credit, in which the commitment fee is 0.5 percent on the unused portion, and Jack's uses $4,000 the first month and $10,000 the second month. The basic equation for calculating the effective annual before-tax interest cost, $k_{effective\ annual}$, is

$$k_{effective\ annual} = \left[1 + \frac{costs - benefits}{amount\ of\ financing} \right]^m - 1$$

Costs:

Interest = (amount borrowed)(annual rate of interest)(number of days/365)

Fees = (fee percent)(base)

Regular interest:

Cost involved is interest. Amount of financing is $10,000.

Interest = ($10,000)(0.10)(60/365) = $164.38

$$k_{effective\ annual} = \left[1 + \frac{\$164.38}{\$10,000} \right]^{365/60} - 1 = 0.1043 \text{ or } 10.43\%$$

Discount interest:

Cost involved is interest = $164.38. Amount of financing is $10,000 – interest = $10,000 – $164.38.

$$k_{\text{effective annual}} = \left[1 + \frac{\$164.38}{\$10,000 - \$164.38} \right]^{365/60} - 1 = 0.1061 \text{ or } 10.61\%$$

Installment loan:

Interest cost = $164.38. The payment is ($10,000 + $164.38)/2 = $5,082.

We can estimate $k_{\text{effective annual}}$ because

$$\text{Loan} = \text{payment } (PVA_{k_{\text{effective annual}},2mo})$$

$$\$10,000 = \$5,082.19 \ (PVA_{k_{\text{effective annual}},2mo})$$

$$PVA_{k_{\text{effective annual}},2mo} = \frac{\$10,000}{\$5,082.19} = 1.968$$

From Table B.2, we can see that this is slightly more than 1 percent per month or 12 percent per year. Using a financial calculator, the rate is 13.95 percent per year.

Compensating balance is $3,000 with normal balance of $1,500:

Cost involved is interest. Amount of financing is $10,000 – compensating balance + normal balance.

$$k_{\text{effective annual}} = \left[1 + \frac{\$164.38}{\$10,000 - \$3,000 + \$1,500} \right]^{365/60} - 1 = 0.1236 \text{ or } 12.36\%$$

Line of credit at 10 percent on $10,000 with 0.5 percent commitment fee on the unused portion:

Jack's uses $4,000 in the first month, and $10,000 in the second month. Costs involved are interest and commitment fee. Loan amounts are $4,000 for the first 30 days, and $10,000 for the second 30 days.

Commitment fee:

1st month: ($10,000 – $4,000)(0.005)(30/365) = $2.47
2nd month: ($10,000 – $10,000)(0.005)(30/365) = $0

Interest:

1st month: ($4,000)(0.10)(30/365) = $32.88
2nd month: ($10,000)(0.10)(30/365) = $82.19

Total costs:

1st month: $2.47 + $32.88 = $35.35
2nd month: $0 + $82.19 = $82.19

Average amount of financing: $4,000(30/60) + $10,000(30/60) = $7,000

$$k_{\text{effective annual}} = \left[1 + \frac{\$35.35 + \$82.19}{\$7,000} \right]^{365/60} - 1 = 0.1066 \text{ or } 10.66\%$$

As you can see, the effective annual before-tax financing cost varies widely, depending upon the terms of the loan. We did not show a variable rate loan. However, if you study the example in the text, you should have little trouble understanding that calculation.

Commercial paper

Rather than paying interest directly, commercial paper is sold at a discount to yield the stated rate. The calculation of the before-tax effective annual cost is similar to calculating the cost of a discount interest loan, with a commitment fee. Suppose Atlantic Motors, Ltd., issued $200,000 in a 90-day commercial paper, sold at $193,000. The company must keep a matching line of credit, which has a commitment fee of 0.5 percent a year. The yield is found using the following formula:

$$k_{\text{effective annual}} = \left[1 + \frac{\text{discount} + \text{commitment fee}}{\text{par value} - \text{discount}} \right]^m - 1$$

$$= \left[1 + \frac{\$7,000 + [0.005\ (\$200,000)\ (90/365)]}{\$200,000 - \$7,000} \right]^{365/90} - 1$$

$$= \left[1 + \frac{\$7,246.575}{\$193,000} \right]^{365/90} - 1 = 0.1612 \text{ or } 16.12\%$$

Secured loans

Secured loans use inventory or accounts receivable as a lien. The calculation of the financing amount or principal depends on how much of the receivables or inventory can be used as a lien. The amount of the loan is stated as a percentage of the inventory or receivables accepted. Secured financing also involves administrative fees. The financing costs are the sum of the interest and the administrative fees. The general formula below is useful for calculating the before-tax effective annual cost of secured financing:

$$k_{\text{effective annual}} = \left[1 + \frac{\text{interest} + \text{fee or commission} - \text{cost savings}}{(\text{receivables or inventory})\ (\text{stated percent})} \right]\left[\frac{365}{\text{number of days}} \right]$$

Selection of Short-Term Financing Sources

Costs, risks, flexibility, and availability vary among sources of short-term financing. In selecting short-term financing sources, managers should consider all these factors in order to meet the objective of value maximization.

Completion Questions

24.1   _____ is a spontaneous form of financing that increases and decreases with the volume of the firm's business.

24.2   To find the relevant financing costs, divide the net costs by the _____ _____ available to the borrower.

24.3   While a firm can employ either the before- or after-tax cost in making short-term financing decisions, its ultimate cost is the _____.

24.4   When firms stretch their payables by not paying on the net date, their before-tax effective annual cost of financing _____, but their credit rating might _____, perhaps resulting in curtailment of _____.

24.5   The key advantages of trade credit are its _____, its flexibility, and its lack of _____.

24.6   The basic interest rate charged by banks to their best business customers is the _____.

24.7   A transaction loan is a bank loan for _____. It requires that a _____ be signed by the borrower.

24.8   Lines of credit often involve a _____ paid to the bank whether or not the firm draws on the line of credit.

24.9   Under a discount loan, the borrower receives _____ _____.

24.10   The firm's _____ can reduce the cost of a loan with a compensating balance agreement.

24.11   _____ is an unsecured promissory note issued by large firms to obtain short-term financing. It can be an alternative or complement to short-term bank loans. Its interest cost tends to be _____ the prime rate.

24.12   _____ of accounts receivables involves using receivables as collateral for a loan. If the borrower defaults on the loan, the funds provided when the receivables are collected go to _____ _____.

24.13 _____ is the sale of accounts receivable. The lender takes on the credit-checking responsibilities. With _____, the factor purchases all the receivables, and pays the seller once a month for them. In _____, the factor provides a loan against the receivables.

24.14 In warehouse financing, the inventories are stored on the premises of _____.

Problems

24.1 Victoria Cooperative purchases vegetables for resale to consumers. It has recently been contacted by two potential suppliers who are willing to offer trade credit. The first, National Vegetable, offers terms of 2/10 net 30. The second, Allied Produce offers terms of 3/15 net 45. If Victoria wishes to minimize the cost of trade credit, which supplier should it choose?

24.2 Atwater Novelties has secured an $80,000, 90-day loan from a local bank. The total interest charge is $4,000. If Atwater's after-tax cost of debt is 14.19 percent, what is its tax rate?

24.3 Hebert Candy Limited wishes to borrow $300,000, and is in the process of negotiating a 180-day loan from a local bank. The bank has offered the company the following alternatives:
   a.   A 16 percent annual interest rate, no compensating balance, and interest paid at the end of the loan.
   b.   A 15 percent annual interest rate with interest discounted and no compensating balance.
   c.   An installment loan with a 12 percent annual interest rate and six payments one month apart. The bank will use add-on interest.
   d.   A 10 percent annual interest rate with interest discounted and a 15 percent compensating balance requirement. Hebert presently maintains no balance at this bank.
   Which loan offers the lowest before-tax effective annual cost?

24.4 McAllistar Chain Saws faces a seasonal demand for its products and hence, has periodic short-term needs for cash. It has arranged for a $750,000 line of credit with the First Alberta Bank to enable it to meet these needs. The terms of this line of credit are a 0.5 percent commitment fee on the unused portion of the line, plus 13 percent annual interest rate on the borrowed portion. The following are the expected monthly borrowings from the line of credit:

Month	Days	Borrowing
January	31	$300,000
February	28	600,000
March	31	750,000
April	30	500,000
May	31	250,000
June	30	150,000

   a.   What are the total costs per month associated with the line of credit?
   b.   What is the effective annual cost of funds obtained from the line of credit?

24.5 Bicknell Electronics is considering the issuance of 270-day commercial paper to finance current inventory needs. The firm plans to issue $2.5 million of paper, which will sell for $2.3 million. The firm will, as well, be required to maintain a line of credit with a commitment fee of 0.75 percent to back the issue. What is the before-tax effective annual cost of this commercial paper?

24.6 Golden Artwork Jewelry Ltd. is considering pledging its accounts receivable to obtain favourable terms on a loan. The bank has offered two alternatives, both of which are for 50 days and provide the same amount of financing. A traditional loan at 16 percent annual interest rate, or the following loan package: (1) stated rate of interest of 14 percent, which is 2 percent above prime; (2) a 1 percent processing fee; and (3) a loan of 80 percent of the amount pledged. Golden Artwork has average credit sales of $3,000 per day, with days sales outstanding of 50 days. Which of the two alternatives has the lowest before-tax effective annual interest cost?

24.7 Martelli Pasta Company averages $350,000 in credit sales per month. By maturity factoring its accounts receivable, it will be able to eliminate the credit and billing department at a monthly savings of $4,000. Martelli cannot accept the factoring arrangement if the effective annual cost before taxes exceeds 18 percent. What is the largest percentage factoring commission per month Martelli would be willing to pay? (Assume 12 equal months, not a 365-day year.)

24.8 Dresden Dinnerware Company employs a 180-day field warehouse agreement to finance inventory. The average amount of inventory is $800,000, the bank lends Dresden 80 percent of the value of the inventory, and the field warehousing fee is $100 per day. If the stated rate on the loan is 3 percent over the prime rate of 14 percent per year, what is the before-tax effective annual interest rate of the loan?

Answers to Completion Questions

24.1 Trade credit
24.2 amount of financing
24.3 after-tax effective annual cost
24.4 decreases; suffer; trade credit
24.5 convenience; restrictive terms
24.6 prime rate
24.7 a specific purpose; promissory note
24.8 commitment fee
24.9 the amount borrowed less interest
24.10 normal bank balance
24.11 Commercial paper; below
24.12 Pledging; the lender to repay the loan
24.13 Factoring; maturity factoring; advance factoring
24.14 a third party

Solutions to Problems

24.1 The cost of trade credit is

$$k_{\text{effective annual}} = \left[1 + \frac{\text{discount percent}}{100\% - \text{discount percent}}\right]^{365 / (\text{date paid} - \text{discount date})} - 1$$

For National Vegetable, the cost is

$$k_{\text{effective annual}} = \left[1 + \frac{2}{100 - 2}\right]^{365 / (30-10)} - 1$$
$$= [1.020408]^{18.25} - 1 = 0.4459 = 44.59\%$$

For Allied Produce, the cost is

$$k_{\text{effective annual}} = \left[1 + \frac{3}{100 - 3}\right]^{365 / (45-15)} - 1$$
$$= [1.030928]^{12.17} - 1 = 0.4486 = 44.86\%$$

National Vegetable's trade credit costs slightly less.

24.2   Step 1. $k_{effective\ annual} = \left[1 + \dfrac{costs - benefits}{amount\ of\ financing}\right]^m - 1$

$= 1 + \left[\dfrac{\$4,000}{\$80,000}\right]^{365/90} - 1 = 0.2188$ or 21.88%

Step 2. $k_i = k_{effective\ annual}(1 - T)$

$14.19\% = 21.88\%\ (1 - T)$

$(1 - T) = 0.6485$

$T = 0.3515 = 35.15\%$

24.3   a.   Step 1.   Interest paid $=$ (amount borrowed)(annual rate)(portion of year)
$= (\$300,000)(0.16)(180/365) = \$23,671.23$

Step 2. $k_{effective\ annual} = \left[1 + \dfrac{costs - benefits}{amount\ of\ financing}\right]^m - 1$

$k_{effective\ annual} = \left[1 + \dfrac{\$23,671.23}{\$300,000}\right]^{365/180} - 1 = 0.1665 = 16.65\%$

b.   Step 3.   Interest paid $= (\$300,000)(0.15)(180/365) = \$22,191.78$

$k_{effective\ annual} = \left[1 + \dfrac{\$22,191.78}{\$300,000 - \$22,191.78}\right]^{365/180} - 1$

$= \left[1 + \dfrac{\$22,191.78}{\$277,808.22}\right]^{365/180} - 1 = 0.1686 = 16.86\%$

c.   Step 4.   Interest paid $= (\$300,000)(0.12)(180/365) = \$17,753.43$

$Payment = \dfrac{\$300,000 + \$17,753.43}{6\ months} = \$52,958.91$ per month

$Loan = payment\ (PVA_{k_{effective\ annual},6mo})$

$\$300,000 = \$52,958.91(PVA_{k_{effective\ annual},6mo})$

$PVA_{k_{effective\ annual},6mo} = \dfrac{\$300,000}{\$52,958.91} = 5.665$

From Table B.2,

$PVA_{1\%,6mo} = 5.795$

$PVA_{2\%,6mo} = 5.601$

So the monthly rate is between 1 and 2 percent, but closer to 2 percent.
Using a financial calculator, $k_{effective\ annual}$ is 21.96% per year.

d.   Step 5.   Interest paid $= (\$300,000)(0.10)(180/365) = \$14,794.52$
Compensating balance $= (\$300,000)(0.15) = \$45,000$

$k_{effective\ annual} = \left[1 + \dfrac{\$14,794.52}{\$300,000 - \$14,794.52 - \$45,000}\right]^{365/180} - 1$

$= \left[1 + \dfrac{\$14,794.52}{\$240,205.48}\right]^{365/180} - 1 = 0.1288 = 12.88\%$

Step 6.   Alternative (d) has the lowest before-tax effective annual interest cost; hence (other things being equal) it should be chosen.

24.4   a.   Step 1.   Monthly interest charge = (amount borrowed)(interest rate)(proportion of year)

Commitment fee   = ($750,000 − amount borrowed)(percent fee)(proportion of year)

January

     Interest charge   = ($300,000)(0.13)(31/365)   = $3,312.33

     Commitment fee = ($750,000 − $300,000)(0.005)(31/365) =   191.10

     Total January charges $3,503.43

Step 2.   *February*

     Interest charge   = ($600,000)(0.13)(28/365)   = $5,983.56

     Commitment fee = ($750,000 − $600,000)(0.005)(28/365) =   57.53

     Total February charges $6,041.09

Step 3.   *March*

     Interest charge   = ($750,000)(0.13)(31/365)   = $8,280.82

     Commitment fee = ($750,000 − $750,000)(0.005)(31/365) =   0

     Total March charges $8,280.82

Step 4.   *April*

     Interest charge   = ($500,000)(0.13)(30/365)   = $5,342.47

     Commitment fee = ($750,000 − $500,000)(0.005)(30/365) =   102.74

     Total April charges $5,445.21

Step 5.   *May*

     Interest charge   = ($250,000)(0.13)(31/365)   = $2,760.27

     Commitment fee = ($750,000 − $250,000)(0.005)(31/365) =   212.33

     Total May charges $2,972.60

Step 6.   *June*

     Interest charge   = ($150,000)(0.13)(30/365)   = $1,602.74

     Commitment fee = ($750,000 − $150,000)(0.005)(30/365) =   246.58

     Total June charges $1,849.32

b.   Step 7.

$$k_{\text{effective annual}} = \left[1 + \frac{\text{total commitment fees + interest}}{\text{average net amount of financing}} \right]^{m} - 1$$

Total commitment fees plus interest = $3,503.43 + $6,041.09

+ $8,280.82 + $5,445.21 + $2,972.60 + $1,849.32 = $28,092.47

Average net amount borrowed per period = $300,000 (31/181)

+ $600,000 (28/181) + $750,000 (31/181) + $500,000 (30/181)

+ $250,000 (31/181) + $150,000 (30/181) = $423,204

$$k_{\text{effective annual}} = \left[1 + \frac{\$28,092.47}{\$423,204} \right]^{365/181} - 1 = 0.1384 = 13.84\%$$

24.5   Step 1.   Interest cost = $2,500,000 − $2,300,000 = $200,000

Step 2.   Commitment fee = $2,500,000(0.0075)(270/365) = $13,869.86

Step 3. $$k_{\text{effective annual}} = \left[1 + \frac{\$200,000 + \$13,869.86}{\$2,300,000} \right]^{365/270} - 1 = 0.1277 = 12.77\%$$

24.6   Step 1.   Cost of traditional loan: stated rate, which is 16 percent.

Step 2.   Cost of the alternative package:

Processing fee = (0.01)($3,000)(50 days) = $1,500

Step 3.   The bank will lend ($3,000)(50 days)(0.80) = $120,000

Interest = ($120,000) (0.14) (50/365) = $2,301.37

Step 4. $$k_{\text{effective annual}} = \left[1 + \frac{\$1,500 + \$2,301.37}{\$120,000}\right]^{365/50} - 1 = 0.2557 = 25.57\%$$

The traditional loan is a much less expensive alternative.

24.7 Step 1. $$k_{\text{effective annual}} = \left[1 + \frac{\text{factoring commission} - \text{savings in expenses}}{\text{accounts receivable per month}}\right]^{m} - 1$$

$0.18 = \{1 + [(\text{commission} - \$4,000)/\$350,000]\}^{12 \text{ months}} - 1$

$[1.18]^{1/12} = \{1 + [(\text{commission} - \$4,000)/\$350,000]\}$

$1.0139 = 1 + [(\text{commission} - \$4,000)/\$350,000]$

$0.0139 = (\text{commission} - \$4,000)/\$350,000$

$\$4,865 = \text{commission} - \$4,000$

$\text{Commission} = \$8,865$

Step 2. Martelli could afford to pay a factoring commission of $\$8,865/\$350,000 = 0.0253 = 2.53$ percent per month.

24.8 Step 1. Field warehousing fee $= (\$100)(180 \text{ days}) = \$18,000.00$

Step 2. Interest $= (0.17)(\$800,000)(0.80)(180/365) = \underline{53,654.79}$

Total fee and interest $\$71,654.79$

Step 3. $$k_{\text{effective annual}} = \left[1 + \frac{\$71,654.79}{\$640,000}\right]^{365/180} - 1 = 0.2401 = 24.01\%$$

Chapter 25
Analyzing Accounting Statements

How This Chapter Relates to the Rest of the Text

Accounting is the language of finance. The analysis of accounting statements prepared under generally accepted accounting principles enables us to ascertain certain information concerning the magnitude, timing, and riskiness of a firm's cash flows, important determinants of its value.

Because of their importance as a source of information, a basic knowledge of balance sheets and income statements is required throughout the text. Developing cash flows arising from long-term capital budgeting projects (Chapters 7–9) is similar to developing an income statement. A large portion of the text (Chapters 21–24) discusses the management of working capital and its components: Current assets and liabilities. Information concerning the firm's capital structure (Chapters 12 and 13) can also be determined from the balance sheet. Additionally, knowledge of how accounting statements are developed helps us in understanding the differences between earnings, as defined under generally accepted accounting principles, and cash flow, which leads to better financial management. The du Pont system shows the relationship between profitability, asset utilization, financial leverage, and its return on equity. In general, accounting statement analysis is a useful tool in developing an understanding of a firm and its characteristics.

Topical Outline

I.   Different statements for different purposes.
      A.   Generally accepted accounting principles (GAAP) guide the recording and reporting to the public of the firm's financial status.
      B.   Firms employ three different sets of financial records.
            1.   GAAP-prepared statements for reporting to stockholders, creditors, and financial publications.
            2.   Statements for tax purposes, employed when dealing with Revenue Canada Taxation regulations.
            3.   Statements for internal management.

II.   The basic accounting statements.
      A.   The income statement presents a summary of revenues and expenses for the firm over a given period of time.
            1.   Sales minus cost of goods sold equals gross margin.
            2.   Operating profit measures earnings after all expenses except interest and taxes and before any adjustments.
            3.   Adjustments can arise from discontinued operations and income from unconsolidated subsidiaries.
            4.   Earnings before interest and taxes (EBIT), are earnings before taxes or financing costs associated with debt.
            5.   Subtracting interest expense from EBIT results in earnings before taxes (EBT).
            6.   Earnings after taxes (EAT), are the base from which cash dividends on preferred stock are subtracted to achieve earnings available to common stockholders (EAC).
            7. $\text{EPS} = \dfrac{\text{net income} - \text{cash dividends on preferred stock}}{\text{number of shares of outstanding common stock}}$
            8.   Fully diluted EPS includes the effects of total conversion of convertible bonds or preferred stock.
      B.   The balance sheet provides a record of the firm's assets, liabilities, and owner's equity at some specific point in time.
            1.   Assets are categorized as either current or long-term.
            2.   Liabilities are categorized as either current or long-term.
            3.   Shareholders' equity includes both preferred and common stock.
            4.   Retained earnings are earnings not paid out as cash dividends; this is not a cash account.

C. The statement of retained earnings keeps track of how earnings were used—as cash dividends or for future internal investment in the firm.

D. Information contained in the statements helps the financial community value the firm and form expectations about the expected returns and riskiness of the firm's cash flows.

III. Accounting statement analysis.

A. Provides clues concerning the magnitude, timing, and riskiness of the firm's future cash flows.

B. Analysis guidelines.

1. Look at trends over 3 to 5 years, since they provide a frame of reference.

2. Compare the firm's performance to that of its industry.

3. All of the accounting statement, including the footnotes, is important.

4. Obtain further information to answer questions raised by the analysis of accounting statements.

C. Common-size statements: Items are calculated in percentage terms to allow for easy comparison of statements from different periods.

1. Income statement.

a. Each component is divided by net sales, so that each item is presented as a percentage of sales.

b. The common-size net income and EBIT are the net profit margin and the gross profit margin respectively.

c. We can compare firm common-size income statements to industry common-size data.

2. Balance sheet.

a. All statement components are calculated as a percentage of total assets.

b. Analysis of balance sheet common-size statements for several years shows trends or changes in these accounts.

c. We can compare common-size balance sheet data to industry data.

D. Ratio analysis.

1. Liquidity ratios (current ratio or quick ratio) indicate an ability to meet short-run obligations.

2. Asset management or efficiency ratios (days sales outstanding, inventory turnover, long-term asset turnover, and total asset turnover) help analysts judge management's skill.

3. Debt management ratios (total debt to total assets, times interest earned, and fixed charges coverage) help in analyzing the firm's capital structure and its ability to meet its legal debt obligations.

4. Profitability ratios (net profit margin, return on total assets, and return on equity) relate net income to sales, assets, or shareholders' equity.

5. Market ratios (P/E, dividend yield, and dividend payout) help investors evaluate the attractiveness of a common stock, considering its price, its earnings, and its cash dividends.

6. The du Pont system relates three ratios—net profit margin, total asset turnover, and total debt to total assets.

IV. Limitations of financial analysis.

A. Accounting data may bear little or no relationship to a firm's cash flows, especially in the short run.

B. There are a variety of legitimate accounting techniques; identical firms may appear to be different due to different accounting methods.

C. Firms may undertake steps, called "window dressing," to make their accounting statements appear better.

D. Multidivisional firms present special problems to analysts; it is difficult to find an appropriate industry benchmark for comparison with multidivisional firms.

E. Inflation and disinflation can have effects on the firm that are not recognized in accounting statements. This can make comparison over time difficult.

F. Firms with international operations face additional reporting problems.

G. Successful firms generally do not operate at industry averages and finding an appropriate industry for comparison is more difficult than it sounds.

Formulas

<u>Performance Measures from the Income Statement</u>

Gross margin on sales = sales − cost of goods sold

Operating profit = sales − cost of goods sold − operating expenses

Earnings before interest and taxes (EBIT):

EBIT = Sales − cost of goods sold − operating expenses − adjustments

Earnings before taxes (EBT) = EBIT − interest

Net income = EBT − taxes

Earnings per share (EPS):

$$EPS = \frac{\text{earnings available to common stockholders}}{\text{number of common stock shares outstanding}} = \frac{\text{net income} - \text{cash dividends on preferred stock}}{\text{number of common stock shares outstanding}}$$

$$\text{Dividends per share} = \frac{\text{total cash dividends paid to common stockholders}}{\text{number of common stock shares outstanding}}$$

<u>Ratio Analysis</u>

Liquidity ratios:

$$\text{Current ratio} = \frac{\text{current assets}}{\text{current liabilities}}$$

$$\text{Quick ratio} = \frac{\text{current assets} - \text{inventory}}{\text{current liabilities}}$$

Asset management ratios:

$$\text{Days sales outstanding} = \frac{\text{accounts receivable}}{\text{sales}/365}$$

$$\text{Long-term asset turnover} = \frac{\text{sales}}{\text{long-term assets}}$$

$$\text{Inventory turnover} = \frac{\text{cost of goods sold}}{\text{inventory}}$$

$$\text{Total asset turnover} = \frac{\text{sales}}{\text{total assets}}$$

Debt management ratios:

$$\text{Total debt to total assets} = \frac{\text{total debt}}{\text{total assets}}$$

$$\text{Times interest earned} = \frac{\text{EBIT}}{\text{interest}}$$

$$\text{Fixed charges coverage} = \frac{\text{EBIT} + \text{lease expenses}}{\text{interest} + \text{lease expenses}}$$

Profitability ratios:

$$\text{Net profit margin} = \frac{\text{net income}}{\text{sales}}$$

$$\text{Return on equity} = \frac{\text{net income}}{\text{shareholders' equity}}$$

$$\text{Return on total assets} = \frac{\text{net income}}{\text{total assets}}$$

Market ratios:

$$\text{Price/earnings ratio} = \frac{\text{market price per share}}{\text{earnings per share}}$$

$$\text{Dividend yield} = \frac{\text{dividends per share}}{\text{market price per share}}$$

$$\text{Dividend payout} = \frac{\text{dividends per share}}{\text{earnings per share}}$$

The du Pont system:

$$\text{Return on total assets (ROA)} = (\text{profitability}) \times (\text{asset utilization})$$

$$= (\text{net profit margin}) \times (\text{total asset turnover})$$

$$= \left[\frac{\text{net income}}{\text{sales}}\right] \times \left[\frac{\text{sales}}{\text{total assets}}\right]$$

$$\text{Return on equity} = \frac{\text{ROA}}{\left[1 - (\text{total debt to total assets})\right]}$$

$$= \frac{(\text{profitability}) \times (\text{asset utilization})}{\text{financial leverage}}$$

What to Look For

Accounting Statements: Limitations and Uses

Limitations

Financial analysts thrive on accounting data. Chapter 25 analyzes the accounting data firms provide in annual reports. Generally accepted accounting principles (GAAP), which rely on the ideas of accrual, realization, matching, and historical cost, guide the reporting of a firm's operating results in accounting statements.

Although the operating data are not necessarily wrong, accounting statements do not give the clearest picture of the firm's potential for generating future cash flows. Accounting statements, since they adhere to GAAP, ignore the timing of cash flows. It is possible for a firm to report a healthy net income while experiencing a severe cash shortage. Such a cash shortage can have significant effects on a firm if interest rates are high or if the firm has used up all its readily available credit.

Analysts use GAAP accounting statements to try to estimate the magnitude, timing, and riskiness of the firm's future cash flows. It is upon this cash flow and risk estimate that analysts base their valuation of a firm. We will suppose that you are a financial analyst, and we will walk through the use of the Loblaw Companies Ltd. accounting statements in the text.

To begin your analysis of Loblaw Companies Ltd., take financial statements for several years and put them into a common-size form. For the income statement, this means you would put all expenses into a percentage of sales revenue. We have reproduced below the actual income statements (in millions) for Loblaw Companies Ltd. and the common-size statements alongside. Notice how much easier it is to see trends when you have a statement in common-size form.

	Actual Income			Common-Size		
	1994	1993	1992	1994	1993	1992
Net sales	$9,999.9	$9,356.1	$9,261.6	100.0%	100.0%	100.0%
Cost of goods sold, selling and administration expenses, and adjustments	9,592.9	9,155.7	9,068.5	97.3	97.9	98.0
EBIT	272.3	200.4	193.1	2.7	2.1	2.0
Interest	62.1	51.3	58.2	0.6	0.5	0.6
EBT	210.2	149.1	124.9	2.1	1.6	1.4
Income tax	83.5	55.7	45.1	0.8	0.6	0.5
Net income	$126.7	$93.4	$79.8	1.3%	1.0%	0.9%

Common-size statements for Loblaw and for the retail industry in Table 25.4 readily tell you that Loblaw's cost of goods sold was lower in 1994 than in 1992 and also lower than the industry average. Operating expenses for Loblaw decreased in 1994 and 1993; but the net result is a higher net profit margin than the industry's. We would need a few more years to get a reasonable trend for Loblaw, but you can see that Loblaw performs slightly better than the retail industry.

For common-size balance sheets, all accounts are calculated as a percentage of total assets. Table 25.5 in the text gives you Loblaw Companies' and the industry's asset, liability, and shareholders' equity accounts in percentage terms. We see that Loblaw's equity has declined, placing more financial risk on creditors. Accounts receivable have also fallen and are significantly below the industry's, suggesting that perhaps Loblaw's credit policy or collection policy has become more strict.

From common-size analysis, we go naturally into ratio analysis. Table 25.6 summarizes the five types of ratios. You will notice that all the information you need to make these calculations is in either the income statement or the balance sheet.

These ratios point out problem areas for managers and financial analysts. Dun & Bradstreet publishes a short pamphlet called "Key Business Ratios," which you can check when you compare your firm's accounting ratios to those of its industry. For example, the average liquidity ratios for the apparel retail sales industry are quite different from those of the automobile industry, as are the turnover ratios. In this way, using your particular industry's average ratios as a benchmark, you can judge the performance of your firm.

Let's look at Table 25.6 in the text. It compares Loblaw Companies Ltd.'s ratios to those of the industry. By taking several ratios—the liquidity ratios, the profitability ratios, and the debt management ratios, for example—we can make some decisions about Loblaw. Note that Loblaw's net profit margin is slightly higher than the industry's, and that more than half its capital structure is debt. We might decide that, as bankers, we will grant Loblaw's a line of credit at a slightly higher than normal rate of interest, due to its profitability and higher debt than the industry. As investors, we might decide that Loblaw has good growth prospects, as reflected by the higher P/E ratio in 1994. In making any judgements with ratios, however, remember that they are based on GAAP statements, which rely on the accrual concept, realization, matching, and historical cost, so there is no direct link to expected cash flows.

In the analysis above, we referred to several ratios in order to make a judgement about the riskiness of a firm's cash flows. The du Pont system incorporates three of these key ratios—profitability, asset management, and financial leverage—so that we can see their contribution to return on equity (ROE).

$$\text{ROE} = \frac{\text{return on total assets}}{\text{financial leverage}} = \frac{(\text{profitability}) \times (\text{asset management})}{\text{financial leverage}}$$

$$= \frac{(\text{net income}/\text{sales}) \times (\text{sales}/\text{total assets})}{1 - (\text{total debt to total assets})}$$

As we know from Chapters 12 and 13, financial leverage is the amount of debt (or other fixed cost sources of financing) used by a firm, in comparison to total assets. Loblaw's financial leverage is 62 percent. When you look at an income statement, you note that interest payments are deducted from before-tax income. In effect, then, interest increases net income when compared to dividends. This effect is called financial leverage. The use of financial leverage has increased Loblaw's return on equity to a point substantially above that of the industry. Anything that changes the profit margin, asset turnover, or financial leverage will affect the return on equity. Remember that the usefulness of the du Pont system is limited, since the GAAP data upon which it is based are not directly linked to expected cash flows.

Completion Questions

25.1   Generally accepted accounting principles (GAAP) underlie consistent and objective accounting statements. But GAAP do not provide a direct link to _____, which are so crucial in evaluating the performance of the firm.

25.2   The payment of taxes is a direct cash _____ for the firm, so separate statements are prepared for tax purposes. These differ from those required for GAAP purposes.

25.3   The _____ is a "snapshot" of the firm's assets, liabilities, and owners' claims as of a specific date. The _____ records the flow of income and related expenses through the firm over a period of time.

25.4   _____ reflects the firm's earnings before costs of financing and income taxes.

25.5   The figures on the balance sheet are presented in terms of _____ costs and do not reflect _____ values or the effects of _____.

25.6   Retained earnings is an account that reflects all prior _____ not paid out as _____ but it does not contain any cash.

25.7   _____ ratios indicate the firm's ability to meet its short-run obligations.

25.8   If we want to know how effective a firm's credit granting and management activities are, we should use the _____ ratio.

25.9   Times interest earned helps measure the ability of a firm to meet its _____. A high ratio is safer, but if too high, it may indicate the firm does not use enough financial leverage.

25.10   The _____ ratio provides an accounting-based indication of the effectiveness of management from the shareholder's perspective. This ratio is directly affected by the return on _____ _____ and by the amount of _____ employed.

25.11   The dividend payout ratio indicates how the firm is splitting earnings between _____ and _____.

25.12   Both common-size statements and financial ratios should be analyzed over time, be compared to those of _____, and be used as a basis for asking further questions about the firm.

Problems

25.1   Baylor Book, Ltd., has the following current portion of its balance sheet:

Baylor Book, Ltd.
December 31
(in thousands)

Cash	$ 30,000	Accounts payable	$ 42,000
Accounts receivable	60,000	Notes payable	78,000
Inventory	156,000	Total current liabilities	$120,000
Total current assets	$246,000		

Sales: $912,500
Cost of goods sold: $585,000

Calculate the current ratio, quick ratio, days sales outstanding, and inventory turnover ratio.

25.2   Using the following balance sheet and other financial information for International Electronics, Ltd., calculate the long-term asset turnover, total asset turnover, total debt to total assets, and times interest earned.

International Electronics, Ltd.
Balance Sheet
as of December 31

Cash	$ 35,000	Accounts payable	$ 36,000
Accounts receivable	45,000	Notes payable	60,000
Inventory	170,000	Total current liabilities	96,000
Total current assets	250,000		
		Long-term debt	1,164,000
Long-term assets	2,000,000	Total liabilities	1,260,000
		Common stock	100,000
		Retained earnings	890,000
		Total shareholders' equity	990,000
		Total liabilities	
Total assets	$2,250,000	and shareholders' equity	$2,250,000

Sales	$4,500,000
EBIT	3,264,000
Interest expense	170,000

25.3   Xtel Ltd.'s common stock is selling for $42.50 per share, pays a dividend of $6.30, and has a dividend payout ratio of 76 percent. What is the P/E ratio?

25.4   Using the information given below, complete the following balance sheet and the sales amount.

Jepson Enterprises, Ltd.
Balance Sheet
December 31

Cash	_____	Accounts payable	$ 10,000
Accounts receivable	_____	Notes payable	20,000
Inventory	_____	Total current liabilities	_____
Total current assets	_____		
		Long-term debt	50,000
Net long-term assets	_____	Total liabilities	
		Common stock	10,000
		Retained earnings	_____
		Total shareholders' equity	_____
		Total liabilities and	
Total assets	_____	shareholders' equity	_____
		Sales	_____

Current ratio: 1.7
Quick ratio: 1.2
Days sales outstanding: 36.5 days
Total asset turnover: 2.0
Total debt to total assets: 0.5

25.5   Engletown Manufacturing Ltd. has set a net profit margin of 4.2 percent, a total asset turnover of 2.5, and a return on equity of 16.8 percent. Using the du Pont formula, determine the company's total debt to total assets ratio.

Answers to Completion Questions

25.1	cash flows
25.2	outflow
25.3	balance sheet; income statement
25.4	EBIT (earnings before interest and taxes)
25.5	historical; current; inflation
25.6	net income (or earnings); cash dividends
25.7	Liquidity
25.8	days sales outstanding
25.9	interest payments
25.10	return on equity; total assets; financial leverage
25.11	common shareholders; reinvesting them in the firm
25.12	the industry

Solutions to Problems

25.1 Step 1.

$$\text{Current ratio} = \frac{\text{current assets}}{\text{current liabilities}} = \frac{\$246,000}{\$120,000} = 2.05$$

Step 2.

$$\text{Quick ratio} = \frac{\text{current assets} - \text{inventory}}{\text{current liabilities}}$$

$$= \frac{\$246,000 - \$156,000}{\$120,000} = 0.75$$

Step 3.

$$\text{Days sales outstanding} = \frac{\text{accounts receivable}}{\text{sales}/365} = \frac{\$60,000}{\$912,500/365} = 24 \text{ days}$$

Step 4.

$$\text{Inventory turnover} = \frac{\text{cost of goods sold}}{\text{inventory}} = \frac{\$585,000}{\$156,000} = 3.75$$

25.2 Step 1.

$$\text{Long-term asset turnover} = \frac{\text{sales}}{\text{long-term assets}} = \frac{\$4,500,000}{\$2,000,000} = 2.25$$

Step 2.

$$\text{Total asset turnover} = \frac{\text{sales}}{\text{total assets}} = \frac{\$4,500,000}{\$2,250,000} = 2.00$$

Step 3.

$$\text{Total debt to total assets} = \frac{\text{total debt}}{\text{total assets}} = \frac{\$1,260,000}{\$2,250,000} = 0.56$$

Step 4.

$$\text{Times interest earned} = \frac{\text{EBIT}}{\text{interest expense}} = \frac{\$3,264,000}{\$170,000} = \$19.20$$

25.3 Step 1.

$$\text{Dividend payout ratio} = \frac{\text{DPS}}{\text{EPS}}, \text{ so EPS} = \frac{\text{DPS}}{\text{dividend payout}}$$

$$= \frac{6.30}{0.75} = \$8.40$$

Step 2.

$$P/E = \frac{\text{market price}}{\text{EPS}} = \frac{\$42.50}{\$8.40} = 5.06 \text{ times}$$

25.4   Step 1.   Total current liabilities = accounts payable + notes payable

$$= \$10{,}000 + \$20{,}000 = \$30{,}000$$

Step 2.   Total liabilities = total current liabilities + long-term debt

$$= \$30{,}000 + \$50{,}000 = \$80{,}000$$

Step 3.   Since total assets = total liabilties + shareholders' equity,

and $\dfrac{\text{total debt}}{\text{total assets}} = 0.5,$

$$\text{Total assets} = \text{total liabilities} + \text{shareholders' equity} = \frac{\text{total debt}}{0.5}$$

$$= \frac{\$80{,}000}{0.5}$$

$$= \$160{,}000$$

Step 4.   Total shareholders' equity = (total liabilities + shareholders' equity) − total liabilities

$$= \$160{,}000 - \$80{,}000 = \$80{,}000$$

Step 5.   Total shareholders' equity = common stock + retained earnings

Common stock = total shareholders' equity − retained earnings

$$= \$80{,}000 - \$10{,}000 = \$70{,}000$$

Step 6. $\text{Total asset turnover} = \dfrac{\text{sales}}{\text{total assets}} = 2.0$

Sales = (2.0) (total assets)

$$= (2.0)\,(\$160{,}000) = \$320{,}000$$

Step 7. $\text{Current ratio} = \dfrac{\text{current assets}}{\text{current liabilities}} = 1.7$

Current assets = (1.7) (current liabilities)

$$= (1.7)\,(\$30{,}000) = \$51{,}000$$

Step 8.   Total assets = current assets + net long-term assets

Net long-term assets = total assets - retained earnings

$$= \$160{,}000 - \$51{,}000 = \$109{,}000$$

Step 9. $\text{Quick ratio} = \dfrac{\text{current assets} - \text{inventory}}{\text{current liabilities}} = 1.2$

Current assets − inventory = (1.2) (current liabilities)

$$= (1.2)\,(\$30{,}000) = \$36{,}000$$

Step 10.   Inventory = current assets − (current assets − inventory)

$$= \$51{,}000 - \$36{,}000 = \$15{,}000$$

Step 11. Days sales outstanding $= \dfrac{\text{accounts receivable}}{\text{sales per day}} = 36.5$

Accounts receivable $= (36.5)\,(\text{sales per day})$

$$= (36.5)\left[\dfrac{\$320,000}{365}\right] = \$32,000$$

Step 12. Current assets $=$ cash $+$ accounts receivable $+$ inventory

Cash $=$ current assets $-$ accounts receivable $-$ inventory

$= \$51,000 - \$32,000 - \$15,000 = \$4,000$

Jepson Enterprises, Ltd.
Balance Sheet
December 31

Cash	$ 4,000	Accounts payable	$ 10,000
Accounts receivable	32,000	Notes payable	20,000
Inventory	15,000	Total current liabilities	30,000
Total current assets	51,000	Long-term debt	50,000
		Total liabilities	80,000
Net long-term assets	109,000		
		Common stock	70,000
		Retained earnings	10,000
		Total shareholders' equity	80,000
		Total liabilities and	
Total assets	$160,000	shareholders' equity	$160,000

25.5 Step 1. Return on total assets $=$ (net profit margin)(total asset turnover)

$= (4.2\%)(2.5) = 10.5\%$

Step 2. Return on equity $= \dfrac{\text{return on total assets}}{(1 - \text{total debt to total assets})}$

$$1 - \dfrac{\text{total debt}}{\text{total assets}} = \dfrac{\text{ROTA}}{\text{ROE}}$$

$$\dfrac{\text{total debt}}{\text{total assets}} = 1 - \dfrac{\text{ROTA}}{\text{ROE}}$$

$$= 1 - \dfrac{10.5\%}{16.8\%} = 1 - 0.625 = 0.375 \text{ or } 37.5\%$$

Chapter 26
Financial Planning and Forecasting

How This Chapter Relates to the Rest of the Text

Cash flow is the single most important aspect in the management and valuation of the firm. Accounting statements (Chapter 25) do not directly provide us with information about the firm's past or future expected cash flow. The value of an asset (or firm) is a function of its cash flow, timing (Chapter 3), and riskiness (Chapter 5). Valuation (Chapter 4) requires the calculation of the cash flow and a recognition of the difference between cash flow and earnings. Cash flow is also an important input in capital budgeting (Chapters 7, 8, and 9). This chapter also deals with the measurement and estimation of cash flow at the firm level and their impact on the firm's strategic planning.

Effective strategic planning contributes to the continual success of the firm. Strategic planning incorporates decisions made relative to short-term financial management (Chapters 21–24) and long-term financial policies (Chapters 12–14), and includes consideration of options to expand, delay, or abandon major projects (Chapter 19) and restructuring (Chapter 16). Long-term financing sources (Chapters 10–11) must be considered in the planning process. Both short- and long-term financial planning requires the use of cash budgets.

Topical Outline

I.   Cash flow analysis.
    A.   The statement of changes in financial position (SCFP).
        1.   The purpose of the SCFP is to provide a statement of the firm's cash flow over an accounting period.
        2.   Determine changes in all accounts from one balance sheet to the next.
            a.   Operating activities pertain to the basic functioning of the firm.
            b.   Investment activities include investment in long-term assets.
            c.   Financing activities involve raising capital from and returning capital to investors.
        3.   Advantages of the statement of changes in financial position.
            a.   Provides a specific focus on the three separate activities of operations, investment, and financing.
            b.   Removes the effects of accruals and restates items such as collectibles or salaries on a cash basis.
            c.   Breaks out gross, as opposed to net, figures for such items as long-term debt transactions.
        4.   Disadvantages of the statement of changes in financial position.
            a.   There are two approaches to developing the SCFP. The direct approach provides more useful information, but the indirect approach has been adopted by most corporations.
            b.   The statement does not reconcile taxes as reported on the income statement and taxes actually paid.
            c.   The statement permits, but does not require separate disclosure of cash flows from discontinued operations.
            d.   Dividends received by the firm and dividends paid by the firm are treated inconsistently, which may be misleading.
    B.   The cash budget.
        1.   Includes all cash inflows and outflows expected by the firm.
        2.   Alerts the firm to future cash needs and provides a standard of comparison for evaluating subsequent performance.
    C.   Procedure for developing a cash budget.
        1.   Create a scenario with an explicit set of assumptions.
            a.   Assumptions concerning the state of the economy, competitors' actions, and conditions in the money and capital markets should reflect future possibilities.
            b.   Scenario analysis enables the manager to see how sensitive cash flow forecasts are to changes in inputs or assumptions.

2. Estimate sales.
   a. Internal sales forecasts are based on past sales or information provided by sales personnel and the marketing department.
      i. Linear regression and forecasting.
         (a) Simple linear regression is used to develop sales forecasts.
         (b) Sales are the dependent variable (Y_t); the time period is the independent variable (X_t). The model is $Y_t = \alpha + \beta X_t$.
         (c) By using future values for time (X_t), we can forecast future values of sales (Y_t).
         (d) Although this approach is simple and inexpensive to implement, it may provide misleading results because sales are often affected by factors not captured by the time component.
   b. External forecasts employ factors such as economic conditions, projected gross domestic product, etc. outside the firm.
3. Determine cash inflows arising from operations.
4. Determine cash outflows from operations.
5. Calculate other cash inflows and outflows.
6. Determine the short-term financing needs or surplus available.

II. Forecasting in practice.
   A. Electronic spreadsheet programs allow for rapid scenario analysis and the ability to update forecasts quickly and easily.
   B. Firm growth must be accounted for. High growth rates may put the firm in a cash bind and require external financing. Failure to plan for future needs is one of the primary shortcomings of many growing firms.
   C. One problem that arises in practice is how to forecast for periods of less than one year when the firm experiences seasonal patterns in cash flows. Adjust the forecasts to reflect the seasonality. For quarterly data do the following:
      1. Employ linear regression to forecast sales.
      2. Do a four quarter moving average on the first four actual observations.
      3. Move down one observation and determine a second four-quarter moving average.
      4. Average the two consecutive four-quarter moving averages.
      5. Repeat steps 2 through 4, moving down one observation at a time.
      6. Calculate the ratio of actual to observation to centred moving average for each period.
      7. Find the average ratio per quarter.
      8. Adjust each forecast using the appropriate seasonal index.
   D. Inflation and disinflation have a profound impact on cash flows. Firms and their suppliers may be required to change strategies in order to cope with these impacts.

III. Pro forma financial statements.
   A. Pro forma statements project expected revenues, expenses, and the firm's financial position at the end of the forecast period.
   B. Approaches to developing pro forma statements:
      1. Use projections arising from the cash budget and modify to reflect GAAP.
      2. The percentage of sales method is based on the historical relationship between balance sheet and income statement entries and sales.
   C. Balance sheet and income statement items are assumed to vary directly with sales or must be forecasted separately.
   D. External funds needed equal required increase in assets less spontaneous increase in liabilities less increase in retained earnings.

IV.   Financial and strategic planning.
    A.   A basic model.
        1.   Reflects dynamic policies that emphasize value creation.
        2.   Long-run strategic planning considers the firm's long-term financing requirements.
            a.   Long-term financing requirements also include the firm's short-term spontaneous financing and its short-term borrowing.
            b.   A cash budget for longer time periods is made in less detail.
            c.   Accurate forecasting and flexibility become more important in long-term planning.
    B.   Things to consider when formulating a strategic plan.
        1.   Any anticipated expansion, replacement, or restructuring of assets.
        2.   Sources of financing and their possible consequences.
        3.   All options to expand, delay, or abandon capital projects.

Formulas

Linear Regression
Notation:
$$Y_t = \text{sales}$$
$$X_t = \text{time}$$

Formulas:

$$\overline{Y} = \sum_{t=1}^{n} Y_t / n$$

$$\overline{X} = \sum_{t=1}^{n} X_t / n$$

$$Y_t = \alpha + \beta X_t$$

$$\beta = \frac{\sum_{t=1}^{n} X_t Y_t - (n)(\overline{Y})(\overline{X})}{\sum_{t=1}^{n} X_t^2 - n(\overline{X}^2)}$$

$$\alpha = \overline{Y} - \beta \overline{X}$$

What to Look For

In this section, we will discuss the measurement and estimation of cash flow. Cash flow is extremely important for financial management. It is a primary determinant of value and the management of day-to-day operations of the firm requires a complete understanding of cash flow: what it is and where it comes from. Financial planning is a discipline of integration. It brings together into a coherent package all the previous and anticipated future decisions of the firm concerning financing and investing.

After-Tax Cash Flow Versus Net Income

The difference between cash flow and net income
As you may have noted from this chapter, earnings figures and cash flow figures often do not agree. Why does this difference exist? The purposes of earnings figures and cash flow figures differ. Earnings figures, whose calculation are guided by generally accepted accounting principles, can be calculated in a variety of ways depending upon which generally accepted procedures are employed. Sometimes the choice of a procedure is an attempt to put forth the most attractive financial picture of the firm. In addition, earnings figures also attempt to match costs and revenues in the

period in which they accrue, based upon historical cost. Earnings are only a clue to the firm's ability to generate cash flows.

Cash flow figures, however, report the inflow and outflow of cash. The value of the firm can be estimated as the present value of the expected future cash flows of the firm. Poor management cannot be masked as easily by cash flow figures as it can be by earnings figures.

In fact, cash flow figures can indicate areas for improvement in management. Let's look at Zeigler Tire Limited, for example. Suppose that Zeigler Tire has annual sales of $700,000, with 75 percent on credit. Credit terms require full payment within 90 days. These sales are relatively seasonal, with about 60 percent in the autumn months. The projected cash flows for the three months ending November 30 are below:

Cash Inflows		Cash Outflows	
Sales in cash	$105,000	Cash expenses	$200,000
Cash on hand	10,000	Taxes	63,000
Credit sales coming in	70,000	Repayment of short-term debt	100,000
Total	$185,000	Total	$363,000

Cash shortfall = $185,000 − $363,000 = −$178,000

As we see, the cash shortfall is $178,000. Now let's compare these cash flow figures with the GAAP balance sheet and income statement. Notice that while the income statement reports a healthy net income of $147,000, Zeigler is actually experiencing a cash shortage of $178,000.

Balance Sheet as of November 30

Assets		Liabilities and Shareholders' Equity	
Cash	$ 10,000	Short-term debt	$100,000
Accounts receivable	70,000	Long-term debt	150,000
Inventory	500,000	Equity	330,000
Total	$580,000	Total	$580,000

Income Statement (for three months ending November 30)

Sales (0.25 in cash)	$420,000
Cash expenses	200,000
Depreciation	10,000
EBT	$210,000
Taxes (0.30)	63,000
Net Income	$147,000

Zeigler has excellent earnings figures but very poor cash flow, since its outflows exceed its inflows. With 75 percent of its tires sold on credit, the cash flow is slowed down. Sales are recorded, but the cash will not be coming in for 90 days. Meanwhile, Zeigler must continue to replace the sold inventory. Zeigler's cash flow figures show a cash shortfall of $178,000 and indicate the need to change its credit terms policy to speed up its cash flow. Zeigler should also consider selling its accounts receivables and cutting the percentage of customers allowed to use credit.

A useful tool in analyzing the firm's cash flow over a period is the Statement of Changes in Financial Position (SCFP). The SCFP categorizes changes from successive balance sheets and items from the income statement as cash flows arising from operations, from investment, and from financing. This classifies cash flows into the three major operations of the firm and makes it easier to analyze how a firm has evolved through time. There are many advantages to the SCFP; it focuses on the three main functions of the firm, it removes the effects of accruals and restates items in terms of cash flow, and it breaks out gross as opposed to net transactions. There are however, several problems with the SCFP. Most notably, there are two methods of developing the statement; the direct approach supplies more information, but the indirect approach has been adopted by most firms.

Cash Flow Analysis

While understanding the difference between cash flow and earnings is important to financial management, it is also important to know how to estimate future cash flows. Cash inflows and outflows can be categorized as arising from operations, investments, or financing. Firms must be sensitive to the balance between inflows and outflows over both the short run and the long run. Excessive cash outflows can ultimately result in the failure of the firm. In order to prevent this, firms often develop cash budgets to provide an indication of future problems and to use as a standard of comparison for evaluating future performance.

The cash budget is a detailed statement of all expected cash inflows and outflows and can be developed for any period of time such as a month or a quarter of a year. The procedure for developing a cash budget includes developing a scenario with explicit assumptions, estimating sales, determining cash inflows and outflows from operations, estimating other cash inflows and outflows, and determining the expected cash surplus or funds needed.

To see how a cash budget can be developed, consider the case of Rand Manufacturing. The firm had sales of $460,000 in January and sales of $396,000 for February, and forecasts sales of $530,000 in March. Fifty percent of sales are for cash, 40 percent are collected in one month, and the remainder are collected in two months.

In order to produce, the company purchases raw materials equivalent to 75 percent of sales. Forty percent of the monthly purchase is paid in cash, the remaining 60 percent one month later. Wages and other expenses are estimated at $125,000 for March; interest expenses are estimated to be $12,000, and the firm expects to pay $35,000 in taxes. At the end of February, Rand has $75,000 in cash on hand and expects to receive $6,000 in dividends on stock owned. The company must maintain a minimum cash balance of $30,000 and has to pay an insurance bill of $50,000 in March. What are Rand Manufacturing's cash needs for March?

First, let us estimate cash inflows from operations. These cash inflows come from either sales or collections on prior sales. Following Table 26.3 we can estimate these cash inflows as follows:

Estimated Cash Inflows from Operations (in Thousands) for Rand Manufacturing

		January	February	March
1.	Total sales	$460.00	$396.00	$530.00
2.	Collections: one-month lag (40% of total sales)			158.40
3.	Collections: two-month lag (10% of total sales)			46.00
4.	Total collections (2 + 3)			204.40
5.	Cash sales (50% of total sales)			265.00
6.	Total operating cash inflow (4 + 5)			$469.40

In a similar fashion, we calculate the net cash outflows from operations.

Estimated Cash Outflows from Operations (in Thousands) for Rand Manufacturing

		February	March
1.	Total sales	$396.00	$530.00
2.	Credit purchases (75% of sales × 0.60)	178.20	238.60
3.	Payment of credit purchases (one-month lag)		178.20
4.	Cash purchases (75% of sales × 0.40)		159.00
5.	Wages and other expenses		125.00
6.	Interest		12.00
7.	Taxes		35.00
8.	Total operating cash outflows (3 + 4 + 5 + 6 + 7)		$509.20

Other cash inflows and outflows are $6,000 from dividends and −$50,000 in insurance expenses, or −$44,000 overall. For March, the net cash inflow is as follows:

		March
1.	Total operating cash inflow	$469.40
2.	Total operating cash outflow	−509.20
4.	Other cash inflow or outflow	− 44.00
4.	Net cash inflow (+) or outflow (−)	−$83.80

Rand Manufacturing has some cash on hand, but is it sufficient? Let's determine the short-term financing needed:

		March
1.	Cash	$75.00
2.	Net cash inflow or outflow	− 83.80
3.	Cash at end of period	− 8.80
4.	Minimum cash balance required	− 30.00
5.	Short-term financing needed	−$38.80

Rand needs to obtain $38,800 in cash in order to maintain operations. In reality, Rand would forecast its financing needs over a longer period of time in order to make arrangements with a lender to prevent any sort of cash crisis.

Forecasting in Practice

Cash flow analysis is obviously a powerful tool for financial managers. In practice, a good cash flow analysis considers a variety of conditions not discussed to this point. Inflation, for instance, has an obvious impact on the firm's cash flows. Also, it may be necessary for a firm to change its strategies to cope with these conditions. The firm may not be able to pass the effects of inflation along to its consumers and may cause suppliers of funds to change strategies. A complete cash flow analysis should consider these possibilities.

Growing firms have special problems that need careful attention. As firms grow, so do their sales. This requires additional assets and, hence, additional capital. High growth rates may put the firm in a cash bind. Internally generated funds may not be sufficient and the firm may need to acquire long-term sources of financing. Failure to consider and plan for the effects of growth is one of the primary shortcomings of growing firms.

Linear regression techniques provide a relatively simple approach to forecasting sales. In this approach, it is assumed that

$$\text{Sales} = \alpha + \beta \times \text{time}$$

By varying time, we can forecast sales for any period in the future. However, this method ignores all factors except time and may yield misleading results. An obvious example of where linear regression may provide misleading results is the case of seasonalities in cash flow. For example, consider Bomber Skis. Ski sales are highly seasonal; people buy new skis during autumn and early winter, then sales drop off markedly. If the firm was trying to forecast cash flow on a quarterly basis, linear regression would likely overestimate cash flow during low sales quarters and underestimate cash flows during high sales quarters. The text presents a method of using moving averages to calculate seasonal indices used to adjust forecasts from linear regression. Failure to do so could leave firms facing seasonal cash flows in financial distress during some quarters due to improper forecasting and planning.

Pro Forma Financial Statements

Other useful tools in estimating expected future cash flows are pro forma accounting statements. These statements project the firm's expected revenues, expenses, and position at the end of the forecast period. Two basic approaches are used in developing pro forma statements. The first uses projections arising from the cash budget and modifies them to reflect GAAP. The second, or percentage of sales method, starts with the historical relationship between sales and various income statement and balance sheet items. These relationships are then applied to the firm's sales forecast to determine net income and external financing needs.

Consider the following abbreviated accounting statement for Voltex Limited, a manufacturer of synthetic fabrics. Voltex believes that sales next year will be $39,000 and wishes to develop pro forma statements to estimate cash needs. The firm also wishes to increase net long-term assets by $3,000 next year.

Income Statement (in thousands)
Voltex Company
Year Ending December 31, 1996

	Actual	% of Sales
Sales	$36,000	
Cost of goods sold	22,320	62.00%
Gross margin	13,680	
Selling, general, and administrative expenses	2,500	6.94
EBIT	11,180	
Interest	1,200	3.33
EBT	9,980	
Taxes (40%)	3,992	-
Net income	5,988	-
Cash dividends	4,491	-
Transferral to retained earnings	$ 1,497	-

Balance Sheet (in thousands)
Voltex Company
December 31, 1996

	Actual	% of Sales
Assets		
Cash	$ 2,000	5.56%
Accounts receivable	3,000	8.33
Inventory	10,000	27.77
Total current	15,000	41.66
Net long-term assets	18,000	-
Total assets	$33,000	
Liabilities and stockholders' equity		
Accounts payable	$ 1,000	2.78%
Notes payable	3,500	-
Accrued taxes and wages	1,500	4.17
Total current	6,000	-
Long-term debt and leases	16,000	-
Deferred taxes	1,000	2.78
Total long-term debt	17,000	-
Common stock	3,000	
Retained earnings	7,000	-
Total shareholders' equity	10,000	-
Total liabilities and shareholders' equity	$33,000	-

The column marked "% of Sales" is simply the line item divided by sales. The percentage is not listed for many items. These are thought not to vary directly with sales or require managerial action to change. An example is notes payable; any change must be negotiated with a lending officer.

By multiplying the percentages from the income statement by our estimated sales of $39,000, we can calculate net income for Voltex.

Pro Forma Income Statement
Voltex Company
Year Ending December 31, 1997

Sales		$39,000
	Cost of goods sold	24,180
Gross margin		14,820
	Selling, general, and administrative expenses	2,707
EBIT		12,113
	Interest	1,299
EBT		10,814
	Taxes (40%)	4,326
Net income		$ 6,488

If the dividend payout ratio remains constant at 75 percent, $4,866 will be paid in dividends and $1,622 will be added to retained earnings. Using this figure and applying the same logic as above, we can estimate the pro forma balance sheet, assuming those entries not affected by sales (except net long-term assets) remain constant.

Pro Forma Balance Sheet
Voltex Company
December 31, 1997

Assets		Liabilities and Stockholders' Equity	
Cash	$ 2,168	Accounts payable	$ 1,084
Accounts receivable	3,249	Notes payable	3,500
Inventory	10,830	Accrued taxes and wages	1,626
Total current assets	16,247	Total current	6,210
Net long-term assets	21,000	Long-term debt and leases	16,000
Total assets	$37,247	Deferred taxes	1,084
		Total long-term debt	17,084
		Common stock	3,000
		Retained earnings	8,622
		Total shareholders' equity	11,622
		Total	34,916
		Additional funds needed to balance total	2,331
		Total to balance	$37,247

Note that total assets do not equal total liabilities and shareholders' equity. The difference, in this case $2,331, is the external funds needed by the firm. The firm could raise these funds through increasing notes payable, issuing long-term debt, or issuing stock. You should see that the method of financing will affect the external funds needed. More notes payable or long-term debt will increase interest expenses; additional stock will require larger dividend payments. Once a method of financing has been decided upon, new pro forma statements should be developed to determine actual financing needs.

Financial and Strategic Planning

The manager of the firm also conducts strategic planning. Managers analyze the investment and financing policies and decisions of the firm, and look for a long-run plan that maximizes the value of the firm, provides sufficient liquidity to meet unexpected needs, effectively handles risk, and avoids options that destroy value. In studying each potential plan, the managers project the consequences of each plan in terms of financing costs, liquidity, flexibility, and value maximization. The manager then selects the plan that best meets the firm's goals and objectives. Financial and strategic planning is, of course, an ongoing process, since today's investments and financial decisions affect tomorrow's growth, investment opportunities, and plans.

Completion Questions

26.1   The statement of changes in financial position classifies cash flows arising from _____, _____, and _____ activities.

26.2   _____ is a method of estimating sales that assumes that sales are dependent only on time.

26.3   Managers must give special attention to the _____, _____, and _____ of the firm's expected cash flows.

26.4   The statement of changes in financial position does not reconcile taxes as reported on the income statement with _____.

26.5   The cash budget is a detailed statement of the firm's expected _____ and _____.

26.6   An external sales forecast is based on factors _____ to the firm, such as the state of the economy.

26.7   Scenario analysis enables a manager to determine how _____ cash flows are to changes in inputs or _____.

26.8   To estimate the firm's cash needs, the firm should take into account internally generated _____, increases in the investment in current assets, the timing and magnitude of the firm's projected _____, repayment of principal, and short-term financing costs.

26.9   The free internally generated funds available for reinvestment depend on the firm's _____ policy.

26.10   In financial planning, GAAP-based accounting statements are not very useful since they are not based upon _____.

26.11   It is possible to adjust for seasonalities using _____.

26.12   The _____ method assumes that certain assets and liabilities increase spontaneously with respect to sales, and can be used to develop pro forma statements.

26.13   _____ forces the firm to bring together all investment and financing decisions into a coherent and workable package.

26.14   The firm cannot evaluate various alternatives, options, and strategies without considering how they will affect the _____.

26.15   Due to uncertainties involved in the firm's internal and external environment, its financial plans should allow for some _____.

26.16   The financial planning process results in the projection of the firm's _____, articulation of its _____, development of its short- and long-run _____, and identification of the amount and timing of the firm's financing needs.

26.17   In addition to spontaneous short-term financing, the firm uses _____ _____ and _____ to meet its financing needs.

Problems

26.1   Essex Industries has approached Dominion First Bank about the possibility of obtaining a $600,000 three-month loan to purchase new manufacturing equipment. Kenneth Lawrence, the company's financial officer, has drawn up a projected three-month income statement for the period of the loan. The income statement does not reflect the impact of the loan.

Projected Income Statement

Sales	$2,000,000
Cash expenses	950,000
CCA	450,000
EBIT	600,000
Interest	50,000
EBT	550,000
Taxes (36%)	198,000
Net income	$352,000

Mr. Lawrence has provided the following information:

1. All sales and expenses are for cash.
2. The new equipment has a CCA rate of 20% and CCA is pro-rated on a quarterly basis.
3. Essex Industries has $400,000 cash on hand.
4. A $500,000 construction progress payment is due this quarter.

If the interest rate is 12 percent annually (3 percent this quarter), will Essex Industries have sufficient funds to repay the loan? Prepare a new income statement and go on to consider the cash inflows and outflows.

26.2   Green's Golf Equipment is a manufacturer of golf balls and is attempting to plan for its future cash flow needs. Historically, 45 percent of sales are for cash, 35 percent are collected with a one-month lag, and 20 percent are collected with a two-month lag. Purchases are 60 percent of sales and are made one month in advance. Forty percent of the purchases are for cash; the remainder is paid after one month. Estimates of wages, interest, and taxes are listed below. The firm also intends to pay an $185 insurance bill in May. Using the data below, forecast Green's cash flow needs for March, April, and May.

	January	February	March	April	May	June
Estimated sales	$1,200	$1,300	$2,100	$2,300	$1,800	$2,500
Wages	250	250	260	280	280	280
Interest	100	100	100	100	100	100
Taxes	20	25	20	20	40	30

26.3   Laird Transit Limited is attempting to forecast its short-term financing needs for the next year. Its cash flow forecasts are as follows:

	Quarter 1	Quarter 2	Quarter 3	Quarter 4
Total operating cash inflow	$300	$400	$250	$180
Total operating cash outflow	− 250	− 320	− 230	− 150
Other net inflow (+) or outflow (−)	− 70	+ 50	− 160	− 20

Laird's starting cash balance is $10, which is the minimum it requires. What are its cumulative short-term financing needs by quarter?

26.4   The following is the 1996 income statement for Clearwater Distillery, a distributor of bottled mineral water:

Sales	$1,450.00
Operating expenses	1,044.00
Income from operations	406.00
Other income	55.00
EBIT	461.00
Interest	120.00
EBT	341.00
Taxes	102.30
Net income	$ 238.70

Sales are expected to increase in 1997 by 12 percent over 1996; other income is expected to remain constant, as is the interest expense. Using the percentage of sales method, estimate the 1997 income statement.

26.5   The 1996 balance sheet for Tyrone Enterprises is as follows:

Balance Sheet
(in thousands)

Cash	$ 70	Accounts payable	$ 100
Accounts receivable	240	Notes payable	220
Inventory	500	Total current liabilities	320
Total current assets	810	Long-term bonds	540
Net long-term assets	1,200	Common stock	600
Total	$2,010	Retained earnings	550
		Total	$2,010

Sales for 1996 were $5,000. The company expects sales to increase by 15 percent for 1997. This increase in sales can be obtained without expanding net long-term assets due to sufficient capacity. The firm's after-tax profit as a percent of sales is typically 2 percent, and the firm pays out 60 percent of net income as cash dividends. The firm will raise additional funds needed through the use of notes payable so long as the current ratio is at least 2.5. Remaining funds needed will be raised by equal amounts of long-term bonds and common stock. Using the percent of sales method and the above limitations, develop a pro forma balance sheet for 1997 for Tyrone Enterprises.

26.6   Becker's Building Supply is trying to forecast sales for 1997. Using the data below, develop a naive forecast using simple linear regression for Becker.

Year	Sales (in thousands)
1987	$170
1988	180
1989	195
1990	225
1991	218
1992	260
1993	245
1994	265
1995	270
1996	290

Answers to Completion Questions

26.1	operating; investment; financing
26.2	Linear regression
26.3	magnitude; timing; risk
26.4	taxes actually paid
26.5	inflows; outflows
26.6	external
26.7	sensitive; assumptions
26.8	funds; capital expenditures
26.9	cash dividend
26.10	cash flows
26.11	rolling forecasts
26.12	percentage of sales
26.13	Financial planning
26.14	value of the firm
26.15	flexibility
26.16	cash flows; corporate strategy; capital budgets
26.17	short-term borrowing; long-term financing

Solutions to Problems

26.1   Step 1.   To determine if Essex Industries will have sufficient cash on hand, recalculate the income statement under the assumption that the loan will be granted.

Sales			$2,000,000
	Expenses		950,000
	CCA: Old	$ 450,000	
	New[a]	15,000	465,000
EBIT			585,000
	Interest: Old	50,000	
	New[b]	18,000	68,000
EBT			517,000
	Taxes (36%)		186,120
Net income			$ 330,880

[a]New CCA: CCA for year 1 = 1/2 capital cost × CCA rate
CCA = (1/2) ($600,000)(0.20)/4 = $15,000 per quarter
[b]New interest expense: The firm wishes to borrow $600,000 at an interest rate of 12 percent per year. The quarterly interest will be Interest = ($600,000)(0.12)/4 = $18,000

Step 2.

Cash inflows	
Sales	$2,000,000
Cash on hand	400,000
Total cash available	$2,400,000

Step 3.   Cash outflows

Expenses	$ 950,000
Interest	68,000
Taxes	186,120
Construction progress payment	500,000
Loan repayment	600,000
Total outflows	$2,304,120

The firm will have a cash surplus of $95,880 ($2,400,000 − $2,304,120) if the loan is made.

26.2   Step 1.   Estimated Cash Inflows from Operations

		January	February	March	April	May
1.	Total sales	$1,200	$1,300	$2,100	$2,300	$1,800
2.	Collections—one-month lag (35% of sales)		420	455	735	805
3.	Collections—two-month lag (20% of sales)			240	260	420
4.	Total collections (2 + 3)			695	995	1,225
5.	Cash sales (45% of total sales)			945	1,035	810
6.	Total cash inflows from operations			$1,640	$2,030	$2,035

Step 2.   Estimated Cash Outflows from Operations

		February	March	April	May	June
1.	Total sales	$1,300	$2,100	$2,300	$1,800	$2,500
2.	Total purchases (60% of sales made one month in advance)	1,260	1,380	1,080	1,500	
3.	Credit purchases (60% of purchases)	756	828	648	900	
4.	Payment of credit puchases (one-month lag)		756	828	648	
5.	Cash purchases (40% of purchases)		552	432	600	
6.	Wages		260	280	280	
7.	Interest		100	100	100	
8.	Taxes		20	20	40	
9.	Total operating cash outflows (4 + 5 + 6 + 7 + 8)		$1,688	$1,660	$1,668	

Step 3.   Net Cash Flow for Green's Golf Equipment

		March	April	May
1.	Total operating cash inflow	$1,640	$2,030	$2,035
2.	Total operating cash outflow	−1,688	−1,660	−1,668
3.	Other net outflows			− 185
4.	Net cash inflow (+) or outflow (−)	−$ 48	+$ 370	+$ 182

26.3   Step 1.   Determine net inflow or outflow:

	Q1	Q2	Q3	Q4
Total operating cash inflow	$300	$400	$250	$180
Total operating cash outflow	− 250	− 320	− 230	− 150
Other net inflow or outflow	−70	+50	− 160	−20
Net inflow (+) or outflow (−)	−$ 20	+$130	−$140	+$ 10

Step 2.   Short-term financing needs:

Cash at start of period	+$ 10	−$ 10	+$120	−$ 20
Net cash inflow or outflow	−20	+130	−140	+10
Cash at end of period	−$ 10	+$120	−$ 20	−$ 10
Minimum balance required	−10	− 10	−10	−10
Cumulative needed (−) or surplus (+)	−$ 20	+$110	−$ 30	−$ 20

26.4   Step 1.   Operating expense as a percent of sales = $1,044/$1,450 = 0.72 = 72%

Tax rate = $102.30/$341 = 30%

Step 2.

Sales ($1,450 × 1.12)	$1,624.00
Operating expenses ($1,624 × 0.72)	1,169.28
Income from operations	454.72
Plus: Other income	55.00
EBIT	509.72
Interest	120.00
EBT	389.72
Taxes (30%)	116.92
Net income	$ 272.80

26.5   Step 1.

Assets as a percent of sales

$$\frac{\text{Cash}}{\text{sales}} = \frac{\$70}{\$5,000} = 1.4\%$$

$$\frac{\text{Accounts receivable}}{\text{sales}} = \frac{\$240}{\$5,000} = 4.8\%$$

$$\frac{\text{Inventory}}{\text{sales}} = \frac{\$500}{\$5,000} = 10\%$$

Liabilities as a percent of sales

$$\frac{\text{Accounts payable}}{\text{sales}} = \frac{\$100}{\$5,000} = 2\%$$

$\text{Sales}_{1997} = \$5,000(1.15) = \$5,750$

$\text{Cash} = (\$5,750)(0.014) = \$80.5$

$\text{Accounts payable} = (\$5,750)(0.02) = \$115$

$\text{Accounts receivable} = (\$5,750)(0.048) = \$276$

$\text{Inventory} = (\$5,750)(0.10) = \$575$

Step 2.   Assets

Cash	$ 80.50
Accounts receivable	276.00
Inventory	575.00
Total current assets	931.50
Net long-term assets	1,200.00
Total assets	$2,131.50

Necessary increase in assets = $2,131.50 − $2,010 = $121.50

External funds needs = $121.50 − ($115 − $100) − [(0.02)($5,750)(1 − 0.60)]

= $121.50 − $15 − $46 = $60.5

Step 3.   Retained earnings = $550 + [($5,750)(0.02)(1 − 0.60)] = $596
The firm needs to raise $60.50 externally. Assuming that the firm wishes to maintain a current ratio of 2.5,

$$\text{Current ratio} = \frac{\text{current assets}}{\text{current liabilities}} = 2.5$$

$$= \frac{\$931.50}{\text{current liabilities}} = 2.5$$

$$\text{Current liabilities} = \frac{\$931.50}{2.5} = \$372.60$$

Current liabilities = accounts payable + notes payable
      $372.60 = $115 + notes payable
Notes payable = $372.60 − $115 = $257.60
The increase in notes payable is $257.60 − $220 = $37.60
The firm still needs to raise $60.50 − $37.50 = $22.90 by using new long-term bonds and common stock.
Since half comes from each source,

$$\text{Increase in common stock} = \frac{\$22.90}{2} = \$11.45$$

$$\text{Increase in long-term bonds} = \frac{\$22.90}{2} = \$11.45$$

Step 4.   The pro forma balance sheet is then

Cash	$ 80.50	Accounts payable	$ 115.00
Accounts receivable	276.00	Notes payable	257.60
Inventory	575.00	Total current liabilities	372.60
Total current assets	931.50	Long-term debt	551.45
Net long-term assets	1,200.00	Common stock	611.45
Total assets	$2,131.50	Retained earnings	596.00
		Total liabilities and stockholders' equity	$2,131.50

26.6

Year	Sales(Y_t)	Time(X_t)	$Y_t X_t$	X_t^2
1987	170	1	170	1
1988	180	2	360	4
1989	195	3	585	9
1990	225	4	900	16
1991	218	5	1,090	25
1992	260	6	1,560	36
1993	245	7	1,715	49
1994	265	8	2,120	64
1995	270	9	2,430	81
1996	290	10	2,900	100
	2,318	55	13,830	385

Means:

$$\overline{Y} = \frac{\Sigma Y_t}{n} = \frac{2,318}{10} = 231.8$$

$$\overline{X} = \frac{\Sigma X_t}{n} = \frac{55}{10} = 5.5$$

$$\beta = \frac{\Sigma X_t Y_t - n(\overline{Y})(\overline{X})}{\Sigma X_t^2 - n(\overline{X})^2} = \frac{13,830 - 10(231.8)(5.5)}{385 - 10(5.5)^2}$$

$$= \frac{13,830 - 12,749}{385 - 302.5} = \frac{1,081}{82.5} = 13.103$$

$$\alpha = \overline{Y} - \beta\overline{X} = 231.8 - 13.103(5.5)$$

$$= 231.8 - 72.066 = 159.734$$

For 1997, $X_t = 11$

$Sales_{1997} = 159.734 + 13.103(11)$

$= 159.734 + 144.133 = \$303.867$

Chapter 27
Small Business Finance

How This Chapter Relates to the Rest of the Text

Small businesses make up a large portion of the Canadian economy. As of 1993, there were more than 855,000 small businesses employing approximately 43 percent of the Canadian labour force. While many of the tools discussed this far, such as capital budgeting (Chapters 7–9) and short-term financial management (Chapters 21–24), are important for entrepreneurs, there are also problems specific to small businesses. Unlike large corporations, small businesses have limited access to capital markets. Entrepreneurs typically cannot issue common stock (Chapter 10) or long-term debt (Chapter 11) as easily as large companies. Financial planning and forecasting (Chapter 26) are also critical to the success of small businesses.

Topical Outline

I.   The issue of small business finance.
   A.   The business plan is important both as a management tool and a vehicle for raising the necessary financing.
      1.   The summary is a brief discussion of the products, services, or technologies of the company, the market potential, a description of management personnel, and abbreviated financial statements.
      2.   The business section should contain a detailed description of the company, its environment, its products or services, and its risks.
      3.   The financial section is the key component of the plan; it should contain projected financial statements for a period of three years.
   B.   Start-up funding commonly comes from the personal resources of the entrepreneur. Once beyond the start-up stage, funding comes in the form of external debt and equity.
   C.   Bank financing often requires a personal guarantee from the entrepreneur. Good relations with a bank are a must for a small business.
   D.   The Income Tax Act may provide incentives for small businesses to be operated as corporations rather than as unincorporated forms of businesses.
II.   Obtaining debt financing.
   A.   Private sources.
      1.   Types of bank loans.
         a.   Operating loans are lines of credit negotiated with the bank and used for day-to-day operations.
         b.   Term loans (of up to five years) are made by chartered banks for plant expansion, renovation, equipment, land and buildings, and other "worthwhile" purposes.
         c.   Equipment financing are loans made by chartered banks using the equipment purchased as collateral.
         d.   Letters of credit are useful in international trade.
      2.   Venture capitalists are more likely to provide mezzanine financing to a small business that is breaking even and ready to expand.
      3.   Short-term financial management is extremely important since small businesses carry higher percentages of both current assets and current liabilities.
         a.   Pledge or factor accounts receivable to secure funds.
         b.   Use inventory financing techniques.
         c.   Trade credit is widely used as a source of funds.
      4.   Leasing allows a small business the use of machines, vehicles, office equipment, and buildings.
   B.   Public sources.
      1.   Business improvement loans are offered under the Small Business Loans Act (SBLA) for new or additional equipment, buildings, and leasehold improvements.

2. Project financing is made available by the Business Development Bank of Canada (formerly the Federal Business Development Bank).

C. Other government programs.

1. Information on government programs can be obtained from the regional offices of Industry Canada, the Business Development Bank of Canada, and provincial development agencies.

2. SBLA loans are guaranteed by the federal government, are secured by the assets financed, and must be repaid within 10 years. The maximum loan is $250,000.

3. The Business Development Bank of Canada (BDBC) promotes and assists small and medium-sized businesses at the start-up or at some other stage in their development.

a. The BDBC provides financial, investment banking, and management services.

b. BDBC loans are usually made for five years and at an interest rate 2 to 3 percent higher than the prime rate.

III. Obtaining equity financing.

A. Small businesses have difficulty going public because of lack of marketability and disproportionately high issue costs.

B. Small companies typically seek private sources of equity first, then enter the venture capital market.

C. Table 27.1 describes various sources of venture capital.

D. As small firms grow, they may raise funds through an initial public offering (IPO). However, IPOs have substantial implicit and explicit costs.

IV. Financial control and planning.

A. Liquidity is crucial to the success of small businesses.

1. A basic need of small business management is the ability to prepare a monthly cash budget.

2. The control of cash calls for a replanning process because of the need to make changes quickly.

B. Controlling credit, collections, and inventory.

1. The most difficult task is establishing a management policy.

2. Two important strategies are ordering economic quantities and establishing re-order points for inventories.

C. Financial performance analysis.

1. Accounting statement analysis techniques discussed in Chapter 25 are appropriate for small businesses as well as large businesses.

2. The most important ratios for small businesses.

a. Current ratio.

b. Quick ratio.

c. Days sales outstanding.

d. Inventory turnover.

e. Total asset turnover.

f. Total debt to total assets.

g. Times interest earned.

h. Net profit margin.

i. Return on total assets.

j. Return on equity.

V. Planning the financial future.

A. Financial planning should be an integral part of the business plan.

B. Financial planning is important because without financing, the firm cannot continue to exist.

C. The basic components of financial planning are the operating statement, the balance sheet, and the capital budget.

D. Financial planning is an indication of what the owner–manager perceives will happen and should reflect the ultimate profits resulting from operations.

E. The goals, objectives, and strategies of the firm should be considered.

F.   A computer may help in financial planning, but any investigation of a computing system should be done with care.

What to Look For

<u>Introduction</u>
While most students intend to work for a major corporation after graduation, others may wish to start their own businesses. In fact, many colleges and universities offer courses in entrepreneurship that concentrate on starting and managing a business. Small businesses are an important part of the Canadian economy; as of 1993, 855,000 small businesses employed 43 percent of the Canadian work force. Although the tools and techniques of financial management discussed in previous chapters are important, small businesses face special problems, such as lack of access to capital markets, that need to be considered. This chapter discusses the difficulties faced by small businesses and the special programs available to them.

<u>Starting a Business</u>
An entrepreneur is a person who recognizes a business opportunity and literally creates something (a business) out of nothing. Since economic growth is so important to the health of the nation, the federal and provincial governments have made small businesses one of their key priorities and continually develop new policies and realign old ones to stimulate business opportunities. An example of this is the lower tax rate on the first $200,000 of corporate income.

A necessity in starting a business is the business plan. The plan defines the objectives of the business, describes the product or services the business plans to offer, discusses the business environment, competition, and target market, and contains detailed financial forecasts for the firm. A business plan is very important. First, by putting things down on paper and applying techniques, such as valuation, that you learned earlier, you can determine if the business idea is worth pursuing. Sometimes things that sounded like good ideas turn out to be less attractive when exposed to concrete analysis.

Second, the business plan provides a benchmark for evaluating the business's future performance. Most small businesses that fail do so because of poor planning or poor management; a business plan enables you to identify potential problems before they arise and difficulties as they occur. Once these have been identified, corrective steps can be taken.

Finally, the business plan is a device you can use to market the firm. Most people do not have sufficient resources for starting a business themselves, and a business plan helps them attract external funding from friends and family, banks, government agencies, or venture capitalists.

Obtaining financing
Once the business plan is developed, most entrepreneurs need to seek start-up financing. The most common form of start-up financing is personal funds from savings, borrowing, or relatives or friends. "Love money" can expose the entrepreneur to considerable personal financial risk or cause considerable friction among family or friends. As such, care should be taken to structure these transactions in a strictly business-like manner.

An owner–manager would like to retain as much control over the business as possible and is likely to attempt to obtain debt financing. There are a variety of places in which funds can be obtained. Chartered banks, which are geared toward business needs, provide operating loans (lines of credit), term loans, equipment financing, and letters of credit to viable small businesses. Small businesses can also make use of short-term financial management techniques such as pledging or factoring accounts receivable, inventory financing, and trade credit to obtain funds. These sources are important to small businesses since current assets and current liabilities are generally bigger than in large businesses.

Because of the importance of entrepreneurship, a variety of government sources are available to small businesses. For instance, SBLA loans are available for new or additional fixed equipment, buildings, or leasehold improvements. The Business Development Bank of Canada also provides loans and services to small and medium-sized businesses. Because there are so many programs, an entrepreneur should contact the regional offices of Industry Canada, the BDBC, or provincial development offices to find out what is available and which programs best suit the firm's situation.

Small businesses have difficulty obtaining equity because of marketability problems, issue-specific risk, and high issuing costs. If private sources of equity are unavailable, the entrepreneur should seek the services of a venture capital firm (Table 27.1). While venture capitalists may be willing to provide equity, they typically demand a say in the operation of the firm. Also, venture capital firms are unlikely to provide start-up funds. They prefer to wait until the business has a proven track record and needs additional cash to support growth.

Operating a Small Business

While the tools and techniques of financial management you have learned to this point are useful in small business management, entrepreneurs need to pay special attention to certain aspects of their business in order to ensure success. Liquidity is crucial to the small business operator. Owner–managers should understand the various aspects of the balance sheet and how they affect cash flows and be able to develop monthly cash flow statements. These statements enable the manager to assess the company's needs for funds, and hence plan ahead for them, and allow the manager to make any changes necessary for the firm's continuing operation.

The entrepreneur also needs to establish policies for dealing with trade credit, accounts receivable, and inventory management. Since working capital is disproportionately larger for small businesses, the owner–manager needs to pay close attention to the management of current assets and liabilities.

If you start or manage a business, it is important to remember the concepts of cash flow, value, and risk and return. These concepts are as valid in discussing small businesses as large ones and should be incorporated into all decisions. And, like the financial market, managers need to be forward-looking. Planning for future financial needs is critical to the success of any business enterprise. No one expects managers to have perfect foresight and, if you err, it is best to err on the side of caution. Remember that finance is both an art and a science; while you should attempt to use all of the tools available to you, including computers if necessary, you should temper your decisions with judgement. Blind faith in tools and technology may be as dangerous as ignorance of them.

Completion Questions

27.1 An _____ is an individual who has the ability to see business opportunities and create something out of nothing.

27.2 The business plan should contain a _____, a detailed description of the proposed _____, and the _____.

27.3 The most common source of start-up financing is from _____.

27.4 _____ refers to loans made by chartered banks to companies wishing to purchase machinery or equipment that is in turn used as collateral.

27.5 Small businesses _____ have the opportunity to obtain equity financing by going public.

27.6 The primary external source of equity financing for small businesses is the _____ _____.

27.7 Small businesses should prepare cash budgets on a _____ basis.

27.8 Before it is possible for owner–managers to make estimates of the growth and future direction of the company, they must decide on what the major _____ and _____ are and what the strategy is to reach them.

27.9 Small businesses have a disproportionately large portion of their balance sheets in _____ _____ and _____.

27.10 The single most difficult problem faced by entrepreneurs is _____.

Answers to Completion Questions

27.1   entrepreneur or owner–manager
27.2   summary; business; financial section
27.3   personal funds
27.4   Equipment financing
27.5   rarely
27.6   venture capital market
27.7   monthly
27.8   goals; objectives
27.9   current assets; current liabilities
27.10   financing